Praise for *Salem Witch Judge*

"A fascinating account of the man and of daily life in colonial America."
—*Booklist*

Winner of the 2008 Massachusetts Book Award for Nonfiction.

"LaPlante's insightful account is fortified with descriptions of . . . New England and its history (including psalms recited by Sewall), creating a vivid sense of place and context. A reformative, assenting spin on Salem's hellfire and brimstone history."
—*Kirkus Review*

Winner of the Winslow House Book Award "for the best book published in 2007 concerning the interaction of early New England (1620-1852) with the wider Atlantic world."
—*Kirkus Review*

"Eve LaPlante's touching biography of Samuel Sewall . . . seems hauntingly familiar. Beneath the sensational title is a figure more familiar than we realize . . . *Salem Witch Judge* upends popular stereotypes about Puritans . . . [and] reminds us how quickly the conventional wisdom can shift, forcing even the powerful to move."
—The *New York Times* Book Review

"LaPlante recounts the life of her ancestor lovingly, but meticulously. In the process, she expertly guides us through the religious life of colonial New England, from well before the 1692 Salem witchcraft episode to long after Samuel Sewall's somber reflections on—and his apology for—his role in that hysteria. LaPlante also reveals the ever enlarging magnanimity of Sewall's spirit, specifically with respect to slaves, Native Americans, and women. His life—and her book—deserve our total and grateful attention."
—Edwin S. Gaustad, Professor Emeritus, University of California, Riverside, coauthor of *The Religious History of America*

"Judge S̶____ is ___ of the ____ public f_____ es of pre-revolutionary America, and his _____ witch trials remains a high and all-too-_____ is example is pertinent to our times."

_____ es, author of *The Good Book*

"LaPlante's splendid biography brings a personal touch to Sewall's story . . . and his efforts to take the difficult but righteous path. . . . After his public repentance, Sewall reconsidered many Puritan teachings and wrote controversial treatises arguing for the equality of Native Americans, women, and slaves. . . . Much as she did in *American Jezebel*, the marvelous biography of her 12th-generation ancestor Anne Hutchinson, LaPlante richly narrates his life . . . drawing on Sewall's diaries and stories told by her Aunt Charlotte."

—*Publishers Weekly*

"The toughest thing in politics is to admit you were wrong and to do something about it. That, remarkably, is what Samuel Sewall did, and in so doing, he fundamentally changed the debate over witchcraft forever. At a time when at least some Americans are arguing that we have to cut back on our civil liberties in the interest of national security, LaPlante's biography of Sewall profiles an early American politician whose example stands out for its courage and its wisdom."

—Michael Dukakis, former governor of
Massachusetts

"Compelling . . . Fascinating . . . *Salem Witch Judge* offers an intriguing journey into a world as far away as colonial America—and yet at the same time as close as the human heart."

—*Christian Science Monitor*

"Historian LaPlante (*American Jezebel*) offers a biography of her controversial Colonial New England ancestor, and it is as well researched, readable, and engaging as her first about Anne Hutchinson. Here, LaPlante examines the radical religious, moral, and philosophical transformations experienced by Samuel Sewall, the only judge presiding over the Salem witchcraft trials who repented for sending more than 20 men and women to their deaths. . . . Recommended . . ."

—*Library Journal*

"Sympathetic and richly detailed . . ."
—*Boston Globe*

"A Highly Recommended Book of 2008"
—*Boston Authors Club Book Awards*

"Affectionate and affecting . . . LaPlante's portrait of a man whose second act became one of atonement as well as contrition is finely drawn . . ."

—*Philadelphia Inquirer*

SALEM WITCH JUDGE

Also by Eve LaPlante

AMERICAN JEZEBEL

SEIZED

SALEM WITCH JUDGE

The Life and Repentance of
SAMUEL SEWALL

———— ⨝ ————

For Mary

Eve LaPlante

Best regards

Eve LaPlante

HarperOne
An Imprint of HarperCollinsPublishers

In memory of

Joseph A. LaPlante
1923–1990
&
Charlotte May Wilson
1895–1980

Cover: Judge Samuel Sewall, a 1729 portrait by John Smibert, appears by gracious permission of the Museum of Fine Arts, Boston.

Frontispiece: *1697, Dawn of Tolerance in Massachusetts: Public Repentance of Judge Samuel Sewall for His Action in the Witchcraft Trials*, mural in the Massachusetts State House, Albert Herter, 1942. Used by gracious permission of the Massachusetts Art Commission.

Unpublished writings of Samuel Sewall appear courtesy of the Massachusetts Historical Society.

Psalm transcriptions by Leo Collins.

HarperCollins books may be purchased for educational, business, or sales promotional use. For information please write: Special Markets Department, HarperCollins Publishers, 10 East 53rd Street, New York, NY 10022.

HarperCollins Web site: http://www.harpercollins.com
HarperCollins®, ■ ®, and HarperOne™ are
trademarks of HarperCollins Publishers.

FIRST HARPERCOLLINS PAPERBACK EDITION PUBLISHED IN 2008

Designed by Joseph Rutt
Maps by Topaz Maps Inc.

The Library of Congress Cataloging-in-Publication Data is available upon request.

ISBN 978-0-06-085960-2

08 09 10 11 12 RRD (H) 10 9 8 7 6 5 4 3 2 1

Men think 'tis a disgrace to change their mind.... But there is not a greater piece of folly than not to give place to right <u>reason.</u>

SAMUEL SEWALL
JANUARY 1689

CONTENTS

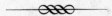

ILLUSTRATIONS

A NOTE ON THE TEXT

This is a work of nonfiction. Dates are old style, using the Julian calendar that English settlers of North America kept until the mid-eighteenth century. Unlike them, however, I begin the year on January 1 rather than March 25. To determine a date from the book in new style, add ten days to it; thus December 21, 1685, in the book is December 31, 1685, by modern reckoning.

I standardize the spelling of names with variant spellings in the seventeenth century, such as Sewell, Susannah, and Thacher, and I use *Jr.* to distinguish children from parents with the same name. Most quotations from Samuel Sewall are from his diary; those from elsewhere, such as his letters or essays, are indicated as such. In quoting from the writings of Sewall and his contemporaries, I make no changes other than modernizing spelling, capitalization, and punctuation. Except when a source used a different translation, all quotations from the Bible are from the seventeenth-century King James Version.

Quotations from the sung psalms are from the 1640 *Whole Book of Psalms, Faithfully Translated into English Meter*, also known as the *Bay Psalm Book*, the first book published in America. The psalm tunes, in modern musical notation, are from the ninth edition of the *Bay Psalm Book*, published in Cambridge, Massachusetts, in 1698. The musical examples contain the original spelling and punctuation. This is the first time that the tune and full text of these psalms have been printed together on a page, enabling readers to sing for themselves what Sewall sang.

An appendix contains Sewall's three important essays, with his spelling and punctuation. Selected excerpts from *Phaenomena quaedam Apocalyptica* represent roughly a quarter of that 1697 essay on the role of America and Native Americans in the apocalypse. Sewall's 1700 pamphlet, *The Selling of Joseph*, America's first public statement against slavery, is printed in full, as is *Talitha Cumi*, his 1724 essay on the resurrection of women's bodies.

SALEM WITCH JUDGE

1697· DAWN OF TOLERANCE IN MASSACHUSETTS PUBLIC REPENTANCE
OF JUDGE SAMUEL SEWALL FOR HIS ACTION IN THE WITCHCRAFT TRIALS

Massachusetts State House mural by Albert Herter, 1942.

INTRODUCTION

Beneath the golden dome of the Massachusetts State House, on a curved wall above the speaker's platform in the Chamber of the House of Representatives, is a large mural of my sixth great-grandfather the Salem witch judge. Titled *1697, Dawn of Tolerance in Massachusetts: Public Repentance of Judge Samuel Sewall for His Action in the Witchcraft Trials,* the mural shows an old man standing at the front pew in a New England meetinghouse. Everyone else in the crowded church is seated except a minister, who reads aloud Samuel Sewall's statement of repentance for executing twenty innocent people.

Five years earlier, in the summer of 1692, Samuel Sewall sat on the Massachusetts court that tried hundreds of people accused of witchcraft. He heard and believed the Salem Village girls who claimed that their neighbors used ghosts to torture and bewitch them. As the scope of the Devil's apparent attack on New England grew, Sewall convicted more than thirty people as witches. He stood by as nineteen women and men were hanged and one man was pressed to death with large stones. Some witchcraft suspects were strangers to him, but others were his friends. One man, a Boston neighbor, was a longtime business associate and fellow member of a private prayer group that met periodically in their homes. Another was a minister who had been a year ahead of him at Harvard College, with whom he corresponded and socialized. In October, after public opinion turned against the court, the governor halted the witchcraft trials. Yet he rewarded Sewall and other Salem witch judges with appointments to a much higher court, and neither he nor the judges made any public statement of regret for the witch hunt. For several years Samuel Sewall struggled with a growing sense of shame and remorse. This private effort culminated in the public moment depicted in the Massachusetts State House mural.

Certain details in the mural are incorrect, although they do not alter its effect. Sewall looks at least seventy years old; he was actually forty-four at the time. Women are scattered among a mostly male crowd; in fact women and men occupied separate sides of a seventeenth-century meetinghouse. Two or three men near Sewall appear to be weeping, yet it is unlikely that his real peers felt much sympathy with him that day. Most of New England's leading men thought he should not take on himself the blame for the witch hunt. They considered the events of 1692 a tragic mistake. In their view it was best to destroy the documents and move forward.

Samuel Sewall thought differently. Alone among the colonial officials who supported the killing of twenty innocent people, he assumed in public "the blame and shame" for the 1692 executions. At the moment captured in the mural, Samuel Sewall began a lengthy process of repentance, both public and private, that involved countless hours of prayer and self-mortification. He spent much of the remainder of his life—more than three decades—trying to restore himself in the eyes of God. This extraordinary urge to acknowledge and make amends for his sin is why he was chosen, along with John Winthrop, John Adams, and John Hancock, as a worthy subject of public art in honor of "Milestones on the Road to Freedom."

The repentance of Samuel Sewall "represents the greatest movement in modern history, not only in theory, but in its practical application," Frank Grinnell, secretary of the Massachusetts Historical Society, observed at the dedication of the mural in 1942. The moment depicted in the Sewall mural marks "the beginning of the recognition of the 'quality of mercy' in human affairs. No principle of Christ has been longer in obtaining whole-hearted acceptance than ... the saying, 'Be ye merciful even as your Father is merciful.'" Grinnell explained, "Massachusetts has been a target for caustic comment for centuries because of the hysterical and brutal outburst of the witchcraft trials and executions in 1692. But it is forgotten how short it was—but five months—with only about a score of hangings, as compared with the thousands burned, hanged or drowned in Spain, France, Germany, England and Scotland in much longer periods. And nowhere, except in connection with Salem, did any of the actors in the tragedy have the moral courage to admit that they were wrong."

The Salem witch trials exposed "many strange phases of humanity," according to their seminal nineteenth-century chronicler, Charles Upham, such as folly, delusion, criminal behavior, heroism, integrity, and "Christian piety." In regard to the last, "The conduct of Judge Sewall claims our particular admiration. He observed annually in private a day of humiliation and prayer, during the remainder of his life, to keep fresh in his mind a sense of repentance and sorrow for the part he bore in the trials."

I first heard of Samuel Sewall when I was a little girl visiting my great-aunt Charlotte May Wilson at the tip of Cape Cod. She lived in the red house beside Provincetown's Red Inn, which she ran. In her spare time she researched the lives of her ancestors, famous and infamous, whose stories she loved to tell. I recall my elderly, childless great-aunt clucking over her forebears like a hen over her brood. On my thirteenth birthday she presented me with a copy of the family tree. Every family, I now believe, has an Aunt Charlotte, the relative who takes the time to learn and share stories about the past.

Our ancestors as described by Aunt Charlotte were formidable figures, and many of them terrified me. There was a surprising number of women writers, from the seventeenth-century poet Anne Bradstreet to Louisa May Alcott, a first cousin twice removed from my great-aunt, who called her "Cousin Louisa." As for the men, there were countless graduates of Harvard College, who mainly grew up to become Congregational or Unitarian ministers. The nineteenth century produced plentiful abolitionists. One of these as a young man fell in love with the daughter of Jefferson Davis, president of the Confederacy. Davis halted the courtship, and his daughter died, according to Aunt Charlotte, of a broken heart. Most memorable to me was the seventeenth-century community organizer Anne Hutchinson, whose defiant expression of her Calvinist theology so unsettled Massachusetts's founding governor that he banished her as a heretic. Aunt Charlotte seemed fascinated by them all, but her obvious favorite was the Salem witch judge.

Samuel Sewall was a great man, Aunt Charlotte always said, though I didn't see why. He was a member of a court that convicted innocent people as witches and executed twenty of them. Somewhere I had learned that another judge left the court in disgust a few weeks after the first hanging. If Nathaniel Saltonstall had the foresight to quit, I wondered, what was so great about our ancestor, who stayed on to hang more people as witches and then waited years before admitting he was wrong?

We don't choose our ancestors, and in some sense we are not responsible for them, but still I would have preferred to find a so-called witch in the family tree. In the modern version of Salem, the witches are the heroes. The court executed only those women and men who refused to confess to witchcraft while sparing hundreds of people who "confessed." Who wouldn't want to emulate those brave souls who died because they refused to confess to something of which they were innocent? The witchlike characters in the modern story of Salem are the girls and young women who started the hysterical accusations that their neighbors were possessed. As for the nine judges who presided over the trials, they seem monstrous.

This legacy of shame afflicted another descendant of a Salem witch judge, Nathaniel Hawthorne. He added a letter to his surname to separate himself from his great-great-grandfather Judge John Hathorne, Sewall's colleague on the court. "I know not whether these ancestors of mine bethought themselves to repent, and ask pardon of Heaven for their cruelties," Hawthorne wrote in *The Scarlet Letter*, which he set in seventeenth-century Massachusetts, "or whether they are now groaning under the heavy consequences of them, in another state of being."

What made Samuel Sewall great, according to Aunt Charlotte, was that he changed. On a religious quest that is both medieval and modern, he tried to make himself more like Christ. Instead of judging others, which is easy, he judged himself. In doing so he became an unlikely pioneer of civil rights for powerless groups. He authored America's first antislavery tract, which set him against every other prominent man of his time and place. Then, in a revolutionary essay he wrote not long after the scene depicted in the Massachusetts State House mural, he portrayed Native Americans not as savages—the standard view then—but as virtuous inheritors of the grace of God. Finally, in a period when women were widely considered inferior to men, he published an essay affirming the fundamental equality of the sexes. To put these ideas into historical perspective, at Sewall's death in 1730 the widespread belief in the equality of races and genders in America lay more than two centuries in the future.

The Salem witch trials had other positive outcomes, in addition to making Samuel Sewall whole. They marked the end in America of hanging people as witches, a practice imported from Europe, where it was widespread. The failures of the Salem witch court led to the creation of America's first independent judiciary, a judiciary separate from the legislative and administrative functions of government, with which it was previously intertwined. The new court, on which Sewall served for decades, still operates today as the Supreme Judicial Court of Massachusetts, now the oldest independent court in the Western Hemisphere. The events at Salem in 1692 also ushered in an era of separation of church and state in Massachusetts, which in turn inspired the formal separation of church and state throughout the United States.

Much of this was lost on me as a child. The most memorable thing Aunt Charlotte said about our ancestor was that he wore sackcloth beneath his clothes from his public apology until his death. She said it rubbed against his skin to remind him of his sin. Aunt Charlotte called it sackcloth, but as an undergarment it was more like the traditionally Catholic hair shirt worn by monks, ascetics, and some pious laymen. In Hans Holbein's 1527 portrait of the forty-nine-year-old English chancellor Sir Thomas More, whom King Henry VIII later beheaded for refusing to accede to his split from the Catholic Church, the edges of More's hair shirt peek out at his neck and wrists.

My aunt's depiction of our ancestor's hair shirt conjured gruesome questions in a child's mind. How often, if ever, did Sewall wash it? Why did he wear it to his grave? Most irreverently, what did it smell like? I never dared broach these questions with Aunt Charlotte, who might have dismissed them with a brusque "Tut tut."

I wish Aunt Charlotte were still alive, as I have many more questions. The Puritans came to America to escape Catholic influences in the English Church, so why would a Puritan mortify himself in the manner of a Catholic ascetic? More broadly, how did a grown man transform himself from a witch judge into a public penitent? How did an extraordinarily prudent man like Samuel Sewall suddenly in middle age put aside the traits that underlay his worldly successes and abandon himself to faith? What aspects of his character enabled him to learn to see, as the apostle Paul required, with the eyes of the heart?

In recent years I've come back to Aunt Charlotte's favorite ancestor, hoping to answer these questions. It was my good fortune that he wrote prodigiously and left behind extensive diaries, poems, essays, commonplace books, annotated almanacs, ledgers, and letters, many of which his descendants donated to the Massachusetts Historical Society. His diary, covering the years 1672 to 1729, was first published in the nineteenth century and is still in print. The historian Henry Cabot Lodge called it "the most important" and "most personal" of all the historical documents of the time." Sewall's diary is the "most intimate" source of information available about English America during the century before the Revolution, according to the scholar Mark Van Doren, who noted Sewall's "genius for self-revelation." In addition to poring over Sewall's lengthy private thoughts and feelings, I have visited all the sites of his life, from the tiny English village where he was born and baptized to the burying ground in downtown Boston where his body lies. In Hampshire, England, I traced the four-mile path from his childhood home to the market town where he learned to read and write and visited the secondary school he dreamed of attending. In North America I explored the remnants of his beloved Boston and saw his haunts in his adopted hometown of Newbury, Massachusetts—his favorite place on earth— much of which has miraculously been preserved. In these physical and literary journeys I have come to know Samuel Sewall as a deeply gifted person who was plagued, as is so common, by self-doubt, insecurity, and ambivalence.

Samuel Sewall's greatest act—his statement of sorrow for doing wrong and his simultaneous promise to improve, as depicted in the Massachusetts State House mural—seems emblematic of a dualism in the American spirit. How American it is to claim, "I can judge right from wrong," and then to admit, "I was wrong"! Like most doubters, Samuel Sewall was most doubtful about himself. His self-criticism and self-reflection make him familiar to us now. In this book I aim to restore flesh to the bones of not only the witches, who are already heroes, but also my Salem witch judge.

1

I HAVE SINNED AGAINST THE LORD

At four in the morning on Monday, December 21, 1685, on the second floor of one of Boston's largest houses, the "faint and moaning noise" of a two-week-old baby forced a father from his warm bed. Wishing to disturb neither his wife nor his child's fitful sleep, he knelt beside the cradle. A bitter wind rattled the shuttered windowpanes of the bed-chamber. Outside, snow blanketed the peninsula known to the settlers as Shawmut, an English corruption of an Algonquian word for "he goes by boat."

Samuel Sewall, a thirty-three-year-old public official, bowed his head over his swaddled baby. The father wore a loose nightshirt. His shoulder-length hair was starting to thin at the crown. In a voice hardly audible, Samuel begged the Lord to extend his grace and favor unto his "weak and sick servant," baby Henry. Reminding God that he loves not only the faithful but also their seed—"not only the sheep of Christ but even the tender lambs"—Samuel asked God "by thine Holy Spirit" to make good his gracious covenant with Sewall's "poor little son."

Samuel Sewall was used to talking freely with God. He had spent seven years at Harvard College studying for the ministry. He knew much of the Hebrew and Christian Scriptures, in both ancient and modern languages, from memory and was familiar with numerous devotional manuals. The words flowed, but still his feeble child moaned.

As Samuel prayed the sun rose as it always did over the Atlantic Ocean, the harbor islands, and the cosseted town. Noting the dawn, Samuel determined to seek help. He dressed quickly and descended the stairs to find a manservant to summon the midwife. Goodwife Elizabeth Weeden, who had attended at all his children's births, soon arrived to examine the baby. As news of the child's precarious state spread across town, a circle of prayer made up mostly of female friends and relatives grew inside the house.

Sewall's wife, Hannah, who was twenty-seven, remained in their bed, where she had spent most of the fortnight since her sixth childbirth. Their firstborn, Johnny, had died seven years before at the age of seventeen months, but their subsequent five children had so far survived. This was a great blessing in a world in which roughly one in two children did not live to see their fifth birthdays.

Hannah Sewall was not by nature frail. When a horse that she and Samuel were riding together fell down abruptly on Roxbury Neck, she scrambled off, brushed the dust from her skirts, and gamely remounted the horse to continue the trip. Only six months before this lying-in, on June 20, Hannah rode pillion behind her husband for four miles from Shawmut Peninsula to Dorchester to visit her friend Esther Flint. After dining on just-picked cherries and raspberries, she and Esther "took the air" in the Flints' orchard overlooking the Atlantic Ocean, leaving Samuel alone in "Mr. [Reverend Josiah] Flint's study reading Calvin on the Psalms." John Calvin (1509–1564), the great theologian of Puritanism, adored the psalms, the Old Testament songs in praise of God, which were essential to Puritan worship. Samuel shared with his spiritual forebear a love of religious music. He sang a psalm or two daily, at home by himself or with his family, with friends in his Bible study group, or at church with the entire congregation, an experience that he likened to "an introduction to our singing with the choir above."

The bedchamber in which Hannah Sewall spent her lying-in was in her childhood home, built by her grandfather, the blacksmith Robert Hull, a half century before. Timber framed in oak and likely covered

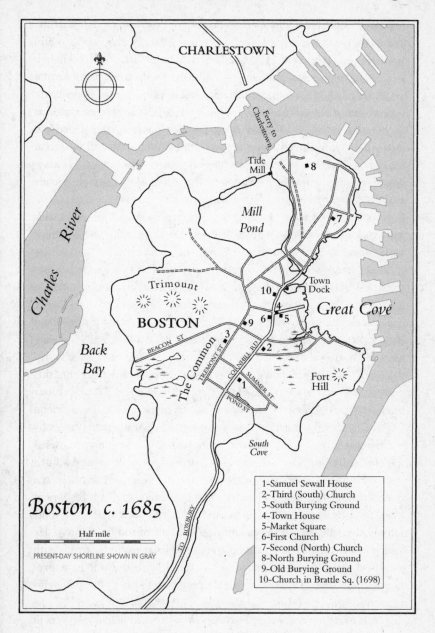

CHARLESTOWN

Ferry to Charlestown

Tide Mill

Mill Pond

● 8

● 7

Town Dock

Great Cove

Trimount

BOSTON

10 ●
4 ●
6 ● 5 ●
9 ●
3 ●
2 ●

BEACON ST

The Common

TREMONT ST

CORNHILL RD

SUMMER ST

POND ST

1 ●

Fort Hill

Charles River

Back Bay

South Cove

TO ROXBURY

Boston c. 1685

Half mile

PRESENT-DAY SHORELINE SHOWN IN GRAY

1–Samuel Sewall House
2–Third (South) Church
3–South Burying Ground
4–Town House
5–Market Square
6–First Church
7–Second (North) Church
8–North Burying Ground
9–Old Burying Ground
10–Church in Brattle Sq. (1698)

with weatherboards, it had a central chimney and a thatched roof. The inside walls were either plastered or covered with wide, upright pine boards. The ground floor contained two large halls and a kitchen, which extended to one side beneath a lean-to roof, with a long hearth. The second floor had numerous bedchambers and closets. Beneath the rafters the loft provided more sleeping space. With additions and improvements made by Hannah's father and husband, the house was more than sufficiently large to accommodate the Sewall and Hull families and their many servants and frequent houseguests. It occupied the southern corner of Washington and Summer streets in modern Boston that later hosted two twentieth-century department stores, first Jordan Marsh and then Macy's. The ten thousand shoppers daily who visit Filene's Basement in Boston's Downtown Crossing enter a space that was once the cellar of Sewall's mansion.

That house, on the town's main street, lay a block east of Boston Common and three blocks south of the central market square, the First Church of Christ in Boston, and the governmental Town House. An iron fence surrounded Samuel's land on the large, then-undivided block east of Washington Street (then Cornhill Road) between Summer and Bedford (then Pond) Streets. The mansion's main gate was on Cornhill, but many of its rear and side windows afforded fine views of Boston Harbor. The house was furnished with oak and mahogany objects imported from England by Robert Hull and Edmund Quincy, fabrics from England and the Far East, and silver vases, beakers, platters, and even chamber pots. Outside there was a kitchen garden full of herbs as well as flower gardens, plots of vegetables, and orchards of apples and pears that Samuel tended with the help of a tenant farmer. In the distance, groves of elm and walnut trees shaded Wheeler's Pond, which no longer exists. There were stables, a coach house, small abodes for the tenant farmer and some of the family's servants, and a building containing the colonial treasury built three decades earlier when Hannah's father became the colony's mint master. Hannah's mother, Judith Quincy Hull, a widow of fifty-nine, lived with the family and shared the management of the household with Hannah. A nanny and servants tended seven-year-old Samuel Jr.; five-year-old Hannah; Elizabeth ("Betty"), who was nearly four; and seventeen-month-old Hull, who had suffered from "convulsion fits" since March.

At supper on Sunday, December 6, during Hannah's most recent labor, little Hull had had a seizure while seated on his grandmother's lap, terrifying the family. That night, as the midwife and other women surrounded Hannah in the bedchamber, Samuel waited downstairs in a chair by the fireplace of the main room of the house, which they called the Great Hall. He was concerned about little Hull, about his wife, about their unborn baby, and about the state of his own soul. Samuel hoped he was saved—chosen by God to be one of his saints— but he did not feel confident that he was. Despite a deep faith in Jesus Christ, Samuel frequently suffered from doubt.

Nine years before, at his public confession of a personal conversion, which was required to join the Boston church, he felt intense anxiety over the adequacy of his faith. Unlike some early Congregationalists, who described a vivid flash of engagement with the divine that converted them to Christ, Samuel's piety was the less dramatic but daily effort to pray sincerely and to understand religious texts. Still, he was often as-sailed internally by a sense of his own sinfulness. And he knew that full communion in the church was limited to "visible saints," those who could convincingly testify to an experience of God's saving grace. On that long-ago day, while standing in the meetinghouse waiting to receive for the first time the sacrament of the Lord's Supper, which was reserved for church members, he became convinced that Jesus Christ would strike him dead at the moment the sacramental bread touched his tongue.

No such thing happened, but his powerful fear of God's wrath per-sisted. He was a man given to reflection, tending to think too much and too long. While turning a thought over and over in his mind, he free-associated possible negative outcomes. This left him beset with worries, especially at moments of change.

During his wife's first four labors, Samuel had been accompanied during this awful waiting period by his father-in-law, John Hull, who distracted him with cordials and conversation. Eight years before, as nineteen-year-old Hannah moaned in labor for the first time, the two men prayed together and shared the first sound of the firstborn: "Father and I sitting in the Great Hall [of their house] heard the child cry," the new father exulted in his diary on April 2, 1677.

"Father Hull," as Samuel called his father-in-law, accumulated vast cash and landholdings during a career as a merchant and as mint master of Massachusetts Bay Colony. The first colonial mint was built in 1652 on Hull's land, where it still stood. Hull also served as the colony's treasurer from 1676 and after 1680 on the governing General Court. Hannah was his sole surviving child—of the five babies born to his wife—so Samuel functioned as his only son. Father Hull had died two years before, on October 1, 1683, at fifty-eight, leaving the management of his enormous estate to his son-in-law. Thus Samuel was alone with his anxieties when Mother Hull emerged from the bedchamber an hour after midnight on December 7 to tell him the good news: Hannah lived, and they had a new baby boy.

The following Sunday, December 13, 1685, Samuel, his mother-in-law, and his children dressed in woolen cloaks and fur muffs for the one-block journey up the main road to the Sabbath service at the Third Church. Nurse Hill carried the six-day-old boy. Everyone in colonial Boston was expected to attend public worship on the Sabbath, which began at sundown Saturday and lasted until sundown Sunday. Colonial law, which was based on biblical injunctions as interpreted by colonial leaders, banned all work, recreation, frivolity, and loud noise during these twenty-four hours. Devout families like the Sewalls spent several hours worshipping at church and observed silence and Scripture study at home. For Samuel and Hannah and their family and servants, the Sabbath was devoted to God.

That day at the meetinghouse, the Reverend Samuel Willard was scheduled to baptize several older children and two infant boys. The meetinghouse was a large, square building of cedar planks with a thatched roof and a square steeple. It was the Third Church of Christ in Boston, built in 1669 by a group of wealthy members of the First Church, including John Hull, who opposed some actions of that congregation and desired a new church with slightly less rigid membership requirements than those of the First (1630) and Second (1650) churches. By virtue of Samuel's high social status and his father-in-law's role in founding the Third Church, the Sewall baby would be baptized first. For the same reason the Sewalls took seats on benches near the pulpit at the front. The congregation divided by gender as well as by class: women sat on the right side of the center aisle, men on the left. Servants, slaves, and young boys clustered in raised galleries to the rear and sides.

Samuel held his new baby before the congregation and named him Henry. This was the name of his father, a well-to-do farmer and erstwhile preacher of seventy who still lived in Newbury, thirty-five miles to the north. During the church service Samuel took pride in his baby's deportment, noting that "Nurse Hill came in before the psalm was sung" to help with the infant "and yet the child was fine and quiet."

The "first sermon my little son hath been present at" was based on John 15:8, "Herein is my father glorified, that you bear much fruit, so shall ye be my disciples," which the Reverend Willard chose specially for the occasion. The Puritan, or Congregational, church had no lectionary, or set list of readings, so the minister could select any Scripture passage he wished on which to preach. Listening to the minister open up this text from John's Gospel, Samuel was reminded of two seemingly opposite truths. On the one hand, his five living children were his fruits. On the other hand, they were not his. They belonged to God, who could at any time take them away.

Over the next few days Samuel watched his newest baby sicken. Little Henry looked and behaved so much like Johnny that at certain moments Samuel felt as though he were reliving the early life of his firstborn, eight years before. Henry was "very restless" Wednesday night. Unable to nurse, he appeared to lose weight. The same night, little Hull had another convulsion fit, waking his father, in whose bed the toddler was sleeping.

The next evening Samuel sang a psalm with his family. Together they finished reading aloud the last book of the New Testament, the book of Revelation, which describes the end of the world as we know it and the Second Coming of Jesus Christ. Like most of his educated peers, Sewall subscribed to millenarianism, the belief that, as suggested in the twentieth chapter of Revelation, Christ will soon return physically to earth and reign here for a thousand years, a millennium, after which the world as we know it will end. No one in the Sewall family or in other homes of Boston's wealthy and powerful citizens doubted that Scripture revealed the imminence of Judgment Day. On that day, as a contemporary minister explained, "Jesus Christ himself will appear with all his holy angels in the clouds of heaven.... All the dead shall rise out of their graves and appear before him ... and Christ himself will give sentence to everyone according to what they have done in this life." On Friday the Sewall family returned to the beginning of the Bible, which they read through "in course" again and again. By reading aloud several chapters every day, a devout family could complete the whole Bible, from Genesis to Revelation, in less than a year.

On Saturday, December 19, Samuel invited the Reverend Willard to the house to pray for baby Henry. Willard, a forty-five-year-old Concord native and Harvard graduate (class of 1659) who served in the frontier town of Groton before being called to Boston's Third Church as its teacher in April 1678, was one of Samuel's mentors. At the time of Willard's installation at the Third Church, Samuel had been just twenty-six, a relatively new member of the congregation, with a sickly baby and a pregnant, twenty-year-old wife. Willard, who was fifteen years Samuel's senior, had previously served twelve years in Groton, until 1676, when Indians destroyed that town and massacred most of its residents. Willard preached and wrote prodigiously. His collected lectures on the Westminster Shorter Catechism, published posthumously in 1726 under the title *A Complete Body of Divinity*, were "a magnificent summation of the Puritan intellect," in the words of the historian Perry Miller. Known for his kindness, Willard spent what little spare time he had brewing an alcoholic drink, "Mr. Willard's cordial," which Samuel Sewall often brought as a gift on visits to friends, especially if they were ill. Of all the ministers in whom Samuel would confide over a long life, Willard was most influential.

Prayer was central to both men's lives. During the gathering at church any man—all of them were "saints"—could rise from his bench to offer a "free prayer," a relic of which can still be heard today in Congregational churches. Members could also nail notes to the meeting-house door requesting public prayers. And there were innumerable set prayers for special needs or occasions, such as in this instance for a seriously ill child. "Lord God, unite this child thereby unto Jesus Christ," begins one prayer in John Downame's devotional manual, *A Guide to Godliness*, published in London in 1622. "That becoming a lively member of his body, he may be partaker of his righteousness, death and obedience, for his justification, and so he may stand righteous in thy sight. Free him from the guilt and punishment of all his sins, and sanctify him in his soul and body, that either he may be fit to glorify thee on earth, or to be glorified by thee in heaven."

As both Samuel and the Reverend Willard were aware, God's support was required whether the child lived or died. "If it be thy blessed will, restore him," the minister continued. "But if thou art purposed to put an end to his days, so fit and prepare him for thy Kingdom, as that he may live with thee in glory and immortality, through Jesus Christ our Lord. Amen."

The next morning, on Henry's second Sabbath, the infant appeared to slip away. Samuel knew from experience that his best option now was prayer. A seventeenth-century doctor could do little or nothing for a seriously ill newborn. Boston had few physicians, and those few men who had come from England with university degrees in "Physic"—the study of the ancient writings of Hippocrates, Aristotle, and Galen—could offer no effective treatments for most illnesses the Sewalls faced: smallpox, influenza, other viruses, and dysentery. Prevailing treatments included bleedings, purgings, the ingestion of concoctions of lavender and other herbs or oil of amber, and for a sore throat the application of the inside of a crushed swallow's nest. The medical profession in its modern sense did not exist.

Samuel was desperate. He wrote notes to the Reverends Samuel Willard and Joshua Moody—a minister in his fifties who had been ejected from England after 1660, settled in Portsmouth, New Hampshire, and now served at Boston's First Church—asking for public and private prayers. A servant raced to deliver the notes. Several hours later, at the December 20 Sabbath service, which Samuel attended without his wife, the ministers mentioned his baby several times. The next evening, when the Reverend Moody called at the house, Samuel dispensed with formality and directed the senior minister right upstairs to "pray with my extreme sick son."

Samuel Sewall was already, at thirty-three, one of New England's most prominent men. He enjoyed both natural endowments and excellent placement in society, the latter due in large part to his prudent choice of a wife. Unlike most other powerful men of Boston, who were born in Massachusetts to the children of the colony's founders, Samuel was born in Old England during the Puritan reign of Oliver Cromwell. (The term *Puritan* referred to Reformed, or nonconformist, Protestants who wished to purify the English church by ridding it of Catholic practices, simplifying the service, vestments, and church ornamentation, and improving clerical education and the quality of sermons.) Samuel came to America with his family when he was nine, a year after the 1660 restoration of the anti-Puritan English monarchy. From childhood on, according to the historian David Hall, Samuel "believed in and defended the peculiar culture of New England." He "inherited from his family a dislike of the Church of England and its 'Hierarchy'"—priests, bishops, and archbishops—and anything else that resembled Roman Catholicism. In the mind of an English Puritan, the Church of Rome was the "whore of Babylon," corrupt, anti-Christian, and idolatrous or, in the words of the Cambridge minister William Perkins, "mere magic."

But Samuel was not the first in his family to cross the Atlantic to avoid offensive religious practices. His grandfather Henry Sewall, a member of England's lesser gentry who was a son and nephew of Coventry mayors, had in 1635 helped settle the coastal farming town of Newbury. Henry Sewall and his son, Samuel's father, Henry Sewall Jr., arrived in Boston on the *Elizabeth Dorcas* in 1634 with money, cattle, and provisions for a plantation. In May 1635, after a winter in Ipswich, Massachusetts, the Sewalls and other English planters rowed north to Plum Island Sound. They landed on the northern bank of the Parker River at a spot that is still marked in Newbury with a granite boulder: *Landing Site of First Settlers.*

While Samuel began his schooling as a boy in southern England— his parents and maternal grandparents had returned there in 1647, three years before he was born—it was here in Newbury, Massachusetts, that he learned to read and write in Latin, Hebrew, and Greek. His teacher, a Cambridge-educated minister named Thomas Parker who gave up preaching in middle age when he lost his sight, was another early settler. Parker petitioned the Massachusetts court for permission to create a parish in Newbury in 1635. As the town's schoolmaster, working from his house on modern-day Parker Street a stone's throw from the Sewall house, he taught Samuel and other boys how to comprehend and anticipate the end of the world as outlined in the Bible's original languages. The Reverend Parker sent fifteen-year-old Samuel off to Harvard, a training ground for ministers and Christian gentlemen, in 1667. Over seven years Samuel earned bachelor's and master's degrees in divinity. At twenty-three, following a year back in Newbury considering his options, Samuel married extremely well and moved into the home of his eighteen-year-old bride.

It was rare in English society for two couples to share one roof, but John Hull needed a male heir. Hannah and Samuel's wedding, in the Great Hall on the ground floor of this house, was performed by the elderly governor Simon Bradstreet, Boston's most esteemed citizen. After the governor and several ministers prayed for the health and happiness of the couple, the company enjoyed English "bride-cake," pears and oranges and other fruit imported from the West Indies, and a variety of spirits: sack-posset (a warm custard of sweet cream and wine), ales, and fine Burgundy and Canary wines. A few months later Samuel abandoned his fledgling career as a preacher to become his father-in-law's junior partner.

Samuel rapidly rose in Boston society. The General Court asked him in September 1681, when he was twenty-nine, to serve as the colony's official printer. Samuel purchased a printing press and hired Samuel Green Jr., of the famous Cambridge printing family, to operate it. During his three-year tenure as printer Samuel learned to set type and oversaw the publication of John Bunyan's Puritan classic, *The Pilgrim's Progress*, as well as pamphlets of laws, reproductions of sermons by Samuel Willard, Increase Mather, and Cotton Mather, and *The Assembly Catechism (The Shorter Catechism Composed by the Reverend Assembly of Divines with the Proofs Thereof out of the Scriptures)*. The press was owned and run by the state. A private property owner with his own press could publish anything he wished so long as he did not offend the government. America's first newspaper, *Public Occurrences*, which appeared in Boston on September 25, 1690, was quickly halted by the governor and council. They banned a second issue of the newspaper because the first issue "contained ... sundry doubtful and uncertain reports...." The concept of a free press was to be an invention of the next century.

Samuel became a freeman, or voter, in 1678, when he was twenty-six. Five years later he joined the government as an elected deputy (forerunner to a modern legislator) to the Great and General Court of Massachusetts, the most powerful ruling body in New England. For

his first term on the court he was a magistrate representing the frontier town of Westfield, nearly a hundred miles west of Boston, which
his father-in-law, who had recently died, represented a decade before.
After six months of service, Samuel became an assistant (forerunner
of our senator) to the same court and was made an overseer of Harvard College. He accepted the largely honorary title of captain in the
local militia and membership in the Ancient and Honorable Artillery
Company, he served in Boston's volunteer police and fire departments,
and he regularly took his turn at the night watch.

Describing Samuel Sewall as a merchant, as he is universally described, is as accurate as calling Thomas Jefferson a farmer. Sewall
did, of course, engage in trade, manage large sums of money, collect
vast tracts of real estate, and amass impressive wealth on both sides of
the Atlantic. For his father-in-law and eventually himself he negotiated with merchants in London and Bristol, England, Bilbao on
Spain's northern coast, other English and French colonies in America,
and the West Indies. He sold shiploads of salt fish, whale oil, lumber,
beaver skins, and cranberries and purchased shiploads of sugar, rum,
cotton, tobacco pipes, oranges, and books. "Some of his letters," an
editor of his diary noted, "read as if they had been dictated in State
Street or Wall Street last week." But Samuel was far more than a businessman. He was a civic leader and a public intellectual, one of the
most educated Americans of his day, who brought to bear on his work
his knowledge of at least four languages, the Hebrew and Christian
Scriptures, and the writings of Horace and Virgil. Today he might be
the sort of judge or attorney who is offered seats on the boards of hospitals, museums, and universities.

Sewall was, in fact, a judge. As a member of Massachusetts's ruling
body, the General Court, he was a magistrate, elected by the freemen
to make and enforce laws. Yet he was not a lawyer. No law school existed in America in Sewall's lifetime, and the day was past when men
with formal training in English common law, such as John Winthrop,
immigrated to the New World. The Great Migration of English Puritans to Massachusetts, which began in 1630 under Winthrop, lasted
only a decade. During the 1640s England offered opportunities for
Puritan reformation. It became a commonwealth, Parliament executed
King Charles I, from whose Catholic leanings twenty thousand Puri

tans had run, and Oliver Cromwell, a Puritan, came to power. These changes kept most English Puritans home. While the first generation of English settlers in Massachusetts included London-trained lawyers, the next several generations of Bostonians, including Samuel, did not.

Blessed with a warm heart and an inquisitive mind, Samuel knew practically everyone in Boston, from the rich and famous to the ordinary folk living in simple houses clustered near his mansion. Boston, with roughly five thousand inhabitants, was the largest town in the colony, which included most of New Hampshire and Maine and still had fewer than a hundred thousand English occupants. (The West Indies, a much smaller territory, had more than a hundred thousand inhabitants in 1692, making it far more thickly settled than New England.) Samuel somehow "managed to get along with everyone," the editor of his diary remarked in a footnote near the end of that lengthy tome. His intimates included the father-and-son team of ministers, Cotton Mather and Increase Mather, who lived in the town's North End, and even "Mother" Elizabeth Goose (1665–1757), who lived across the road. Mother Goose's son-in-law, the Boston printer Thomas Fleet, purportedly published the clever rhymes she told her grandchildren as *Mother Goose's Melodies for Children* in 1719, although no copies of the broadsheet exist. Besides his many outside contacts, Samuel was devoted to his large family—wife, children, parents, in-laws, siblings, and cousins. "Perhaps better than any one late seventeenth-century Puritan, Samuel Sewall combined worldly success and piety," Charles Hambrick-Stowe, a professor of Christian history, wrote in the late twentieth century. The historian Mark Peterson added, "Sewall's religious beliefs and practices remained constantly at the center of his busy engagement in worldly affairs." A century earlier the biographer Nathan Chamberlain deemed Sewall "the very type of the Puritan," whose life was "thoroughly colored by" his faith.

Samuel Sewall was also a poet and musician, a man who often had a tune in his head. "I am a lover of music to a fault," he confessed in a letter. One of his favorite activities was to lead his family in singing a psalm or two after supper. His wife was musical too. She played a virginal, an instrument similar to a harpsichord, which he retrieved from a repair shop in Boston in December 1699. He noted every wedding party and event at which he encountered a "consort" of instruments or even a single dulcimer, violin, flute, oboe, or harp. He often gave a friend or relative a gift of a Psalter, a book of musical psalms. At the death of the musician Jacob Eliot, a founding member of Samuel's church, he rued the loss of "such a sweet singer."

Music was a deeply felt aspect of Puritan life, and more so in a singer such as Samuel, who for years served as the precenter, or deacon, of his church, leading the congregation in song by "lining out" the melody of the chosen psalm. The members of the Boston churches could sing English translations of the hundred and fifty psalms of David, as the Hebrew psalms are known, to one or more suitable psalm tunes. (Even Jesus sang psalms, according to the Gospels of Matthew and Mark.) Many of the psalm tunes that Samuel knew were named for places, such as Windsor, Oxford, Low Dutch, Litchfield, York (or Stilt), London, and Saint David's. Puritan congregations memorized and sang by rote these tunes, which were fitted to the metrical verse of the psalm text. The first English settlers of America had brought with them a dozen or so tunes. The first book ever printed in the New World was the 1640 *Bay Psalm Book (The Whole Book of Psalms, Faithfully Translated into English Meter)*, the first New England Psalter, which is the equivalent of today's hymnbook although it included no musical notes. The musical notes first appeared in the ninth edition of the *Bay Psalm Book*, published in 1698. These melodies, which John Calvin and other sixteenth-century Protestants had commissioned from composers such as the great Louis Bourgeois, are eminently singable. Some are still familiar as hymn tunes, such as the well-known Old Hundredth ("All creatures who on earth do dwell..."). Rejecting the set liturgy of the Catholic and Anglican mass and lectionary, the Puritans pared down their worship service to only three elements: prayer, preaching, and psalm singing. The prayer was improvisational, or free, and the preaching and psalm singing were solely from the Bible. Lacking pipe organs and other musical instruments, they relied for their music on the human voice.

Few people today know the emotional depth of this sacred music— it contradicts the dreary image of the dour Puritan—and no book in print contains both the melodies and words in English meter. "It is difficult for us today," the music historian Percy Scholes wrote, "to realize the intensely personal application which the Puritans, and... all countries under Calvinist influence, made of the psalms." The Puritans' devotion to music may be forgotten now, but it was so well known then as to be mocked. In London in 1610, while composing *A Winter's Tale*, William Shakespeare had a clown describe the men in a chorus as "three-man-song men all," meaning they could sing skillfully in three parts. Shakespeare's clown continues, in act 4, scene 3, "and [they are] very good ones; but they are most of them means [tenors] and basses, but one Puritan amongst them, and he sings psalms to hornpipes." The only man able to sing the melody, a countertenor, was also a Puritan, who would set a psalm even to a popular dance tune.

Samuel's mornings almost always began with a psalm. Tuesday, December 22, 1685, broke even colder than the days before. Samuel woke early, anxious over little Henry. "The child makes no noise save by a kind of snoring as it breathed and, as it were, slept," he wrote in his diary. The sky was still dark. Servants built a fire in the kitchen downstairs and began preparing the morning meal of oatmeal or cornmeal mush, with milk or molasses, and johnnycakes.

Leaving Hannah to rest, Samuel gathered with his children and their nanny at the long oak table near the hearth for their morning devotions, reading from and discussing the Bible. That day's Old Testament reading was the sixteenth chapter of First Chronicles, which Sewall read aloud. The children and nanny repeated it silently. After the fifteenth verse, "Be ye mindful always of his covenant; the word which he commanded to a thousand generations," Samuel reminded Sam Jr., Hannah, and Betty that God's covenant included even little Henry.

For Samuel and his peers, their Bible Commonwealth was the contemporary equivalent of the Promised Land, a place specially chosen by God for his people on earth. It was a visible sign of the covenant that Massachusetts's founder, John Winthrop, described to the thousand Puritans who had followed him to America in 1630: "Thus stands the cause between God and us; we are entered into a covenant with Him for this work...." Winthrop's remarkable sermon "A Model of Christian Charity," which he delivered either on board the *Arbella* while crossing the Atlantic or on the dock before the ship set sail, states his spiritual aim in creating New England: We must "do justly," "love mercy," and "walk humbly with our God," he told the crowd. "We must entertain each other in brotherly affection; we must be willing to abridge ourselves of our superfluities, for the supply of others' necessities.... We must delight in each other, make others' conditions our own, rejoice together, mourn together, labor and suffer together: always having before our eyes our ... community as members of the same body." In this way "the Lord will be our God and delight to dwell among us, as His own people, and will command a blessing upon us.... He shall make us a praise and glory, that men shall say of succeeding plantations: 'The Lord make it like that of New England.' For we must consider that we shall be as a city upon a hill, the eyes of all people are upon us."

More than half a century later, in a warm kitchen in the heart of that same city upon a hill, Samuel read and "went to prayer" on the fourteenth chapter of John's Gospel. The first two verses related directly to his family's experience. Jesus tells his followers, "Let not your heart be troubled: ye believe in God, believe also in me. In my Father's house are many mansions: if it were not so, I would have told you. I go to prepare a place for you." Samuel told his little children that Jesus was preparing a place in heaven for each of them. They listened, amazed.

The room grew light as the sun rose over the steely sea, revealing a bank of clouds. After morning prayers Samuel went up to check on Henry, whose faint breaths were far less robust than he wished. Though he resisted his son's decline as much as possible, he did not doubt it was the will of God. One challenge of his faith was to accept every event as the work of an all-knowing, all-powerful God. Puritan preachers found numerous ways of expressing this idea, which Jesus had encapsulated in his prayer to his divine father in the Garden of Gethsemane the night before he was crucified: "Thy will be done." Years before, on a trip to survey a herd of wild horses that Father Hull kept in the wilderness of Waquoit on Cape Cod, in October 1677, Samuel had noted the autumn beauty of the South Shore beaches, cliffs, and meadows: "Seeing the wonderful works of God in the journey, I was thereby more persuaded of his justice, and inability to do any wrong." Whatever happened, whether for good or for ill, was the just work of God. God's justice is, of course, easier to appreciate when nature pleases than when it hurts.

Little Henry Sewall died in Nurse Hill's arms that Tuesday morning as she was rocking him. "About sunrise, or a little after," Samuel wrote in his dairy, "he fell asleep, I hope in Jesus."

Despite the confidence Samuel had displayed in describing to his other children the place Jesus prepared for baby Henry, he could not be sure that his innocent child's soul was actually in heaven. In Calvinist theology—the foundation of Puritanism—the sin of Adam and Eve stains even a newborn baby, so an infant's salvation is not assured. Calvinism is founded on the belief that humanity is totally depraved (Samuel and contemporaries often used the word *vile*), and God is omnipotent. As the Reverend Cotton Mather phrased this equation, "God is all, I am nothing." Salvation comes from God alone, not from human efforts, and before birth every person is chosen, or elected, by God for salvation or damnation, a phenomenon called double predestination. This theological foundation gave Puritans and other Calvinists deep anxiety about their spiritual estate. Am I saved? they wondered. Did God choose me? How can I be assured of my salvation? What are true signs of God's great and mysterious grace?

Despite Samuel's worries over his spiritual estate, he felt hopeful that God embraced his innocent baby. He, the child's father, was a full member in good standing of the Third Church of Christ in Boston, as he had been since Hannah's first pregnancy. He and Hannah and many other saintly souls and godly ministers had prayed fervently for the child's salvation during its brief life. Now, for themselves, all they could do was continue to pray.

Nurse Hill washed and laid out the baby's body. The older children gathered around the five-pound corpse. Except for their grandfather Hull two years before, the children had little direct experience of death. By way of comforting them and himself, Samuel reminded them that "a mansion is ready for Henry in the Father's house."

That evening after the children were asleep, Samuel and Hannah and Nurse Hill prayed together. Samuel began with John 15, "out of which Mr. Willard took his text the day Henry was baptized." The eighth verse, "Herein is my Father glorified, that ye bear much fruit," seemed providential. His and Hannah's fruit had died, so one or both of them must have failed in their duties to God. This was his conclusion. He noted that Hannah concurred.

The next reading, Matthew 3:8–10, filled Samuel with foreboding. It began, "Bring forth therefore fruits meet for repentance." These were the words of John the Baptist to prepare the "way of the Lord." Both Jesus and John began their ministries with a call to repentance. John said, "Repent! For the kingdom of heaven is near." Then he warned the Pharisees and Sadducees, "You brood of vipers! Who warned you to flee from the wrath to come? Every tree which bringeth not forth good fruit is hewn down, and cast into the fire." As Samuel considered this Scripture, he felt increasing fear, not for his innocent baby, whom he had entrusted to God, but for the state of his own soul.

The next morning he attended a private prayer and Scripture study meeting at the home of a neighbor, as was his habit on alternate Wednesdays. This gathering, by invitation only, was Puritan Boston's equivalent of today's home-based book club, prayer group, or soiree. It included women and could be hosted by a woman, but the discussion was always led by a man. Noted men who attended this gathering regularly included the merchant and sea captain John Alden, who was the oldest son of the Pilgrims John and Priscilla Alden, several ministers—Willard and James Allen—and Josiah Franklin, who in 1706 became Ben Franklin's father. At each meeting one member chose a Scripture passage for reading and explication. Samuel had attended these meetings for almost ten years, since the summer after his wedding, often in the company of his father-in-law and sometimes with his mother-in-law or wife.

That Wednesday in December 1685 the group gathered at the nearby home of Nathaniel Williams, a forty-three-year-old deacon of the Third Church. Williams was married to a daughter of the Reverend John Wheelwright, whom the General Court banished from Massachusetts for sedition in 1637 just before it banished Wheelwright's outspoken sister-in-law, Anne Hutchinson, for heresy. (Wheelwright and Hutchinson's crimes entailed questioning the judgment of ministers of the colony who were allied with John Winthrop.) As its first order of business, the prayer group agreed to observe a fast day on account of various losses, including the death of the Sewall baby.

Fast days were the colony's most important civic and spiritual events. The ruling court, one or more ministers, and even individuals or small private groups, as in this case, could call a fast day. Along with occasional public days of thanksgiving, public fast days effectively replaced the "popish" saints' and holy days that the Puritans had left behind in Old England. "Public fast days were held in response to dire agricultural and meteorological conditions, ecclesiastical, military, political, and social crises," the historian Charles Hambrick-Stowe noted. Samuel's group intended this fast day as a sacrifice to God, to show the colony's eagerness to reform and repent so that God might cease punishing them.

Some years later Samuel described one of his own private fast days, providing what his diary's editor considered "the most full and minute existing record of a private fast-day as kept by the devout of that time." In preparing to pray and fast for "important matters," Samuel retreated from family life. He went alone to the upper room at the northeast end of his house. He closed the door and fastened the shutters above Cornhill Street, the town's nosiest thoroughfare. He may have prostrated himself on the floor, as Cotton Mather sometimes did in prayer, but he surely did not kneel, for Puritans considered kneeling a violation of the Second Commandment: "Thou shalt have no other gods besides me. . . ."

"Dear God," Samuel prayed, "perfect what is lacking in my faith and in the faith of" Hannah, "my dear yokefellow. Please convert and recover our children," whom he named. "Requite the labor of love of my kinswoman Jane Tappan," his thirty-three-year-old niece, who had boarded with the Sewalls for years, helping with child care and household duties. Hoping she might be settled in marriage, he said, "Give her health and find out rest for her." He prayed for two of his servants: "Make David a man after thy own heart; let Susan live and be baptized with the Holy Ghost, and with fire."

Moving outside his household, he asked God to "steer the government in this difficult time. . . . Bless the company for the propagation of the Gospel" among the Indians. Through his life Samuel was committed to evangelism, in particular among the native tribes, which he referred to as "gospelizing the ungospelized places." He personally planned and paid for the building of an Indian meetinghouse in Sandwich, on Cape Cod, in 1688 and arranged for the Reverend Thomas Tupper to be its first minister.

He prayed for his own church. "Bless the South [Third] Church in preserving and spiriting our pastor, in directing unto [us] suitable supply, and making the church unanimous." Moving outward, he continued, "Save the town, the college [Harvard], [and Massachusetts] province from invasion of enemies, open and secret, and from false brethren. Defend the purity of worship. Save Connecticut and the New York government. Reform all the European plantations in America—Spanish, Portuguese, English, French, and Dutch. Save this New World, that where sin hath abounded, grace may superabound, that Christ who is stronger would bind the strong man and spoil his house, and order the Word to be given, Babylon is fallen.... Save all Europe. Save Asia, Africa, Europe and America." After this lengthy and roaming meditation he observed that "through the bounteous grace of God I had a comfortable day."

Samuel and his peers were aware of the random nature of the natural world, yet they tended to see in frightening occurrences such as droughts, epidemics of smallpox, and children's deaths a sign of divine vengeance—signs that God was displeased with human action. The reverse was generally accepted: good health and fine weather suggested God's approval. Even as Samuel and his peers saw the world this way, they acknowledged that discerning the real meaning of natural events is difficult and not exact. Thus Samuel could pray heartily and feel that his prayers had been answered, but he could never be certain that he had even been heard. As a result the essential Christian virtues were accepting the will of God and preparing well for one's own death. At death, at least, one could hope for security in union with Christ. The terrifying alternative was eternal damnation.

At the prayer meeting with his friends and neighbors, Samuel prayed to God to "prepare me and mine for the coming of our Lord, in whatsoever way it be." He found the gathering surprisingly consoling until the late arrival of William Longfellow, his improvident brother-in-law from the North Shore, who appeared "so ill conditioned and outwardly shabby." In a flash Samuel felt angry and embarrassed by his connection to this awkward man, who was married to his younger sister, Anne.

A moment later Samuel's irritation at Longfellow turned to shame on his own account. His brother-in-law had come to the meeting to pay his respects upon the loss of the baby, Samuel realized. He remembered Longfellow arriving in the same manner at much more formal occasions, such as "upon the funeral of my father," John Hull, and Samuel's firstborn, Johnny. Silently he begged the Lord to "Humble me."

In thinking of his own sin, he envisioned not so much a certain evil action as a general turning away from God. More than a specific behavior such as pride, deceit, lack of faith, laziness, envy, or rage, sin was for him a broader sense of failure to love and serve God. In Calvinist theology, every man and woman is tempted to turn away from God because we are descendants of Adam and Eve, who did not obey God. Sin is unavoidable. In response to one's sin, repentance offers a path back to God's grace.

Baby Henry's funeral was to be the next afternoon, following Samuel Willard's regular Thursday lecture at the Third Church. During that service Scripture again addressed Samuel's predicament, as it often seemed to. This time it happened during the singing of the Twenty-first Psalm, chosen by Willard, which describes God's destruction of his enemies. Male and female voices gathered on the first note of the eighth verse, which begins, "The Lord shall find out all that are thine enemies...."

Psalm 21

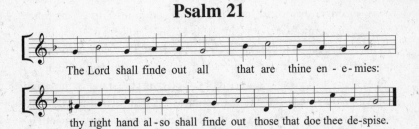

The Lord shall finde out all   that are   thine en - e - mies:

thy right hand al - so shall finde out   those that doe thee de-spise.

Cambridge Short Tune

8 The Lord shall finde out all
   that are thine enemies:
   thy right hand also shall finde out
   those that doe thee despise.

9 Thou setst as fiery oven
   them in times of thine ire:
the Lord will swallow them in's wrath
   and them consume with fire.

10 Thou wilt destroy the fruit,
   that doth proceed of them,
out of the earth: & their seed from
   among the Sonnes of men.

11 Because they evill have
   intended against thee:
a wicked plot they have devis'd,
   but shall not able bee.

12 For thou wilt as a butt
   them set; & thou wilt place
thine arrows ready on thy string,
   full right against their face.

13 Lord, in thy fortitude
   exalted bee on high:
and wee will sing; yea prayse with psalmes
   thy mighty powr will wee.

The 1640 *Bay Psalm Book*, containing all the psalms in English verse, was open before Samuel, but he had no need of it. In the tenth verse, as he sang of God punishing his enemies and their descendants, his face flushed: "Thou wilt destroy the fruit that doth proceed of them out of the earth, and their seed from among the sons of men."

The words stung. In taking Henry, God was punishing Samuel and Hannah. After the psalm singing Samuel prayed internally, "The Lord humble me kindly in respect of all my enmity against Him, and let His breaking my image in my son be a means of it."

2

———— ⁕⁕⁕ ————

SYMPTOMS OF DEATH

The cold ground that received the body of three-week-old Henry Sewall on that bitter December 24 is still marked. Near the rear of the Old Granary Burying Ground on Tremont Street in Boston, between the tomb of Paul Revere and that of Ben Franklin's parents and siblings, is a large, rectangular nineteenth-century monument marked SEWALL. (The Franklins were regular members of Samuel's prayer group and attended his church.) Carved atop the great tomb are the words "Judge Sewell [*sic*] tomb / Now the property of his heirs." Beneath this monument lie the remains of three-week-old Henry Sewall, fifty-eight-year-old John Hull, and forty other members of the family.

This burying ground, Boston's third, was originally part of the common on which cows, bulls, and pigs grazed. Gravediggers deposited eight to ten thousand bodies on this two-acre plot in the hundred years after 1660, when the cemetery opened. In 1737 a digger complained of having to bury bodies four deep. The ground does not drain well, so bodies decomposed quickly. The cemetery's modern name comes from its proximity to a wooden granary, a warehouse for up to twelve thousand bushels of grain for the poor, erected by the town around 1730 at the present site of the Park Street Church, which had previously been the site of an almshouse. In 1685 this cemetery was known as the New, Central, or South, Burying Ground, and this spot was the Hull and Quincy family tomb.

At the close of the lecture service, at around four in the afternoon of December 24, the funeral procession began. It started at the Third Church. According to a contemporary account, the meetinghouse was "large and spacious and fair," with three large porches, or raised galleries, square pews, a side pulpit, a bell, and a steeple. Sheet lead covered the roof. It was on Boston's main road in the same spot as today's Old South Meeting House, which was erected in 1730 as a stone replacement for the cedar building.

Describing the short walk from here along a snow-covered road to the burying ground, Samuel wrote, "We follow little Henry to his grave: Governor and magistrates of the country here, 8 in all, beside myself, eight ministers, and several persons of note." Samuel's grief did not dull his awareness of social status. The governor, who still served in that post if only in name, was the esteemed eighty-two-year-old Simon Bradstreet, who had presided at the marriage of the deceased baby's parents. Bradstreet was now one of only two survivors of the original twenty thousand English people who had settled Boston a half century before.

In acknowledgment of their central role in his baby's short life, Samuel had asked two women to bear the tiny chestnut coffin to its final resting place. The coffin weighed so little that Elizabeth Weeden, the midwife, and Nurse Hill took turns carrying it. The nurse had wrapped the body in a linen pall, but she saw no need to add tansy, thyme, or other herbs, as she would have in summer.

Samuel followed the coffin. He held the hand of his oldest son and namesake, now age seven, whose three younger siblings stayed home. His mother-in-law, Judith Quincy Hull, came next, arm in arm with Ephraim Savage, the forty-year-old widower of her niece, Mary, a daughter of Judith's only sibling, Edmund Quincy. "Cousin Savage," as Samuel termed Ephraim because his late wife was Hannah's first cousin, was a member of the Harvard class of 1662, a son of another Third Church founder, Colonel Thomas Savage, and a grandson of the banished heretic Anne Hutchinson. "Cousin" Jeremiah Dummer, a distant maternal relative of Samuel's who had apprenticed to John Hull as a silversmith, came next, leading Ann Quincy, whose husband, Daniel, Judith Quincy Hull's nephew, another silversmith, was ill. The term *Cousin*, which Samuel used frequently, was broader in meaning than it is now.

Although not himself of Boston's elite, Samuel was intimate with the grandchildren of the wealthy, powerful first Bostonians, mostly because of his wife, a granddaughter of early settlers Edmund Quincy and Robert Hull. Beyond that marital connection, Samuel was close with grandsons of such founding figures as Governor John Winthrop, Governor Thomas Dudley, First Church minister John Cotton, and Anne Hutchinson. In this insular culture, the progeny of the founders, who had battled over control of the nascent country, took each other's hands in friendship or marriage. It was also a tribal aristocracy or, perhaps more accurately, a self-perpetuating oligarchy: prominent men whose wives died looked for new wives among the widows of their deceased friends. Similarly, it was not uncommon for someone to marry his own stepsibling, as the Reverend Increase Mather did when he wed Mary Cotton, the daughter of his stepmother, Sarah Cotton Mather. Hannah Hull Sewall's parents were also stepsiblings who lived in the same house before they married. One benefit of familial intermarriage of this sort was keeping wealth within a family.

More than a hundred mourners attended little Henry Sewall's funeral that day, but the child's mother and paternal grandparents were absent. Henry and Jane Dummer Sewall could not travel easily from Newbury in winter weather. Hannah was still lying in at home. A woman of a considerable estate could lie in indefinitely. Hannah's mood, which her husband did not record, could not have been good.

At the cemetery the gravedigger had already dug the hole inside the Hull family tomb, a mausoleum enclosing a burial chamber that was now half-full of water despite the general freeze. As the coffin was placed in the ground, the Reverend Willard prayed for the souls of those left behind. Someone threw lime on the baby's coffin. Samuel and Sam Jr. covered it with dirt and tears. At around five o'clock most of the mourners proceeded two by two along the dark and icy roads to the Hull-Sewall house, where they feasted on bread, meat, and cheese and drank beer, hard cider, and wine.

Another foot of snow fell that night. While Samuel's neighbors slept, the grieving father stayed up with Little Hull, who had "a sore convulsion fit" that continued "wave upon wave" into the morning. On Friday Samuel Phillips, a Harvard-educated minister from Rowley, the North Shore town where Sewall's paternal grandfather had spent the few years before his death in 1657, visited the family and went to "pray with Hullie."

Friday was Christmas Day, which the Sewalls were careful not to observe. Puritans had left feast days behind in England, along with many other features of the state church they still reproached for its "popish injunctions," in the words of Samuel's father-in-law. Puritans, who were known in England as nonconformists, viewed the Bible with a strict and frequently literal eye. The Sabbath was the most important day. To honor other days, as Anglicans and Catholics did, profaned the Sabbath and violated God's Fourth Commandment, to "remember the Sabbath day and keep it holy." In 1659, in keeping with its goal of creating a Bible Commonwealth, the Massachusetts General Court banned all Christmas celebrations. The statute reads, "For preventing disorders ... by reason of some still observing such festivals as were superstitiously kept in other countries to the great dishonor of God and offence of others ... whosoever shall be found observing any such day as Christmas and the like, either by forbearing labor, feasting, or any other way ... shall pay for every such offence, five shillings as a fine...." The same week that Henry Sewall died, the Reverend James Allen of the First Church reminded his congregation yet again that Christmas celebrations are "anti-Christian heresy."

Even as Samuel mourned his son, he could savor his town's avoidance of holiday festivities. Carts bearing food, other goods, and firewood traveled into and out of Boston along the bumpy road before his house. Shops were "open as usual," he noted on Christmas Day, as he would do every Christmas for decades. The few Bostonians who "somehow observe" the day "are vexed, I believe, that the body of the people profane it. Blessed be God" there is "no authority yet to compel them to keep" the holiday.

His *yet* is telling. The authority that would compel Bostonians to keep holidays they opposed was coming to New England in the form of English governors and laws. Christmas festivities and Anglican worship were on their way. The Puritan world that Samuel and his Puritan peers knew and loved was falling apart. "The symptoms of death are on us," he observed in his diary in January 1686 as his peers in the Massachusetts General Court viciously debated their next move. The Puritan experiment of creating a New Canaan in the wilderness of America, where they could worship as they believed God wanted, had begun "palpably to die." Indeed, that death was not just beginning. The colony was already defunct.

That story begins in England more than half a century earlier, when John Winthrop and colleagues secured a royal charter from King Charles I to create a trading company, the Massachusetts Bay Company, which they used to found the colony of Massachusetts Bay. In a break with colonial tradition, they carried on board ship with them in 1630 the paper document that was the charter rather than leaving it with the English court. Today, almost four hundred years later, that paper document is the crown jewel of the collection at the Commonwealth of Massachusetts archives on the Boston waterfront.

Winthrop and other early colonial leaders used—even exploited— that charter to create their own government and militia and to build their own towns, schools, and churches. One of their central goals was to worship freely, but they did not seek religious freedom in the modern sense of permitting the expression of varying views. They wished to worship in their own way—without the Anglican Book of Common Prayer, the cross at baptism, the surplice worn by clergy in the Church of England, and the requirement of kneeling at the Lord's Supper and keeping holy days. They felt entitled to expel from their society not only nonconforming Puritans, such as Roger Williams, John Wheelwright, and Anne Hutchinson in the 1630s, but also people of other faiths, including Anglicans, Catholics, Quakers, and Baptists. The colonial leaders, who were called magistrates, also felt entitled to grant themselves and each other vast parcels of American soil.

Within a few years of arriving with their open-ended charter, most leading men held vast expanses of land, far more than they could have afforded or even imagined owning in England. At the same time, troubling reports of the colonists' excessive freedoms as well as disloyalty to the Crown reached the court of King Charles I. The king sent an order for the return of the Massachusetts charter in 1635. Governor Winthrop ignored this and similar requests from the parent country, a tactic that would prove effective for nearly five decades.

In the minds of the colonists, the creation of Massachusetts was the will of God. Like the Jews in ancient Egypt, the Puritans in England were enslaved by an idolatrous state church. The bishops and arch-bishops of the Church of England were the pharaohs, and the English Book of Common Prayer demanded they worship false gods. God had "moved the hearts of many" English nonconformists "to transport themselves far off beyond the seas into ... New England," Samuel's father-in-law, John Hull, explained in 1649. "And [God] brought year after year such [people] as might be fit materials for a commonwealth ... some of the choicest use, both for ministry and magistracy. Military men, seamen, tradesmen, etc., and of large estates and free spirits to spend and be spent for the advancement of this work that the Lord had to perform and to make this wilderness as Babylon was once to Israel, as a wine cellar for Christ to refresh his spouse in...." Just as the Jews were refreshed and purified in Babylon, so the Puritans were improved by their exodus to America. Christ's spouse was their own Congregational Church, a covenanted community of "saints."

In 1649 when John Hull wrote this, Boston was a thriving, nineteen-year-old mercantile town of about a thousand souls. The town was the heart of a much larger English settlement, reaching all the way from Maine (then part of Massachusetts) to Connecticut, with a population of slightly more than twenty thousand English settlers, about 10 percent of them living in Boston, Roxbury, Dorchester, and Charlestown. Oliver Cromwell and his Puritan-led Parliament, which beheaded King Charles I in London in 1649, felt no need to interfere with a Puritan colony. During the 1650s, according to the eighteenth-century historian Thomas Hutchinson, Massachusetts "approached very near to an independent commonwealth," with a "system of laws of government" that "departed from their charter."

This was Winthrop's intent. As a trained lawyer he respected English common law, but he wished to create a new legal system in Massachusetts. Instead of making common law the ground of their legal code, as in England, the Puritan leaders relied on the law of Moses, as outlined in the Ten Commandments from the Hebrew Bible. These men created a governing body, the Great and General Court of Massachusetts, which served as their legislature, administration, and judiciary—to use terminology of a later period, for they did not perceive these divisions. (As a precedent, the English parliament functioned as both high court and legislature.) The General Court initially limited the vote in Massachusetts to male members of the Congregational Church, but the magistrates soon extended the franchise to all land-owning men, or roughly half the English males. Women, Native Americans, Africans, and other nationalities could not vote. The author of the first draft of Massachusetts's body of laws, in 1635, was none other than the Reverend John Cotton, the influential teacher of the First Church, formerly England's most celebrated Puritan divine, who had no prior experience writing laws. Most colonial law came directly from the Bible, but Winthrop and his peers also borrowed from English common law. Winthrop admired the English principle of relying on legal precedent, for instance, as well as aspects of English statute law, which prohibited witchcraft. In 1604 under King James I, England's parliament passed a statute that made witchcraft a felony, punishable by death. The General Court of Massachusetts enacted a similar statute in 1642. By the mid-seventeenth century the Massachusetts magistrates could take freely from both Scripture and the English legal system with little interference from England.

But their sense that they could freely govern themselves ended abruptly in 1660, when the English monarchy was restored. King Charles I's son Charles II ascended the throne. Puritans on both sides of the Atlantic viewed Charles II with particular repugnance because of his links to Catholicism and France. Through his mother, Henrietta Maria of France, Charles II was a first cousin of the Catholic French king Louis XIV. This distrust was mutual. One of Charles II's hopes was to fulfill his father's 1635 order for the return of the colonial charter, but he was initially distracted by several colonial wars. He fought the Netherlands for control of New Amsterdam, which England took and renamed New York. He helped to finance New England's bloody war with the Indians, King Philip's War, in 1675. So it was not until the 1680s that Charles II finally had time to consider the defiance of Massachusetts Bay Colony, which behaved toward its mother country like a wayward adolescent flouting parental rules. Finally, from the king's perspective, on October 23, 1684, England's High Court of Chancery revoked the colony's 1630 charter. From that day on Massachusetts Bay Colony was no more.

Slightly more than a year later, at the time of little Henry Sewall's funeral, New England had no clear government. The charter that gave

Governor Simon Bradstreet his power had been vacated, but the new governor, who would be appointed by the Crown rather than elected by the freemen of the colony, had not yet arrived. The General Court of Massachusetts on which Samuel served continued stubbornly to meet four times a year, as it had since 1630. But it no longer had power to make or enforce laws. The former colony was now a province of England—*province* suggesting far more deference to the Crown— and all the rights and privileges enjoyed by men like Samuel were in question.

In the wake of these two traumatic deaths—of his colony and of his son—Samuel had several memorable dreams. In his diary, which he kept beside his bed, he recorded at dawn those he could remember. The most unusual dream occurred during the night of Friday, January 1, 1686, which for him was not the first day of the first month of a new year. Protestant England and its colonies still used the old Julian calendar, which begins each year on March 25, although much of Europe had followed Pope Gregory XIII in adopting the modern, or Gregorian, calendar in 1582.

In one of Samuel's dreams Jesus Christ appeared in human form in colonial Boston. "Our Savior, in the days of His flesh when upon earth, came to Boston and abode here," Samuel reported. Like countless friends, relatives, and servants of the Sewalls, Jesus Christ chose to stay at Father Hull's house. While dreaming, Samuel "admired the goodness and wisdom of Christ in coming hither and spending some part of His short life here" in Congregational, nonconformist Boston, which was in fact under threat. Placing first-century Christ in seventeenth-century Boston, as Samuel did in his dream, may have suggested the mutual possibility of resurrection from death. This visitation was not Jesus Christ's Second Coming, which Samuel and his peers often discussed, but his first incarnation, at the start of the Christian era. As Samuel observed later, the "chronological absurdity" of this appearance in Boston "never came into my mind."

What did occur to him while dreaming was that if Jesus Christ were in Boston, "how much more Boston had to say than [Catholic] Rome boasting of Peter's being there." This idea, that true Christianity is American and Congregationalist, was a core New England belief. Boston's first generation of nonconformist ministers, the men who created the Congregational Church—the Reverends John Cotton, John Wilson, Richard Mather, John Eliot, and Thomas Shepard—considered themselves and their flocks a literal gathering of saints. It was Samuel's dream to follow them in creating a Bible Commonwealth where their savior, Jesus Christ, might actually "wish to dwell."

Samuel's pleasure in this dream was tempered by his inborn sense of regret. Seeing Jesus in the flesh, he rued "the great respect that I ought to have showed Father Hull since Christ chose when in town to take up His quarters at his house." This was natural for Samuel—to feel he had not done what was right.

3

3

HAVE MERCY UPON ME

Even without the charter that gave them the power to make and enforce laws, the magistrates of Massachusetts still needed to maintain order. Blasphemy, rape, murder, and other violations of the Ten Commandments did not end with the revocation of the charter, and may even have increased because of the general insecurity accompanying that loss. Samuel and his colleagues had no choice but to continue to enforce their law, even if its foundation was in doubt. As much as possible, they continued to wield power as they had before, in the vain hope that other matters might again distract the king.

Early on the morning of Thursday, March 11, a lecture (or sermon) day in Boston, Samuel could hear the multitudes gather in the market square. Boston was about to have its first public execution in years. The event, a hanging at the gallows on Boston Common for murder, was to be the subject of the compulsory lecture service that day at the First Church. The lecturer was the famed Reverend Increase Mather, forty-six, the senior minister of Boston's Second (also North) Church. The guilty party, who would be displayed before the congregation in chains, was a thirty-year-old indentured servant, James Morgan. In a drunken fight the previous December Morgan had stabbed another man, James Johnson, in the abdomen with an iron spit. Johnson died.

At a Boston trial at which Samuel Sewall had presided, James Morgan confessed to the crime and showed a spirit of repentance. The court convicted him of murder, a capital offense, and sent him to jail to await execution. During his imprisonment Morgan requested and was granted time for counsel and prayer with the young minister Cotton Mather, Increase's son. Five days before Morgan's scheduled hanging, Cotton Mather preached on Morgan's sin at the Second Church on Sunday morning. The same afternoon, at the Third Church, the Reverend Joshua Moody took Morgan's execution as his sermon text.

In the minds of the Puritan ministers, public punishment of a sinner was a public service. It demonstrated to the community the wages of sin. But many people considered it simply a celebrated spectacle, a chance to skip work and have fun, as a ball game or a parade is regarded today. Twenty-seven years later, at the public execution of another convicted murderer on Boston Common, Samuel rearranged his schedule to give his servant Tom Lamb a day off, "as 'tis promised him," so Lamb could attend the event and share in the crowd's "general satisfaction." During a visit to Cambridge, England, in 1689 Samuel noted that the gallows of that university town was suitably located on "a dale, convenient for spectators to stand all round on the rising ground."

On March 11 at the Sewall house several blocks from the First Church, Samuel donned his overcoat and headed for the market square, where the First Church was. The size of the gathering crowd amazed him. Standing apart from the mob, Samuel watched men and women shove through the main entrance of the Old Meeting House, as he called the First Church. During a lull he slipped into the church through a side door. Morgan, fresh from jail, stood at the front of the meetinghouse near the pulpit. Iron chains encircled the convicted murderer's arms, yet he clasped a Bible, making a visual image of a penitent sinner. This was standard during an execution sermon. As much as the Puritans hated "popish" symbols like stained glass and ornate statuary, they understood the power of imagery. Penitents in church sometimes wore sackcloth over their clothes as a symbol of repentance or covered themselves with ashes. These practices had biblical roots. In the Old Testament the prophet Daniel displays sorrow and anguish by wearing sackcloth and ashes. Job sews a garment of sackcloth to wear beside his skin. Humbled by God, he says in chapter 42, "I abhor myself, and repent in dust and ashes." In Jonah 3:3–10 God sends Jonah to Nineveh to warn the city that God will punish its sins. In response to this warning the king of Nineveh proclaims a fast and orders his people to cover themselves with sackcloth, "cry mightily to God," and "turn from" evil and violence. "When God saw what they did, how they turned from their evil way, God repented of the evil which he had said he would do to them; and he did not do it." The Salem minister John Higginson affirmed in 1686 that sackcloth "signifies the sad afflicted and mournful condition that the churches and witnesses of Christ shall be in."

Public repentance was essential to Puritan devotional life. Despite the seeming bleakness of the core belief in humanity's fundamental depravity, Puritan theology always left a door open to sinners. If a sinner would only repent, he might return to grace. The practice of course had biblical roots. The Hebrew word for repentance means "to return" and "to feel sorrow." The New Testament word for repentance is the Greek *metanoia*, which means "a change of mind," "to think again," or "to see in a new way." Thus repentance is a change of mind and heart that occurs after the fact. Repentance was so important to Puritans that the question of innocence or guilt became secondary. If a person confessed and seemed to repent, he was given another chance. Repentance might not prevent punishment, but it enabled a sinner to be reconciled with God. If repentance happened in public, as with James Morgan, the community could benefit. Thus the Reverend Mather's sermon on Morgan's misbehavior was not only to reform Morgan but also to instruct the crowd.

As Samuel watched the rabble, the Reverend John Eliot approached him. Eliot, who was known as the Indian Apostle because of his commitment to evangelizing Native Americans, was now eighty-one years old. One of Boston's first and best known ministers, he had arrived in 1631 on the ship carrying Governor John Winthrop's family. He began preaching at Roxbury the next year. His attentions always honored Samuel, who considered "Mr. Eliot" a mentor.

"Captain Sewall, a crazed woman has caused a panic in the gallery of the meetinghouse," the ancient minister greeted him, using Samuel's military title. As a captain of the Ancient and Honorary Artillery Company, Samuel led the troops in their monthly exercises on Boston Common. The crazed woman, later revealed to be the daughter of Morgan's master, who resented losing her servant, had disrupted the meeting by crying "Fire!" from the balcony of the meetinghouse. This prompted people to "rush out with great consternation," according to Eliot, who feared the gallery might fall under the weight of the crowd. Eliot asked Sewall's permission to move the meeting a block up the road to the larger Third Church.

Sewall consulted with Governor Bradstreet, who had been a member of the Third Church since 1680, and the Reverends Cotton and Increase Mather. All consented to the move, which took an hour to accomplish. In the Third Church, the Reverend Increase Mather led James Morgan, still in chains, to the pulpit. Mather was a tall, thin man with a long, thin face, a prominent nose, and a solemn look due partly to poor eyesight. A serious man, he had a tendency toward depression or, some historians say, manic depression. The experience of partaking in the Lord's Supper sometimes overwhelmed him with such a sense of God's generosity to humanity that he was moved to tears. For this execution sermon he had chosen a relevant text, Numbers 35:16: "If he smite him with an instrument of iron, so that he die, he [is] a murderer: the murderer shall surely be put to death."

After the lecture the congregation sang the first part of Psalm 51, a song of penitence that calls for deliverance from sin. King David composed this psalm after recognizing, through the interventions of the prophet Nathan, that his behavior with Bathsheba—committing adultery and arranging for her husband to be murdered—was sinful. The story of King David's growing awareness of his wrongdoing was meant to help turn a sinner toward God. Their Latinate English translation from the biblical Hebrew was the second version of this psalm offered by the *Bay Psalm Book*.

Psalm 51

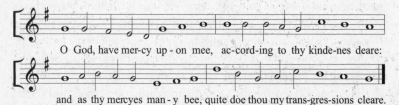

O God, have mer-cy up-on mee, ac-cord-ing to thy kinde-nes deare:

and as thy mercyes man-y bee, quite doe thou my trans-gres-sions cleare.

Old Hundredth Tune

O God, have mercy upon mee,
    according to thy kindenes deare:
  and as thy mercyes many bee,
    quite doe thou my transgressions cleare.

2 From my perversnes mee wash through,
    and from my sin mee purify.
3 For my transgressions I doe know,
    before mee is my sin dayly.

4 Gainst thee, thee only sin'd have I,
    & done this evill in thy sight:
  that when thou speakst thee justify
    men may, and judging cleare thee quite.

5 Loe, in injustice shape't I was:
    in sin my mother conceav'd mee.
6 Loe, thou in th'inwards truth lov'd haz:
    and made mee wise in secrecie.

7 Purge me with hyssope, & I cleare
    shall be; mee wash, & then the snow
8 I shall be whiter. Make me heare
    Joy & gladnes, the bones which so

Thou broken hast joy cheerly shall.
9   Hyde from my sins thy face away
  blot thou iniquityes out all
    which are upon mee any way.

For his final walk from the meetinghouse to the Boston gallows, James Morgan requested the company of the Reverend Cotton Mather. The two men prayed together as they traveled the two rutted blocks to the broad slope of the common, where the gallows stood. The young minister, who is now considered Massachusetts's most famous Puritan preacher, was then just a promising third-generation legacy, the son and grandson of more famous ministers, with the insecurities attendant on that status.

Cotton Mather's double surname indicates his dual descent from the founding generation of divines. John Cotton, his mother's father, was the celebrated English Puritan preacher. In 1633, after the Church of England archbishop, William Laud, suppressed him, John Cotton sailed to Boston, where he was immediately given the plum position of teacher at its First Church. John Cotton died in 1652. Four years later his widow married Richard Mather, the Dorchester minister, who had arrived from England in 1635 after similar persecution for his religious nonconformity. Richard and Sarah Cotton Mather lived together with their younger children in the Cotton house on Cotton Hill, which is now known as Pemberton Hill and faces Boston City Hall. (A brass plaque on the plaza before the John Adams Courthouse marks the site of that house.) Cotton's daughter Mary married her stepbrother the Reverend Increase Mather in 1662 and nine months later gave birth to Cotton Mather. A brilliant child, he could read and understand Greek and Latin at age eleven, when he was admitted to Harvard College, roughly four years younger than most of his classmates. The summer that eleven-year-old Cotton Mather entered Harvard, Samuel Sewall graduated at twenty-two with a master's degree in divinity. Four years later, when he was only fifteen, Cotton Mather received an undergraduate degree. In his early twenties he preached often at his father's church in the North End, and his father ordained him in May of 1685. Now, in 1686, Cotton Mather was just twenty-three. He had a rounder face than his father, a prominent nose, and large, intense, widely spaced eyes. He wore the black preaching gown and skullcap favored by Puritan divines.

A crowd of onlookers followed the minister and the condemned servant, enjoying the spectacle and the anticipation of more. At the gallows Mather and Morgan continued praying for so long that most of the crowd departed for the midday meal. Morgan's repentance did not prevent his punishment, and at five-thirty James Morgan was finally "turned off," as Samuel noted that evening in his diary: "The day was comfortable but now, [at] 9 o'clock, rains."

Although Samuel apparently lost no sleep over Morgan's soul, he regretted the loss of saintly men and women. Only twenty-four hours after Morgan's execution Samuel reported that "Father Porter," who was "acknowledged by all to have been a great man in prayer," was "laid in the Old Cemetery."

Hardly a month after Morgan's execution, the leading men of Boston were again called to punish misbehavior, this time by one their own. The offender was a young minister, twenty-eight-year-old Thomas Cheever, a son of the Boston schoolmaster, Ezekiel Cheever, whom Samuel and his colleagues knew intimately as the teacher of their sons. Young Cheever preached in Malden, northeast of Cambridge. Townspeople accused him of committing adultery and using obscene language "not fit to be named." The former involved "shameful and abominable violations of the Seventh Commandment" ("Thou shalt not commit adultery"). The latter, a violation of the Third Commandment ("Thou shalt not take the Lord's name in vain"), occurred in a public house in Salem.

A group of powerful magistrates and ministers had agreed to sit in justice on this case, as was standard in the Congregational Church. Samuel and his friend and minister, Samuel Willard, of the Third Church, were asked to join this ad hoc church court, and both consented. At four in the morning of April 7, 1686, the two Samuels met at the front gate of Sewall's house to walk together to the Charlestown ferry. They had no horses because the trip to Malden could be accomplished mostly by water. Before dawn they had crossed the Charles River by ferry and hired another boat to take them up the Mystic River to the Malden River. From the Malden dock they walked to a private house owned by Cornet Henry Green, where the church court would meet.

The court comprised representatives of Boston's three churches (First, Second, and Third) and several members of the General Court, including Samuel and John Richards, who would later serve with Samuel on the witchcraft court. Several additional men crowded into the parlor of the Green house, including Samuel Parris, a pale man of thirty-two with long brown hair who was considering becoming a minister. Parris wanted to learn about church discipline. A few years hence, in November 1689, Parris would be ordained and installed as the preacher of Salem Village, where he would lead the charge against suspected witchcraft in 1692. Ezekiel Cheever, the father of the accused, had requested permission to be present and was allowed, as befitted his high status. The ministers, teachers, and judges of early New England had intentionally left behind many trappings of life in Old England, yet they had perhaps inadvertently created new versions of aspects of that world. They developed an oligarchy, for instance, in which the sons of the leading citizens in one generation became the leaders, often the Congregationalist ministers, of the next.

The Reverend James Allen began the meeting of the church council with prayer. Allen, an Oxford-educated Puritan in his early fifties who had sailed to America in 1662 after the Church of England ejected him, had served at Boston's First Church since 1667. The group quickly chose as its moderator Increase Mather, who commenced to pray. Increase Mather was the rare Harvard-educated Bostonian who had sailed east across the ocean. After taking a master's in divinity at Trinity College, Dublin, he had returned to Boston in 1661. Since 1664 he had preached twice weekly at the Second Church, as he would do for nearly four decades, often to a congregation of a thousand.

Following a brief debate over procedure, the judges called in young Cheever and several witnesses to his misbehavior. The witnesses recounted what they had observed—adultery and obscene language. Cheever said he was innocent of all the charges: the accounts the court had heard were false. The Reverend Joshua Moody of Boston's First Church spoke for the council in admonishing Cheever for "grievous" behavior. Moody advised Cheever to repent. Cheever said he could not repent because he was innocent. Moody said he should sleep on the council's recommendation. That evening, before Samuel Sewall, John Richards, and the Greens' other houseguests could retire to bed, Increase Mather prayed with them for another hour. Private houses often served as inns, as bed-and-breakfasts do today. Lodging was also available at many public houses, which served as taverns and inns every day except the Sabbath, when they were required to close.

Early the next morning Mather prayed over his notes of the proceedings before sending for the accused. Mather told Cheever that the council believed the accusations against him. Cheever replied, "If I ever did violate any of the Commandments, I have no memory of it."

Angrily the older minister said, "The council, at the request of this church in Malden, declares Thomas Cheever guilty of great scandals, by more than two or three witnesses.... We have cause to fear that he has been too much accustomed to an evil course of levity and profaneness. Also we find that as to some particulars he pretends he does not remember them. Nor," he emphasized, "have we seen that humble penitential frame in him when before us, that would have become him."

Repentance, that key ingredient for Puritans, was lacking. A few years later an exemplary Massachusetts minister, Joseph Green, who took the pulpit of Salem Village in the troubled period after the witch trials, enumerated in his diary the steps to living rightly as a Puritan. Repentance was essential to his list.

1. Pray to God in secret.... Pray to God that he would pardon your sins.... Pray to Jesus Christ to pardon you ... and save you from hell fire, and from eternal misery....

3. Keep holy the Sabbath day. Do not speak your own words nor think your own thoughts on the Sabbath, but spend the whole day in reading and praying and other holy duties....

5. Remember Death; think much of death; think how it will be on a death bed, whether then you will not wish that you had prayed....

6. Think much of the Day of Judgment, when ... all secret sins shall be discovered and shall be punished with eternal burnings....

7. Think ... seriously of eternity. Think of those that are in hell, that must abide under all the pain imaginable to eternity, and those that are in heaven shall live in the greatest happiness with God forever....

9. Do not put off your repentance 'til tomorrow; but today while the day of grace lasts give all diligence to secure your souls; for you know not you may be in hell before tomorrow if you defer your repentance.

Sin is a natural consequence of humanity's fall in both Jewish and Christian traditions. As descendants of Adam and Eve, humans cannot avoid sin. But after sinning must come repentance, turning away from the sin. That is the only way to redemption. At Malden that day the ministers urged Cheever to do what was right. They prayed that he would turn away from his sin and toward God. Cheever refused.

Seeing young Cheever fail to manifest "that repentance which the rule requires," the Reverend Increase Mather spoke for the council.

"We suspend Mr. Thomas Cheever from the exercise of his ministerial function" and "keep him from the Lord's Table" for six weeks. In addition to losing his work as a preacher, young Cheever lost his enjoyment of one of the two sacraments of the Congregational Church. Reformed churches had left behind most of the seven Roman Catholic sacraments, preserving only two, baptism and communion. (They called their sacraments *ordinances*, also to separate themselves from the Catholic Church.) Baptism could be granted to children of the elect in the Puritan church, but communion was reserved for the elect, those people who could convincingly show they were under God's grace, which Cheever no longer could.

The church council met again six weeks later, this time in Boston, to determine if Cheever could be brought back into communion. Brought before the ministers and judges, Cheever again refused to acknowledge guilt. In response, the council unanimously found him guilty and dismissed him as Malden's pastor. He would later move east to Rumney Marsh, which is now Revere, and find work as a teacher. The church council also urged a fast day in Malden so the congregation could "humble themselves by fasting and prayer before the Lord."

4

DEADLY ENEMIES

Samuel "came home well" from the council meeting in Malden—thanking God in his usual way by noting in his diary *"Laus Deo"*—but all was not well at home. Little Hull's seizures were worse. They had grown more frequent in recent weeks. One morning Samuel arose to discover that his now-youngest son had had "a sore fit in the night," soiling himself and his parents' bed.

The exact cause of Hull's convulsions is not clear, although children commonly contracted infections that led to diarrhea, vomiting, high fever, and sometimes seizures. Two of Samuel's intimates, his brother Stephen and his friend Elisha Hutchinson, had recently lost infant sons who had suffered multiple convulsions, probably due to infections that spread to the brain. Samuel and Hannah's first two sons had also had febrile convulsions. Baby John's first two seizures occurred when he was two months old. Asleep in his cradle on Sunday, June 16, 1677, the child "suddenly started, trembled, his fingers contracted, his eyes starting and being distorted." This prompted his twenty-five-year-old father to ride to Charlestown for the doctor. Two days later the baby had another seizure. Johnny died fifteen months later of unknown causes. Hoping to avoid this result with Sam Jr., in May 1680 Samuel "carried" his almost two-year-old namesake "to Newbury where his grandmother [Sewall] nurses him,... to see if [the] change of air would help him against convulsions." It was

reasonable to remove a frail child from a crowded port town that
received ships bearing sailors who might be infected with smallpox,
malaria, typhus, influenza, dysentery, or other scourges. Sam Jr. experienced no seizures while with his grandparents, returned to his
parents healthy a year later, and was now approaching his eighth
birthday.

Hullie, who still had a serious fit about once a week, nevertheless
began to walk and talk. His first word was "apple," which his grandmother Hull and a servant named Eliza Lane heard him utter in the
kitchen on Sunday, February 1, 1686, when he was eighteen months
old. This news filled Samuel with hope and joy. In late March, however, Samuel noted that while he was visiting the Reverend Increase
Mather at home in the North End, Hull had a "very sore" seizure.

The next week, hoping to cure his fits, Samuel and Hannah decided
to send little Hull to stay with his paternal grandparents in Newbury,
Samuel's adopted hometown. Sewall did not set eyes on this region
until he was nine, yet he considered himself a "Newbury man." The
region's hold on him was due, in part, to its landscape. Horses and
cattle grazed on fields of salt marsh dotted with haystacks that
stretched to the sea. At the shore a slender barrier island, Plum Island,
provided protection for mackerel, sea bass, and migratory birds. "Plum
Island lies, like a whale aground, / A stone's toss over the narrow
sound," the nineteenth-century poet John Greenleaf Whittier wrote.
"Beyond are orchards and planting lands, / And great salt marshes
and glimmering sands." The hills of Newbury afforded magnificent
views of Cape Ann, New Hampshire's Isles of Shoals, Mount Agamenticus in Maine, and the vast Atlantic. This was a magical world to
which Samuel delighted in bringing his children.

Early on April 26, 1686, Samuel and Hannah and their smallest
living son set out for Newbury. The driver of their coach was Samuel's
clerk, Eliakim Mather, the Reverend Increase Mather's nineteen-year-
old nephew, who lived with the Sewalls. As the coach headed north
through Charlestown, the "chippering" sparrows "proclaimed" to
Samuel the arrival of spring. The travelers met Samuel's brother
Stephen at the intersection of the Boston and Cambridge roads. On
horseback, he accompanied them to his house in Salem, where they
spent the night.

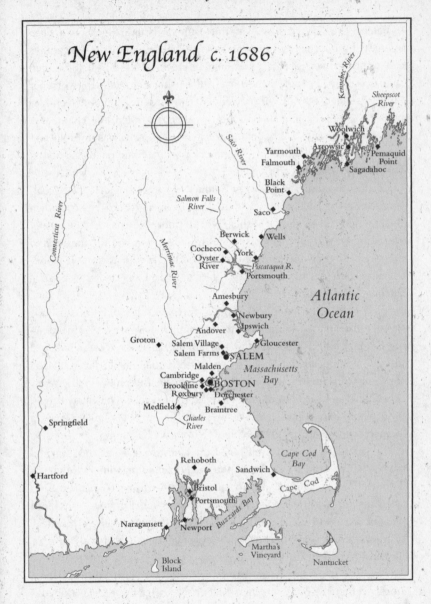

New England c. 1686

Kennebec River

Sheepscot River

Woolwich

Saco River

Arrowsic

Pemaquid Point

Yarmouth
Falmouth

Sagadahoc

Black Point

Salmon Falls River

Saco

Merrimac River

Berwick   Wells

Cocheco   York
Oyster River   *Piscataqua R.*
                    Portsmouth

Connecticut River

Amesbury

Newbury
Ipswich

Andover

Groton   Salem Village   Gloucester
          Salem Farms
          SALEM
          Malden   *Massachusetts Bay*
Cambridge
Brookline   **BOSTON**
Roxbury   Dorchester

Atlantic Ocean

Medfield   Braintree

Springfield   *Charles River*

          Rehoboth   Sandwich   *Cape Cod Bay*

Hartford

          Bristol   *Cape Cod*
          Portsmouth

Naragansett   Newport   *Buzzards Bay*

          Block Island   Martha's Vineyard   Nantucket

Salem, the largest town on the colony's North Shore, had been founded by English settlers two years before Boston. The Indians called it Naumkeag, a word for a fishing place, but its English founder, John Endicott, renamed the port town using the Hebrew word for peace. Stephen Sewall, who attended Harvard briefly as a teenager before becoming apprenticed for five years to a Salem merchant, was trusted with various important roles in town. He was the clerk—scribe—of several courts, the register of probate and deeds for Essex County, and a justice of the peace.

Salem was home to not only Samuel's brother but also many colleagues and friends. Samuel visited often, usually on trips between Boston and Newbury or other North Shore towns. He generally stayed overnight with his brother, who was five years his junior, and Stephen's twenty-one-year-old wife, Margaret, who were still grieving the death of their first baby. They lived just off the main road of the bustling town.

That evening at Stephen's house, three old North Shore friends "kindly entertained" Samuel and his wife. One was thirty-nine-year-old Colonel John Hathorne, a wealthy, pious Salem-bred merchant and justice of the peace who had served with Samuel as a magistrate on the General Court for three years. Captain Bartholomew Gedney, another local man in his midforties, was a physician. The third friend, with whom Samuel was closest, was the Reverend Nicholas Noyes, a former schoolmate from Newbury. Noyes was a chubby fellow five years Samuel's senior. A member of the Harvard class of 1667, he had been a fellow student of the famous blind schoolmaster of Newbury, Thomas Parker, who was his great-uncle. Since 1683 Noyes had been assistant minister of the Salem church. For Samuel, relaxing with old friends, a hearty meal, and invigorating conversation in his dear brother's house gave him a welcome opportunity to turn from his worries over little Hull.

The graves of his three intimate friends are now clustered in a single cemetery in downtown Salem, the Charter Street Burying Ground, then known as the Burying Point. A sign at the cemetery entrance notes these three men's "connection with the witchcraft" trials. The Reverend Noyes, who would still be preaching in Salem in 1692, officiated at many hearings that year and openly challenged the

accused witches at their executions. Hathorne and Gedney both
served as judges on the witchcraft court, Hathorne proving the most
aggressive interrogator. The nineteenth-century historian James
Savage deemed Hathorne the "most active magistrate in the prosecution of witches, exceeding mad against them." Judge Hathorne's father
had come to America in 1630, with John Winthrop. His most famous
descendant, Nathaniel Hawthorne, added a *w* to his surname to disso-
ciate himself from the ancestor whom he felt had "inherited the perse-
cuting spirit, and made himself so conspicuous in the martyrdom of
the witches, that their blood may fairly be said to have left a stain upon
him."

After a good night's sleep in Salem, the Sewalls rose early to prepare for the second leg of their trip. They shared a morning meal with
Stephen and Margaret before continuing north in their coach. Stephen
had borrowed a spry horse for them, "exceeding fit for our purpose,"
to replace their horse, which had been slow the previous day. They got
to Newbury "very well in good time."

Samuel's parents' house, which still stands and is occupied today,
was in Newbury center just opposite the meetinghouse and north of
the Town Green. It was a timber-framed, hall-and-parlor-style house
with two large main rooms flanking a central chimney, multiple fireplaces, and additional rooms beneath a lean-to and on the second floor.
The basement contained a dairy, where Samuel's mother churned milk
into cream and butter. Henry Sewall, a gentleman farmer, owned
thousands of acres in Newbury, which he both purchased and inherited and was gradually passing to his sons and sons-in-law. The first
Sewall estate, in the 1630s, consisted of several acres near the old
landing place on the Parker River, a few miles south of this house, and
five hundred acres inland along the Parker River, which the natives
called Quascacunquen.

Newbury began in the 1630s as a tight village around the Lower
Green along today's Route 1A between the Parker River and Old
Town Hill. This is where Newbury's first English settlers, about a
hundred immigrants from Wiltshire and Hampshire in southern England, chose house lots and farmed in common. Among these settlers
were Samuel's father and grandfather, who arrived with "a plentiful
estate in money, neat cattle [bovines]," and provisions "for a new

plantation." They sowed the inland soil with English grass seed for grazing. On the extensive salt meadow, now known as wetlands, they harvested salt-marsh hay, a valuable commodity. During the seventeenth century North Shore men cut and dried hundreds of thousands of tons of salt-marsh hay and loaded it onto barges, which they poled through the marsh at high tide to creeks leading to towns, where the hay was moved to ships headed for Boston and the wider market. Salt-marsh hay was used throughout the colonies for bedding and feeding cattle, sheep, and pigs.

The Reverend Parker preached his first American sermon here in 1635, and the settlers started to build a meetinghouse. But they soon realized the far greater value of the land to the north along the wider, deeper Merrimac River. So in 1646 the town center moved a few miles north, to the area of the extant Sewall house. That same year Samuel's parents—thirty-two-year-old Henry Sewall and Jane Dummer, who was not quite twenty—were married by Judge Richard Saltonstall of the General Court. (Almost a half century later Saltonstall's son Nathaniel and the Sewalls' son Samuel would serve together on the witchcraft court.) The newlywed Sewalls returned to England in 1647 with Jane's parents, who found New England's climate "not agreeable"—too cold. In 1657, learning that his own eighty-year-old father had died, Henry Sewall Jr. (his father's only child) returned to Massachusetts to claim his land and estate. While he was there the English monarchy was restored, so in 1661 Henry called for his wife and children to join him.

In the quarter century since then Samuel's parents had raised eight children, and they now helped with raising a growing brood of grandchildren, soon too numerous for Samuel to count. There were ultimately forty-three grandchildren, according to a modern genealogist, Eben Graves. Samuel had one brother besides Stephen. John Sewall had a wife and several children and ran a sawmill in Newbury Falls, now Byfield, on the North Shore. Every one of Samuel's five sisters married a local man and stayed on the North Shore. The oldest, Hannah, now thirty-seven, was married to Jacob Tappan, of Newbury, with whom she had had eight children. Jane, twenty-six and married to Moses Gerrish of Newbury, had five children so far. Twenty-three-year-old Anne was married to William Longfellow, with four children.

Mehitabel, twenty, the wife of William Moody, of Newbury, had a baby girl. Samuel's youngest sister, seventeen-year-old Dorothy, was not yet married, although she would wed Ezekiel Northend, of Rowley, in 1691.

Samuel and Hannah had packed for a week's stay in Newbury, to ensure Hullie's comfort with his grandparents, whom he had seen only a few times before. His grandmother, Jane Dummer Sewall, had come to Boston by boat to wean him—in an earlier, unsuccessful attempt to cure his seizures—but he seemed not to remember her. During the week that Samuel and Hannah spent with Hullie in Newbury, the child seemed to do well. He had no fits. God was answering their prayers, Samuel thought, "graciously" helping his family.

Samuel and Hannah left twenty-two-month-old Hullie in Newbury with his grandparents on May 6, breaking their trip home with another night in Salem. On May 7, during the trip's final leg, Hannah became painfully ill with the "flux"—diarrhea and intestinal distress, probably due to a bacterial or viral infection or to spoiled food. She often suffered from flux, especially during pregnancy. That day she felt so poorly that they chose not to stop for a sermon in Lynn that both would have enjoyed. Arriving home, they learned of the "great wedding" three days earlier of the Reverend Cotton Mather to fifteen-year-old Abigail Phillips at the elegant Charlestown home of the bride's parents. The judge who officiated, Major John Richards, had served with Samuel on Thomas Cheever's church court and would join him on the witchcraft court.

Aside from the nuptials of the pedigreed minister, most news that May was bad. Every week, it seemed, another boat from England arrived with another powerful, unwelcome guest. The unpopular new governor of New England, Edmund Andros, whom locals knew from his earlier term in Boston as a royal emissary, had been appointed by a new and even more repugnant king, James II, who succeeded his childless older brother, Charles II, in February 1685. Whereas Charles II remained Anglican and only privately received the last rites of the Catholic Church, James II actually converted to Catholicism, provoking a crisis among Protestants in England and its colonies, who were already troubled by Catholic France's mistreatment of the Huguenots under Louis XIV. James II, wishing to consolidate his colonial holdings, decreed a new English province, the Dominion of New England, to oversee the chartered colony of Massachusetts Bay. The king's ministries ruled this new dominion, which extended from northern Maine to New Jersey. Throughout this vast territory Edmund Andros had the power to seize land, levy taxes, and eliminate or alter local governments. Most irksome to Samuel, Andros and his cronies could impose Anglican services, even at Samuel's church.

Andros's assistant, Edward Randolph, was also unpleasantly familiar. In Boston on a royal mission in 1676, Randolph had earned the locals' hatred for his support of the revocation of the charter. In May 1686 he returned again, as secretary and registrar for the Dominion of New England, carrying the royal commission for a new government. The town crier proclaimed this document from the balcony of the Town House in the market square. Massachusetts was now to be governed by a president and deputy president (replacing the colony's governor and deputy governor) and sixteen counselors, who replaced the former "assistants," a term used since 1630. Randolph and Andros offered the top positions to local judges who seemed capable of moderation, as they put it, and loyalty to the Crown. William Stoughton, fifty-four, was asked to become deputy president of Massachusetts. A graduate of Harvard, class of 1650, Stoughton had studied for the ministry at Oxford, preached during the Cromwell years in England, and been ejected from the pulpit after the restoration of the monarchy. Returning to Massachusetts, he had served as a magistrate of the General Court and a colonial agent to London. The new president of Massachusetts was to be Joseph Dudley, the thirty-eight-year-old son of the colony's second governor, Thomas Dudley. A member of the Harvard class of 1665, Dudley lived on a large farm in Roxbury, where he'd been born. He had spent several years in London working to maintain the old charter. In recent months, however, he had quietly changed course, recommending to the king that he revoke the charter and appoint Dudley president of Massachusetts.

Unaware of Dudley's subversion, Samuel Sewall and the Reverend Willard urged Dudley on May 18 to refuse the presidency, to stall the offensive new government. Dudley and Willard were brothers-in-law; their wives were sisters. Sewall and Dudley would later be related through the marriage of their children, Sam Jr. and Rebecca. Dudley ignored their advice and accepted the royal appointment.

To console himself, Samuel avoided the Town House, the seat of government. With friends he bewailed the colony's losses over wine and spirits at public houses across Boston. He spent time alone singing psalms. "The foundations being destroyed, what can the righteous do?" he wondered. Still, he remembered to thank God for "our [colony's] hithertos of mercy 56 years."

On May 16 Samuel had been horrified to see Edward Randolph, a member of the Church of England, attend services at his own Third Church. That was only the beginning of the Anglican invasion. Two days later Randolph audaciously arranged for his personal chaplain, Robert Ratcliffe, to perform an Anglican wedding at the Third Church. Ratcliffe wore a surplice, the loose-fitting white ceremonial vestment used by Anglican and Catholic clergy, which Puritans rejected as a symbol of the Catholic mass and priestly role. On June 6, "in his surplice," Samuel noted with regret, Ratcliffe publicly read the Book of Common Prayer liturgy. This was heresy in Massachusetts, whose founders opposed the Book of Common Prayer and all it signified—the mass, a liturgical calendar and set list of readings, requiems, evensong, and holy days such as Easter and Christmas. By mid-June, to Samuel's great distress, Ratcliffe made plans to erect an Anglican church in Boston. That was to be King's Chapel, which still stands today.

Samuel deplored the Anglican presence in Puritan Boston. He believed that God created the Bible Commonwealth and protected it from all evils, such as disease and hunger, and every enemy. Those enemies, as he saw them, were Indians (some were "Friend Indians," but many were not), the French, the Catholic Church, Anglicans, and royalists. The list of enemies also included witches, antinomians (literally "against the law," referring to heretical Puritans), Quakers, and Baptists. There were even more distant enemies, "Turks," or Muslims, whose progress Samuel tracked. He feared the Turks would defeat Christian Europe and take over the world, a fear that lessened after the 1683 defeat of the Turks at Vienna, which ushered in more than three centuries of European dominance. Ultimately, as Samuel saw the world, all these enemies stood in for the true enemy of Samuel's America: Satan, the prince of darkness, Antichrist.

One legacy of John Winthrop, John Cotton, and other Bay Colony founders is the myth of America as a land specially favored by God, a myth we still live with today regardless of political ideology. In the spring of 1686, to preserve the spirit of that America in the face of its dying, Samuel Sewall paid the printer Samuel Green to produce hundreds of copies of a pamphlet containing the farewell sermon that John Cotton delivered on the docks in Southampton, England, in April 1630 before Winthrop's fleet set sail. The Scripture was 2 Samuel 7:10: "I will appoint a place for my people Israel, and will plant them, that they may dwell in a place of their own, and move no more; neither shall the children of wickedness afflict them any more...." By August of 1686 Samuel had donated copies of *God's Promise to His Plantation* to every magistrate of the new provincial court and to every member of the local militia.

Not long after arranging for this printing, on the morning of May 25, he read the seventeenth psalm aloud to his family. It is a prayer for deliverance from persecutors:

> O Lord, attend unto my cry, give ear unto my prayer.... I have called upon thee, for thou wilt hear me, O God: incline thine ear unto me, and hear my speech.... Keep me as the apple of thy eye, hide me under the shadow of thy wings, from the wicked that oppress me, from my deadly enemies, who compass me about.... Arise, O Lord, disappoint him, cast him down. Deliver my soul from the wicked....

This was "a precious, seasonable prayer," he told Hannah, "exceedingly suited to this day."

5

―――――⦿⦿⦿――――――

THE DEVIL AMONGST US

Sad affairs of state turned Samuel's attention inward, to his children and their accomplishments. "My son," seven-year-old Sam Jr., "reads to me Isaiah 22," he noted proudly on May 19. Samuel, the oldest son of an oldest son, had high hopes for his own oldest boy. The expectation was partly cultural: an oldest son inherited all of a father's wealth in England, whose system of primogeniture maintained large estates. A few days later, on Sunday, May 30, he heard Sam Jr. read the twenty-sixth chapter of Isaiah: "In that day shall this song be sung in the land of Judah: We have a strong city.... Open ye the gates, that the righteous nation ... may enter in." Together they sang Psalm 141, which begins, "O God, my Lord, on thee I call, do thou make haste to me." And then, "moved to sing" more, Samuel chose the seventeenth and eighteenth verses of chapter 3 of the book of Habakkuk.

Although the fig tree shall not bloss'm
neither shall fruit be in the vines;
the labour of the ol've shall fail,
and the fi-elds shall yield no meat;
the flock shall be cut off fro' the fold,
and there shall be no herd in-th' stalls:
Yet I will rejoice in the LORD,
I will joy in the God of my salvation.

Sam Jr. was to attend school for the first time the next September, at Ezekiel Cheever's house on Schoolhouse Lane, now School Street, two short blocks away. Ezekiel Cheever, father of the unrepentant minister Thomas Cheever, was master of Boston Latin, a public secondary school founded in 1635. "Mr. Cheever received him gladly," Samuel would report with pride that September. But the gladness did not last. Sam Jr. was not a gifted scholar. Within two years of admitting him Cheever would send him off to Eliezer Moody in hopes that someone else might teach him to write.

All the Sewall children, girls as well as boys, began to learn their letters at age three or four. A few years later they were expected to join the family's daily readings from catechism and Scripture. In December 1697, when Joseph was nine, he began "to read the Psalm" with the family, "by the intercessions of his mother, and his brother's concession." Joseph had started school at the tender age of two and a half. His cousin Jane Tappan walked him to Mistress Townsend's house and "carried his hornbook," a small board marked with the alphabet, the Lord's Prayer, and Roman numerals. Samuel's daughters studied with Dame Walker and, after her death, Mistress Deborah Thayer, who taught knitting, embroidery, reading, and writing. Samuel noted that "Little Betty can read and spin passing well—things very desirable in a woman." When Hannah Jr. was eight she was hit by a cart one autumn morning as she crossed a lane on her way to school. Though it knocked her to the ground, she was not seriously injured; her teeth "hurt a little."

The children's health constantly worried Samuel, who recorded far more than seizures. At six Hannah broke "her forehead grievously just above her left eye" while climbing a chair to reach atop a cupboard. A horse ran over Judith when she was three. One winter when the children were in a sleigh "the Indian who drove it struck [nine-year-old] Betty with his goad on the side of the head so as to make it bleed pretty much and swell." In 1687 Sam Jr. contracted the measles, which spread to his sisters, to several servants, including Eliakim Mather and Betty Lane, and to Samuel and his brother Stephen. Smallpox ran periodically through the town and sometimes through the family. Hannah Jr., Sam Jr., and Betty had smallpox in May 1690. A week later their cousin Jane Tappan vomited and "brings up three great worms, and much foul matter," and then developed the pox. Tape-worms, roundworms, and other parasites grew in contaminated food and also in human waste, which servants emptied from chamber pots into a privy in the yard. "Betty vomits up a long worm," he noted when his daughter was six. A few years later she "takes a vomit and brings up" three impressive worms, the longest "about eleven inches."

Early on Saturday, June 5, 1686, one month after having left Hullie in Newbury, Samuel set out alone on his horse to visit "my little Hull." He timed his trip "prudently" to avoid the Anglican takeover of his meetinghouse on the Sabbath and "to keep out of the way of the Artil-lery election." On training day, usually one Saturday a month, the sol-diers of the Ancient and Honorable Artillery Company, the militia founded in 1638, marched around Boston Common with muskets, swords, and pikes. The men practiced shooting volleys, doublings, and facings. Following their drills they retired to a public house for a "treat" such as beer, bread, and a custard of sweet cream and wine called Syllabub. This military activity had pleased Samuel when it served the colony, but it was a burden now.

On Sunday, after attending meeting with his parents and his littlest boy, who seemed well, Samuel rode to West Newbury to visit his sister Anne. "Sister Longfellow" fed him "strawberries and cream" at "the Falls," a waterfall on the Old Newbury River, now the Parker River. The Longfellows farmed five hundred acres that had been granted to Henry Sewall Sr. in the 1630s.

Samuel began his return trip as soon as the elections in Boston were over, stopping in Salem "for the sake of" hearing his old friend "Mr. Noyes's lecture" on the virtue of humility. That Friday, in Boston, Samuel walked to the Town House for the meeting of the new council. Government chambers filled the second-floor gallery of the Town House, which rose on ten-foot-high pillars above a merchants' exchange where vendors peddled their goods. The Town House cellar contained a small jail and a room for a bellman. He was charged with ringing the bells of the adjacent First Church for services and beating drums three times a day—to wake the town at five in the morning, to call merchants to work at eleven, and to send tavern-goers home by nine.

Unhappily, Samuel took the oath of allegiance to the new govern-ment. He demonstrated discontent by taking the oath in the "New

England fashion," holding the Bible in his left hand and holding up his right hand to heaven. The "English fashion" of taking an oath, which entailed holding or kissing the Bible, seemed to violate the Second and Third Commandments. Samuel was again commissioned a captain in the militia. His close friend Captain Elisha Hutchinson, a grandson of the heretic Anne Hutchinson, refused to take any oath to the Crown, so he received no public role and no military commission. Samuel's tenure as captain would not last long. In an argument over whether or not to include the cross of Saint George, a symbol of England, on the colonial flag, he would resign. New Englanders had left the "popish" cross out of their flag since 1634 with the exception of the flag flying over the castle on the harbor, which English ships could see. After wrestling with the question, Samuel concluded that to allow the cross on the flag could "hinder my entrance into the Holy Land."

On Saturday, June 19, just before six in the morning, his brother-in-law Jacob Tappan arrived at the front door of the Sewall house. Tappan had left Newbury at dusk Friday and ridden through the night. He spoke to a servant, who relayed upstairs the awful news, which Samuel recorded in his diary: "My dear son, Hull Sewall, dies at Newbury about one o'clock" the previous day.

Within an hour Samuel was prepared to join his brother-in-law for the trip to Newbury for the boy's funeral. The other children were too young for the trip. Hannah, again pregnant, stayed home. Samuel and John rode north all day and arrived as the sun set over the sultry hills of West Newbury. Relatives and friends, including the Harvard-educated ministers John Woodbridge, Joshua Moody, and John Richardson, awaited him at his parents' house. Samuel asked two of their sons, John Moody and Johnny Richardson, his nine-year-old nephew John Tappan, and a local boy named Samuel Thompson to be Hullie's pall-bearers. The crowd moved "very quickly" to the meetinghouse for the evening burial, which began with the minister saying a prayer for Hullie. It was dusk before the four young pallbearers carefully laid the little coffin in the ground. Samuel had brought black kid gloves to give to mourners, but it seemed "too late"—perhaps he was just too heartbroken—to distribute them to anyone but pallbearers. Family members at seventeenth-century English funerals customarily handed out black scarves, gloves, or hatbands and sometimes black and gold enamel rings as reminders of not only the deceased but also our common end.

Early the next morning Samuel and his father and mother, who were seventy-two and about sixty-seven, returned to the cemetery for the burial of an old Newbury man, Richard Collicut. At this longer ceremony the Reverend Richardson preached from 1 Corinthians 3:21–23: "Therefore let no man glory in men, for all things are yours; whether Paul, or Apollos, or Cephas, or the world, or life, or death, or things present, or things to come; all are yours; And ye are Christ's; and Christ *is* God's." (The italics are his.) Samuel observed that the minister seemed to go "something out of his order by reason of the occasion ... singling out those words *Or Death.*"

The bereaved father headed home late Monday by way of Salem, where he slept at his brother's and distributed the balance of his funeral gloves. At four on Tuesday morning, in the "flaming" heat, he headed south from Salem to Winnisimmet (now Chelsea), arriving even before the ferrymen. He was the only passenger on the ferry across the Mystic River to Charlestown. He crossed Charlestown on foot and took the ferry across the mouth of the Charles River to Shawmut. His house was only a mile farther, so he was home by eight. He found "all well" and thanked God.

Despite his gratitude, he was acutely aware that the past six months had been among the worst he had ever known, which he considered a sign from God. In just six months he had lost not only his country but also two of his children. In a moment of solitude later that day, he recorded the latest news in his diary, a litany of death and loss both intimate and communal.

Hullie was taken ill on Friday morn. Mr. Clark of Cambridge had a son of nine years old drowned the Tuesday before. Two women died suddenly in Boston. James Mirick that lived just by my father at Newbury had his house suddenly burnt down to the ground on Sabbath even[ing] before this Friday.

Betty Lane's father dies suddenly.... Mistress Chauncy, widow, died having been sick a day or two, of a flux. Her body is carried in the night to Roxbury there to be buried. Mr. Richard Collicot buried. Mr. Thomas Kellond [a neighbor in Newbury] dies, is to be buried....

He tried, finally, to explain the most personal loss. "The Lord sanctify this third bereavement." By taking three of his babies, God was surely sending him a message. The challenge was to decipher it.

It was natural for Samuel and others of his time and place to see meaning—even divine purpose—in bad weather, house fires, and deaths. His usual response to bad news was to ask, Could this have happened by accident? David Hall of Harvard Divinity School, a renowned scholar of Puritanism, describes Samuel's mental world as Elizabethan, medieval, and "very different from our own." It was a "world of wonders" and "prodigies and portents." Samuel tracked daily events and his spiritual reading in his diary in hopes of comprehending their meaning. In the book of Revelation thunder and trumpets herald the Second Coming of Christ, so he recorded these sounds. An eclipse of the moon, which Samuel observed in 1676 during King Philip's War, seemed to him "metaphoric, dismal, dark and portentous, [like] some prodigy appearing in every corner of the skies." A lunar eclipse on November 30, 1685—extremely late in Hannah's pregnancy with Henry—drove Samuel into his house to read a chapter of Revelation. In his diary he wrote exactly what he saw in Boston's hazy sky, hoping later to comprehend it: "In the total obscuration [the moon] was ruddy, but when [it] began to receive some light, the darkish ruddiness ceased." Did this have some connection to him or to the child soon to be born to Hannah?

In a larger sense, were the events foretold in Revelation finally coming true? Would the darkness of the final days described in Revelation come as a cosmic phenomenon or a physical disaster? When and how would the symbolic actions of Revelation, such as pouring out of vials and unfolding of seals, occur? At any moment, he believed, the Second Coming could happen, bringing heavenly rapture to the elect and banishing the rest to hell. This worldview, shared by many of his peers, underlay the perfectionism, moral absolutism, and fatalism of Puritan culture.

Years before, about a month after the birth of his first baby, Samuel observed several "omens" at the Third Church. On June 21, 1677, in an early act of civil disobedience, a Quaker woman named Margaret

Brewster, naked except for a frock of penitential sackcloth, and several Quaker men ran through Samuel's meetinghouse at sermon time. Quaker missionaries had since the late 1650s openly questioned Congregationalist authority. They believed in an "inner light" from God rather than divine election. They supported toleration of other faiths. They opposed the use of sung or instrumental music in services. Rejecting the need for ministers and formal church services, they believed women as well as men could lead worship. For all these reasons the General Court under Governor John Endicott banished Quakers as heretics upon pain of death in 1659. The court hanged several Quakers on Boston Common under this law. (Later, faced with a Quaker petition to fence in their martyrs' graves, Samuel voted with the majority of the court to deny the request.) After 1660 the Crown revoked the 1659 law. Quakers continued their attacks on Puritan rule, marching through the town and calling for the magistrates to repent. In 1676 the General Court ordered constables to "search out and arrest all Quakers."

The scene in the Third Church "occasioned the greatest and most amazing uproar that" twenty-five-year-old Samuel "ever saw." It seemed to him "the Devil was amongst us." He noted the woman's "loosened hair" that "straggled wildly down her neck and shoulders," uncovered by a standard bonnet, and her face "besmeared with soot," a biblical symbol for repentance. This "apparition" reminded him of lines from the first chapter of Isaiah: "Bring no more vain oblations; incense is an abomination unto me; the new moons and sabbaths, the calling of assemblies, I cannot away with; [it is] iniquity, even the solemn meeting. Your new moons and your appointed feasts my soul hateth: they are a trouble unto me; I am weary to bear [them]."

To Samuel's amazement, Margaret Brewster shouted at the minister, "God is displeased at you! He will show his displeasure soon." Church members seized her and dragged her out to jail. The next day she was tried, convicted of disturbing the peace, and whipped, tied to a cart, and dragged through town.

During another sermon that month, a man gave "a sudden and amazing cry which disturbed the whole assembly," Samuel noted. "It seems he had the falling sickness. 'Tis to be feared the Quaker disturbance and this are ominous."

Recording such events allowed Samuel to "perceive and profit from coincidences that in hindsight might become important," according to David Hall. Seen through the lens of Scripture, "the rhythm of historical time" provided clues to "interventions of the supernatural." News "from abroad fell in order as evidence that the sequence described in Revelation was rapidly unfolding. Historical time ... was really prophetic time, and [Puritans] struggled to decipher the relationship between the two." This urge explains the large number of diaries and memoirs of high-status Puritan men, including John Winthrop, Thomas Shepard, Increase Mather, Cotton Mather, and John Hull.

Samuel Sewall's diary in printed form takes up more than a thousand pages in two volumes. The original comprised fourteen volumes, which are now at the Massachusetts Historical Society, in Boston. They vary in size from tiny pocket almanacs to volumes twelve inches high. Some he carried in his waistcoat pocket. Others he kept at home. Many were thin blank books with leather covers in which he also recorded notes of sermons and negotiations and figures from his work as a merchant and judge of probate. His strong, legible handwriting quavers with age. His entries span fifty-six years, from December 1673 until October 1729, although a volume covering the years 1677 to 1684 is inexplicably missing. He often reread earlier notations and added notes of clarification for future rereadings. On the page describing December 1685, for instance, he added in the margin beside baby Henry's birth the single word *Natus*, and he inscribed *Mortus* at the baby's death. Now and then he turned over a used volume and began anew from the back. Some journals have a gap of empty pages at the end or, if he wrote from both ends, in the middle.

This diary, an internal record of his spiritual career, was truly a memoir in that he wished to remember and find meaning in his life. He left his accumulated diaries to his son Joseph, who saved them and passed them down the generations. Yet Samuel wrote mainly for himself, never imagining that anyone besides himself and perhaps his children and grandchildren might read his entries. He engaged in mild self-censorship, as is natural. He omitted things he considered unimportant or, in rare cases, so troubling as to be inexplicable. M. Halsey Thomas, an editor of the published diary, intuited that Samuel was basically honest in his entries because of his devout Calvinism: "Under the eye of an all-seeing and all-knowing God it was useless to try to cheat." The literary scholar Mark Van Doren has remarked on this diary's "frankness, its simplicity of mind and heart, [and] its willingness to tell the truth even at the expense of the author's dignity," which "justify its comparison with the immortal diary of [Samuel] Pepys."

Samuel's drive to keep a diary for more than half a century flowed from his theology, according to his nineteenth-century biographer Nathan Chamberlain. "Protestantism at its core is the apotheosis of individualism, and the most relentless of democracies." Its "enthronement and canonization of the individual, accepted gradually but infallibly by English Puritanism, rested upon a religious idea ... that as an incarnate God, while wearing our flesh, had once died for every man, so no man thus redeemed could, without sacrilege, be abased by any tyranny of prelate or kings...." The individual conscience was the "supreme authority in religion," Chamberlain concluded, and the "right of private judgment was, and remains, one of the root ideas of logical Protestantism."

To a Puritan, the history of an individual or a people is a history of God's providence. Everything that happens is from God, so everything matters. As David Hall explained, "The person who listened closely to the sounds of the universe could hear the spirit speak." Yet diary keeping was complicated by the desire to create a compelling, meaningful narrative. The problem, as Kierkegaard noted, was that life is lived forward but understood only in reverse. "The grace of God, as most men experience it, is elusive," observed Perry Miller, another scholar of early New England. Although "certainty is written in the tables of divine election," that "book remains inaccessible to mortals. The creature lives inwardly a life of incessant fluctuation, ecstatically elevated this day, depressed into despair the next. The science of [auto]biography required clinical skill in narrating these surgings and sinkings, all the time trying to keep the line of the story clear."

Samuel never doubted that natural events had divine meaning, even if he could not discern it. Having lost three sons, he could not help but wonder, Are these events random? Is God punishing me for my sins? Are these trials intended to make me stronger? How shall I respond?

His wife shared this experience. She too was a pious Puritan who had endured the loss of three sons—Johnny, Henry, and now Hullie. Yet we have almost no information about her response. Her feelings were doubtless no less intense than her prolific husband's, yet they were not documented and saved, in keeping with the practice of her place and time. In the written record of early New England, most women appear only at birth, marriage, and death. The few women whose thoughts survive include the dissident Margaret Brewster, the Quaker martyr Mary Dyer, and the banished heretic Anne Hutchinson, who made history only because their behavior seemed witchlike and Satanic.

It is thus a measure of Hannah Hull Sewall's extremely high social status that we have any information from her about her babies' demise. Her descendants saved a letter she wrote from her desk at home on July 15, 1686, a week after the day on which the family would have celebrated Hullie's second birthday had he lived.

A gift lost at sea occasioned Hannah's unexpectedly lighthearted missive to a distant relative on Bermuda. Some months earlier the relative, Love Fowle, had sent fine foods to Hannah on a ship that was waylaid by pirates, who trolled the colonial seas. Not receiving a thank-you for the gift, Fowle had written to inquire if it had arrived.

"Good Cousin," Hannah began in her strong hand. "On June the 10, I received your kind letter dated the 4th of May upon which I made enquiry after the loving token you sent me, and the account I had was that they [the gifts] were half stolen before they came on board and the rest delivered to Mr. Prout, who told us he received so few, would but in a manner pay the freight, and knew not but they were for himself, and had eaten them up or near eaten them."

Hannah, who may have smiled in considering the sea captain's appetite, continued elegantly, "I am sorry for the frustration of your intended kindness to me; but your desire is kindness and that I have received and gratefully accepted and would entreat you to prevent the inconvenience of being so deceived for the future, by forbearing to give yourself the trouble of sending."

Hannah's wit, which must have appealed to the more heavy-handed Samuel, is evident, as are her fluency and manners. In reply to her cousin's mention of offspring, Hannah added, "I am glad to hear of God's blessing you with children. I buried two sons lately.... I have one son and two daughters living. The Lord do me good by his various ways of Providence towards me." Confident and pragmatic, she does not belabor her loss. As she knew, she and Samuel were more fortunate than many parents, including her own, who buried every baby save one.

In a time and place in which most women could not write their names, Hannah Hull Sewall could read and write in English and likely also in Latin. From the age of four or five she had studied with the "pious, prudent, and skillful" John Sanford, a private schoolmaster. She doubtless penned hundreds of letters to family and friends in England, America, and the West Indies, which had a population almost double that of New England. Still, Hannah's arch comment on the nonarrival of an unidentified edible gift is our only record of her thoughts.

Nor is there any surviving painting or drawing of Hannah Hull Sewall, despite several of her husband and sons. She is not mentioned in her father's lengthy diary except inferentially; her husband makes several appearances. In Samuel's diary, which he kept regularly through their forty-two-year marriage, she is mentioned occasionally, sometimes with feeling. Yet she does not appear during her and Samuel's eighteen-month courtship and first several months of marriage. During that period Samuel made entries every two or three days, frequently mentioning former classmates, many of whom became lifelong friends. He described pushing a nail into his brother John's new house for good luck. He noted his mother's tears after he felled an oak tree growing close to her house. He commented on Hannah's father, with whom he was considering a career.

Samuel's first mention of Hannah came with his first awareness, seven months after they wed, that she was pregnant. At dawn on Saturday, September 30, 1676, Samuel noted, "H. Sewall is called up by the flux, which it seems troubled her Friday in the afternoon, though unknown to me." He had known her for at least two years and shared a bed with her for seven months, yet she remained "unknown." He did not comment on her in his diary because he did not see her as worthy of mention. Women were secondary to men in his world. Men viewed women's bodies as vessels for reproduction. In heaven, it was thought, only male bodies would be resurrected.

This is not to say that Samuel failed to love his wife. Rather it suggests that, despite her birth to far greater wealth than Samuel, which greatly enhanced his access to power, Hannah was largely outside the world of power and meaning, which was male. The model seventeenth-century Englishwoman was obedient, submissive, virtuous, and kind. New England's women were "the hidden ones," Cotton Mather said. They ran households, raised and taught children, grew and harvested crops, did brewing and dairying and spinning, bargained with neighbors, birthed babies, and traveled about on foot, on horseback, and in canoes. Yet, as the historian Laurel Thatcher Ulrich has pointed out, using a biblical metaphor, "women performed their work under a bushel," whereas "men's candles burned on the hill." Books and complex discourse were thought to tax a woman's mind. In 1645, commenting on a learned woman who suffered a breakdown, John Winthrop Sr. wrote in his journal, "If she had attended her household affairs, and such things as belong to women, and not gone out of her way and calling to meddle in such things as are proper for men, whose minds are stronger, she [would have] kept her wits, and might have improved them usefully and honorably in the place God had set her."

The Sewalls' world remained a patriarchy. Women were outside the thrust of life with the single exception of childbirth, the brief interval in which midwives and other women assumed power. During Hannah's fourteen labors Samuel remained outside the bedchamber, which was filled with female friends and relations. Acknowledging this realm as feminine, he asked two women to serve as little Henry's pallbearers in December 1685.

Samuel loved and admired both his parents. Nevertheless, the words he wrote and hired an engraver to carve on their gravestone in Newbury made his father prominent, other men worthy of mention, and his mother recede.

Mr. Henry Sewall (sent by Mr. Henry Sewall his father in the ship *Elizabeth Dorcas*, Captain Watts, commander) arrived at Boston 1634, wintered at Ipswich, helped begin his plantation

1635, furnishing English servants, neat cattle, and provisions, married Mrs. Jane Dummer March the 25, 1646, Died May the 16, 1700, Age 86, His fruitful vine being thus disjoined [she] fell to the ground January the 13 following Age 74.

As for the female pronoun, Samuel simply left it out.

6

ORIGINAL SIN

Women may have been invisible in colonial Massachusetts, but they still had eyes to see. Hannah Hull first saw Samuel Sewall on August 11, 1674, when she was sixteen years old. One of the most desirable catches in New England, she had come in a horse-drawn coach from Boston with her parents for the Harvard commencement. Harvard College was in a decline, its few buildings in ruins and its class size shrinking to single digits, but it was still the best place for Hannah Hull to scout a suitable spouse.

Harvard College, set on an open plain in today's Harvard Square, was thirty-six years old, the first university in English North America. It opened in 1638 as a training ground for ministers, but its 1650 charter called for it also to educate future civic leaders "in all manner of good literature, arts, and sciences." The curriculum involved two years of Greek, Hebrew, and logic, a year of ethics, and a final year of metaphysics, math, rhetoric, oratory, and theology. The college in 1672 consisted of the president's timber-framed house, a small, two-story brick Indian College (so named because the Corporation for the Propagation of the Gospel Among the Indians paid for it) that served as a printing house, and the main College Hall, in which the commencement was held. College Hall was a decrepit two-story wood building containing a library, recitation hall, dormitory, and study hall. It would be replaced by a brick building, then under construction, called New Hall. None of these buildings stands today.

Hannah Hull felt at home at Harvard. Its president was practically her uncle. Leonard Hoar, who became the college's third president in 1672, was the brother of her aunt, the late Joanna Hoar Quincy, wife of Edmund Quincy, Hannah's mother's only sibling. When Hannah visited Harvard she stayed at the president's house.

That August morning, seated between her parents as the graduates read aloud their theses in College Hall, Hannah was doubtless aware of her unusual status as the sole child of the colony's wealthiest man. Her parents could deny a match she might wish to make, but they would respect her wishes. They gained nothing if she chose poorly, for her husband would inherit the vast Hull estate. Had she had a brother, the family property and business would have been his. As it was, John Hull would pay a large dowry to his daughter's husband, who would function as Hull's only son. The man she had to convince of a suitor's suitability was not so much the suitor as her father.

Harvard's class of 1674 consisted of only three bachelor's candidates: Edmund Davie, Thomas Sergeant, and Joseph Hawley. But there was a bonanza of candidates for the master's degree. Ten of the eleven men of 1671 had stayed on for three more years to earn the advanced degree that qualified them for the ministry. They were Isaac Foster, Samuel Phipps, Samuel Danforth, Peter Thatcher (youngest son of the Reverend Thatcher of the Third Church), William Adams, Thomas Weld, John Bowles, John Norton, Edward Taylor (a poet as a well as a preacher), and Samuel Sewall.

These young men sat before President Leonard Hoar, who would hand them their degrees. Now in his early forties, Hoar had immigrated to Braintree, Massachusetts, as a boy. After graduating from Harvard in 1650 he returned to England, preached in Essex, and was ejected from the pulpit in 1662 after the restoration of the monarchy. The young Puritan studied medicine at Cambridge, earning a doctorate in physic in 1671. The following summer he and his wife sailed to Boston, where they stayed for several months with the Hulls. They joined the Third Church, where Leonard preached briefly as the Reverend Thatcher's assistant. Harvard offered him the presidency in November 1672 after the death of its second president, Charles

Chauncy. Hoar soon moved to Cambridge with his wife, who was pregnant with their first child.

Bridget Hoar, his wife, who sat alongside the Hulls at the 1674 commencement, had a flamboyant family. Her father, an aristocratic Puritan lawyer, was "the regicide" John Lisle. In 1649, as President of the High Court of Justice and Lord Commissioner of the Great Seal for Cromwell, John Lisle drew up the indictment and death sentence of King Charles I. Fifteen years later, while in exile in Switzerland, Lisle was shot and killed by two Irishmen hoping for a reward from Charles II. His widow, Lady Alice Lisle, was still alive in England, but she would also die violently. In southern England in the late summer of 1685, after the Battle of Sedgemoor, in which King James II defeated his illegitimate Protestant nephew, the Duke of Monmouth, Lady Lisle was accused of treason for having hidden some of Monmouth's soldiers. Nearing seventy, Lady Lisle was beheaded in the Winchester market-place.

In the summer of 1674, at the time of Samuel's commencement, Harvard College was struggling to stay alive. The incoming class of 1678 had only four students. One of them, eleven-year-old Cotton Mather, would later remember Leonard Hoar as a scholarly, pious man who could not control disorderly students: "The young men in the college took advantage" of Hoar and "ruined his reputation." Hoar's goal as president, he told his friend the English chemist Robert Boyle, was to bring about Harvard's "resuscitation from its ruins."

When it was Samuel Sewall's turn to receive his master's degree in divinity, he rose from his seat and approached Hoar. A compact young man of middling height, Samuel had thick brown hair cut to his shoulders, ruddy cheeks, a Roman nose, and deep-set, intelligent eyes. His master's thesis, part of which he read aloud in Latin, was on sin, a most compelling subject. No copy of the thesis, composed entirely in Latin, remains. But the question he addressed survives. *"An Peccatum Originale sit & Peccatum & Poena?"* Or, "Is original sin both sin and punishment?" His answer was a resounding yes. For him, as for most devout Calvinists, original sin was not a theoretical construct but a real force with which he grappled daily.

Hannah Hull listened to every word of the twenty-two-year-old scholar's Latin peroration on damnation and "set her affection on" him, he would learn. In a letter to one of their sons decades later, Samuel would recall, "Your honored Mother ... saw me when I took my [master's] degree and set her affection on me, though I knew nothing of it till after our marriage."

A commencement party followed the granting of degrees. Cake and sliced meats, including cow's tongue, were served, along with great quantities of rum from the West Indies and wine from the Portuguese island of Madeira. Whether or not Hannah or her parents spoke directly to Samuel is a fact lost to history. But there is no doubt that Samuel was aware of Hannah's parents. Judith Quincy Hull, the only daughter of New England's first Quincy, had arrived in the New World at age five in 1633 on the same ship as the renowned divine John Cotton. The Quincys settled on a large farm in Braintree, Massachusetts, part of which later assumed their family name. After the early death of Judith's father, Edmund Sr., her mother, Judith Pares Quincy, married a widowed blacksmith named Robert Hull and moved with her two children into the Hull house on the Shawmut Peninsula. At the time of their parents' marriage, Judith Quincy Jr. and her stepbrother John Hull, Hannah Hull Sewall's future parents, were young teenagers.

John Hull, born in December 1624 in Market Harborough, Leicestershire, had arrived in Massachusetts in November 1635 with his parents, his older half brother, Richard Storer, and his younger brother, Edward. Prior to this trip young John had twice nearly died, experiences that intensified his sense of God's watchful protection. On one occasion he was careless with fire. Even earlier, at only two years old, he was run over "while playing in the street. A number of pack horses came along and the foremost horse stroke me down upon my back with his knee, and yet when I was down"—Hull later explained, seeing divine intervention in his own life—"God so ordered it that" the horse "held up his foot over my body and moved not, until some of my relations came out of the shop and took me out of his way."

John Hull's formal education, which had begun at an English grammar school, continued at Boston Latin, America's first secondary school. An indifferent student, Hull left school in his early teens "to help my father plant corn" in Muddy River, a farming village just west of Boston. "By God's good hand," as he put it, "I fell to learning (by the help of my brother) and to practice the trade of a goldsmith," which his older brother had learned during a six-year apprenticeship in London. A silversmith—the term was used interchangeably with *goldsmith*—was "somewhat akin to the banker of today," the historian Hermann Frederick Clarke wrote. "John Hull, in adopting the craft of a silversmith, took the first step toward his diversified career of silversmith, merchant, mint-master, and banker, as well as ... honored public servant."

The ambitious young goldsmith also courted his stepsister, who agreed to marry him when she was twenty and he was twenty-two. The wedding of John Hull and Judith Quincy, in the Old Hall of their late parents' house on May 11, 1647, was performed by none other than the sixty-year-old founder of the colony. "Mr. John Winthrop married me and my wife, Judith, in my own house," Hull noted. A year later Hull joined the First Church of Christ in Boston, where the Reverend John Cotton, founder of the Congregationalist Church, still preached.

Hull's star continued to rise. He became a corporal in the militia in 1649 and four years later was promoted to sergeant. His biggest boost came in 1652, when the General Court asked the twenty-eight-year-old goldsmith to set up a colonial mint. Counterfeit coinage was damaging trade, so the court asked Hull to standardize the coin by "fineness" and weight. Hull requested that his friend, Robert Sanderson, an experienced, London-trained goldsmith in his midforties from Watertown, become his partner. The two men converted bullion, Spanish pieces, and imported silver plate into shillings that bore the stamp of a tree on one side to indicate denomination. Their best-known coin was the pine tree shilling. When King Charles II objected to the colony's presumption in coining its own money, someone was said to placate him by pretending the pine tree was a royal oak, symbol of royal longevity.

Pine tree shillings made John Hull rich. The court allowed him to keep one of every twenty shillings he coined. Nathaniel Hawthorne, who based a short story in *Grandfather's Chair* (1840) on Hull, explained, "The magistrates soon began to suspect that the mint master would have the best of the bargain. They offered him a large sum of money if he would but give up that twentieth shilling which he was continually dropping into his own pocket. But Captain Hull declared himself perfectly satisfied with the shilling. And well he might be; for so diligently did he labor, that, in a few years, his pockets, his money-bags, and his strong box were overflowing with pine-tree shillings." This generous allowance was later reduced, but not before Hull had raised what historian Thomas Hutchinson called "a large fortune by it." Twenty-two years later, at Samuel's commencement, Hull's great wealth was widely known.

Throughout the day following his commencement, Samuel packed his books and clothes and prepared to leave College Hall, where he had studied and slept since he was fifteen. Three years before, with bachelor's degree in hand, he had decided to stay on for the master's. Since then he had served as a resident fellow, tutoring younger students, and as keeper of the college library, which included the volumes bequeathed by a dying John Harvard in 1638. In recent months Samuel had begun his diary. His first entry, made the previous December, concerned his teaching. "I read to the Junior Sophisters the 14th chapter of Heereboord's Physic," or *Philosophia Naturalis*, published in 1663. "I went to the end, and then read it over from the beginning" over four months. He recorded haircuts, local news (such as the execution of a seventeen-year-old Roxbury boy for "bestiality with a mare"), visits with friends and family, purchases of pipe tobacco, wine, beer, and "an hourglass and penknife," and a gift of money to a slave.

By August 14, three days after commencement, Samuel was back in Newbury. For several months he helped his parents with the farming chores he had done as a boy, moving and milking cows, feeding cattle and hogs, shearing sheep, and repairing fences. For a farm family on the North Shore, late summer brought long days of harvesting corn, root vegetables, and salt-marsh hay.

But Samuel did not abandon the town. He rode to Boston and Cambridge several times to answer questions from the General Court regarding Harvard College's "languishing and decaying condition." In October the court dismissed every salaried officer of the college except President Hoar, and the college closed temporarily. Every student but three left the college in November. The following March Hoar resigned the presidency. He developed consumption, died that November, and was buried among the Quincys in Braintree.

During these months Samuel did not have a firm sense of his future plans or any apparent eagerness to clarify them. In the fall of 1674 he received a letter from Woodbridge, New Jersey, asking him to serve as that town's first minister. This was an inside offer. Newly incorporated Woodbridge was named for an ancient acquaintance of his. The "learned and ingenious" Reverend John Woodbridge, as Samuel described him, an Oxford-educated nephew of the Newbury minister Thomas Parker, had served on the Massachusetts General Court, returned to Puritan England until the Restoration, and comfortably retired in Newbury. In November Samuel wrote a letter declining the pulpit in New Jersey. The only time he is known to have preached was the following April, when his beloved schoolmaster, the Reverend Parker, whose health was declining, asked Samuel to fill in at the Newbury parish. During the sermon an hourglass rested on the pulpit for the minister's use. Samuel was "afraid to look on the glass, ignorantly and unwittingly," he noted with regret, so his preaching wandered for "two hours and a half."

We do not know how often, if ever, he saw Hannah Hull during that fall, but we do know he contacted her father. John Hull first appears in Samuel's diary on November 14, when Samuel needed to deliver letters he had written to relatives in London and Northampton, England. He asked his younger brother Stephen to take the packet of letters to Boston so that "Mr. Hull" might convey them on one of his ships crossing the Atlantic.

In considering Samuel as the future husband of their only child, John and Judith Hull did not have to struggle to discern virtues. He was evidently of fine character, well educated, and from a solid background. Perhaps most important, they shared religious views. Both the Hulls and the Sewalls were deeply committed to Puritan theology, Congregationalism, and the "New England way."

As for Samuel's thinking, his choice of a partner was even more prudent than his forebears' had been. Hannah, an heiress, "brought her husband a powerful family connection," the biographer Nathan Chamberlain observed, so that Samuel would live "off the higher rank all his life." Hannah Hull's dowry, which John Hull paid Samuel in installments, was five hundred pounds, a massive sum. (For contrast, a minister's annual salary was sixty to eighty pounds, plus several cords of firewood.) Dowries, popular in medieval and early modern Europe, maintained class divisions, helped to secure a wife's future, and gave couples a solid start financially. They existed in civil law in most of the world until the nineteenth century and still exist in some countries. To some degree a family's wealth determines the age of the bride: the more wealth, the younger the bride can be because a young woman with a healthy dowry need not delay marriage.

"The Pine-Tree Shillings," chapter six of *Grandfather's Chair*, Nathaniel Hawthorne's fanciful nineteenth-century account of early New England, concerns "the mint-master of Massachusetts" who "coined all the money...."

When the mint-master had grown very rich, a young man, Samuel Sewall by name, came a-courting to his only daughter, [whom] we will call ... Betsey ... [with whom] did Samuel Sewall fall in love. As he was a young man of good character, industrious in his business, and a member of the church, the mint-master very readily gave his consent.

Following a long aside about the imagined plumpness of the "fine, hearty" Hull daughter, whose actual first name does not concern Hawthorne, the story continues:

On the wedding day, we may suppose that honest John Hull dressed himself in a plum-colored coat, all the buttons of which were made of pine-tree shillings. The buttons of his waistcoat were sixpences; and the knees of his small-clothes were buttoned with silver threepences.... On the opposite side of the room ... sat Miss Betsey ... blushing with all her might....

There, too, was the bridegroom, dressed in a fine purple coat and gold-lace waistcoat, with as much other finery as the Puritan laws and customs would allow.... .

The mint-master also was pleased with his new Son-in-law; especially as he had courted Miss Betsey out of pure love, and had said nothing at all about her portion. So, when the marriage ceremony was over, Captain Hull whispered a word to two of his men-servants, who immediately went out, and soon returned, lugging in a large pair of scales. They were such a pair as whole-sale merchants use for weighing bulky commodities; and quite a bulky commodity was now to be weighed in them.

Hawthorne's Hull orders his daughter "into one side of these scales." She obeys. He orders his servant to bring in a "huge, square, iron-bound, oaken chest."

Captain Hull then took a key from his girdle, unlocked the chest, and lifted its ponderous lid. Behold! It was full to the brim of bright pine-tree shillings, fresh from the mint; and Samuel Sewall began to think that his father-in-law had got possession of all the money in the Massachusetts treasury. But it was only the mint-master's honest share of the coinage.

Then the servants, at Captain Hull's command, heaped double handfuls of shillings into one side of the scales, while Betsey remained in the other. Jingle, jingle, went the shillings, as handful after handful was thrown in, till, plump and ponderous as she was, they fairly weighed the young lady from the floor.

"There, son Sewall!" cried the honest mint-master, resuming his seat in Grandfather's chair, "take these shillings for my daughter's portion. Use her kindly, and thank Heaven for her. It is not every wife that's worth her weight in silver!"

7

MY CHILDREN
WERE DEAD

During the six weeks following Samuel and Hannah's actual wedding, on February 28, 1676, he found not a single free moment to sit quietly with his journal recording his thoughts. Samuel's first postnuptial note in his diary referred to public, not personal, affairs. "Governor Winthrop dies," he reported on April 5. The deceased was not the first John Winthrop, who had officiated at Hannah's parents' wedding, but his son John Winthrop Jr., first governor of colonial Connecticut and the father of Samuel's close friend Wait Still Winthrop. Wait Still, as he was called, had been Samuel's Harvard classmate, although he left after two years without a degree, and was a member of Samuel's church. Samuel attended the funeral and saw John Winthrop Jr. interred beside his father in the Old Burying Ground.

Samuel's former college classmates were becoming his intimate friends. This phenomenon, now common, was just beginning, according to Harvard's historian, Samuel Eliot Morrison: "It was … in [President Henry] Dunster's day [1640–54] that the Class became an organic unit of Harvard College, with consequences affecting both the social and scholastic aspects of American higher education." On May 24, after a lecture by Samuel Willard at the Third Church, Samuel was touched to be joined in his pew by his classmates Sam

Phipps, Tom Weld, and Edward Taylor. "God grant we may sit together in heaven," he said. Of his ten classmates, seven became ministers. Isaac Foster preached in Hartford, Connecticut, and Samuel Mather served in nearby Windsor. In Massachusetts, Thomas Weld preached in Dunstable, Peter Thatcher in Milton, William Adams in Dedham, John Norton in Hingham, and Edward Taylor in Westfield. Taylor became "one of the choice figures of American colonial literature," the scholar M. Halsey Thomas noted. One of Taylor's 1682 meditations on the Canticle of Canticles, or the Song of Solomon, begins,

My dear, dear, Lord I do thee Savior call:
Thou in my very soul art, as I deem,
So high, not high enough, so great; too small:
So dear, not dear enough in my esteem.
So noble, yet so base: too low, too tall:
Thou full, and empty art: nothing, yet all.

Winthrop and other founders of the Bay Colony had always intrigued Samuel. Nine years before his wedding, as a fifteen-year-old scholar new to Harvard, he had walked four miles from Cambridge to Boston to hear the Reverend Richard Mather's 1667 funeral sermon for the Reverend John Wilson, the first minister of the First Church of Christ in Boston. Richard Mather, Increase's father, another founding divine, was the primary author of the essential *Bay Psalm Book*. Decades later, in a 1706 letter to Salem's elderly minister John Higginson, who had arrived in 1629, Samuel would write, "I account it a great favor of God that I have been privileged with the acquaintance and friendship of many of the first planters in New England; and the friendship of yourself has particularly obliged me."

Foreign affairs also affected Samuel, who felt himself a citizen of the world. News from Europe arrived eight weeks after the fact and was sometimes incorrect. One day in 1696 Samuel reveled in news from an English ship that Louis XIV, the powerful French king, was dead—an event that did not actually occur until 1715. The most significant political occurrence in the year he married Hannah was King Philip's War, which had started the year before. "King Philip" was the

English name of the Wampanoag leader Metacomet, who battled the English for control of southern New England. Members of other native tribes fought on both sides.

Samuel tracked war news. On April 21, two weeks after the Winthrop funeral, "about fifty men" were "slain 3 miles off Sudbury." Three days later at Braintree "a woman [was] taken, and a man knocked in the head." On May 19 Captain William Turner of Boston killed "200 Indians" near the Connecticut River. Near Hatfield, Massachusetts, on June 7 "ninety Indians [were] killed and taken by [the] Connecticut ferry." He learned on July 1 that Narragansett Indians had killed and scalped an Englishman, Hezekiah Willet, near Bristol, Rhode Island. "Jethro, his Negro [slave], was then taken" by Indians and then "retaken by Captain Bradbury." Jethro "related that the Mount Hope Indians that knew Mr. Willet were sorry for his death, mourned, [and] combed his head."

King Philip's War ended in August 1676 when an Indian serving the English shot Metacomet in Bristol, Rhode Island. English troops beheaded and quartered Metacomet. Thousands of Native Americans and hundreds of English died in King Philip's War, which had more casualties per capita than any other war on American soil, according to the historian Jill Lepore. Many frontier towns in Massachusetts, including Groton, Medfield, and Rehoboth, were burned to the ground. Fighting came within twenty miles of Boston, terrifying its people, many of whom lost relatives or friends. To the ministers, the war indicated God's anger with New England for failing to keep to the covenant. As the Reverend Increase Mather reminded his congregation, the Lord afflicts those who do not obey.

Eventually, domestic matters demanded Samuel's attention. Hannah was pregnant by late summer, and her subsequent episodes of flux became a recurring theme. At dawn on September 30, 1676, she rose from their bed to seek help from servants. That night she could not sleep. The next day, the Sabbath, she "had sundry stools." Her mother was also ill, prompting Dr. Brackenbury to come to bleed Judith. The letting of blood, a standard treatment for various ills, was based on the Greek physician Galen's theory that health results from a balance between bodily "humors," which included phlegm, yellow bile, black bile, and blood.

Two days later Samuel wrote, "Hannah S. had an extreme restless night. 8 or 10 stools. Dr. Brackenbury advises [her] to [take] diacodium ... and approves pepper boiled in milk and water, alike of each." Hannah received six ounces of diacodium, a syrup of boiled sugar and poppy heads. The next day she had "two stools. Considerable sleep. Six ounces diacodium."

Samuel moved out of their room temporarily, choosing to sleep in "the chamber over the kitchen." Dr. Brackenbury, who visited daily, "was loath to give an absolute purge unless necessity required."

Hannah improved on October 5, so Samuel returned to their bedchamber. "Nurse Hurd watches [her]. But one stool ..." He counted her stools until October 8, when he reported, "Last night no stool: and three sick persons"—Hannah, Judith, and a servant, Betty Lane—"had a very good night, praised be God."

A few days later Hannah was feverish and "slept not so well as formerly." He wrote to a relative, "My wife hath been dangerously ill, yet is now finely recovered and gaining strength. It has been a sick summer with us."

Now that the couple expected a child, he had finally to decide on a career. During the fall of 1675 his father-in-law and several other prominent merchants of Boston had advised him, as he noted, "to acquaint myself with merchants, and invited me (courteously) to their cabals." Samuel was deeply impressed by the advice of Hannah's cousin-in-law the Reverend John Reyner, who advised him "not to keep over much within, but [to] go among men, and that thereby I should advantage myself." Samuel was attracted to the businessmen and their ways, as well as to the challenge of burnishing a public image. After talking with Reyner, Samuel determined to begin his life as a merchant.

On January 10, 1677, while walking to Dorchester for a meeting of his prayer group, Samuel prayed fervently to God to "show me favor at the meeting" and "set home those things that were by You carved for me."

The chosen text that day was the Canticle of Canticles, from the Old Testament, which the group considered a description of the marriage of Christ and his church, to which they belonged. In discussing Canticle 1:7—"Show me, O thou whom my soul loveth, where thou feedest, where thou liest in the midday, lest I begin to wander after the flocks of thy companions"—the Reverend Josiah Flint pressed each member "to look to your own souls." Samuel did so earnestly. What work should I choose? he asked himself. More important, How can I be closer to Christ?

"Be sure not to deceive yourselves as to your union with Christ," the Reverend Samuel Torrey warned the gathered souls.

Samuel felt that this "preaching and praying" was intended by God "for me."

Three days later he went out to the chicken coop below the garden at the bottom of the property to feed his chickens. The birds gathered, clucking, at his feet as he did his twice-daily chore of mixing ground maize with water. Setting the porringer on the dirt, he thought to himself, "I give them nothing save Indian corn and water, yet they eat it and thrive very well. This food, however mean it may be, is necessary."

He was convinced of his own need for "spiritual food," something that would do for him what the maize did for his chickens. It occurred to him that his daily devotions—morning and evening prayers—lacked sufficient reverence and consistency. From now on he would pray more earnestly.

To a Puritan, prayer was essential. One reason was that human nature is sinful. Samuel may have sometimes doubted God, but he never doubted that we are born in sin, we die in sin, and the only escape from sin is God. However, as he often noted, sin can be difficult for the sinner to discern.

One chilly evening the previous month, he had been in the kitchen after supper. Through a window he could see an unfamiliar, bedraggled dog wandering by. It looked dangerous. "I am afraid we shall be troubled with that ugly dog," he said to his father-in-law's apprentice John Alcock, a man of nineteen who boarded with the family.

"Which way did he go?" Alcock asked.

"At the street door," Samuel replied. The dog appeared to be near the front gate, on the main road. Alcock found a thick staff. He went out the front door. Seeing a low shape moving in the darkness, he sneaked toward it and swung the staff.

The "dog," a nine-year-old boy who had just come to live in the Hull-Sewall house, dropped and screamed. A large weal rose on the boy's forehead. Samuel felt grief and shame. Only by "God's mercy" did "the stick and manner of the blow" not spill the boy's "brains on the ground," Samuel realized. "The Devil (I think) seemed to be angry at the child's coming to dwell here." The boy, nine-year-old Seth Shove, son of a frontier minister, boarded with Samuel's family while preparing for Harvard College. Several years hence Samuel, who paid for Shove's education, would deliver him to Harvard. Financing the schooling of promising English and Indian boys was one of his many benefices, as was inviting young relatives and needy boys to live with his family.

Hannah, Samuel, and their families and servants spent much of January and February 1678 preparing for Hannah's first birth. The Sewalls now needed their own maid, so Samuel hired his seventeen-year-old sister, Jane. She worked for him and Hannah until September, when she returned to Newbury to be married. In February, with help from servants, Samuel brewed the groaning beer to serve to guests who would visit during Hannah's lying-in.

As he awaited the arrival of his first child, Samuel sought the counsel of Thomas Thatcher, minister of the Third Church and the father of his classmate. A minister's son born in Salisbury, England, in 1620, Thomas Thatcher had studied medicine and theology with the Reverend Charles Chauncy, Leonard Hoar's predecessor at Harvard, and become pastor of the new church in 1669. With Thatcher's support, Samuel became a member of the Third Church on March 30, 1677, two days after he turned twenty-five. All that day he was overcome privately with his own "sinfulness and hypocrisy." Before the congregation he and another man, Gilbert Cole, expounded on their personal experience of God's saving grace. Following the testimony of the two men, a minister read aloud statements of two women who wished to join the church, Anne Gannett and Rebecca Hackett. This was the custom in a church that did not permit women to speak, following the apostle Paul's rule, "A woman must be silent in church." With a show of hands, the congregation voted to embrace the four new saints. Together they made a solemn covenant "to take the Lord Jehovah for our God, to walk in brotherly love, and to be watchful to edification." The congregation joined them in prayer.

Three days later, on the evening of April 2, 1677, Hannah, who would not join the Third Church as a member until 1689, although she regularly attended services, gave birth to a boy. Samuel did not observe her during labor and childbirth, but the process intrigued him. As he walked the midwife, Elizabeth Weeden, home at two in the morning, he was entranced by her portable stool, whose three detachable legs fit neatly into a bag, which he carried for her. He carefully recorded the names of the midwives who delivered his children and the women in addition to Hannah who suckled them. Several weeks postpartum he listed the treats that Hannah served her nurses and helpers in gratitude. One such menu included boiled pork and "fowls," roast turkey and beef, minced pies, pastries, tarts, and cheese.

Hannah did not attend their baby's baptism, which came within a few days of his birth. On Sunday, April 8, at the Third Church, Elizabeth Weeden carried the infant into the church halfway through the Reverend Thomas Thatcher's afternoon sermon. At the close of the sermon Samuel held up his baby before the congregation. Thatcher prayed for him. "Then I named him John," after the child's maternal grandfather, "and Mr. [Thomas] Thatcher baptized him into the name of the Father, Son, and Holy Ghost." Samuel added a prayer that his son might be "washed from sin in the blood of Christ."

Samuel's new role as a father did not prevent him from feeling the need of God's paternal protection. Early in May 1677 he made the mistake of going out one windy Friday morning "without private prayer." Riding across Boston Common, where a company of soldiers was training, he tried to avoid the troops "because of my fearful horse." But the soldiers "so transported" his horse that Samuel "could not govern him, but was fain to let him go full speed, and hold my hat under my arm. I took great cold in my ear thereby, and also by wearing a great thick coat of my father's part of the day, because it rained, and then leaving it off." He developed a sore throat and grew "very sick." Only on Monday, after a prayerful visit from Increase Mather, was Samuel finally "mended."

As he and Hannah adjusted to family life, he learned the ways of his father-in-law's business. Samuel handled John Hull's complicated accounts and much of his correspondence. Several merchants usually jointly invested in a ship, sharing the risk and the profit. They paid for and outfitted the fleet, hired captains, and purchased goods to export, such as dried and salted mackerel and codfish, hogsheads of alewives,

cedar shingles, barrel staves, wax candles, tar, beaver skins, cranberries, cattle, and horses. In addition, they purchased goods from Europe
and the West Indies for sale here. These included dry goods—sieves,
hooks, shot, nails, tobacco pipes, scythes, knives, needles, lead, chairs,
books, cotton, and silk—as well as sugar, molasses, cotton, rum, salt,
oranges, sweetmeats, and chocolate.

Samuel also helped his father-in-law manage his landholdings. Hull
owned large tracts in Maine (then "the eastern part of Massachusetts
Bay"), New Hampshire, Martha's Vineyard, many parts of the Massachusetts mainland (including Boxford, Wilmington, Braintree, Winchester, Brookline, and Sherborn), and Rhode Island. During the
1680s Samuel purchased a sawmill in Salmon Falls, now Berwick,
Maine, and a large interest in an iron works in Braintree, Massachusetts. Even today there is a lovely promontory in Narragansett, Rhode
Island, called Point Judith, which Hull bought in 1657 for 151 pounds
from Narragansett Indians and named after his wife.

Property claims were among Samuel's greatest worldly concerns.
"There was never a time in American history when land speculation
had not been a major preoccupation of ambitious people," the historian
Bernard Bailyn noted. "Within a single generation of the first settlements, the acquisition of land had taken on a new form and a new
purpose; speculation in land futures was fully launched as a universal
business, and it developed quickly. By 1675, politically influential individuals in Massachusetts had been granted personal gifts by the legislature totaling 130,000 acres, in parcels far larger than any conceivable
personal use could justify and beyond any possible personal use by
their children and grandchildren." Land was wealth, and land value
could be expected to rise with the population. Men acquired land "not
for its use but for its resale value as a commodity in a rising market."

John Winthrop's founding sermon, "A Model of Christian Charity,"
almost seems to contradict this worldly aim. "If we break this covenant with God *and seek for ourselves in this present world valuable and
wealthy goods,*" Winthrop cautioned, "the Lord will surely break out in
wrath against us, for that is the price of breaking the covenant." He
was trying to define the essential covenant between God and the Puritans. "Thus stands the cause between God and us.... We are entered
into a covenant with him for this work and with each other.... He will

expect a strict performance of the articles contained in it...." Amassing possessions was allowed only in the service of God. This was a fine line, but a line nevertheless, which seemed to justify the accumulation of material wealth. Winthrop and his colleagues, the grandfathers of Sewall's best friends, enjoyed vast estates that made them, in Old English terms, functional aristocrats, whereas in England their families were of the yeoman or gentry classes.

Schoolchildren learn that the Puritans came to America for religious freedom, but the truth is more complex. The Englishmen who settled America had aims both spiritual and secular. Magistrates and ministers both collected land. Some of Samuel's Muddy River acreage had once been John Cotton's farm, a gift from the ruling court to the politic First Church minister. The records of land tracts granted by the magistrates of the Great and General Court to themselves and their allies show the roots of real estate speculation in America.

Over the years Samuel, like his and Hannah's male forebears, expanded his family's real estate. "The care and sale of [land] took much of his business time and energy," Nathan Chamberlain noted. In 1687, in imitation of the leading men of the first generation, Samuel purchased most of an island in Boston Harbor. That May eight men witnessed "my taking livery and seisin of [nearly five hundred acres of Hog] Island by turf and twig and the house," along with seven oxen and steers, eight cows, one hundred sixty sheep, thirteen swine, two horses, one mare, "four stocks of bees," some fowl, and a sailboat with oars and a fishing rod. A tenant farmer occupied the island, which Samuel used for family picnics and for grazing sheep and cattle. He built a wharf there and planted many trees. Sometimes he spent the night on the island under the stars.

In the summer of 1688 Edmund Andros, the provincial leader, would try to unsettle Samuel's claim to the island. "There is a writ out against me for Hog Island," Samuel noted that July, "and against several others ... as being violent intruders into the king's possession." Samuel fought back and maintained his deed. An excellent judge of real estate, horses, and people, Samuel was not afraid to say his mind. Ten years after lending a man from Barbados ten pounds, he wrote to him in 1700, "Sir, I presume the old verity 'If knocking thrice, no one comes, go off' is not to be understood of creditors in demanding their just debts. The tenth year is now current since I let you ten pounds, merely out of respect to you as a stranger and scholar.... I am come again to knock at your door to enquire if any ingenuity or honor dwell there...." He advised an agent of his on Barbados, "Recover the money and remit it to Mr. John Ive, merchant in London, for my account."

At home, though, Samuel sometimes had to bite his tongue. John Hull was master of the house as long as he lived, which would be seven years after Samuel joined the family. The two men shared a deep respect, yet conflicts occasionally arose. One evening in February 1677 the two men were talking together in the parlor before a fire. Hull mentioned his irritation that someone in the colonial treasury, which he ran as treasurer, had allowed a man to pay his taxes in oats. Samuel threw some logs on the hearth. To Samuel's amazement, his father-in-law lashed out at him for wasting wood. "If you should be so foolish," Samuel later quoted his father-in-law as saying, "then I should have no confidence in you, for your mind would be as unstable as the wind."

Samuel knew that Hull's anger was misdirected, but he still felt hurt. Saying nothing, he retreated to his bedchamber to console himself with Scripture. He found reassurance in 1 Peter 1: 6, "Wherein ye greatly rejoice, though now for a season, if need be, ye are in heaviness through manifold temptations." This reminded Samuel that "no godly man hath any more afflictions than what he hath need of." Singing several verses of Psalm 37, which reassures those who "fret" because of evil that the wicked shall soon die, further improved his mood.

Psalm 37

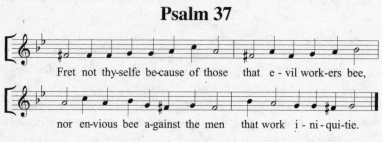

Fret not thy-selfe be-cause of those   that e - vil work-ers bee,

nor en-vious bee a-gainst the men   that work i - ni - qui-tie.

Oxford Tune

Fret not thyselfe because of those
    that evill workers bee,
nor envious bee against the men
    that work iniquitie.

2 For like unto the grasse they shall
    be cut downe, suddenly:
and like unto the tender herb
    they withering shall dye.

3 Upon the Lord put thou thy trust,
    and bee thou doing good,
so shalt thou dwell within the land,
    and sure thou shalt have food.

4 See that thou set thy hearts delight
    also upon the Lord,
and the desyres of thy heart
    to thee he will afford.

5 Trust in the Lord: & hee'l it work,
    to him commit thy way.
6 As light thy justice hee'l bring forth,
    thy judgement as noone day.

7 Rest in Jehovah, & for him
    with patience doe thou stay:
fret not thy selfe because of him
    who prospers in his way,

    Nor at the man, who brings to passe
    the crafts he doth devise.
8   Cease ire, & wrath leave: to doe ill
    thy selfe fret in no wise.

9 For evil doers shall be made
    by cutting downe to fall:
but those that wayt upon the Lord,
    the land inherit shall.

Inspired by his father-in-law's land acquisition, Samuel developed a concern for his parents' properties in England. In 1677 he wrote to Stephen Dummer, a maternal uncle in Hampshire, England, asking him to "take care of my father's lands, especially at Lee, writing down all his receipts and payments." Two years later the Boston selectmen made Samuel a perambulator of Muddy River, Roxbury, and Cambridge. Perambulators met regularly to walk around grazing lands to ensure public order, land claims, and property boundaries. Samuel discharged this responsibility once a month in good weather, "chiefly," he admitted in June 1687, "that I may know my own" land, which "lies in so many nooks and corners."

The extent of Samuel's holdings in Muddy River are no longer known. The twenty-five acres granted to Hannah's grandfather in 1636 had expanded through further purchases by John Hull to more than three hundred acres that extended east to the Muddy and Charles Rivers and northwest to the Cambridge line. This land was tillable southeast to the old Cedar Swamp, now known as Hall's Pond. Sewall's farm, as the growing parcel was called by the 1680s, included much of modern-day Coolidge Corner and Brookline Village. Samuel called his farm Brooklin—short for Brook-lying—in honor of the waterway marking its northern border, a tributary of the Charles River known as the Smelt Brook. Years later, when residents of this region, then called Muddy River, voted to incorporate themselves as a town, they named the new town Brookline, after Sewall's farm.

Samuel rode to Muddy River on March 16, 1686, to survey land and "adjust the matter of fencing" between Thomas Danforth, a former deputy governor, and his neighbor Simon Gates. Muddy River, a "rolling landscape of some picturesqueness," according to a historian, served as Boston's "back cow pasture." Since the 1630s, by court order, all barren cattle, weaned calves, and swine more than three months old were removed from the Shawmut Peninsula to save its house gardens. The village of Muddy River, situated two miles west of the town, had "good ground, large timber, and stores of marshland" and meadow, and fewer than a hundred English and Indian inhabitants.

Samuel met Danforth and Gates alongside the Muddy River (another tributary of the Charles) at a creek near the juncture of the towns of Boston, Roxbury, and Cambridge. The three men agreed to measure a line "from a stake by the creek 16 rods [of] marsh" upland to "a little above the dam" and "about a rod below an elm growing to the Boston-side of the fence." The deputy governor would "fence thence upward above the dam" and Gates would "fence downwards to the stake by the creek where by consent we began." After noon the men dined at Gates's farmhouse. Dinner, the main meal of the day, was usually a meat stew or pottage (commonly beef, deer, hare, squirrel, pigeon, turkey, or pheasant) and root vegetables such as parsnips, carrots, turnips, and onions. Desserts were apples, peaches, berries with milk and sugar, and yokeage, a mix of parched, pulverized Indian corn and sugar borrowed from Native American cuisine. Breakfast and supper consisted of oatmeal or cornmeal mush mixed with milk or molasses. Most meals were accompanied by beer and hard cider, according to the historian Keith Thomas: "Beer was a basic ingredient in everyone's diet, children as well as adults.... Each member of the [seventeenth-century English] population, man, woman, and child, consumed almost forty gallons a year," or nearly a pint of beer a day. Water was often unclean and not potable, so people drank alcohol. The food at Gates's pleased Samuel, as did Danforth's offer to let the Gates family "go on foot to Cambridge Church directly through his ground." Such courtesies could arise only when men of property felt their claims of ownership were respected, especially now that all claims were in question due to the loss of the charter.

Arriving home from his farm that day, Samuel learned that smallpox was again in Boston. The previous November an acquaintance had succumbed to the virus. Samuel himself almost perished from smallpox at twenty-six, two years after his wedding and not long after his firstborn died. Bedridden for six weeks in the autumn of 1678, "I was reported to be dead.... But it pleased God of his mercy to recover me. Multitudes" in Boston died then, including John Noyes and Benjamin Thirston, "two of my special friends."

Despite Samuel's many anxieties, some news was simply good. He learned in the late spring of 1686 that Hannah, now twenty-six, was pregnant for the seventh time in ten years. The new baby, another boy, arrived on January 30, 1687. At his baptism, by the Reverend Willard at the next Sabbath day, "the child shrunk at the water but cried not." Eight-year-old Sam Jr. "showed the midwife" Elizabeth Weeden, who carried in the infant, "the way to the pew." Samuel held up his new son and named him Stephen, after his own brother. Stephen seemed healthy. He suffered no convulsions. He cut two teeth in June, when he was five months old. A month later, though, he was "very sick."

Samuel called on the Reverend Willard. The minister and his wife came to the house to pray with the baby on the evening of Monday,

July 25, and again the next morning. Tuesday afternoon, in his grand-mother's bedchamber, as Nurse Hill rocked him in her arms, Samuel and Hannah's "dear son Stephen Sewall" expired.

The family rushed to burial on account of the summer heat. Early Wednesday evening four young boys close to the family bore little Stephen's coffin from the Third Church to the graveyard. As usual, the family walked two by two. Samuel led his wife. His brother Stephen led the grandmother Judith Hull. Sam Jr., nine, led his sister Hannah, seven. "Billy Dummer," a ten-year-old cousin who would become Massachusetts's governor in 1723, led Samuel's five-year-old daughter, Betty. "Cousins" Quincy and Savage and many other mourn-ers followed, in pairs.

Samuel asked two strong men, Samuel Clark and Solomon Rainsford, to carry Stephen's coffin inside the tomb. While descending the steps into the burial chamber, Rainsford slipped on a loose brick and dropped his end of the coffin. It landed on Samuel's firstborn "John's stone," which was "set there to show the entrance." Samuel, who missed nothing, felt relief that Clark "held his part steadily" and so the crowd heard "only a little knock."

After the short ceremony, as people drifted away, Sam Jr. turned back to peer into his family tomb. He saw "a great coffin" inside, that of his grandfather John Hull, which terrified him. Later, in his diary, Samuel noted his compassion for his son. His deep faith in salvation through Christ did not always prevail over his anxiety about death. While away from home in 1689 he woke from a nightmare in which his wife, Hannah, was dead, "which made me very heavy." Six years later he dreamed that all but one of "my children were dead," which "did distress me sorely." Ten years after that, in 1705, he had a "very sad dream" in which "I," like a felon, "was condemned and to be exe-cuted." He too was afraid.

Sam Jr. cried all the way home from his baby brother's funeral. His sisters, Hannah and Betty, burst into tears. Their parents and servants "could hardly quiet them" at the mourners' feast. A few days later Samuel's brother Stephen came to visit. He said the French had seized two ships from Salem, including one in which Stephen had invested. The ship's "whole fare [was] due to him," Samuel noted, "so that his liveli-hood is in a manner taken away. Here is wave upon wave" of bad news.

Consolation following desolation, Hannah conceived another child in November 1687. She gave birth to a son on August 15, 1688. Samuel and Hannah now had four living children and four children who had died. On August 19 Samuel carried the new baby to the Third Church, where the Reverend Willard preached a sermon before baptizing him. Samuel named this son Joseph "not out of respect to any relation" but for the "first Joseph," Jacob's beloved son, and "in hopes of the accomplishment of the prophecy, Ezekiel 37 and such like." In this Old Testament passage the Lord says, "Behold, I will take the stick of Joseph, which [is] in the hand of Ephraim, and the tribes of Israel ... and make them one stick.... I will take the children of Israel from among the heathen,... I will make them one nation in the land upon the mountains of Israel.... I will save them out of all their dwelling places, wherein they have sinned, and will cleanse them: so shall they be my people, and I will be their God."

Samuel, who could already see that Sam Jr. would not be a scholar, attached those paternal hopes to this tiny new boy. The thought of a daughter becoming a scholar or theologian did not occur to him. He sent his daughters to dame schools, but secondary or tertiary education was not offered to girls.

Joseph "was baptized with Mr. Stoughton present," Samuel noted with pride. This seemed auspicious. Fifty-eight-year-old William Stoughton, deputy governor of the Province of New England, was a man of power and grace. After studying for the ministry at Harvard and Oxford, he had preached on both sides of the Atlantic. The Massachusetts court had granted him the honor of preaching the election sermon of 1668. Unlike most ministers, Stoughton "would not confine his powers to the pulpit," the historian James Savage wrote. Stoughton served as a magistrate of the General Court during the 1670s and 1680s and, after 1686, as deputy governor, with the strong backing of Increase Mather. In 1692, when a new governor would need a man sufficiently wise to lead a court charged with hearing and judging multiple cases of suspected witchcraft, it would be Stoughton to whom he would turn.

Meanwhile, Samuel was planning to leave on a voyage that would keep him from home for most of little Joseph's early life.

8

GLORIOUS REVOLUTION

In September 1688, at the request of the Provincial Council, Samuel prepared to return to his country of birth. Increase Mather and other Massachusetts leaders were already in London trying to renew the old charter or at least to secure a new charter preserving some of their liberties. Samuel's mission was to assist the Reverend Mather in securing New Englanders' property rights.

Although the great majority of Americans could not afford transatlantic sojourns, Samuel's father-in-law had made the same roundtrip two decades before. In November 1669, when Hannah was eleven, John Hull and another Third Church founder sailed to the homeland in search of a minister. Hull returned eleven months later to find his "wife, daughter, servants, and all in health and safety." His servants, indentured household employees who worked for a term, included relatives from England and America and unrelated people of English and African origins.

In 1688, as thirty-six-year-old Samuel anticipated the same voyage, he found the prospect of leaving his wife and four young children for months—possibly years—discomfiting. At the same time, he was intrigued to see his birthplace, which he could barely remember. He spent weeks packing. He set aside rounds of cheese, casks of Madeira wine, and live geese and sheep to slaughter on board and share with other passengers. His wife baked and packed plum cakes (stewed plums in pie crusts) and pasties (meat and herbs in pastry shells). In October Gilbert Cole, who was admitted to the Third Church the same day as Samuel, bottled him "a barrel of beer for the sea."

Samuel also packed books. He would read or reread them to pass the time on the ship, then give them away. He filled a trunk with a dictionary of biblical Hebrew, volumes by theologians Thomas Manton, Desiderius Erasmus, and John Preston, as well as stacks of pamphlets and sermons published at the Harvard College press, mementos of the New World that he hoped to share. He did not list every book he carried with him, but he took special care with one book, carefully wrapping it before adding it to the trunk. He did not yet know to whom he would give it.

This book, the latest edition of the complete Indian Bible, bound in calves' leather, was so valuable it could not be bought. It was an evangelical work and as such could only be given away. The Indian Bible, one of the most important historic artifacts of seventeenth-century North America, remains an emblem of Puritan missionary zeal. Only twenty Indian Bibles exist in the world today. Each one is valued at more than two million dollars although they are unlikely to be available for sale.

The Indian Bible was John Eliot's brainchild. Back in 1655, when the Cambridge-educated Roxbury minister was fifty, he developed sufficient fluency in Algonquian, after years of study, to begin translating the Gospel of Matthew into this Native American language. "I do very much desire to translate some parts of the Scriptures into their language and print some Primer in their language where to initiate and teach them to read." He was pursuing a cultural goal: the seal of Massachusetts Bay Colony shows a Native American man ringed by the words, from Acts 16:9, "Come over and help us." In 1646 the General Court ordered that "efforts to promote the diffusion of Christianity among aboriginal inhabitants be made with all diligence." Three years later England's Puritan-run Parliament enacted an Ordinance for the Advancement of Civilization and Christianity Among the Indians, which created the Corporation for the Propagation of the Gospel Among the Indians in New England, the first Protestant missionary society.

With the help of his Indian teachers—John Sassamon, Job Nesutan, and Cochenoe—Eliot translated the Gospel of Matthew. He sent this sample translation to the Corporation for the Propagation of the Gospel Among the Indians in New England. Delighted, the corporation provided funding; a printing press; a printer from London, Marmaduke Johnson; and permission to translate the whole Bible into the Indian language. Eliot published the whole New Testament in Algonquian in 1661. Every copy was given away—one to King Charles II, some to English and American supporters of the Corporation for the Propagation of the Gospel, and hundreds to the Algonquian people. Missionaries on Martha's Vineyard, the Kennebec River region in Maine, and Natick, Massachusetts, used this text to preach to and convert countless Native Americans.

Eliot's crowning achievement was the complete Indian Bible including the Old Testament. It was a quasi-phonetic translation, intended for reading aloud by an English speaker to a listener who understands Algonquian. Thus the words "The Holy Bible, containing the Old Testament and the New," became "Mamvsse wunneetupanatamwe up-biblum God naneeswe nukkone testament kah wonk wusku testament." Marmaduke Johnson and the local printer, Samuel Green, published the first edition of the whole Indian Bible in 1663 at the Indian College in Cambridge. Each printing cost five hundred pounds. The amount of paper used in printing Indian Bibles exceeded that in all other seventeenth-century American publications combined. Eliot arranged for a second edition of the whole Indian Bible in 1685. It was from this second printing, which Samuel Sewall had supported financially, that he took his intended gift.

A few days before Samuel's ship, the aptly named *America*, was to sail, his servants began carrying his luggage aboard. Samuel met the captain, to whom he gave a gift, and he chose the starboard cabin for himself. He called for a day of prayer at his home, at which the Reverend Willard preached on Psalm 143:10: "Teach me to do thy will; for thou are my God: Thy spirit is good; lead me into the land of uprightness." Hannah was too ill with "the ague in her face" to venture downstairs to join the gathering, but Samuel led the group in singing Psalm 86, verses three to seven, in the Cambridge tune.

On October 29, as a sort of farewell gift, Samuel took his children Sam Jr., Hannah, and Betty, four of their young friends, and several other men to Hog Island for a picnic. He landed his boat "at the point"

Psalm 86

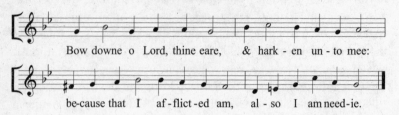

Bow downe o Lord, thine eare,   & hark - en un - to mee:

be-cause that I   af - flict -ed am,   al - so I   am need-ie.

Cambridge Short Tune

Bow downe o Lord, thine eare,
    & harken unto mee:
    because that I afflicted am,
      also I am needie.

2 Doe thou preserve my soule,
    for gra-ci-ous am I:
    o thou my God, thy servant save,
      that doth on thee rely.

3 Lord pitty me, for I
    daily cry thee unto.
4 Rejoyce thy servants soule: for Lord,
    to thee mine [soul] lift I do.

5 For thou o Lord, art good,
    to pardon prone withall:
    and to them all in mercy rich
      that doe upon thee call.

6 Jehovah, o doe thou
    give eare my pray'r unto:
    & of my sup-pli-ca-ti-ons
      attend the voyce also.

7 In day of my distresse,
    to thee I will complaine:
    by reason that thou unto mee
      wilt answer give againe.

of the island "because the water was over the marsh and wharf, being the highest tide that I ever saw there." The party dined on turkey and other fowls, cooked over an open fire. They had "a fair wind" home, arriving at sunset.

On November 16, just before he was scheduled to leave Boston, an elderly Irish washerwoman named Mary Glover was hanged as a witch on Boston Common. Some months earlier, children in a house where Goodwife Glover worked began to act strangely. Their father, a Boston mason named John Goodwin, told them to stop. They said they were unable; Goody Glover had put a spell on them. She spoke in a foreign tongue, her native Irish, and she kept rag puppets, which were considered incriminating. The Reverend Cotton Mather was called in to investigate. He concluded that witchcraft was responsible and wrote it up as a 1689 essay, *Memorable Providences Relating to Witchcrafts and Possessions.* Mary Glover was brought to trial for witchcraft in Boston. Hoping to save herself, she confessed she was a witch. The court found her guilty and sentenced her to hang. Cotton Mather resolved then "never to use but just one grain of patience with any man that shall go to impose upon me a denial of devils and witches." At eleven on the morning of her hanging, Samuel glanced out a window of his house and noted that "the widow Glover is drawn by to be hanged."

The *America* set sail for England on November 22, an hour before sunset. As Samuel watched the town he loved fade into the distance, he poured himself a glass of Madeira and began to pray. Scripture and the Psalms would be his best companions at sea. A day later he observed, "I ate my wife's pasty, the remembrance of whom is ready to cut me to the heart. The Lord pardon and help me."

Traversing the Atlantic was treacherous and uncomfortable even for a wealthy merchant with a private cabin. The weather was bad for much of the trip. Wind, hail, snow, and huge waves pelted the ship. The ship took on water, prompting the captain to warn it might capsize. A storm sent Samuel's chest flying across his cabin, breaking some glassware.

On the first of January 1689 news came from a passing ship that the Glorious Revolution, a major event in English history, had occurred. England had a new king. Leading English politicians who were unhappy with James II had invited the Dutch prince William of Orange, a Protestant who was James II's nephew and son-in-law, to challenge James II for England's throne. William of Orange had landed at Torbay in England on November 5 and defeated James II, who fled to France, where he was welcomed by Louis XIV. William and his wife, James II's daughter Mary, were now king and queen of England, which would now be run as a constitutional monarchy.

In the wake of the Glorious Revolution, Samuel's peers in Boston, including Cotton Mather, Samuel Willard, other prominent ministers, and many merchants, would soon stage a revolution of their own. On April 19, 1689, eighty-six years before the April 19 famed for "the shot heard round the world," they rallied local militia and imprisoned Governor Edmund Andros, his secretary, Edward Randolph, and several of their supporters in the fort overlooking Boston harbor. They placed Joseph Dudley, who was now seen as a conspirator, under house arrest in Roxbury. Within a few months the men of Boston would ship the Andros crowd back to England. Emboldened by the Glorious Revolution, which put two Protestants on the throne, New England's leaders returned Governor Simon Bradstreet and the former deputies and assistants of the General Court to the offices they had held in 1686. This provisional government, which included Samuel, would last until a new royal governor, Sir William Phips, arrived with a new charter in 1692.

In England Samuel would not learn of Boston's "quiet, well-bred, and bloodless revolution," as his diary's editor termed it, until late June, while on a visit to Cambridge with the Reverend Increase Mather and his fifteen-year-old son, Samuel. The New Englanders enjoyed Cambridge, Sewall reported: their innkeeper served them a boiled leg of mutton, "colly-flowers," and "carrots, roast fowls, and a dish of peas. Three musicians came in, two harps and a violin, and gave us music." Departing Cambridge early on June 29, the men headed to London in a coach with four horses, breakfasting at Epping. By late morning they reached a coffeehouse where mail awaited them. Tearing open a letter, Samuel Sewall "read the news of" the revolution in Boston. He gave the letter "to Mr. Mather to read. We were surprised with joy." Yet another event at home that Samuel was absent for, of a more personal nature, was the admission of his wife to full membership in the Third Church on January 1, 1689.

That same January week, on board his ship to England, Samuel sighted shorebirds—"a gray linnet and a lark, I think." One foggy morning the captain "trimmed sharp for our lives," narrowly avoiding "horrid, high, gaping rocks" off the Isles of Scilly. Arriving at Dover on January 13, Samuel stepped on land for the first time in seven weeks. It was the Sabbath, so he walked to a malt-house to hear a Puritan minister preach from Isaiah 65:9: "And I will bring forth a seed out of Jacob, and out of Judah an inheritor of my mountains: and mine elect shall inherit it, and my servants shall dwell there."

Samuel felt like a tourist in England. He introduced himself to people as "a New England man," and after six months he wrote, "I am a stranger in this land." His base of operations was a room above a London shop owned by his wife's "Cousin Hull," the son of John Hull's late brother, Edward. Edward Hull Jr. ran a haberdashery, the Hat-in-Hand, in Aldgate, a neighborhood just northeast of the Tower of London. At that time London was the world's largest city, with half a million inhabitants. Its city center, destroyed by the Great Fire of

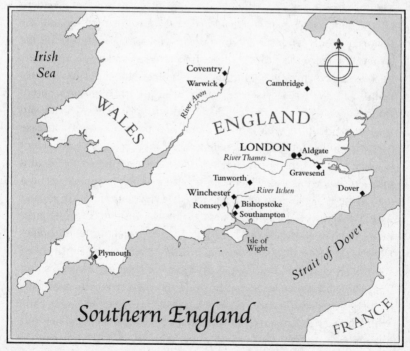

Southern England

1666, was now mostly rebuilt. London, the seat of English government, was already famous for its media, culture, and markets.

In contrast to London, most of England's cities were small, with fewer than ten thousand residents. Most of the nation's five million inhabitants lived in the countryside and grew their own food. Their average life span was less than forty years. Many women died in childbirth; one of every two children died before turning five. Bubonic plague, malaria, and leprosy were common. Few people traveled far from home. A boat was the most efficient mode of transport. Roads were poor and, in winter, often impassable. England was a highly stratified society in which nearly half the people lived at subsistence level. The gentry and nobility, who controlled most land and wealth, comprised less than 5 percent of the population. In the middle were yeomen—substantial farmers and tradesmen—and a small rising professional class of clergy, lawyers, merchants, and officials. While most people could not read or write, the percentage of Englishmen receiving higher education at Oxford, Cambridge, or the Inns of Court was greater—at 2.5 percent—than at any time until the twentieth century. Of the wide range of privileges in seventeenth-century England, the historian Keith Thomas has observed, "Not every under-developed society has its Shakespeare, Milton, Locke, Wren and Newton."

Samuel had three goals for his stay in England: to see his kin and country of birth; to oversee his family property in Hampshire; and to assist Increase Mather in restoring colonial privileges. During his time in England he took in many familiar tourist sites. At the Tower of London he toured the fourteenth-century mint and the royal armory, admired the crown scepter, and noted the "lions [and] leopards" in the menagerie, which also housed giraffes, baboons, and even a polar bear in the moat. Samuel visited Parliament and took a barge up the Thames to Hampton Court Castle several times "to wait on the king," with whom he hoped to discuss the protection of colonists' rights. "We were dismissed *sine die*," without having fixed another date to meet, he wrote on one such occasion, which was typical of his success. Samuel took the barge in the other direction to see the night sky from the observatory at Greenwich, where he spoke at length with John Flamsteed, England's first Astronomer Royal. One particularly hot summer day Samuel dived into the great river "in my drawers" for a "healthful and refreshing" swim, an activity he also enjoyed on sultry August afternoons in Boston's Back Bay.

On a mid-March perambulation east of Aldgate in London he toured the Jews' Burying Place at Mile End. Like many devout Puritans, Samuel had a special interest in Jews, not only because they were a covenanted people but also because their conversion to Christianity would be a sign that the end of the world was near. He and the grave keeper had a friendly chat over glasses of beer amid the graves. As Samuel prepared to leave he said to the man, "I wish we might meet in Heaven."

"And drink a glass of beer together there," the grave keeper replied.

Eager to see the places of his boyhood, Samuel hastened to Hampshire's county town of Winchester—where Leonard Hoar's mother-in-law, Bridget Lisle, had been beheaded—within a month of his arrival in London. At the Winchester market on February 19 Samuel purchased a bay horse, boots, a saddle and saddlecloth, a bridle, and other equipage, as a tourist today would rent a car.

Hampshire "has always been an open gate for English discovery and enterprise towards the west," according to Nathan Chamberlain. "The sun is warmer there than in the North Land, and its gardens and orchards fuller." Cattle, ponies, pigs, donkeys, and deer still roam its forests, heaths, and lowland moors. Winchester was once England's capital, and it is still heart of Hampshire County. Better preserved than many English towns, Winchester retains a medieval feel on account of its surrounding Roman wall, narrow cobbled streets, thirteenth-century castle, magnificent Gothic cathedral, and few modern high-rises. The town straddles the Itchen River, which is crossed by stone bridges.

Nestled near the river is the campus of Winchester College, a secondary school for clever boys. The school's ancient barrier wall and dark Gothic buildings seem to say to the world, "Keep out." Winchester College is fifty years older than Eton. It was founded in the late fourteenth century by William of Wykeham, bishop of Winchester and chancellor to Richard II, to educate seventy "poor and needy scholars." William of Wykeham, who also founded New College, Oxford, supervised the creation of the medieval campus, which still stands beside a meadow dotted with eighteenth-century plane trees.

Samuel visited Winchester College on February 25 and requested a tour. A man led him through a cloister to "the chapel on the green," an architectural oddity existing nowhere else in the world. A chantry, a medieval structure in which monks chanted for the dead, was set in the middle of a cloister, surrounded by grass. Samuel entered the chantry and followed the man up a spiral of marble stairs to the "library around the stairs," a large room with timber beams, white plaster walls, and delicately mullioned Gothic windows.

In this light-filled medieval chamber, Samuel encountered a remarkable collection of books, which William of Wykeham had begun in the fourteenth century. Samuel saw Peter Comestor's *Historia Scholastica*, from around 1175, and a four-volume vellum songbook published in 1564 and inscribed by a suitor to Queen Elizabeth I. An early-thirteenth-century manuscript, *Life of St. Thomas Becket*, possibly by William of Canterbury, contained the earliest known portrait of Becket. In Ranulf Higden's 1380 work, *Polychronicon*, the librarian showed Samuel a remarkable oval map of the world that places Jerusalem at the center and Paradise, in the east, at the top. Samuel admired several books donated in 1600 by Sir Robert Cecil, secretary of state and treasurer to King James I, including a 1587 Heidelberg Bible and many works of Luther, Zwingli, and Calvin.

Startled by the quality of this collection, Samuel decided on the spot to leave his Indian Bible here. "Samuel Sewall, like modern donors, may have been animated by the idea of being remembered in a library that has one of the longest continuous histories in the Anglo-Saxon world," a later keeper of the Winchester College library conjectured. Beyond that, Samuel had a personal reason for wanting to leave his Indian Bible at Winchester College. His alternative English life—the life he'd have lived had he not sailed to America in 1661—might have continued at Winchester College, which then admitted scholars as young as ten years old. Doubtless aware of this, he handed his Indian Bible to the college librarian, confident that this precious token of the delights and possibilities of the New World had found its home in the old.

The text of Samuel's Indian Bible, which is now the most valuable object in the collection at Winchester College, begins:

Negonne Oosukkuhwhonk Moses, ne asoweetamuk

GENESIS

Chap I

1. Weske kutchinik ayum God kusuk kah Ohke.

2. Kah Ohke mo matta kuhkenauunneunkquttinnoo kah mon-teagunninuo, kah pohkenum woskeche moonoi, kah Nashauanit popomshau woikeche nippekontu.

3. Onk noowau God wequi, kah mo wequai.

4. Kah wunnaumum God wequai neen wunnegen; kah wutchadchanbeponumun God noeu wequai kah noeu pohkenum.

The words INDIAN BIBLE appear in gold leaf on the spine. One of its two original clasps is missing. Below the Algonquian title, MAMUSSE WUNNEETUPANATAMWE UP-BIBLUM GOD, are the words "John Eliot, Cambridge. Published by Samuel Green, printer, MDCLXXXV, second edition, Boston." Atop the title page, in his confident hand, Samuel penned his name and the date he received the book from the printer: "Sam. Sewall January 2, 1685/6"—January 12, 1686, by modern reckoning—which was three years before he deposited it at Winchester College. The Bible is stored in a locked vault and displayed once every five years. It has never left Winchester College.

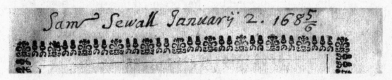

In the months following Samuel's tour of the college, he visited his boyhood villages and towns. He saw many cousins in the village of Baddesley (pronounced "Bad-ess-ly"), where he had spent several years in the 1650s. At Baddesley's medieval parish church he stood before the grave of his Aunt Rider, who had died in 1688. He walked to nearby Lee, a village of about a dozen thatched houses, to see his father's land and farmhouse, which still produced a modest income, twenty pounds a year.

During the few years that his parents had spent in Puritan England, they possessed the means to move several times. While there is no record of Henry Sewall's schooling, his status as a cattle farmer who occasionally preached indicates education and material comfort. Given the tendencies of Puritan boys of his background, Henry had likely attended English grammar schools before coming to America at nineteen, in 1634. He and his wife lived first in Warwick, northwest of London, near Coventry, where Henry's grandfather, a wealthy linen draper, had been mayor. To be closer to Jane's family, the Dummers, Henry and Jane Sewall moved south to Hampshire. By May of 1649, when she delivered their first child, Hannah, they were in the village of Tunworth. Before their second child was born they moved again, to the village of Bishopstoke, which lies between Winchester and Southampton.

The Sewall house in Bishopstoke, which probably still stood when Samuel visited this ancient parish in 1689, was a hundred or so yards northeast of the Bishopstoke church. On the rising ground east of the River Itchen, it was one of forty or fifty similar abodes—seventy hearths, according to a 1665 census survey—whose occupants were farmers and millers. The sort of thatched house still common in rural England, it was timber framed and coated with wattle and daub, a mixture of the hair of a horse, goat, or cow; lime; and mud plaster. It had a brick-lined chimney and one or two fireplaces. A parlor and spacious kitchen with a long table and benches occupied the ground floor.

In a bedchamber on the second floor of this house, a little before daybreak on Sunday, March 28, 1652, Samuel Sewall had been born. "The light of the Lord's Day was the first light that my eyes saw," he wrote decades later of his origins. Samuel was, or hoped to be, with God from the start.

Five weeks later, on May 4, 1652, Henry and Jane carried their new son to the parish church, set on a knoll on the eastern bank of the River Itchen. Swans swam amid the bulrushes in the river. A mill stream lapped against the churchyard. The church, which appears in the 1086 Domesday Book, a survey of English land and landholders, stood until 1891, serving for most of that time as the physical and social center of the village. Medieval paintings of biblical scenes decorated its interior walls. On that May morning in 1652, a Cambridge-educated Puritan minister named Thomas Rashly preached a sermon before baptizing the Sewalls' baby. Henry held up his first son and named him Samuel, after the Old Testament leader who judged Israel and "built an altar unto the Lord." Following the service the Reverend Rashly and many other family and friends of Henry and Jane crowded into the Sewall house for "an entertainment" in honor of the new baby.

Before Samuel was two the family moved to the neighboring village of Baddesley, where three younger siblings were born and baptized, John in October 1654, Stephen in August 1657, and Jane in October 1659. Baddesley is also mentioned in the Domesday Book. It consisted of a medieval church, in whose yard Samuel's Aunt Rider lies, and a nearby common surrounded by thatched farmhouses. Baddesley was even smaller than Bishopstoke, with fewer than forty houses (fifty-six hearths in the 1665 census). Samuel's lengthy education began here: at "Baddesley, by the merciful goodness of God, I was taught to read English" and to write. At age five or six Samuel began a daily four-mile walk from Baddesley to the market town of Romsey, which was dominated by a monumental twelfth-century Norman abbey that survived King Henry VIII's dissolution of the monasteries only because a clever Benedictine abbot sold it to the townspeople in 1544, transforming it into a parish church. Samuel's daily route to school went from the South Baddesley Church across Baddesley Common through a forest to Romsey Common fields, where cattle grazed.

Samuel's grammar school was called the Romsey Free School even though the boys' parents paid tuition. Located on the abbey grounds, it may have been inside the abbey, according to a local historian, Phoebe Merrick. Graffiti initials around a window high on the nave's northwestern wall are considered the work of schoolboys in the seventeenth century, when a schoolroom sat within the nave on an upper floor that no longer exists. The schoolmaster, whom Samuel remembered fondly, was Mr. Figes ("Fid-ges"). By the 1680s, when Samuel visited as an adult, the boys at the Romsey Free School wore a uniform of "blue coats, puckered, no pockets" and a flat cap with a white tassel and band.

In 1659, during Samuel's second or third year of study with Mr. Figes, Henry Sewall grew troubled by the "very little" rents he received from his land in Newbury, Massachusetts. Leaving his wife and children in Baddesley, he sailed back to New England, where his father still lived, to try to improve his returns. In Baddesley that October, when Jane gave birth to a baby girl, also named Jane, Henry was not present. Seven-year-old Samuel was the oldest male in the house.

Puritan politics may have influenced the timing of Henry's trip. Oliver Cromwell, the Puritan leader, died in 1658. His son, Richard, succeeded him but lacked his father's political skill. The Puritans lost power in 1660 when the decapitated king's oldest son, Charles II, retook the throne. Learning of this, Henry Sewall decided to stay in Puritan America. He sent money and instructions to his wife, who once again began packing to move.

In late April of 1661, amid the "thunder and lightening" that accompanied the English coronation of King Charles II, nine-year-old Samuel and his older sister and three younger siblings and mother left Baddesley with two servants, John Nash and Mary Hobbes. They traveled to Winchester to await the pool wagons to London. Samuel never mentioned if he looked longingly at the handsome college where he might have been a ten-year-old scholar. He recalled a gaggle of Dummer relations taking leave of his family "with tears." One man "treated us with raisins and almonds." The Sewalls continued on to London and their ship, the *Prudent Mary*, which set sail from Gravesend in May.

In early July, after eight weeks at sea, Samuel grew anxious, he noted years later in his diary. The boy had tired of the ship's cramped quarters, awful boredom, and horrendous smells. A hundred passengers and crew members slept on bunks hanging from rafters. Cattle and other beasts crowded the hold below. On deck there was "nothing to see but water and the sky." Samuel "began to fear that I should never get to shore again."

He did not discuss his fear with his mother, who had smaller children to manage. Quietly over several days he pondered it on his own. Suddenly he realized he need not be afraid. "The captain and the mariners would not have ventured themselves, if they had not hopes of getting to land again." If the men in charge of the ship could hope for a safe landing, so too could the logical boy. Samuel eased into the final stretch.

On July 6, 1661, the *Prudent Mary* sailed into Boston harbor, which was dotted with islands. On first seeing the well-situated town that he would later call his home, Samuel observed a slender peninsula stretching several miles out to sea, almost entirely hemmed in by water. To the south lay the Bay of Roxbury. To the north flowed the Charles River, which Governor Winthrop's crew had named for Charles I, whom they hated but hoped to mollify. To the west of the town lay a vast marsh and the tidal waters of the Back Bay. Several hundred timber-framed, thatched houses, two churches, a market square, and a Town House were perched on a square outcropping at the head of Boston's "neck."

The "greatest wants" of a town with such a setting, the explorer William Wood had noted in 1634, were wood and meadow lands. Bostonians had to fetch "building-timber and firewood from the [harbor] islands in boats, and their hay in loiters." Yet there were benefits to Boston's paucity of trees: its residents were "not troubled with three annoyances, of wolves, rattlesnakes, and mosquitoes."

What the town lacked in forest it made up for in hills. On its south side was "a great broad hill," Wood observed, "whereon is planted a fort, which can command any ship as she sails into any harbor within the still bay. On the north side is another hill, equal in bigness, whereon stands a windmill." Roughly between them to the northwest was "a high mountain with three little rising hills on the top of it," which prompted John Winthrop to call Boston "Trimountaine." From here a person could "overlook all the islands which lie before the bay, and descry such ships as are upon the seacoast." William Wood concluded, "This town although it be neither the greatest, nor the richest, yet it is the most noted and frequented, being the center of the plantations where the monthly courts are kept. Here likewise dwells the governor: this place hath very good land, affording rich cornfields, and fruitful gardens; having likewise sweet and pleasant springs." This was the region's "chief place for shipping and merchandize."

In the harbor on July 6, 1661, the boat carrying Samuel waited under anchor as the tide receded and the boat was finally grounded. The captain "kept aboard" Samuel's mother and siblings. But Samuel, as the oldest boy, was "carried out in arms" by a man he did not know. He roamed the rocky shoreline, explored tidal pools, and picked berries. An earlier arrival, Francis Higginson, had noted this coastland's teeming edible wildlife: "Excellent … mulberries, plums, raspberries, currants, chestnuts, filberts, walnuts, smalnuts, hurtleberies and hawes of whitethorn near as good as our cherries in England, they grow in plenty here." Samuel spent one more night on the ship with his mother and siblings. The next morning, at high tide, the crew rowed the Sewalls and their luggage to shore. Boston celebrated a Thanksgiving Day that week while Samuel's father "hastened to Boston and carried his family to Newbury by water," where Samuel was "carried ashore in [a] canoe."

Twenty-eight years later, he again made the journey across the Atlantic, this time returning to his own wife and four children. The *America* left from Plymouth in Devon on October 10 and landed at Piscataqua, New Hampshire, on November 29 and Boston on December 2. Like the voyage to England, the return was difficult. In November Samuel composed an impromptu will. "If it should please God … to put an end to my life before I come to Boston," he wished to leave volumes of books to friends, his watch to his wife "as a token of my love," his new suit "with the chamlet cloak" to his brother Stephen, and his whole estate to "my dear Mother [Hull] and Wife."

Samuel arrived home on the evening of December 2, 1689, laden with gifts. Among them were eight dozen silk stockings from Salisbury in three sizes (men's, women's, and youth); leather gloves and riding whips for his daughters, purchased at Romsey; linen from Oxford; nine gross of buttons (a gross is twelve dozen); silver spoons; small trunks marked with each of his children's initials and year of birth; hooks and lines; hats, muffs, and mittens; biscuits and cheeses; maps of London, England, Scotland, and Ireland; and Bibles in Hebrew and Greek.

A few days later he took the oath of office as a magistrate of the Great and General Court of Massachusetts. At a public house in Boston he drank toasts to the health of New England with fellow magistrates Wait Still Winthrop, William Stoughton, John Richards, and John Hathorne, all of whom would serve with him on the witchcraft court. In early February 1690 a ship departed Boston bearing the prisoners of the recent rebellion. Sir Edmund Andros, Edward Randolph, Joseph Dudley, and several other royalists were "sent home to the king."

During his year abroad Samuel had done what he could to help Increase Mather restore the colonial rights and ways of New England. He had written letters to government officials who seemed likely to offer support. In April 1689 he had sent a missive to a Puritan member of Parliament, Thomas Papillon, who came from a Huguenot family that had escaped France's persecution of Protestants. Explaining New England's predicament in highly personal terms, Samuel wrote to Papillon, "Captain John Hull of Boston in New England ... died in September 1683, leaving a widow and a daughter who is my wife, by whom I had an estate that might afford a comfortable subsistence according to our manner of living in New England." This was polite understatement from such a wealthy man.

"But since the vacating of the charter ... the title we have to our lands has been greatly defamed and undervalued; which has been greatly prejudicial to the inhabitants, because their lands, which were formerly the best part of their estate, became of very little value and consequently the owners of very little credit...." As a result, Samuel wrote, I "have little heart to go home before some comfortable settlement obtained whereby we might be secured in the possession of our religion, liberty and property." Sewall's final triplet echoes the "life, liberty, and property" coined by the English Puritan Samuel Rutherford in 1644 and copied by John Locke in his *Second Treatise*, and it predates by nearly a century Thomas Jefferson's "life, liberty, and the pursuit of happiness." The letter to Papillon continued, "I am informed some favorable votes have been passed in the House of Commons wherein New England was mentioned. I entreat your forwarding of such votes, as you have opportunity, in doing which you will be a partner with God who is wont to be concerned in relieving the oppressed...."

With such efforts Samuel had worked to secure his and others' land titles. Now, back in Massachusetts, he was poised to lead.

9

GREAT HEAVINESS
ON MY SPIRIT

The guest list for the party thrown by Samuel and Hannah Sewall on Monday, February 24, 1690, is a veritable who's who of upper-crust devotees of the New England way. Simon Bradstreet, age eighty-six, "and Lady," his younger second wife, Anne, were present at the long dinner table. There were daughters of the late John Cotton and the late Edmund Quincy Sr.—Mary Cotton Mather, whose husband, Increase, was still in London, and Samuel's widowed mother-in-law. The Reverend Cotton Mather and his wife were present, along with the Reverends Samuel Willard and Joshua Moody with their wives— representatives of all three of Boston's churches. Major Elisha Hutchinson and his wife sat next to the Reverend James Allen, who preached at the church that had cast out Hutchinson's grandmother. Thomas Brattle, a merchant who had been in London on colonial business during Samuel's time there, sat nearby. Brattle, a mathematician, astronomer, and member of the Harvard class of 1676, was serving with remarkable effectiveness as the treasurer of the still-troubled college. His father, of the same name, had been a founding member, with John Hull, of the Third Church. Brattle and Deputy Governor William Stoughton, who was also present, were both bachelors, a rare phenomenon in Puritan society. The common course for a high-status gentleman was to marry in one's early twenties and, following the death of that wife (likely in childbirth), to marry again and, if necessary, again.

During the party, a celebration of Samuel's safe return from England, the Sewall children were elsewhere, unheard, in the care of servants. Most of the family's servants were kept busy in the Great Hall, racing to prepare, deliver, and retrieve platters of delicacies for the guests. Wine bottles moved quickly around the long table. Samuel led the singing of portions of the sixth and fiftieth psalms to the Windsor tune. The mood was gay.

Or, rather, gay to a point. At some point—no one recorded whether at that moment they were enjoying roasted meats, stewed fruits, or cheeses—a servant delivered to Governor Bradstreet a dispatch just arrived from Albany in New York.

Simon Bradstreet scanned the dispatch with growing horror. To a stunned audience, he read aloud the "amazing" news, which Samuel called "bitterness in our cups." Two weeks previous, around midnight, French and Indian forces raided Schenectady, twenty miles north of Albany, one of England's northern frontiers in America. The French and Indians killed sixty English people—they "ripped up" children and "dashed out" their brains—and destroyed their village. Bradstreet was shocked. Only days earlier he had written with confidence to London that the winter cold "forbids the stirring of our Indian enemies."

In the days following the doomed dinner party, Samuel learned that New England's enemies, the allied French and Indians, planned more attacks. A large group of French and Indian soldiers was moving south from Quebec, the French stronghold, to New England. At dawn on March 19 the French and Abenaki Indians raided Salmon Falls in the eastern part of Massachusetts (now Berwick, Maine) and wreaked "dreadful destruction." They burned twenty houses and the English fort there and killed or captured nearly a hundred people. This was "doleful news," Samuel wrote. Even worse, the French and Indians appeared to be headed farther south, toward Boston.

The magistrates anxiously discussed the proper response. On the streets and in the Town House, they wondered, What can be done to stop these acts of terror? When will the French and Indians arrive in Boston to wreak destruction?

William Stoughton proposed "prosecuting vigorously the business against the Eastern French." Stoughton, who is remembered now for his "cold-blooded" ferocity in prosecuting suspected witches, was a large man with small eyes, pursed lips, and straight hair parted in the center. Several years earlier, while serving as a councillor under Andros, he was considered too moderate toward the Crown, but he had gained Increase Mather's favor by opposing Edmund Andros in 1689, prompting Mather to nominate him as deputy governor.

John Alden Jr. and Bartholomew Gedney also urged a strong response. They proposed to send English ships and soldiers to defeat the French at Quebec. This was an expensive proposition that the government could not afford. So the merchants and other wealthy men of Boston raised the money, largely among themselves, to pay for ships, supplies, and troops. Samuel donated hundreds of pounds and was one of the cabal that chose Sir William Phips, a forty-year-old sea captain from Maine, to lead the troops to Canada.

Phips was a colorful character. Born in 1651 on a farm alongside a saltwater tributary of the Sheepscot and Kennebec Rivers in what is now Woolwich, Maine, he was an unschooled son of Maine planters whose English ancestors had a sixteenth-century coat of arms. Following a five-year apprenticeship to a sea captain, Phips settled in Boston, where he gained a reputation for boldness. His "inclination," Cotton Mather wrote, was "cutting rather like a hatchet than like a razor." According to Edgar Bellefontaine, a legal librarian at the Social Law Library in Boston, "Phips was a pirate—with the management style and language skills of a pirate." In the early 1680s, hoping to achieve wealth and social mobility, Phips sailed to the Caribbean in search of buried treasure. South of the Bahamas he discovered more than two hundred thousand English pounds of gold—"a great deal of money then," Bellefontaine noted. Phips carried the treasure to England and turned it over to the government around the time of the ascension of King William and Queen Mary. In return the Crown knighted William Phips and gave him 10 percent of the bounty, transforming him into one of Massachusetts's wealthiest men. Sir William Phips purchased a magnificent house in the North End of Boston, where he was an ally of the Mathers. Cotton Mather baptized Sir William, who had not been baptized as an infant, in March 1690 and welcomed him into the Second Church. Increase Mather, who was then still in England, encouraged the Crown to make Phips the next governor of Massachusetts. That appointment would occur in London on January 26, 1692, after which the elder Mather and the new governor would sail back to Boston on the same ship.

In 1690, in the wake of Indian attacks on Maine, the Massachusetts General Court swore in Phips as major general of the provincial army. Samuel was present at the Town House that March day. He observed "eight companies and troops" training and joined his own South Company in prayer at the Common. Three days later, on March 25, 1690, "Drums beat through the town for volunteers."

Increasing attacks by French and Indians prompted New York's acting governor, Jacob Leisler, to demand that Massachusetts send two "commissioners" to New York for a joint colonial conference on "common safety." Samuel Sewall and William Stoughton volunteered for the trip. They set out on horseback on April 21, each waited on by several attendants. They left their horses (but not their bridles and saddles) in Newport, Rhode Island, and paid a sloop's captain to take them across the sound to Oyster Bay, Long Island. On rented horses they rode to Jamaica, in modern-day Queens, Brooklyn, and by ferry to Manhattan. Samuel was not sanguine about Leisler's public safety meeting, which "brought great heaviness on my spirit." Yet he relished the chance to learn to sing a psalm in the Dutch language while visiting a Dutch Reformed church. It was Psalm 25: "Unto thee, O Lord, do I lift up my soul…. Let me not be ashamed, let not mine enemies triumph over me…." This seemed "extraordinarily fitted for me in my present distresses, and by which [I] have received comfort."

That month Major General William Phips led more than seven hundred soldiers in eight small ships north to Port Royal, Nova Scotia. Meeting little resistance, he seized the town on May 11. Samuel, who had contributed a hundred pounds to the expedition, wrote on May 22, "We hear of the taking [of] Port Royal by Sir William Phips … which somewhat abates our sorrow for the loss of Casco" in Maine.

French and Indian forces had continued to attack towns along the New England coast. They hit the coastal village of Saco, Maine, on April 21, killing people and animals, taking human hostages, and burning houses. Four days later they routed Cape Porpoise. A group of Madockawando Indians and French soldiers burned the English settlement of Falmouth near modern-day Portland, Maine, on May 20, killing some people and capturing others. A month later they raided Cocheco, across the river from Salmon Falls, at the Maine–New Hampshire border. They seized the English fort at Pemaquid in Maine, raided Sagadahoc, and headed south through North Yarmouth, Black Point, Saco, and Oyster River. The latter, now the town of Durham, New Hampshire, is hardly thirty miles from Boston's North Shore. With a sense of growing fear, the Massachusetts court dispatched two councillors, John Hathorne and Jonathan Corwin, to investigate in Maine and New Hampshire. Hathorne and Corwin recommended sending more troops and supplies to Maine garrisons and warning frontier settlers not to be "surprised by the enemy and suddenly destroyed as other places have been."

These many battles were the start of King William's War, the first of a series of battles now collectively known as the French and Indian Wars. These battles between Britain and France over their colonies would last more than seventy years, into the second half of the eighteenth century. King William's War, which was fought on American and European soil between 1689 and 1697, was ultimately pointless: the September 1697 Treaty of Ryswick, which ended it, restored all colonial possessions to their prewar status, as if no war had been fought.

But to the French, Indian, and English people who lost friends and family in King William's War, it felt as devastating as King Philip's War almost twenty years earlier. For Samuel, a member of the governing council who supported the war with hundreds of pounds of his own money and feared every day for his community's safety, the war was another blow to the New England way.

In the midst of this chaos, on May 19, 1690, John Eliot, the Indian Apostle, died at eighty-six. "This puts our election [next week] into mourning." More bad news followed. In July Samuel was "alarmed" to hear "of Frenchmen being landed at Cape Cod, and marched within ten miles of Eastham." Meanwhile his brother Stephen and a hundred fifty other local volunteers sailed to Canada. Samuel prayed, "The good Lord of hosts go along with them." Smallpox spread through

Boston, prompting a quarantine. On July 25, when Nathaniel Saltonstall, one of the magistrates, tried to come to town to discuss the war
with his colleagues on the court, he was not allowed to cross the river
from Charlestown. Samuel and Wait Still Winthrop took the ferry to
Charlestown to converse with Saltonstall there. A fire in early August
destroyed fourteen houses and many warehouses along the docks in
the North End.

On August 8 Samuel rode his horse to Nantasket, a peninsula south
of Shawmut, to watch thirty-two ships and two thousand English soldiers gather in the harbor in preparation for Phips's second expedition
to Canada. Following his great success at Port Royal, Major General
Phips planned to attack the stronghold of Quebec. Samuel watched as
a "Lieutenant General muster[ed] his soldiers on George's Island."
As a magistrate, Samuel was invited on board a warship, which sailed
him and other notables "up to town." Late that night in Boston, he and
Wait Still Winthrop and two other men ceremoniously rolled two-
wheeled "carriages for field-pieces" such as cannons down to the dock
for delivery to warships anchored at Nantasket.

The following day Samuel rode south to Hull, near Nantasket, to
dine with "Sir William [Phips] and his Lady" as the major general
waited for the wind to "spring up." Phips would have preferred to
delay his trip further—he had not secured a pilot for the mission and
was short on supplies and ammunition—but the coming winter urged
him on. At about six that evening, Samuel noted, the "wind veered and
the fleet came to sail. Four ships of war and twenty-eight" other ships
left Boston harbor, headed up the coast to the mouth of the Saint Lawrence River.

Samuel gallantly "carried" Lady Mary Phips home to Boston that
evening on his horse or, more likely, in her coach. En route they
stopped briefly in Braintree to see Samuel's wife's cousin Daniel
Quincy, who was extremely ill. Continuing on, he left Lady Mary in
Boston's North End at her brick mansion, which was nearly as large
as the nave of the North Church. The Phipses lived on Charter Street,
around the corner from Increase and Mary Cotton Mather's house at
the site of Caffé Vittoria on modern-day Hanover Street.

The next day, during the service at the Third Church, a rider came
from Braintree to tell Samuel that Daniel Quincy was close to death.

Daniel, the oldest son of Judith Hull's brother Edmund and Joanna Hoar Quincy, was a silversmith who worked with John Hull. Samuel slipped out of the church and galloped to Braintree. "Cousin Quincy" was surrounded by family, including his wife and his Aunt Judith, Samuel's mother-in-law. Samuel prayed and read psalms at the bedside. He sent for the Reverend Willard, who arrived with more prayers. As Samuel watched Daniel, who was only thirty-nine, pass from this life, he prayed silently, "The Lord fit me for my change and help me to wait till it come." The family laid Daniel's body in John Hull's tomb in Boston two days later. Samuel led the widow, Ann, followed by the children, who included one-year-old John Quincy— grandfather of Abigail Quincy Adams and great-grandfather of John Quincy Adams, sixth president of the United States—and many relatives and friends.

Hannah Sewall, who was about eight months pregnant, took ill during Cousin Quincy's funeral. "She had a great flux of blood, which amazed us both," Samuel reported. He hurried her home and called for a nurse and the midwife, Elizabeth Weeden. That night he prayed for hours, fearing the worst.

The next morning his wife was still alive and they had a new baby girl, born before dawn. At Sabbath service on August 24 the Reverend Willard baptized her and six other babies. Samuel's new daughter "cried not at all, though a pretty deal of water was poured on her by Mr. Willard." Samuel named her Judith, "for the sake of her grandmother and great grandmother, who both bore that name." During the service he prayed inwardly to be a better Christian: "Lord, grant that I who have thus solemnly and frequently named the name of the Lord Jesus may depart from iniquity." He asked God "that mine"—his children—"may be more Yours than mine, or their own."

Two months later the new baby was dead. On the evening of September 20, inexplicably, "my little Judith languishes and moans, ready to die." Samuel rose from his bed at two in the morning to "read some psalms and pray with her." The Reverend Willard, who had buried one of his own children just three days earlier, arrived before eight in the morning to pray. The vigil at the Sewall house lasted until baby Judith died just before eight that night. "I hope [she] sleeps in Jesus," Samuel said.

Solomon Rainsford carefully steadied her little coffin while setting it in the family tomb on September 23. Mourners included Wait Still Winthrop, John Richards, the Bradstreets, the Willards, the Moodys, Increase Mather and his wife, and three generations of Samuel's family.

Alone at home, Samuel wondered what God was saying to him. In five years he had buried four of his last five babies. So many deaths intensified his sense of unworthiness. He felt impotent in the face of medical conditions that were not yet identified or understood. Typical of his peers, according to the historian Keith Thomas, Samuel had "no satisfactory contemporary explanation for the sudden deaths which are today ascribed to stroke or heart disease," viral or bacterial infections, tuberculosis, convulsions, or cancer. Lacking a germ theory of disease—which would not be established until the mid-nineteenth century with the work of scientists such as Louis Pasteur—people considered most sickness inexplicable. They presumed that God or other supernatural forces were agents of disease and death.

October brought more bad news. Sir William Phips's second military expedition to Canada ended in disaster. The expedition had been planned the previous spring as part of a wide attack on the French in Canada and their Indian allies. To divert the French, Iroquois and English forces from New York and Connecticut headed to Montreal. A separate English expedition aimed to threaten Indians "at the East," in Maine. Meanwhile, Phips's massive force was to surprise Quebec. To Samuel's dismay, though, both the Montreal and Maine attacks stalled. Phips reached Quebec in early October but lost his courage and delayed his attack. The French, under Louis de Baude, Comte de Palluau et de Frontenac, forced back the English and killed an estimated two hundred soldiers. Numerous English ships were lost on the St. Lawrence River.

This disaster bred others. Massachusetts's treasury, which had borrowed fifty thousand pounds to fund this expedition, was empty. The New England economy would suffer for twenty years. Currency was devalued. Foreign trade declined dramatically, in part because of the war with the French. Some prominent Bostonians blamed Phips. Samuel defended him in a letter he sent to Increase Mather in London in December 1690. "You will hear various [negative] reports of Sir William Phips.... I have discoursed with all sorts, and find that neither activity nor courage were wanting in him [at Quebec], and the form of the attack was agreed on by the Council of War" in Boston. In this instance Samuel felt comfortable sharing the blame for the disaster.

Despite all the world's upheaval, God still blessed him and Hannah. Within a few months she was again pregnant. Samuel began arranging to build a large addition to their house. Early in 1692 he consulted with his minister, asking "whether the [difficult] times would allow one to build an" addition. Encouragingly, the Reverend Willard replied, "I wonder you have contented yourselves so long without one." Only later did Samuel realize that while he was discussing his house renovations with Willard, French and Indian warriors were destroying the entire English settlement at York in Maine. Ashamed, Samuel admitted, "I little thought what was acted that day at York."

Worldly matters would continue to interfere with his renovation plans. Not until January 1694 would he finally stick a pin, for good luck, into the frame of the addition, which contained several large chambers and a new kitchen. Construction was not complete until the summer of 1695, when Samuel gathered several ministers for a private fast in "our new chamber. Mr. Willard begins with prayer, and preaches," and the Reverends James Allen and John Bailey prayed too. Together the group sang part of Psalm 27, chosen by Samuel.

Psalm 27

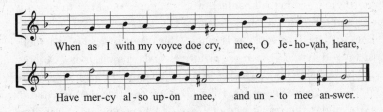

When as I with my voyce doe cry, mee, O Je-ho-vah, heare,
Have mer-cy al-so up-on mee, and un - to mee an-swer.

Windsor Tune

7 When as I with my voyce doe cry,
     mee, O Jehovah, heare,
   Have mercy also upon mee,
     and unto mee answer.

8 When thou didst say, seek yee my face,
  my heart sayd unto thee,
thy countenance, O Jehovah
  it shall be sought by mee.

9 Hide not thy face from mee, nor off
  in wrath thy servant cast:
God of my health, leave, leave not mee,
  my helper been thou hast.

10 My father & my mother both
   though they doe mee forsake,
  yet will Jehovah gathering
   unto himself me take.

11 Jehovah, teach thou mee the way,
   and be a guide to mee
  in righteous path, because of them
   that mine observers bee.

12 Give mee not up unto the will
   of my streight-enemies:
  for witnesse false against me stand,
   and breath out cruelties.

13 *I should have fainted,* had not I
   believ-ed for to see,
  Jehovahs goodnes in the land
   of them that living bee.

14 Doe thou upon Jehovah waite:
   bee stablish-ed, & let
  thine heart be strengthened, & thine hope
   upon Jehovah set.

"I set Windsor Tune and burst into tears that I could scarce continue singing," confessed Samuel, who struggled mightily to keep his family and community safe.

Back in the fall of 1691, as Hannah's due date approached, Samuel's pleas to God for aid grew more plaintive. At dawn on Sunday, October 25, he prayed alone in a little second-floor chamber of his house before going to the Sabbath service. He asked God to "give me a pardon of my sins under the broad seal of Heaven. I hope and do thirst after Christ.... I am sensible of my own folly and loathsomeness, that I value Him no more, and am so backward"—cautious—"to be married by Him." His caution toward God was consistent with the prudence that helped him realize his worldly goals.

Hannah roused him on Wednesday morning at four to say her labor had begun. He called for the midwife. As always, Elizabeth Weeden was prompt. Hannah delivered her and Samuel's tenth child, a girl, by eight that morning.

Samuel named the baby Mary at the next Sabbath meeting. The Reverend Willard baptized her and "enlarged" her in prayer. Samuel, asked to set the tune for three psalms, chose "Martyr's, St. Davids, Oxford." All in all, "a very pleasant day."

Still, the country's decline continued. That month a flock of sheep was found murdered in Cambridge. People suspected Indians. The culprit turned out to be wolves, but that did nothing to lessen the fear of attacks by Indians and French. On Christmas Day the General Court passed a law "prohibiting Frenchmen" from "being in seaports or frontier towns" of New England "except by license from the Governor and Council."

A few months earlier, as Hannah was laying their three-year-old son, Joseph, in his cradle, the child said to her, "News from Heaven. The French are coming. Canada." Astonished, Hannah reported this to Samuel. He wondered if someone, perhaps one of the older children, had "tampered with him." No one had.

Then this was an omen. God had spoken through Samuel's toddler, sending the same message Samuel heard from ships' captains on the docks and in the Town House. The enemy French were spreading across America, seeking more Jesuit missions and more French forts. They had reached the Great Lakes, the Mississippi River, the Allegheny Mountains, the Ohio and the Susquehanna Rivers, and now they had designs on New England.

As a member of the Provincial Council, Samuel felt responsible for his country. He regretted the failed expedition to Quebec. He wondered why God was assailing his homeland, "our Israel." What have we done wrong? he asked himself. Who, or what, is to blame?

Samuel was not alone. Many New Englanders felt anxious and afraid during this period at the start of the French and Indian Wars. Thomas Hutchinson, who wrote his history of Massachusetts in the 1760s, when the children of many participants in the Salem witch hunt were still alive, described the early 1690s as a terrifying time. "The sea coast was infested with privateers [private commerce raiders], so that few vessels could escape them. The inland frontiers east and west were continually harassed by French and Indian enemies." The government had "a heavy debt." People "were seized with gloom and horror." The "greatest misfortune" was "an apprehension that the devil was let loose among them, that many had entered into a league with him, and others were afflicted, tormented, and the subjects of diabolical rage and fury."

Early on January 25, 1692, the same day that Samuel consulted with his minister about expanding his house, French and Abenaki Indian warriors attacked York, Maine. The Abenaki had guns and ammunition, which prompted rumors that some English had traded with enemy French and Indians. Fifty English men, women, and children were killed, and nearly a hundred were taken prisoner. Every house in York was burned to the ground.

Thirty miles to the south, panic gripped Massachusetts's North Shore. Many English residents had moved to the North Shore as refugees from Maine, pushed south by earlier French and Abenaki attacks. Numerous families had close ties to the frontier, where the terror was. This war panic in northeastern Massachusetts contributed to the outbreak of suspected witchcraft, historians agree.

If the country's afflictions came from Satan, then that could explain everything—the loss of the old charter, the loss of life and property to the French and Indians, and the loss of so many settlers and their children through disease. If Satan were at fault, then Samuel and the other magistrates were not.

If the Devil were behind all their troubles, the enemy was clear. Now they could begin to fight back.

10

∞∞∞

IN SATAN'S GRIP

The witchcraft trouble started, as every schoolchild knows, in Salem Village, a small, rural parish of a seaport town. Salem was the largest town in Essex County, then the wealthiest and most populous part of Massachusetts outside Boston.

Salem Village, like so many poor, isolated, frontier settlements, was beset by squabbles. Neighbor battled neighbor over land boundaries, crops, and grazing rights. One ongoing feud pitted a family named Nurse, which held lots of land, against some branches of the Putnam family, which held less. Meanwhile, successive ministers of the parish battled the congregation over compensation. Two successive ministers in the 1680s, James Bayley and George Burroughs, had left the pulpit, taken the parish to court, and won settlements. The preacher who followed Bayley and Burroughs, Deodat Lawson, avoided such struggles only by quickly departing for a better post.

Lawson's successor, Samuel Parris, arrived at the end of 1689 with no pastoral experience. At thirty-eight, he had failed as a merchant in the West Indies, and this was his first ministerial job. Like his predecessors, Parris complained about his meager salary and firewood allotment. In the fall of 1691 he angered his congregation by seizing permanent possession of the church's parsonage, which he occupied, and its two-acre lot. Many parishioners refused to supply him with firewood. During the bitter winter that followed Parris composed and preached a series of sermons on the gulf in the world between good and evil, and between Christ and Satan.

The actual trouble began inside the parsonage. Parris and his wife, Elizabeth, who was in her early forties, had a nine-year-old daughter, Elizabeth, who was called Betty, and possibly a younger child, and they were raising Parris's eleven-year-old niece, Abigail Williams, who was presumably an orphan. The minister owned a couple of middle-aged, married slaves, John and Tituba, purchased on Barbados, who lived with the family. While the slaves' exact backgrounds are not known, John Indian and Tituba Indian, as they were sometimes known in English culture, are believed to have been Carib Indians and perhaps partly African.

Tituba was a gifted storyteller. In the warm kitchen on cold evenings, she amused Betty Parris and Abigail Williams with tales of other worlds. She read their palms, told them their fortunes, and performed tricks. When the girls asked her to divine the careers of their future husbands—to them, equivalent to their fates—Tituba drew circles in ashes on the hearth, burned locks of their hair, and muttered incantations to the Devil and his imps.

Tituba's talents may have seemed exotic to Betty and Abigail, but folk magic was standard in English culture. Pious Puritans routinely employed "white witchcraft" to counteract the effects of "black magic," or *maleficium*, which came from outside themselves. Naturally, these labels shifted with perspective: two neighbors feuding over a land boundary could each use their "white magic" to counteract the other's *maleficium*.

Belief in witchcraft—"the alleged exercise of magical powers through the gift of supernatural beings other than God and His angels," according to the *Oxford Dictionary of the Christian Church*— was common throughout the Christian world, as it still is in many places and has been from the beginning of recorded history. Witchcraft was often "a rather mundane affair—a cause of strange or unexpected illness, sudden misfortunes, and marital problems," the historian Keith Thomas wrote. In seventeenth-century English culture the "inadequacies of orthodox medical services left a large proportion of the population ... dependent upon traditional folk medicine." Commonsense remedies, herbal medicines, and midwifery mixed with "ritual healing, in which prayer, charms or spells accompanied the medicine." Magical healing was performed either by the sufferer, the sufferer's family, or a local wise man or woman. The latter was alternately called a wizard (from *wise man*, as in the biblical magi), a charmer, a conjurer, a sorceress, or a witch. The term *witch* also applied to someone—usually a woman—who hurt others by touching them, giving them a potion, or placing a curse over them. "Usually she was suspected of causing physical injury to other persons, or of bringing about their death," Thomas added. "She might also kill or injure farm animals or intervene with nature by preventing cows from giving milk, or by frustrating such domestic operations as making butter, cheese or beer."

Throughout the first Christian millennium, according to the *Oxford Dictionary of the Christian Church*, the Church and European courts largely ignored witchcraft. In the twelfth century "learned, ritual magic, derived from Hellenistic and Arabic sources, reached the West." The Church condemned these rites but did not arrest and try witches and sorcerers unless they were found "conspiring to criminal damage." A thirteenth-century pope went so far as to forbid the Inquisition from dealing with witchcraft unless it involved heresy.

The situation changed in the fourteenth century, when the number of witchcraft trials in western Europe began to increase. From the fourteenth to the seventeenth centuries, scholars estimate, fifty thousand Europeans were executed for witchcraft—about a hundred seventy people per year. More than 80 percent of the victims were female. During these centuries the concept of witchcraft changed in a manner that intensified the public demand for legal action against witches, according to Keith Thomas. The "notion that the witch owed her powers to having made a deliberate pact with the Devil" was added. Witchcraft was now Devil worship, a Christian heresy, "the greatest of all sins, because it involved the renunciation of God and deliberate adherence to his greatest enemy." With this change the witch now "deserved to die for her disloyalty to God."

The number of witchcraft trials and executions in England increased dramatically in the sixteenth and seventeenth centuries. "In medieval England," Thomas explained, "a man need not be hurt by witches, so long as he observed the prescriptions of the Church." After the Reformation, however, that "ecclesiastical magic crumbled, and society was forced to take legal action against" witchcraft. "Witchcraft prosecution in England ... was made possible by the law of the land. Until that law was repealed, or at least until judges and juries tacitly refused to administer it, the formal prosecution of witches" continued. "There is no reason to believe that the [witchcraft] trials were ever more than indirectly affected by religious conflict or by the greater or lesser zeal of different religious groups."

Nevertheless, aspects of Puritanism aligned with the belief in witchcraft. Puritanism emphasized a personal Devil who could tempt people, sometimes even with God's permission and oversight. Satan was portrayed as seeking cleverly to entrap God's saints, testing their faith. Do not stray from the "strait and narrow way," ministers warned. The Puritan emphasis on "the tortures of the afterworld led to self-consciousness, introspection, and morbidity," the historian David Hackett Fischer wrote. "Anyone outside of or contrary to that church was an agent of the devil.... It was the responsibility of the church to help such a person by inducing him to confess the indwelling of an evil spirit and free himself. If he did not confess, it were better that he be killed, lest he be a vehicle through which the devil contaminate others."

Moreover, the Calvinist sense of humanity's overwhelming sinfulness aligned with the dogma of Satan. "Where the modern mind now refreshes itself in New England with the beauties of the seashore, the forest, and the sunset," Fischer noted, "the Puritan saw only threatenings of terror." To quote the seventeenth-century minister Michael Wigglesworth, New England was a "howling wilderness" inhabited not only by bears, wolves, moose, and wildcats, but also by "hellish fiends and brutish men that devils worshipped." In Europe the Puritan theologian John Knox called the Devil "the prince and God of this world." Meanwhile, other Protestants and Counter-Reformation Catholics focused on the Devil. While Satan is not significant in the Old Testament, Christianity and later Judaism raised him to become God's antagonist, a tempter of humanity and instrument of God's judgment. Over time Christians both Catholic and Protestant came to view Satan as Antichrist, or the opposite of good. Their world split into dichotomies: good versus evil, Satan versus Christ, darkness versus light.

In the mind of a seventeenth-century European or American, witches were as devoted to Satan as Christian saints were devoted to God. Witches gathered in the forest at night to worship and perhaps copulate with their master. In "Young Goodman Brown," a story that Nathaniel Hawthorne set in Salem Village just before the witchcraft frenzy, the eponymous character observes a witches' Sabbath in the woods.

Irreverently consorting with these grave, reputable, and pious people, these elders of the church, these chaste dames and dewy virgins, there were men of dissolute lives and women of spotted fame, wretches given over to all mean and filthy vice, and suspected even of horrid crimes. It was strange to see that the good shrank not from the wicked, nor were the sinners abashed by the saints. Scattered also among their pale-faced enemies were the Indian priests, or powwows, who had often scared their native forest with more hideous incantations than any known to English witchcraft.

"Welcome, my children," said the dark figure [Satan], "to the communion of your race.... Evil is the nature of mankind. Evil must be your only happiness...."

Samuel Sewall never saw anything like that scene, invented in the nineteenth century. But as a seventeenth-century Puritan he believed firmly that a witch was a soul in whom the Devil abides, just as a saint—a God-fearing English Congregationalist—kept Christ in his soul.

In the Salem Village parsonage at the end of January 1692, the Reverend Samuel Parris began to observe disturbing changes in his nine-year-old daughter and eleven-year-old niece. Betty would not pray when she was supposed to. She refused to do chores. She had fits of kicking and screaming. Abigail and a playmate, twelve-year-old Anne Putnam, began to have strange fits and spasms of pain. The three girls would creep under a table on their hands and feet, barking like dogs, mewing like cats, and grunting like hogs. The minister had never seen such strange behavior.

Suspecting an evil spirit, he sent for a physician, William Griggs, who examined the girls at the house. Griggs could find no medical reason for their afflictions. When he asked, "Who tortures you?" the girls said three women "afflicted" them. They named the first three "witches" of 1692, Sarah Good, Sarah Osborne, and Tituba Indian.

These three women were typical victims of witchcraft accusations. In both America and Europe, suspected witches were mostly women, in their forties or older, who lacked social power or violated social norms or both. Tituba Indian was a slave. Her tawny skin made her suspect to the English, whose Satan was "dark" or "black." Sarah Osborne, a destitute old Englishwoman, begged at neighbors' doors. Sarah Good, though only in her thirties, was visibly pregnant and so haggard she looked almost as old as Osborne.

"How did they bewitch you?" the doctor wondered. The girls said the women's ghosts, which they called "specters," urged them to sign the Devil's book. It was common knowledge that the Devil could assume any shape except that of an innocent person. So if someone's ghost, or disembodied spirit, was observed doing ill, that person was considered a witch. And everyone knew that Satan carried a black book in which he induced his followers to write their names in their own blood. The notion of a witch making a pact with the Devil was the comprehensible antithesis of the covenant a Puritan made with God.

The girls told the doctor that they resisted the Devil and refused to sign his book. In response to their defiance, the girls reported, the witches—or perhaps their ghosts—hurt the girls, making them act like animals and flinging their bodies around.

Dr. Griggs, horrified, told Parris that the girls in his house were "under an evil hand." The news that the Devil was assailing the occupants of the Salem Village parsonage spread rapidly, to Salem Town and Andover, then Gloucester and Newbury, and finally to Boston. To most of those who heard it, the next question was, When will the Devil arrive here?

Samuel Sewall may have spoken briefly to the Reverend Parris during Thomas Cheever's church trial four years before, but he did not know the minister (who had attended but not graduated from Harvard) or his family. When Sewall first set eyes on the two girls from the parsonage, ages nine and eleven, in the Salem Village meetinghouse in early April, he too found their testimony chilling. "It was awful to see how the afflicted persons were agitated."

The girls' symptoms spread as fast as news of their affliction. Before long more girls and young women, many of them servants, reported similar troubles. The tales of affliction spun by older teenagers—Mary Walcott, Mary Lewis, Elizabeth Hubbard, Elizabeth Booth, and Susanna Sheldon—and Mary Warren and Sarah Churchill, who were twenty, gave these young women access to public power they had never known. The doctor, minister, and local authorities recorded their every word.

Spurred on by the attention, these "victims" of witchcraft "became quite skilful and expert in the arts" of magic and spiritualism, the historian Charles Upham observed. They "put themselves into odd and unnatural postures, make wild and antic gestures, and utter incoherent and unintelligible sounds. They would be seized with spasms, drop insensible to the floor, or writhe in agony, suffering dreadful tortures, and uttering loud and piercing outcries." They were objects of "compassion and wonder." When they shrieked in church they were not punished for their rudeness but pitied. The Devil was to blame.

By late February the people of Salem Village were "alarmed to the highest degree," Upham wrote. Looking back from the late twentieth century to this widespread hysteria, which would be considered delusional a year later, even by active participants, the historian Elizabeth Reis wrote, "We will never know exactly why, but whether accusers and witnesses sincerely believed that the accused had signed a devil's pact and afflicted others, whether they contemplated political or familial revenge, whether they simply continued to play a game that had gotten out of hand, whether they pursued a strategy to deflect suspicion from themselves, or whether they calculated fraud, they knew that their stories would be believed." Accusations of witchcraft, "particularly against women," were "credible and demanded action."

In the face of an attack by the Devil, local authorities quickly mounted a response. In the informal but highly centralized system of justice that had evolved in Massachusetts, two local justices of the peace, John Hathorne and Jonathan Corwin, issued warrants for the arrest of Sarah Good, Sarah Osborne, and Tituba Indian. On the last day of February a sheriff arrested the three women and brought them in carts to Ingersoll's ordinary, an inn and tavern in Salem Village, where they would be questioned by Judges Hathorne and Corwin.

Hathorne and Corwin both served with Sewall on the General Court, although Samuel knew Hathorne better. Samuel's longtime friend the Reverend Nicholas Noyes was also present at the hearing as the officiating minister, offering prayers.

"Are you a witch?" Judge Hathorne asked Tituba Indian.

The slave denied it repeatedly. The judges ridiculed her until she said, "I am." She went on to implicate the other two women. "I go to witch meetings riding upon a stick, with Sarah Good and Osborne behind me. We ride taking hold of one another." At a later hearing she told the judges that Good and Osborn "are very strong and pull me and make me go with them.... Last night they tell me I must kill somebody...."

One might suspect Tituba of irony. Long afterward, however, she revealed that her master, the Reverend Parris, had flogged her before the hearing and ordered her to confess and implicate the other women named by the girls. Parris's goal was to deflect the blame for the devilish affliction, which so far affected only members of his family, in his house.

It is human enough to imagine that pointing to someone else's fault may conceal one's own. Countless Puritans and other Christians accused their opponents of worshiping Satan. "This was said by Protestants of Catholics, by Catholics of Protestants, and by Christians of" Native Americans, Keith Thomas observed. People "saw the Devil in any manifestation of social wickedness or religious unorthodoxy. A Protestant iconoclast in 1540 could describe the image of Christ in the [medieval Catholic] roodloft as a picture of the Devil, while in 1704 a Yorkshire Nonconformist [Puritan] declared that people who received the sacrament according to Anglican rites were serving not God but the Devil."

Tituba Indian had a second compelling reason to confess to witchcraft. As the local judges likely told her, the court's policy was to spare those who confessed. A confession would guarantee she faced no trial, no prosecution, and no punishment. After the witch hunt, one of the bewitched and afflicted girls, Margaret Jacobs, admitted to authorities that the judges had "told me if I would not confess" to being a witch that "I should be put down into the dungeon and would be hanged, but if I would confess" and name others "I should save my life." In August, in a letter to the court, more than fifty citizens of Andover signed a letter stating that local women suspected of witchcraft were innocent. They wrote that "confessing was the only way to obtain favor" with the court, which "might be too powerful a temptation for timorous women to withstand."

Hathorne and Corwin wanted and expected to hear confessions. To them, a confession was the best evidence of witchcraft although the word of two credible witnesses was also acceptable. Hathorne and Corwin considered themselves inspired for having rejected the classic European method of discerning a witch, which involved tying a suspect's thumbs to her toes and throwing her into deep water. If she floated she was deemed guilty and executed. If she sank and drowned, she was innocent, though unable to enjoy her exoneration. Cotton Mather derided that barbaric method as "the invention of Catholics and Episcopalians."

Throughout the summer, as scores of suspects came to trial for witchcraft and the nineteen who refused to confess were hanged, Tituba, the first to confess, remained alive. Following the hearing she was carted along Essex Street, Boston Street, and Aborn Street to the Salem jail. The jail, a wooden building about twenty feet square, is long gone, but an iron marker at the corner of today's Federal and Saint Peter's Streets marks the spot. Tituba was chained to the wall of the basement dungeon, which was inhabited by a colony of large rats. A tidal river flowed nearby. The air stank. Without clean water and healthy food, many prisoners became ill and some died. Jailers forced the witch suspects to remove their clothes so their private parts could be searched for a Devil's teat—an extra nipple for suckling a familiar, or devilish beast.

Many suspects were tortured until they confessed. "Prisoner confessed without torture," the clerk of court noted from time to time. A desire to avoid the noose motivated many to confess. Mary Clements of Haverhill, for instance, told the judges she "signed the Devil's book," took "the Devil to be my God," agreed to "serve and worship him," was "baptized by the Devil," renounced her former Christian baptism, and "promised to be the Devil's, both body and soul forever."

A few months later, after the witch hunt ended, she retracted this confession before Increase Mather. Some of the Salem confessors remained in prison. Others were freed. No confessors were hanged.

Forced confession and repentance is a perversion of Puritan theology, which relied so heavily on the free confession of saving grace and the process of repentance. Some of the accused made a partial confession, saying their nature was depraved, as is standard Calvinist belief, and suggesting that past sins might have led them to the Devil. This too saved them from the noose. But the judges invariably condemned all who denied that they were filled with sin.

Judge John Hathorne came to these hearings with two convictions, scholars observe. One was that the Devil could use witches to undermine the Puritan church. The other, which arose from his experience as a local justice, was that all (or almost all) the suspects who came before him were guilty. Therefore, a suspect who confessed to witchcraft was immediately less threatening to the judge. In his view, she had begun to turn from the Devil. A confession seemed to offer hope of repentance and a return to God. In this way, the confessions that he and his colleagues elicited from witchcraft suspects had a paradoxical function. They both confirmed the judges' suspicions and also, strangely, exonerated the confessor.

This twisted pattern of justice endured throughout the 1692 witch trials. Suspects who confessed avoided trial. Those who professed innocence were guaranteed a trial, conviction, and death at the gallows. "None who confessed, and stood to their confession, were brought to trial," Charles Upham concluded. "All who were condemned … maintained their innocence" to the moment of death.

After disposing of Tituba Indian, Judges Hathorne and Corwin called for the next suspects. As Sarah Good entered the chamber, Samuel's friend the Reverend Noyes remarked, "She is indeed a miserable witch."

But Good told the court, "I am falsely accused." She stated, "I do not torment the children.... I serve God."

"Who tormented the children?" Hathorne wondered.

"It was Osborn," Sarah Good replied.

The judges questioned several witnesses, including Good's husband, who had recently abandoned her. Good's husband called her "an enemy of all good," probably unaware of his pun. The judges called the Goods' four-year-old daughter, Dorcas, to testify against her mother. Some of the afflicted girls had said that the little girl had bitten them. Prompted by Hathorne and Corwin, Dorcas Good said, "My mother had three birds ... that hurt the [afflicted] children."

The judges found the four-year-old and her mother guilty of witchcraft. Mother and child were sent to jail, where they too were chained to the floor. Sarah Good's baby was stillborn a few months before she was hanged, on July 19, with several others who refused to confess. Good's little girl eventually confessed, probably at the coaxing of her mother, who hoped to save her life. Dorcas Good was released from jail in 1693, at five. She was no longer normal, according to her father, who could not care for her.

As a constable brought in Sarah Osborne, the afflicted girls, who attended hearings en masse as witnesses, screamed out in terror. Osborne testified she was not guilty, had "no familiarity with evil spirits," and hardly knew Sarah Good.

Why had she missed so many meetings at church? the judges asked.

She replied, "Because I was sick."

The court found Osborne guilty and sent her to jail, where she died in the month of May.

Meanwhile, Samuel Sewall's peers headed north and east to serve in the war. The court ordered Captain Elisha Hutchinson to Maine to lead the troops. Hutchinson departed on February 18 on a horse that belonged to Samuel. Standing at the ferry landing in the North End watching his dear friend depart for the battlefield in Maine, Samuel consoled himself with the thought, "I gave him my horse."

Captain John Alden Jr., a member of Samuel's prayer group, sailed to Maine from Boston in March on a mission to save English captives, including his own son. Alden carried money collected in Boston's churches and several French prisoners of war, which he intended to exchange for imprisoned Englishmen.

On the North Shore the number of witch suspects mounted quickly. Hathorne and Corwin now scheduled hearings in the Salem Village meetinghouse to accommodate the growing crowd of afflicted people and spectators. On March 21 the judges questioned Martha Corey, a "saintly" woman who was openly skeptical about the witch hunt. Each time Corey answered a question from the court, the assembled girls shrieked. The girls claimed to see satanic creatures hovering around her, a yellow bird and a man who whispered in her ear. The judges asked the girls to describe these visions more clearly.

Abigail Williams, the minister's eleven-year-old niece, called out, "Look where Goody Corey sits ... suckling her yellow bird between her fingers."

"I am a gospel woman," Martha Corey stated.

"You are a gospel witch," shouted the impertinent Mercy Lewis, a teenage servant of the Putnam family.

Hathorne asked Corey, "How does the Devil come in your shape and hurt the children?"

Unfortunately, Martha Corey laughed. The historian Charles Upham noted that she "repudiated the doctrines of witchcraft, and expressed herself freely and fearlessly against them" at the price of her life.

The Reverend Noyes, who had great faith in his ability to see into others' souls, remarked, "It is apparent she practiseth witchcraft in the congregation."

There is no record of any seventeenth-century New Englander doubting Satan's desire to control the world and destroy God's people. Satan was as real to them as the dirt beneath their feet. Yet he had magical powers. He could slip through a pinhole, turn into an earthly creature, and possess a person's mind. Many pious Christians felt the Devil tempt them. The Puritan notion of visible saints—that people could recognize in themselves, and possibly in others, election by God—seemed to imply that people could recognize Satan's allies too. This aspect of Puritan theology fueled witch hunts on both sides of the Atlantic. England's worst witch hunt had occurred during its civil war, when Puritans ruled. In Essex, England, in 1645 a man named Matthew Hopkins accused three hundred people of witchcraft and executed about a third of them. In Essex, England, as in Essex County, Massachusetts, the trials and hangings quickly evolved into "the unraveling of the witchfinders' deeds and lives," the historian Malcolm Gaskill wrote. In his view, witch hunts require governmental chaos and social upheaval.

By the end of March 1692, when Samuel celebrated his fortieth birthday, scores of suspected witches crowded the jails of Salem and other towns, including Boston. The number of witches grew so fast that more judges were needed to conduct hearings. To address the problem, the Governor's Council—Samuel was finally willing to call the General Court by this name in deference to the new governor, Phips—decided to convene in Salem on April 11. By mutual consent, Deputy Governor Thomas Danforth and four assistants—James Russell, Isaac Addington, Samuel Appleton, and Samuel Sewall—traveled to Salem for this meeting.

At this point in his life, forty-year-old Samuel had much to be grateful for: five living children, a loving wife, a rich spiritual life, a comfortable estate, and a powerful role in the government of a country he loved. Prudence had served him well.

Yet he wrote nothing in his diary during the two weeks prior to this visit to Salem, omitting even his customary mention of his birthday. He was tongue-tied, too uncomfortable with current events to set down a thought. Even after he began to comment on the witch hunt he was tight-lipped. In a typical six-month period his diary writing takes up more than fifteen published pages. During the dramatic six-month period of the witch hunt, from April 1 to October 1, 1692, he filled only six pages—less than half his usual output. Clearly, he did not know what to say.

Well before dawn on Monday, April 11, 1692, Samuel and his horse ferried across the mouth of the Charles River. They headed along the bank of the Mystic River toward Salem, a route his horse knew by heart. Samuel wore leather boots, cotton drawers, a linen shirt, warm breeches held up with a sash, a heavy waistcoat, a cravat or neck cloth, and a dark felt skullcap. Having entered middle age, he had a soft belly and long brown curls touched with gray.

Traveling to the North Shore usually filled Samuel with hope. This time, though, his heart was heavy. The Devil was assailing the region he called home. As a judge of the court, he was required to take seriously any charge of witchcraft. Colonial laws against witchcraft arose from a 1604 English civil statute, enacted by Parliament with King James I's support, that defined witchcraft as a felony punishable by hanging. Over the past half century New England courts had tried about a hundred people for witchcraft. Five women—Achsah Young in Connecticut and Margaret Jones, Elizabeth Kendall, Anne Hibbens, and the Irish washerwoman Mary Glover in Massachusetts—had been convicted and hanged. Looking to the Bible for guidance, Samuel found a strong message in the book of Exodus: "One must not suffer a witch to live."

Samuel reached Salem town by ten o'clock that April morning. The court was to convene at eleven in the meetinghouse, which was larger than the Salem courthouse, to accommodate the crowd. Samuel turned his horse over to a manservant and spoke briefly with his brother

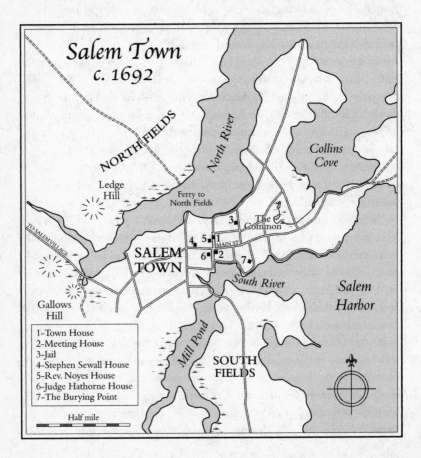

Salem Town
c. 1692

NORTH FIELDS

North River

Collins Cove

Ledge Hill

Ferry to North Fields

TO SALEM VILLAGE

3

The Common

4 5 1
      MAIN ST.

SALEM TOWN

6 2

7

South River

Salem Harbor

Gallows Hill

Mill Pond

SOUTH FIELDS

1-Town House
2-Meeting House
3-Jail
4-Stephen Sewall House
5-Rev. Noyes House
6-Judge Hathorne House
7-The Burying Point

Half mile

Stephen, who was present as a scribe and as the clerk of court. The bulk of the records of the witchcraft court would later be destroyed by persons unknown. Of those records that survive, most are believed to have been penned by Major Stephen Sewall.

Leaving his brother, Samuel joined his colleagues from the Governor's Council, who would be asked to judge the validity of the complaints against the suspects. Marilynne Roach, a historian of Salem, wrote that the deputy governor and "out-of-town assistants"—Sewall, Russell, Addington, and Appleton—"presumably observed" the proceedings "while John Hathorne and Jonathan Corwin presided as local magistrates." Men, women, and children flowed into the meeting-house. Watching the "very great" crowd gather, Samuel had a sense of foreboding. He had never before seen such excitement over a preliminary hearing of suspects.

His friend Nicholas Noyes quieted the crowd and began the meeting with a prayer for colony's health in the face of "devilish powers." Samuel prayed in earnest that the Devil would be destroyed. The Reverend Samuel Parris moved to the front of the room. He produced three new suspects for questioning. Unlike the earlier suspects, these people were widely respected and comfortable financially, and one of them was male.

One of the three, fifty-four-year-old Sarah Cloyse, the wife of a Topsfield farmer, Peter Cloyse, was the youngest and feistiest of three aging sisters who would go to jail that summer. Her oldest sister, Rebecca Nurse, a Salem Village grandmother, was already in jail. Cloyse would be the only sister to escape death on the gallows. During the previous winter she had offended Parris by leaving his meeting-house while he preached, slamming the door. During this hearing John Indian stated that Cloyse "choked me and brought me the Devil's book to sign." Questioned by Hathorne and Corwin, Cloyse said she had done no such thing. Parris's eleven-year-old niece described an elaborate vision of forty witches, including "Goody Cloyse," gathering to "take communion." At this, Sarah Cloyse fainted. The judges ordered her to jail to await trial.

John Proctor, a respected sixty-year-old farmer, had a considerable estate in Salem Farms (now Peabody, Massachusetts), a wife, Elizabeth, who was also present for questioning, and several children. His nine-teen-year-old servant, Mary Warren, had implicated both Proctors after John chastised her for saying that a neighbor was a witch.

Proctor's testimony had a profound effect on Samuel. As the farmer spoke, several girls in the meetinghouse screamed and gasped. Some girls fell on the floor of the meetinghouse and seemed to suffer con-vulsions. While Samuel had been told of these outbursts, he had not understood how frightening they could be.

Until now, Samuel's experience of witchcraft was secondhand, through reading or gossip. Six years earlier a relative had mentioned "a maid at Woburn who 'tis feared is possessed by an evil spirit." Actu-ally seeing the phenomenon was more troubling than he had imag-ined. That afternoon, as soon as the Reverend John Higginson completed his closing prayer, Samuel rode straight home to Boston. Meanwhile, the Proctors and Sarah Cloyse were put in chains in the Salem jail.

Later, in the margin of his diary entry for April 11, 1692, Samuel added the words, "Vae"—"woe to"—"Vae, Vae, Witchcraft," as if the sins of that day could be commanded away.

To an educated seventeenth-century Englishman, questioning the existence of witches and spirits was akin to questioning the existence of God. The invisible world of witches and spirits was considered evi-dence of another invisible world, that of God. Defending the mystery of both worlds, Increase Mather wrote in his *Essay on Illustrious Provi-dence*, "There are wonders in the works of creation as well as provi-dence, the reason whereof the most knowing amongst mortals, are not able to comprehend." Joseph Glanvill, a seventeenth-century English minister who compiled witch stories, observed that to deny witchcraft "is equivalent to saying, 'There is no God.'..." Roger Hutchinson, a sixteenth-century Puritan theologian, wrote, "If there be a God, as we most steadfastly must believe, verily there is a Devil also; and if there be a Devil, there is no surer argument, no stronger proof, no plainer evidence, that there is a God." The Puritan divine John Weemes added that if people will "grant that there are devils, they must grant also that there is a God."

Decades after 1692, the great eighteenth-century English legal theorist Sir William Blackstone would state, "To deny the possibility, nay, the actual existence, of witchcraft and sorcery is at once flatly to contradict the revealed Word of God, in various passages both of the Old and New Testament; and the thing itself is a truth to which every nation in the world hath in its turn borne testimony, either by examples seemingly well attested, or by prohibitory laws, which at least suppose the possibility of commerce with evil spirits." As late as the early nineteenth century the English physician and philosopher Samuel Hibbert wrote that "giving up of witchcraft is, in effect, giving up the Bible."

That was something that Samuel Sewall and many others were not willing to do.

11

SPEEDY AND VIGOROUS PROSECUTIONS

On the evening of Saturday, May 14, 1692, the frigate *Nonsuch* sailed into Boston harbor, bringing Increase Mather and the province's new governor, Sir William Phips, home from England. Sailors rowed Mather and Phips ashore. Eight companies of soldiers escorted the two men to the Town House, where candles burned in every window. As the twenty-four-hour Sabbath had already begun, Samuel and others ensured that there were no volleys of guns.

On Sunday morning troops escorted Phips from his North End mansion back to the Town House, where "commissions were read and oaths taken," Samuel noted. Eighty-seven-year-old Simon Bradstreet stepped aside as governor, and Sir William was sworn in. Phips, despite his failure at Quebec, remained popular: at Boston's recent annual election of town meeting members and court deputies on May 4, for which he was not present, he received the most votes, 969. He delivered to the province its new charter, issued by King William and Queen Mary the previous December. This Second Charter—second to Winthrop's—was not what the men of Boston wanted but it was what they had.

The new charter dramatically reduced their right to self-government. Under the old charter local freemen chose the governor and other members of the General Court, which in the 1640s split into two houses, the lower consisting of deputies and the upper consisting of assistants, or councillors. The new charter called for England to appoint the governor—with some prompting, as in this case, from provincial emissaries. If conflicts arose in Massachusetts, its citizens could now appeal to the Privy Council in England, which now superseded the General Court as the highest administrative, legislative, and judicial power in New England.

The new charter also changed the structure of the provincial government, splitting and dividing many powers previously held by the Great and General Court. It called for an independent judiciary—that is, judiciary bodies separate from and independent of the administrative and legislative functions of government. This change would have a profound effect on the evolution of American government, which enshrines the notion of the separation of these powers. Prior to May 1692 New England had "no court system in the modern sense," according to Elizabeth Bouvier, the early-twenty-first-century archivist of the Massachusetts court. Prior to the new charter the colony's "judicial, administrative, legislative, and executive functions—as well as the religious authority—were all intertwined in the General Court." After 1692 the royal governor was empowered to create new independent courts as he saw fit. The new charter also called for grand juries to be elected locally each year and a system of county courts to meet every month or two to handle conflicts within regions.

Another change was that the chartered province acquired far more territory than before. All of Massachusetts Bay, Plymouth Colony, Nova Scotia (Acadia), Maine, the Elizabeth Islands, Nantucket, and Martha's Vineyard were consolidated under the Province of Massachusetts, which also had control of the armies of Connecticut and Rhode Island. "A vast exposed frontier must bring heavy burdens upon a government," the historian Thomas Hutchinson noted in the next century. While the old charter gave English settlers clear rights to the soil of New England, this charter left open the question of land ownership.

Finally, and most offensive to Puritans like Samuel, the new charter encouraged religious tolerance. That is, it allowed freedom of religion for all except Catholics. As always, politics was local; the English court could countenance the Baptist Church and the Society of Friends but not its closer enemy, the Catholic Church. To the men of Boston this change was a direct attack on the New England way. The General Court of Massachusetts had so desired religious purity that it had banished Anne Hutchinson as a heretic in 1637 and executed Baptists and Quakers on Boston Common in 1660.

In May of 1692 Sir William Phips was quick to realize that his first challenge as governor of the province was to drive the Devil out. When he arrived, the jails of Salem, Ipswich, other North Shore towns, and Boston were overflowing with suspected witches. The new charter gave him the power to create a court system with the consent of the legislature, or General Court. Finding himself faced with an emergency, Phips created a new court, a Court of Oyer and Terminer, which in Latin means "it listens and decides." Legally he was justified: England had a precedent for such courts, and New England was a common-law jurisdiction of England. This Court of Oyer and Terminer was to be a circuit court, meaning that its judges would ride from town to town hearing testimony and presiding over trials in meetinghouses, private houses, inns, and occasionally taverns. By late May Phips had selected nine judges, of whom five had to be present for the court to sit. The legal librarian Edgar Bellefontaine noted that "Phips appointed the most prominent people he could find."

In the centuries since then the Salem witch court—as the Court of Oyer and Terminer is commonly known—has been perceived as a North Shore phenomenon. In fact, the witchcraft court was created in and from Boston, the center of power in Puritan New England. Fewer than half of its judges lived on the North Shore. They were John Hathorne, Jonathan Corwin, and Bartholomew Gedney, all of Salem, and Nathaniel Saltonstall of Haverhill. The majority—Wait Still Winthrop, John Richards, William Stoughton, Peter Sergeant, and Samuel Sewall—were wealthy merchants, landowners, church members, and magistrates of the ruling court in Boston, on which the North Shore men also served. Long after the witch hunt ended, the Boston judges would try to minimize their involvement by referring to a "delusion" in Salem, Essex County, or the North Shore. The truth was that these nine men were leaders in Boston. Five had attended Harvard College. As a group they had fought to retain and restore the old charter. As a group they had shipped the royalist and Anglican invaders Andros and Randolph back to England. As a group they believed deeply in the New England way.

On May 27, when Samuel learned that Phips had appointed him to the new court, he did not question whether to serve. The appointment was yet another opportunity for him to aid his beleaguered country and to advance himself.

He knew the other judges well, as they knew each other, from their work on the ruling court, which was now alternately called the General Court, Provincial Council, or Governor's Council. Wait Still Winthrop, whom historians consider "of ordinary talent," unlike his remarkable father and grandfather, was one of Samuel Sewall's closest friends. Winthrop and Sergeant were fellow members of the Third Church. Most of the judges were intimate with the Mathers, father and son. John Richards, now the treasurer of Harvard College, had belonged to the Second Church for three decades, contributed generously to the salary of Increase Mather, and officiated at Cotton Mather's wedding in 1686.

Toward the new court's chief justice, William Stoughton, who is generally remembered now for his "ferocious" prosecution of witches, Samuel felt great warmth. The two of them had ridden to and from New York two years before. Samuel often visited Stoughton at his farm in Dorchester, which overlooked the ocean, as he would continue to do after the witch hunt. In the fall of 1697, for instance, Samuel and the Reverend Samuel Torrey breakfasted in Dorchester with Stoughton, who was then the acting governor of Massachusetts. As Samuel arrived that October morning, he observed William Stoughton "carting ears of corn" from his "upper barn." Stoughton served his friends fresh venison and chocolate, which Samuel spelled "chockalatte." Relishing the local meat and the warm drink imported from far away, Samuel said to Stoughton, "Massachusetts and Mexico meet at Your Honor's table." These men would remain friends as long as they lived.

On June 2, 1692, in the courtroom on the second floor of the Town House of Salem, the Court of Oyer and Terminer convened for a trial. The defendant was a middle-aged innkeeper from Salem Town named Bridget Oliver Bishop. At a prior hearing an afflicted girl had said she saw Bishop—or her specter—nursing a familiar. Several men testified that Bishop's ghost visited them in bed at night, pressing a great weight on them. Women who examined her body at the court's request found on her a "preternatural teat," presumably for nursing imps. Bishop was known for loose morals. She allowed gambling at her tavern, which she often kept open past the curfew. She had been accused of witchcraft before, in 1679, by the brother of a competing innkeeper. That time she was acquitted; this time she was not.

Samuel said nothing during Bishop's trial, according to the existing records. But his colleagues, particularly Hathorne, found the evidence against her convincing. During her initial examination, when Hathorne had asked Bishop, "How do you know that you are not a witch?" she had said, "I know nothing of it." He felt he had "caught [her] in a flat lie." Stoughton, as chief justice, urged the other judges to accept spectral evidence against Bishop, which he found compelling. Spectral evidence was testimony of a crime committed by the ghost of a person who is not physically present. Throughout the trials Stoughton would argue strongly for admitting spectral evidence although it had no basis in biblical or English common law.

Before adjourning with a prayer, the court found Bridget Bishop guilty of witchcraft and sentenced her to death by hanging. Court records suggest that some judges were silent during proceedings while others, particularly Stoughton and Hathorne, were loquacious. Nevertheless, the whole court decided to convict and execute people for witchcraft. According to archivists and historians, these decisions were unanimous.

The court set June 10 as the date of Bridget Bishop's execution. Bishop went to the gallows first, historians agree, because of her bad reputation and the apparent strength of the evidence against her. The celebrated event of Massachusetts's first execution for witchcraft in several years was to take place on Gallows Hill, now known as Witch Hill, Salem's highest point. This ledge atop a wooded hill on the town's southwestern side was chosen to afford Satan a fine view of his minions swaying in the wind.

Gallows were found in most New England towns, as was the custom in England. A gallows was a wooden scaffold balanced on a

frame above the ground with a crossbeam above it. On June 10 Bridget
Bishop climbed a ladder to the scaffold and stood below the crossbeam. The hangman placed a noose around her neck, leaving a bit of
slack rope. The other end of the rope went over the crossbeam and
was held firmly or tied below. The hangman knocked out the scaffold,
causing the victim to drop. Either the fall killed Bishop instantly by
severing her spinal cord or she suffocated while dangling from her
neck. Fifteen years later, while viewing an execution on board a ship
in Boston harbor, Samuel noted that the scaffold on the deck was "let
sink," causing the convict to hang.

Bishop's death scene, which some of the judges likely attended,
deeply disturbed Nathaniel Saltonstall, who had sat in justice on her.
He was not confident in the authority of the spectral evidence. As a
result he questioned the morality of her execution. Several ministers
who were present would raise similar concerns in the coming days.
Learning of this, Governor Phips asked prominent ministers of Massachusetts to meet to consider spectral evidence. In their report,
"Return of Several Ministers Consulted," which appeared June 15,
they recommended "speedy and vigorous prosecutions." At the same
time, they suggested that a person is not necessarily responsible for
spectral acts. Satan can possess a person's body, they affirmed, but the
person may not have granted his or her permission.

This was not Stoughton's view of spectral evidence, which was the
view that dominated the Court of Oyer and Terminer during the
summer. Stoughton influenced the other judges because of his elevated
position as chief justice, his forceful personality, and his unstated conviction that if not for all of Sir William Phips's gold and silver he himself would be governor of Massachusetts. The other judges followed
Stoughton in assuming that Satan cannot control a person without
that person's consent and therefore that spectral evidence was allow-
able. In the process the judges studiously ignored the English
common-law principle that a crime must be observed by two credible
witnesses, not a gaggle of shrieking girls. As for Samuel, he made no
entries in his diary throughout the month of June.

At the end of that month, according to court records, Samuel returned to Salem to sit with the court. Presumably he enjoyed visiting
his brother's family and seeing other relatives and the Reverend

Noyes, as he always did in Salem. He likely met nine-year-old Betty Parris, who was now staying indefinitely with Stephen and Margaret Sewall. The Sewalls, who had three children under age five and were expecting a baby, had taken in Betty in March, when she remained "under an evil hand." Her father apparently hoped to cure her by removing her from Salem Village, and the Sewalls were willing to help. Margaret Sewall observed several of Betty's fits, which prompted her to fear the girl would die. She asked Betty to describe her visions. The nine-year-old reported "a dark man" who promised her anything. Margaret reassured Betty that Satan "was a liar from the beginning" and encouraged her to report if the dark man returned. "And so she must have," the historian Marilynne Roach surmised, "for Betty did recover." In contrast, her cousin Abigail, who stayed in the Parris household, continued throughout the summer and early fall to provide the court with names of more suspects.

In late June Samuel and several other judges of the court met again at the Salem courthouse. On June 29 the court convicted and condemned to death Sarah Good and four other women—Rebecca Nurse, Sarah Wildes, Susanna Martin, and Elizabeth Howe. Rebecca Nurse was a seventy-year-old, English-born "gospel woman" from Salem Village. Her husband, Francis Nurse, had tussled with the Reverend Parris over how much land and firewood the pastor should expect. The Putnam family, whose daughter Anne was one of the most severely afflicted girls, had engaged in a long feud with the Nurses. Before the court Nurse firmly denied she made a covenant with the Devil. One judge asked her if she was without sin. "Well, as to this thing"—accusations of witchcraft—"I am innocent as the child unborn. But," she continued honestly, "what sin God hath found out in me unrepented of that He should lay such an affliction on me?" After her conviction, thirty-nine of her neighbors petitioned the court to save her life. As a result, Nurse was briefly acquitted. Stoughton reversed the acquittal. Phips reprieved her but soon, under pressure from Stoughton and others, withdrew his reprieve.

The other three suspects on June 29 were from other North Shore towns, Amesbury and Topsfield. The spread of the problem seemed to confirm that this was Satan's work. Stoughton and Hathorne felt they could not cease fighting now.

Meanwhile, Nathaniel Saltonstall resigned from the court "in dis-gust at the outrages on justice," in the words of the nineteenth-century historian James Savage. Saltonstall himself said, "I am not willing to take part in further proceedings of this nature." He could see no legal or moral justification for spectral evidence.

Saltonstall was a grandson of Sir Richard Saltonstall, who had come to Boston with Governor Winthrop in 1630 and settled in Water-town. Sir Richard soon returned to England on account of the poor health of some of his children, but his son Richard Jr. stayed, became a magistrate of the General Court, and officiated at the 1646 wedding of Samuel's parents in Newbury. Richard Jr., who had been educated at Cambridge prior to immigrating, returned to England in 1672 after his father's death. His son Nathaniel attended Harvard College with the Reverend Samuel Willard in the class of 1659.

In leaving the court just a month after it began, Nathaniel Saltonstall took a stand against the governor who appointed him, the colonial establishment, and most of his colleagues and friends. One year later, after the trials and executions were halted, at the annual election of the members of the Massachusetts court Saltonstall would receive fewer votes than several of his colleagues on the witchcraft court, including Winthrop, Richards, and Sewall. In that May 1693 election, the historian Kenneth Murdock observed, "every [Salem witch] judge received the stamp of popular approval." The "most popular name was that of Samuel Sewall."

Samuel did not describe in his diary his reaction to his older col-league's decision to quit the court. In February 1693, however, after hearing gossip that Saltonstall himself was a witch, Samuel sent him a letter. "I have sympathized with you and your family as to the report that went of some being afflicted by a person in your shape.... I fully believed the letter asserting your innocence."

However, "I was grieved" recently "when I heard and saw that you had drunk to excess; so that your head and hand were rendered less useful than at other times." Recollecting the details, Samuel went on, "You may remember, you were sitting in the south side of the Council chamber, on the bench; I drew near to you, and enquired concerning Mr. Ward," a relative of Saltonstall's wife. "You answered, He was better, which made you so merry. You also told me of the breaking up of the ice of the River Merrimac.... Let me entreat you, Sir, to break off this practice" of drinking to excess. "Don't furnish your enemies with arms," Samuel warned the man who had abandoned the witch-craft court. "I write not of prejudice but kindness; and out of a sense of duty as indeed I do. Take it in good part from him who desires your everlasting welfare. S.S." Saltonstall read this letter in Samuel's presence at the Town House of Boston, thanked him for it, and requested his prayers.

In June of 1692 Samuel was no longer young, but he was not yet old enough to stand apart from his society. He did not think of leaving the court. He would get along, serve his country, and advance himself. A few months hence, when Governor Phips created the new Superior Court of Judicature, it would be Samuel Sewall, not Nathaniel Saltonstall, who received an invitation to join the first independent judiciary in the Western Hemisphere. In this world, at least, prudence was rewarded.

Samuel returned to Salem almost three weeks later, on July 19, for the execution of Sarah Good and the four women whom he had condemned in late June. Most of the judges were present, along with several ministers, including Noyes, and numerous townspeople. Samuel stood by as Sarah Good, whose recent pregnancy had ended with a stillbirth in jail, climbed the ladder to the gallows. He saw the hangman place the rope around her neck. He heard Sarah Good's last words.

"Liar!" she shouted at Noyes, who stood in prayer on the earth below the gallows. "I am no more a witch than you are a wizard," she cried. "If you take my life away, God will give you blood to drink." Years later, when Noyes suffered an internal hemorrhage and died choking on his own blood in 1717, people in Salem would remember these words and call them prophetic.

Later, after the crowd dispersed, the bodies of Sarah Good, Rebecca Nurse, Sarah Wildes, Susanna Martin, and Elizabeth Howe were buried in shallow, unmarked graves on the hill. A witch could not be laid in hallowed ground.

Back in Boston the next day, in a strange twist, Samuel visited the house of a suspected witch. Within hours of returning from the hangings he attended a fast for his old friend Captain John Alden Jr., who was in the Boston jail.

Alden was an unlikely witch. This son of Pilgrims—Puritan settlers of Plymouth Plantation who arrived in Massachusetts nine years
before John Winthrop—was a well-to-do, seventy-year-old Bostonian
more established even than Samuel. Alden's father, the "ancient of
Plymouth," came to America on the *Mayflower* and prior to his death
in 1687 was the last surviving signer of the Mayflower Compact.
Many merchants, including John Hull and Samuel Sewall, had trusted
John Alden Jr. to sail their ships across the ocean. He had "nobly"
commanded armed vessels for Massachusetts during King William's
War. With John Hull he had been a founding member of the Third
Church in 1679. Alden and his wife, Elizabeth, who was now fifty-two,
had several children and were longtime members of the neighborhood
prayer group. Back in 1677 after a March prayer meeting, then
twenty-five-year-old Samuel had noted, "Mr. Alden spake to 1 Samuel
15:22" on how "to obey" is "better than sacrifice." Now it was Alden
who desperately needed Samuel's prayers.

The Court of Oyer and Terminer had sent for Captain Alden on
May 28 after several Salem Village girls named him. They had heard
rumors that he had traded with the French and Indians before the
attack on York. He had appeared in Salem on May 31 before Hathorne,
Corwin, and Bartholomew Gedney. Just two years before, Alden and
Gedney had been allies jointly leading the effort to finance the expedition against the French in Quebec.

During his hearing someone told the afflicted girls, who had never
before seen John Alden, that the tall man in the courtroom was John
Alden of Plymouth fame. One girl cried, "There stands Alden, a bold
fellow, with his hat on before the judges. He sells powder and shot to
the Indians and French and lies with the Indian squaws, and has
Indian papooses." Alden had in fact made many trips to and from
Maine and Acadia in the previous four years as an agent of the province and as a private trader. There were rumors that he supplied goods
to the French and Indians although evidence of actual collaboration
with enemy forces was scanty. His recent effort to retrieve prisoners
of war in the north had met with only partial success—he freed some
captives, but others were already dead and his son was out of reach, in
prison in Quebec—leading some in Massachusetts to criticize Alden
for bungling the mission.

Alden's relatives, who included Quakers and other supporters of religious freedom, may have aroused suspicion, the historian Louise Breen conjectured. His wife, Elizabeth Phillips Alden, was the step-daughter of Anne Hutchinson's daughter Bridget, who went into exile with her banished mother in 1638. Bridget's first husband, John Sanford, backed Anne Hutchinson and signed the Portsmouth Compact that guaranteed freedom of religion in Rhode Island: "No person within the said colony, at any time hereafter, shall be in any wise [ways] molested, punished, disquieted or called into question on matter of religion—so long as he keeps the peace." After Sanford's death in 1653, Bridget married the widowed Major William Phillips, a Boston wine merchant of a Quaker family. Bridget and William Phillips moved to Maine, where he amassed a fortune in land. His daughter, Elizabeth, married Captain John Alden Jr. in 1660. "One function of witchcraft accusations was to punish those individuals who had close dealing with Quakers, Indians, or Anglicans at a time when altered imperial circumstances made it increasingly awkward to act against any one of these groups," Breen noted. "If Quakers, like Indians, stalked the perimeters of [the] settlement, seeking to pollute the true ordinances of God…, then the Phillips family, to which Alden belonged, was a catalyst of New England's defilement and ruin."

In Salem, at John Alden's witchcraft hearing, the justices of the peace tested the power of his sorcery by asking him to "look upon the accusers." The old sea captain turned toward the girls, who promptly collapsed on the floor. Aghast that the hysterical "wenches" could move the court, Alden stared at Judge Gedney. "Why did my glance not strike *you* down?" he demanded of his old ally, who made no reply. A little later Gedney said to Alden, "I have known you many years, and been at sea with you, and always looked upon you to be an honest man. But now I do see cause to alter my judgment." He encouraged Alden to "confess and give glory to God." Alden replied, "I hope I should give glory to God, and never gratify the Devil, and that God will clear up my innocency." Gedney, Hathorne, and Corwin sent Alden to jail as a witch.

At the gathering at the Alden house on the afternoon of July 20, the Reverend Willard prayed for Alden. Samuel Sewall, who did not mention feeling any discomfort, read aloud from a treatise by the late English divine John Preston on the "first and second uses of God's all-sufficiency," which he earnestly hoped would help his friend in jail. Another merchant, Captain Joshua Scottow, prayed until a "brave shower of rain" interrupted him, pleasing all, as New England was suffering through a drought. Two other ministers, James Allen and Cotton Mather, dropped in to pray for Alden, followed by Captain James Hill, a deacon of the Third Church. The meeting ended before five o'clock with the men singing the first part of Psalm 103.

Psalm 103

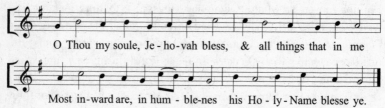

Low Dutch Tune

> O Thou my soule, Jehovah bless,
> & all things that in me
> Most inward are, in humblenes
> his Holy-Name blesse ye.

> 2 The Lord blesse in humility,
> o thou my soule: also
> put not out of thy memory
> all's bounties, thee unto.

> 3 For hee it is who pardoneth
> all thine iniquityes:
> he it is also who healeth
> all thine infirmityes.

> 4 Who thy life from destructi-on
> redeems: who crowneth thee
> with his tender compassi-on
> & kinde benignitee.

5 Who with good things abundantlee
  doth satisfie thy mouth:
so that like as the Eagles bee
  renew-ed is thy youth.

6 The Lord doth judgement & justice
  for all oppress-ed ones.
7 To Moses shew'd those wayes of his:
  his acts to Isr'ells sonnes.

Several Boston ministers continued to believe that the new court was not equipped to handle witchcraft allegations. More than a hundred people were now in prison. They included several men and women of evident piety and good estate. The Reverend James Allen, who knew the family of Francis and Rebecca Nurse, believed spectral evidence was wrong. He and other clergymen representing Boston's three churches wrote to the Court of Oyer and Terminer to protest the imprisonment of Captain Alden. Their letter was penned by Samuel Willard, who had faced a case of witchcraft two decades before, in Groton. In 1672 Willard's sixteen-year-old servant had suffered strange fits, spoken in Satan's voice, and said a neighbor bewitched her. Willard had advised his servant to pray with the suspect neighbor, which she did, and her fits soon stopped. In the 1692 group letter Willard argued that a person whose shape the Devil assumes may be innocent. The court ignored the ministers' pleas.

"All summer," the historian Marilynne Roach wrote, Samuel Willard's sermons "urged compassion for the accused, because the Devil delighted in lies." According to Benjamin Wisner, a historian of the Third Church, "Though three of the judges who condemned the persons executed for witchcraft"—Sergeant, Winthrop, and Sewall—"were members of his church, and to express doubts of the guilt of the accused was to expose one's self to accusation and condemnation, [Willard] had the courage to express his decided disapprobation of the measures pursued, to use his influence to arrest them, and to aid some who were imprisoned awaiting their trial, to escape from the colony."

In a pamphlet titled *Some Miscellany Observations on our present Debates respecting Witchcraft*, printed secretly and anonymously in autumn 1692, the Reverend Willard criticized the legality of the court's procedures. During several sermons that summer he preached on a relevant Scripture passage, 1 Peter 5:8, "The devil walketh up and down seeking whom he may devour." According to sermon notes taken by the Boston merchant Edward Bromfield, one of Sewall's close friends, on Sunday, June 19, the Reverend Willard warned against the "raising of scandalous reports" because "those that carry up and down such reports are the Devil's brokers." Openly assailing the value of spectral evidence, Willard told his congregation, "The Devil may represent an innocent, nay a godly person, doing a bad act" and magically assume "the image of any man in the world."

12

REIGN OF TERROR

By July the witchcraft crisis had spread to Andover, an inland town northwest of Salem, and east to Gloucester. Across the North Shore people were afraid and distracted. Farmers neglected their cattle and fields. Families began moving away.

In the Salem jail one accused witch made a valiant effort to solve the problem. John Proctor, who was chained to the dungeon floor, penned a letter to five prominent ministers of Boston's three churches: Increase Mather, James Allen, John Bailey, Joshua Moody, and Samuel Willard. "Reverend Gentlemen," the sixty-year-old farmer began, on behalf of himself and other condemned prisoners, we "implore your favorable assistance of this our humble petition to his Excellency," Governor Phips, "that if it be possible our innocent blood may be spared, which undoubtedly otherwise will be shed, if the Lord doth not mercifully step in; the magistrates, ministers, juries, and all the people in general, being so much enraged and incensed against us by the delusion of the Devil.... We are all innocent persons."

Aware that the court and community were deluded, Proctor implored the ministers to attend the trials. He requested that the trials be moved to Boston, the center of population. He informed the ministers that many suspects were tortured and coerced into confessing, in violation of English common law. Proctor cited as examples the sons of his neighbor Martha Carrier, another accused witch, and his own child.

"My son, William Proctor, when he was examined, because he would not confess that he was guilty, when he was innocent, they tied him neck and heels till the blood gushed out at his nose.... These actions are very like the Popish cruelties." He requested that accusers be questioned separately, rather than as a group, to maintain credibility. "If it cannot be granted that we can have our trials at Boston, we humbly beg that you would endeavor to have these magistrates changed, and ... that you would be here ... at our trials, hoping thereby you may be the means of saving the shedding of our innocent blood."

Proctor received no response. In early August he and his wife, who was eight months pregnant, and four other suspects were brought to trial in Salem. Based largely on the spectral testimony of the Proctors' resentful servant, Mary Warren, Samuel Sewall and his colleagues convicted both Proctors and sentenced them to hang. In a moment of mercy the judges commuted Elizabeth Proctor's sentence until after she gave birth.

The churches of Boston called for a public fast day on August 4 to beg God for help in fighting witchcraft. In his fast-day sermon the Reverend Cotton Mather chose as his text Revelation 12:12: "Woe to the inhabitants of the earth, and of the sea; for the Devil is come down unto you, having great wrath; because he knoweth that he hath but a short time." The Last Judgment was near at hand, the minister prophesied. He expected it in 1697. In the meantime, he warned, Satan plotted to overthrow the world.

Satan cannot accomplish this work alone, Cotton Mather told his congregation. He needs "an army of devils." His cadres of witches need an earthly leader, "the head actor at ... their hellish rendezvouz," someone who "has the promise of being a king in Satan's kingdom." By now, with the testimony of several witnesses, Mather could identify the witches' leader. It was, appropriately, a man who appeared to be dedicated to God.

The Reverend George Burroughs, formerly a minister in Salem Village, had been arrested on May 2 at his home in Wells, Maine, while sharing a meal with his wife, Mary, and eight children. Since then he had been kept in irons at the Boston and Salem jails. He and several other accused witches were to be tried on August 5. Samuel rode to Salem on the fourth to prepare for the frontier minister's trial. Of all the witchcraft suspects who had come before him, Burroughs was the one he knew best.

Samuel and the Reverend Burroughs had been students together at Harvard, Burroughs graduating a year ahead of Samuel. In a list of Harvard graduates at the back of a commonplace book, Samuel had recorded both "Georgius Burrough (1670)" and "Gulielmus Stoughton, Master Oxoniae (1650)." Samuel and Burroughs had kept up a friendly correspondence. Burroughs, now a short, dark, muscular man of forty, had visited the Sewall mansion as recently as November 18, 1685, when Samuel noted in his diary, "Mr. G. Burroughs dined with us."

Samuel was not the only player in the drama with personal links to George Burroughs. Judge Hathorne, who had served on the Salem Village committee to find a replacement for Burroughs in 1686, was related to Burroughs by marriage. Sarah Ruck Hathorne, the young widow of the judge's younger brother, had become Burroughs's second wife in 1682. The judge had heard stories that Burroughs was "unkind" to Sarah, and they "fell out." One afflicted teenager, Mary (Mercy) Lewis, had lived as a child with Burroughs's family in Salem Village. She was now a servant for Thomas and Anne Putnam, who with their daughter, Anne, made scores of accusations. Mary Lewis testified that Burroughs killed his wife. When Burroughs first arrived in Salem Village to preach, he and his wife briefly boarded with relatives of the Putnams, who recalled him being "very sharp" to his "dutiful" wife. A neighbor recalled his wife saying she was afraid of him. Anne Putnam Jr. claimed to see ghosts of Burroughs's late wife wearing sheets. The ghost told the twelve-year-old that Burroughs had killed her and that Putnam should report this to the court.

A man named William Baker, himself an accused witch, testified before the judges that George Burroughs and Bridget Bishop had summoned more than a hundred young men armed with knives and swords to attack Salem Village, to "destroy the village, destroy the church of God, and set up Satan's kingdom."

Burroughs's physical strength struck some people as suspicious. Four people testified they saw Burroughs carry a barrel of molasses with only two fingers, an impossible feat. A man named Thomas Greenslit reported that the minister lifted up a heavy, six-foot-long gun with only "the forefinger of his right hand." Burroughs had been in Falmouth, Maine, on May 20, 1690, when the Indians attacked that English settlement. Simply surviving the slaughter made people think he must be in league with the Devil.

Burroughs had unorthodox opinions too. A free-thinking Puritan, he was relaxed about how often one should partake of the Lord's Supper. One judge asked him when he last received that sacrament. "It was so long since, I could not tell," Burroughs replied. The historian Bernard Rosenthal conjectured that Burroughs inclined toward the Baptist faith. He no longer believed in baptizing infants, he told the court, and he had not baptized his younger children. Being a Baptist was no longer a capital offense in Massachusetts, as it had been thirty-three years earlier, but witchcraft was.

Samuel voted with the court to convict and execute Burroughs on August 5, but he chose not to attend Burroughs's execution. On the day scheduled for the execution of Burroughs and four other convicted witches, Samuel arranged to be in Watertown on business, advising townspeople on whether to "settle a minister" and "where the [new] meeting house should be set." He may not have relished the spectacle at Salem of the hanging of a college friend and erstwhile dinner companion whom he had just sentenced to death.

Several days after condemning Burroughs, whose trial he did not record in his diary, Samuel made this mundane note: "I carried my mother, Mrs. Jane Sewall," who was visiting from Newbury, "to visit Sam [Jr.] at Mr. Hobart's at Newton," the school where the fourteen-year-old now boarded. For Sam Jr. this placement with the Reverend Nehemiah Hobart (Harvard class of 1667), an old friend of his father, "was the indifferent scholar's last hope for becoming qualified for admission to the college," the historian Judith Graham surmised. Samuel also recorded the wedding of his fellow Salem witch judge John Richards to Anne Winthrop, Wait Still's sister, "before William Stoughton, Esquire, the Lieutenant Governor, at the house of Madame Usher." The latter, practically a member of Samuel's family, was the former Bridget Hoar, who had taken as her second husband the Boston merchant Hezekiah Usher Jr.

Even before the day of George Burroughs's hanging, an unrelated event threw Samuel into mourning. His friend Nathaniel Gookin, the thirty-six-year-old minister who served as Harvard College's acting president, died suddenly in Cambridge on August 14. Nathaniel's brother, the Reverend Daniel Gookin, was married to Hannah Sewall's cousin Elizabeth Quincy. The Gookins' father, Major General Daniel Gookin, an ally of the Reverend John Eliot who had been one of Samuel's mentors, was the author of *An historical account of the doings and sufferings of the Christian Indians in New England, in the years 1675, 1676, 1677.* The elder Gookin was born in England in 1612, arrived in Boston in 1644, and served the colony as a soldier, magistrate, and "protector of Indians" until his death in 1687. A year later, as thirty-six-year-old Samuel Sewall headed for England on board the *America*, he dreamed of the late Daniel Gookin Sr. In the dream the major general, "well clad from head to foot" in a "coat and breeches of blood-red silk" and "of a very fresh, lively countenance," beckoned Samuel "out of the room where I was—I think 'twas the Town House—to speak to me." The death of Gookin's son Nathaniel, "one of the best friends I had left," particularly affected Samuel. Faced with so much bad news, he could not tell if God were punishing New England for its sins or if Satan were finally taking over.

Three days after Gookin's funeral, on Friday, August 19, the constable of Salem carted five condemned witches to Gallows Hill to be executed. To the amazement of the throng of spectators, the doomed men and women not only proclaimed their innocence but also remained calm.

John Proctor steadfastly declared he was innocent. Centuries later Arthur Miller would make Proctor the heroic central character in his play *The Crucible.* (The love triangle involving the Proctors and Abigail Williams is the playwright's invention.) Elizabeth Proctor, nearly nine months pregnant, remained in fetters in the jail.

John Willard, another farmer of Salem Village with a family and a comfortable estate, died beside Proctor that day. Willard (who was not related to the Reverend Willard of Boston) had been implicated by a teenager named Susanna Sheldon who claimed he told her he was a wizard. He—or his ghost, she couldn't be sure—suckled two black pigs. One day she saw him kneel in prayer to a "black man with a long-crowned hat" and then magically vanish.

Yet another prosperous farmer joined John Willard and John Proctor on the gallows. George Jacobs Sr., a tall, white-haired man of eighty, had, like Proctor, been named by a teenage servant. During the old farmer's trial he had knelt before the witch judges and begged them to believe he was innocent. Realizing that was impossible, he had told them, "You tax me for a wizard.... You may as well tax me for a buzzard. I have done no harm. Well, burn me or hang me. I will stand in the truth of Christ."

Martha Carrier, the Andover woman whose sons were tortured into confessing, was also hanged on August 19. As she approached the gallows, having spent several months in jail, Cotton Mather called her a "rampant hag." He added, "The Devil promised her she should be Queen of Hell."

Mather's description of Martha Carrier as a "rampant hag," which recalls Nicholas Noyes's description of Sarah Good as a "miserable witch," captures the emotional content beneath the false legalities. To men in power, women could be terrifying. In a culture dominated by men, according to the historian Laurel Thatcher Ulrich, a belief in witchcraft "confirms the social nature of the maternal role.... Because women were perceived to have real, though mysterious, power, they could become the focus of communal fear and anger." The perceived reality of witches expressed "the depth of conflict and need for security in this often incomprehensible world. There should be no surprise in finding witchcraft in the same time and place as idealized motherhood."

Meanwhile, the crowd awaited the killing of a minister for witchcraft. This new challenge would be one reason the frenzy would soon end.

The hangman led George Burroughs to the gallows, his hands and legs in chains. Cotton Mather was said to be perched on his horse, high above the mob. The Reverend Burroughs turned to the crowd, which included most of the judges of the special court, and quietly stated his innocence. Then he bowed his head.

"Our Father, which art in heaven," he said in a firm voice, beginning the Lord's Prayer. "Hallowed be Thy name. Thy kingdom come." The minister appeared placid. But everyone knew that a wizard cannot pray rightly. Satan invariably trips up his tongue.

"Thy will be done, in earth as it is in Heaven," Burroughs continued, the prayer seeming to strengthen his resolve. Everyone wondered what small mistake would prove his alliance with Satan.

"Give us this day our daily bread. And forgive us our debts, as we forgive our debtors." He paused, conscious of his debtors who were

present. "And lead us not into temptation, but deliver us from evil."
Deliver us from evil.

He stopped, sensing tension in the crowd, which had turned eerily
silent. "For thine is the kingdom, and the power, and the glory, for
ever," he said, solemnly. "Amen."

Someone began to cry. A few sobs grew into wails, which spread
through the crowd. George Burroughs had prayed flawlessly. Scores
of people heard it. Many wondered now, if they had not already, Is it
possible he is not a witch? Should he live?

The judges sensed danger. If the crowd hindered the execution of
Burroughs, that could prevent future executions and even trials. Then
Satan would win. An unidentified official motioned to the hangman,
George Corwin, who quickly knocked the scaffold from beneath the
minister's feet. Burroughs's neck snapped.

"Burroughs is no ordained minister!" Cotton Mather cried out to the
crowd. "He was duly convicted," he reminded them. "It was a fair trial."
He cautioned that the "Devil may appear among us as an angel of light."

The weeping subsided. Who could argue with the Reverend
Mather?

The bodies of George Burroughs, George Jacobs Sr., John Proctor,
John Willard, and Martha Carrier were left for hours, swinging in the
wind. Somehow the family of George Jacobs was able to remove his
corpse, carry it on horseback to his farm, a mile west along a river,
and bury it beneath a tree.

In Boston, Sewall wrote in his diary, "This day George Burroughs,
John Willard, John Proctor, Martha Carrier, and George Jacobs were
executed at Salem, a very great number of spectators being present....
They all said they were innocent, Carrier and all." Referring to a private
conversation he had just had with Increase Mather, Samuel reassured
himself, "Mr. Mather says they died by a righteous sentence." Samuel
was sorry to have heard that "Mr. Burroughs, by his speech, prayer,
[and] protestation of his innocence, did much move unthinking persons." Later, in the margin, he added the words, "Doleful! Witchcraft."

On the North Shore September was a pivotal month. Even as the
virus of accusation continued to spread south to Marblehead and
west to Reading, public sentiment turned away from the judges. The
Court of Oyer and Terminer met twice that month, on the ninth and

the seventeenth, and convicted fifteen more witches, but opposition to its procedures intensified and the frenzy was soon to end.

But first, nine more people died, more victims than in any other month. Giles Corey of Salem Farms (now Peabody) was next. This "large landholder ... of singular force and acuteness of intellect," in the words of Charles Upham, was the husband of Martha Corey, who had made the mistake of laughing out loud at the accusations against her. Her husband, who was not then charged, attended her trial and after her conviction asked the court's permission to go with her to jail. The judges refused but decided to examine him too.

The judges hammered him with questions about witchcraft and the Devil, but he refused to speak. Giles Corey was aware of the English law that stated, "No person shall be tried for any offence, but high treason, until he enters a plea." If he remained silent, he might preserve his last will and testament. "In the belief that his will would be invalidated and his estate confiscated, if he were condemned by a jury after pleading to the indictment," the editor of Sewall's diary noted, Corey "resolutely preserved silence, knowing that an acquittal was an impossibility" unless he confessed.

Corey was aware of the immediate consequence of his silence. In English law a person who remained mute before a court received *peine forte et dure*, or a "slow crushing under weights," until a plea was forthcoming. In Salem on September 17, with the local judges in attendance, a sheriff led Giles Corey out of the dungeon into a nearby field. He ordered the old man to strip to the waist and lie flat on the earth in a pit dug in the field. Corey complied. Several men lifted a door on top of his chest. They piled boulders atop the door. The sheriff asked Corey if he pleaded guilty or not guilty to the charge of witchcraft. Corey said nothing.

The judges urged him to plead. So did several friends. Corey remained silent. Men added rocks to the pile. Corey's ribs broke. His tongue hung out. His eyes bulged from their sockets. For more than forty hours, until noon on Monday, September 19, the old man continued to breathe.

Giles Corey succeeded in protecting his land and possessions from the sheriff, who had ransacked the houses and barns of many other convicted witches. Without a plea from Corey, the sheriff had no legal justification for invading his property.

In Boston Samuel learned of Corey's death later that day. He noted in his diary, "Giles Gory was pressed to death for standing mute. Much pains [were] used with him two days ... but all in vain." It occurred to Samuel that the old man's torture was a fitting judgment of God. The next day he heard news that seemed to confirm this.

"About eighteen years ago," he learned, Giles Corey "was suspected to have stamped and pressed a man to death, but was cleared. 'Twas not remembered till Ann[e] Putnam [Jr.] was told of it by said Corey's specter [ghost]" on Sunday night. This gossip came by post from Thomas Putnam, the Salem Village man whose family members were responsible for roughly half of the accusations of witchcraft. Putnam's letter asserted that his daughter was "grievously tormented by witches" and spirits on the Monday evening after Corey died. She told her father that a man appeared to her in a white sheet saying Corey had pressed him to death years before.

The same day that Samuel received this information from the Putnams, the *Swan* arrived in the harbor, "a rich French prize of about 300 tons, laden with Claret, white wine, brandy, salt, linen, paper, etc." Meanwhile, in the North End, Cotton Mather penned a letter to Stephen Sewall in Salem, reminding him as clerk of the special court to give Mather the transcripts of the witchcraft trials. In light of declining public support for the proceedings of the court, the growing number of accusations against socially influential people, and the urgings of the governor, Mather wished to study these documents and attempt to explain their meaning to the world. The report he would later write, which was rushed into print by November, although the title page says 1693, was *The Wonders of the Invisible World*.

"My dear and my obliging Stephen," Cotton Mather began on September 20. "That I may be the more capable in lifting up a standard against the infernal enemy,

I must renew my most importunate request, that you would please quickly to perform what you kindly promised, of giving me a narrative of the evidence given in at the trial of half a dozen, or if you please a dozen, of the principal witches that have been condemned.

Please also [speak] to ... some of your observations about the confessors and the credibility of what they assert, or about things evidently preternatural in the witchcrafts, and whatever else you may account an entertainment, for an inquisitive person, that entirely loves you and Salem.

... your grateful friend, C. Mather

P.S.... His Excellency the Governor laid his positive commands upon me to desire this favor of you; and the truth is, there are some of his circumstance with reference to this affair, which I need not mention, that call for the expediting of your kindness....

The next day Stephen and his wife arrived in Boston to stay with Samuel and his family. Stephen likely carried the transcripts with him. On September 22 Cotton Mather called at Samuel's house, where Mather, Judge Stoughton, Judge Hathorne, and the Sewall brothers jointly discussed whether and in what form to publish "some trials of the witches." Stoughton departed the gathering early but returned because "it began to rain and was very dark." Samuel offered him a room for the night, which the chief justice accepted, but "he went away early in the morn." Before Samuel fell asleep that night he studied John 1: "In the beginning was the Word, and the Word was with God, and the Word was God."

In Salem on September 22, three days after the death of her husband, Martha Corey and six other women and one man were hanged. Samuel, who was not present, was told that Goodwife Corey walked to the gallows in prayer. The other people who were killed that day, most of whom he and his colleagues had convicted in September, were a fisherman's wife from Salem named Alice Parker; Samuel Wardwell, an Andover farmer; Ann Pudeator, of Salem Village; Margaret Scott, of Rowley; an Andover widow, Mary Parker; a Marblehead woman named Wilmot Reed; and Mary Esty, a mother of seven in her late fifties from Topsfield.

Esty's older sister Rebecca Nurse had preceded her to the gallows, and her younger sister Sarah Cloyse was still in jail, convicted and condemned. "I know not the least thing of witchcraft," Mary Esty had told Samuel and the other judges during her examination. They condemned her to death. She wrote to them from jail. "I would humbly beg of you, that Your Honors would be pleased to examine these afflicted persons strictly, and keep them apart some time, and likewise to try some of these confessing witches...." If the court tried the confessed witches, many of whom were accusers, then there would be no incentive to make false confessions. Similarly, the testimony of the accusers would not hold up if they testified separately and without the accused being present. If the court adopted these practices, she added, "I question not but you will see an alteration of these things."

After these executions, which would turn out to be America's final executions for witchcraft, the Reverend Nicholas Noyes studied the eight bodies hanging from ropes. Loud enough for the crowd to hear him, Samuel's old friend remarked, "What a sad thing it is to see eight firebrands of hell hanging there."

13

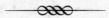

GOD SAVE
NEW ENGLAND

The witch court adjourned on September 22 and never met again. The witch hunt ended, but not because the judges came to realize their course was wrong. In fact, "there is no doubt of there ever having been any doubts or misgivings on the bench," Charles Upham, Salem's seminal chronicler, concluded in the nineteenth century. "It is not probable, and it is scarcely possible, that any considerable number could be at once doubters and accusers."

The witch hunt ended because the tide of public opinion turned. By late summer many powerful people openly questioned the reliability of the evidence accepted by the court. Summing up the change, Thomas Brattle—merchant, mathematician, and Harvard College treasurer who had attended the Sewalls' doomed dinner party in February 1690—wrote on October 8, 1692, "There are several about the Bay, men for understanding, judgment, and piety, inferior to few (if any) in New England that do utterly condemn the said proceedings." Brattle mentioned former governor Simon Bradstreet, former deputy governor Thomas Danforth, the Reverend Increase Mather, the Reverend Samuel Willard, and Judge Nathaniel Saltonstall, who "left the court, and is very much dissatisfied with the proceedings of it. Excepting Mr. [John] Hale [of Beverly, Massachusetts], Mr. [Nicholas] Noyes, and Mr. [Samuel] Parris, the Reverend elders, almost throughout the whole country, are very much dissatisfied" with the witchcraft court, and so too "several of the present justices; and in particular, some of the Boston justices...." While no one doubted the existence of witches and satanic spirits, many questioned the court's methods of determining guilt. Most of the convictions by the Court of Oyer and Terminer were based solely on spectral evidence, which had no basis in any system of law, including the Bible.

In early October Governor Phips disbanded the Court of Oyer and Terminer, dismissed its judges, freed most of the accused on bail, and stayed all further indictments. He justified the timing of this decision by noting, in an October 12 letter to the English court, that he had been away all summer fighting French and Indians in Maine. "As soon as I came from fighting against their majesties's enemies" at the frontier, he wrote, only half-truthfully, "and understood what danger some of their innocent subjects might be exposed to, [I] put a stop to the proceedings of the court." In fact, during the four months the witchcraft court sat, throughout the summer and into early fall, Phips spent as much time in Boston as in Maine. In addition, according to the historian Mary Beth Norton, "Phips was well informed about the trials and firmly supported them while they lasted." The significant change in the fall was that his wife joined the ranks of the accused.

The precursor to the accusation of Lady Mary Phips is believed to have been her effort to free an imprisoned witchcraft suspect from the Boston jail. During one of her husband's absences in August or September, and apparently without his knowledge, Lady Mary signed an order to release an accused witch whose name is lost to history. The jailer followed the order, which cost him his job. This daring act on the part of the governor's wife led to gossip and ultimately to her being named as a witch.

Lady Phips was not alone. By October many well-placed people stood accused of witchcraft. They included Dudley Bradstreet, an Andover justice of the peace whose father was the beloved old colonial governor. Judge Jonathan Corwin's mother-in-law was said to be a witch. Ministers' families were suspect. The witchcraft court had tried and sentenced two daughters of Andover's senior minister, Francis Dane, in September, and both were now in jail. Close relatives of the

Reverends Joshua Moody, Samuel Willard, Increase and Cotton Mather, John Hale, Nicholas Noyes, and the late Thomas Thatcher were named. One woman said the Reverend Willard himself "afflicted" her, prompting the judges of the Court of Oyer and Terminer to dismiss her as "mistaken." The witchcraft accusers and witnesses became "over-confident, and struck too high," the historian Charles Upham explained. It was obvious, according to Elizabeth Reis, another historian, that "if the delusion ... lasted much longer under the rules of evidence that were adopted," then "everybody in the colony except the magistrates and ministers" would be charged with witchcraft. Everyone in the country—high or low, rich or poor, saved or damned—was at risk.

Nearly every leader of Massachusetts welcomed Phips's decision to halt the witchcraft trials. The notable exceptions were Cotton Mather, William Stoughton, and John Hathorne, who believed the trials and executions should continue. But most men of power were now willing openly to attack the procedures and proceedings of the court. Still, no one blamed the individual judges. Less than two months later, when Governor Phips created a new and far more important court, four of its five members would be former Salem witch judges.

In October, even after the Court of Oyer and Terminer was disbanded, the witchcraft problem was not solved. More than 150 suspects remained in prisons, where three women and one baby had already died. Roughly 50 people, including many accusers, had confessed they were witches. Some accusers were now retracting their accusations against people who had been hanged or remained in jail. At the same time new accusers emerged, naming more names. In total, 185 people—141 women and 44 men—were accused of witchcraft. Of the 59 people tried, 31 were convicted and 20 were executed. Of those executed, 14 were women and 6 were men. Some of them were humble, but many were prosperous and respected.

Many socially prominent victims had managed to escape from jail, most of them to New York. Mary English, the wife of a wealthy Salem merchant, Philip English, slipped out of the Boston jail with assistance from the Reverend Moody. Mistress Elizabeth Cary, of Charlestown, was released from the Cambridge prison in late July after her husband, Captain Nathaniel Cary, gave his life's savings to the jailer.

Captain Cary told Samuel Sewall, whom he knew, that the jailer tortured her: he put eight-pound "irons on my wife's legs," causing her to develop "convulsion fits." Fearing she would die, he had begged the jailor to remove the irons but "in vain."

In the middle of September, after fifteen weeks of incarceration, John Alden Jr. broke out of the Boston jail. Influential friends helped him travel to Duxbury, where he had grown up among the Pilgrims, and relatives hid him for several months. The following April he returned to Boston, surrendered to authorities, and was discharged of "suspicion of witchcraft" by the new court. Six weeks later, on June 12, 1693, Samuel visited Alden and his wife at home, hoping to make amends for his role in the witch hunt.

Samuel Sewall said to John Alden, "I am sorry for your sorrow and temptations by reason of your imprisonment. I am glad of your restoration." These words, which Samuel recorded in his diary, are one of the earliest signs of his growing shame and remorse. In the coming years Samuel would often call at the Alden house by way of making restitution to someone he had harmed. On March 14, 1702, Samuel "happened to be there" when the eighty-year-old sea captain died.

In the autumn of 1692, as the judges, ministers, and governor of Massachusetts struggled to set their troubled land aright, most of the documents pertaining to the witch hunt were destroyed. Persons unknown contributed to this "suppression and destruction of the ordinary material of history," the historian Charles Upham wrote. Unlike most colonial court records, which have been carefully preserved, the journal of the Court of Oyer and Terminer disappeared. The parish records for Salem Village contain a thorough accounting of every other period in the church's history but no mention of witchcraft trials or executions. Upham believed that most participants in the witch hunt, except perhaps the victims and their families, wished to "obliterate the memory of the calamity."

On October 26 the Governor's Council called for a fast day so that, in Samuel's words, the province "may be led in the right way as to the witchcrafts." Two days later Samuel observed Chief Justice Stoughton pressure Governor Phips to restore the Court of Oyer and Terminer. "It must fall," the governor replied. Phips was acutely aware of the continuing danger of King William's War in Maine, where he and his wife had family. Moreover, according to the historians Emerson Baker and John Reid, the witch hunt was especially "threatening to Phips and his authority because a significant number of those involved," both accusers and accused, "were connected with his family or that of his wife, or were known to them through their former association with the Casco Bay region and adjoining settlements" in Maine. The safest course for the governor was to ensure public safety by working to create a court system for the province, as the new charter required. Still, the vote of the Governor's Council to end the proceedings of the witchcraft court was close—thirty-three in favor, twenty-nine opposed.

Regarding the gradual nature of the shift in public opinion and public policy, the historian Richard Weisman wrote, "The Court of Oyer and Terminer was the first judicial commission in over thirty years to have acted decisively to protect villagers against malefic harm. And while some residents may have been troubled by the imprisonment of their more respectable neighbors, others were undoubtedly relieved to be spared further contact with persons whom they had suspected for years." People like John Alden, Philip English, and Rebecca Nurse "did not ordinarily participate in witchcraft proceedings,... and it was largely through their efforts that the court was dismantled. But those of their neighbors who were less prosperous and who were forced to deal directly with reputed practitioners of malefic magic ... had a different outlook. The Court of Oyer and Terminer was one of the very few official tribunals to have taken their suffering seriously. It is not so surprising, after all, that requests for legal protection [against witchcraft] continued well into November of 1692 and that, for some members of the village laity, the court was terminated before it had finished its work."

At the Sewall mansion on Sunday, November 6, 1692, Samuel Sewall, whose tenure as a witch judge was over, was called to judge and punish his younger son. Four-year-old Joseph "threw a knob of brass and hit his [ten-year-old] sister Betty on the forehead so as to make it bleed and swell." Their grandmother Hull, who observed the toss, called on Samuel to discipline the boy. Entering the room, Samuel noted that little Joseph "sought to shadow and hide himself from me behind the head of the cradle, which gave me the sorrowful remembrance of

Adam's carriage," referring to the first Adam's awareness of original sin. Samuel "whipped" his son "pretty smartly" for hurting his sister "and for his playing at prayer-time" on the Sabbath, "and eating when [he was supposed to] return thanks."

Throughout November the governor and members of the General Court discussed how to structure the new court system. Meanwhile, on Tuesday, November 22, Samuel observed a private day of prayer and fasting. The witch hunt troubled him. In addition, he worried that he might not be able to continue in his role as a judge.

"God, pardon all my sinful wandering, and direct me for the future," he pleaded. "God, save New England as to enemies and witchcrafts, and vindicate the late judges [of the Court of Oyer and Terminer] with fasting [and] with your justice and holiness.... Bless the assembly [the Governor's Council, formerly the General Court] in their debates, and that [they] would choose and assist our judges." He knew he was under consideration for the new court.

Three days later, on November 25, 1692, Phips formally created the Superior Court of Judicature, America's first independent judiciary— independent, that is, of other governmental bodies. The new charter, which made Massachusetts dependent on England, "with highly centralized executive power conferred upon an appointee of the Crown," according to the legal scholar Arthur Ruggs, empowered Phips, as royal governor, to create a court system. He ordered a new court, the Superior Court of Judicature, to handle major civil and criminal matters, leaving smaller matters to local justices of the peace. While local justices' opinions could be appealed to the Superior Court of Judicature, the latter's decisions could be appealed only to the Privy Council, in England. The Superior Court was to meet at set times throughout the province, from Maine to Rhode Island, and to follow English common law. In fact, according to Russell Osgood, author of *The History of the Law in Massachusetts*, this court would operate "carefully within the ambit of colonial statutes, while filling in blanks based on English common law practice and manuals, such as Dalton's *Countrey Justice*."

More than three hundred years later that new court, now referred to as the Supreme Judicial Court of Massachusetts, is the "oldest court in continuous service in the hemisphere," Osgood wrote. Its creation

as an independent court is now considered the first step in the separation of powers in American government. In 1780, decades after Phips
formed the Superior Court of Judicature, the Massachusetts Constitu-
tion formalized this separation of powers by creating a representative
government with three separate branches: legislative, executive, and
judicial. While 1692 lives in infamy because of the witch hunt, it lives
in legal history as the date of the birth of the oldest independent court
in the land as well as of the separation of powers.

Governor Phips rewarded Samuel for his service to the colony with
a seat on this court. On December 22, after the lecture service at the
Third Church, the governor swore in Samuel Sewall, John Richards,
Wait Still Winthrop, and Thomas Danforth as justices of the new
court. William Stoughton took the oath of office as the court's chief
justice. For Samuel Sewall the witchcraft trials served as a stepping-
stone, even as they burdened his soul.

Phips may have been slow to start the new court, but once he did so
he and the court collaborated in quelling the witchcraft crisis. The
new court "dealt humanely" with accused and condemned witches,
Russell Osgood noted. The first meeting of the Superior Court of Judicature was held despite bitter cold in early January 1693 in Salem,
where the stream of witchcraft accusations still flowed. Samuel and
his colleagues heard fifty indictments that day. They acquitted forty-
seven people. They ordered that the three suspects they convicted of
witchcraft not be executed. They ignored all spectral evidence.

The chief justice, Stoughton, had reservations about this new
course. "He held on to spectral evidence" even after everyone else
abandoned it, Charles Upham noted. "He would not admit that he, or
anyone concerned, had been in error." As long as he lived, "he never
could bear to hear any persons express penitence or regret for the
part they had taken in the proceedings."

In mid-January, at a meeting of the Superior Court of Judicature in
Charlestown, Stoughton ordered that several condemned witches who
were still in the Salem jail should "be hanged as soon as possible."
Someone notified Governor Phips, who sent a reprieve to Salem. The
executions were stopped.

Stoughton was enraged. "We were ... to have cleared the land of
them [witches]," he said. "Who it is that obstructs the cause of justice, I

know not. The Lord be merciful to the country!" He stormed off the bench. Stoughton's anguish was genuine, according to the legal scholar Edgar Bellefontaine. "The members of the Court of Oyer and Terminer really believed the Devil influenced daily events, and they believed in spectral evidence, but now they could no longer consider spectral evidence. This meant they *should not have* condemned and hanged all those people. Spectral evidence, the legal basis for all those convictions, was cut out from under them. The judges' strength of character is impressive. Phips told them the law did not permit them to consider evidence that they knew in their heart to be true."

Cotton Mather's wife gave birth to their first child in March 1693. The baby, Joseph, lived only three days due to the lack of "a postern for the voidance of excrements," Samuel Sewall reported. Cotton Mather observed the autopsy of his infant son, noted rectal abnormalities, and concluded that there was "great reason to suspect a witchcraft in this preternatural accident." The rumor arose that the infant was a monster with a cloven foot, suggesting the Devil was involved. People whispered that Cotton's wife was a witch. That accusation came to nothing, though, because there was no longer a witchcraft court.

That spring Governor Phips granted a general pardon and signed an order to release all witchcraft suspects who were still alive. More than a hundred men and women flowed from the jails of Salem and Boston. "Such a jail-delivery has never been known in New England," Thomas Hutchinson remarked a century later. However, jailers did not release prisoners until their families paid for their prison expenses, which included the cost of chains, fetters, food, and portions of the salaries of jailers, judges, and court officials. If a prisoner died in jail, the family had to pay for the body. The Reverend Samuel Parris would pay nothing for Tituba's release, so the court sold her, as a slave, to someone else.

One positive effect of the witch hunt was a changed view of Satan. After 1692 Satan was seen as less physical and more psychological or spiritual. Sermons and conversion narratives described "a less proximate Satan, one who tempted sinners and physically presided over hell, rather than one who preyed on people and possessed souls in the immediate, living world," the historian Elizabeth Reis wrote. Samuel's minister Samuel Willard said in a 1701 sermon that while Satan can assume a human shape, his temptations are incorporeal. "Men and angels are of two distinct kinds, and were not made for sensible communion ordinarily one with the other." As a result, "apparitions" of Satan "are beside the order of ordinary providence."

After the witch hunt, Reis added, people believed that Satan "could be conquered spiritually" rather than physically. Thus "Puritans took more responsibility for their own sins and their own souls." Rather than blaming Satan for sins, the ministers emphasized the role of humanity's essential depravity and focused on how someone might choose to change himself. As Reverend Willard preached at the Third Church in 1694, sin is "all voluntary; there is no outward force laid upon them to cause them thus to do, but [sin] is a fruit of the native corruption which is in them."

In the months and years following the witch hunt, the situation in Massachusetts did not dramatically improve. King William's War continued for several years, at the cost of many lives on both sides. In 1693 alone French privateers seized scores of fishing and commercial vessels from Salem, depleting its fleet.

As for the judges of the witch court, the temptation was to look ahead, try to forget what happened, and never look back. All but one of them appear to have taken this path. Samuel Sewall, according to the historian Mary Beth Norton, was "the only judge who ever changed his mind about the trials."

Some years earlier, while approaching his native country on board the *America*, Samuel had been reading *A Practical Commentary, with Notes, upon the Epistle of James* by the Puritan theologian Dr. Thomas Manton. "Blessed be God who in my separation from my dear wife and family hath given me" Manton's treatise, which was published in London in the year of Samuel's birth. Wishing to leave the book on the ship as a gift to the captain, he jotted some notes in his diary. "Look then not to the earnestness of your motions, but the regularity of them; not at what you would, but at what you ought. Men think 'tis a disgrace to change their mind.... But there is not a greater piece of folly than not to give place to right reason."

14

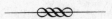

I AM BEYOND
CONCEPTION VILE

Samuel had often considered the biblical story of King David, who is at first unaware that he has sinned. He takes Bathsheba, a married woman, as his wife and then, to conceal his adultery, arranges for the murder of her husband, who is away fighting David's war. Not until Nathan, the prophet, describes to him his actions in impersonal terms does David become aware that his behavior was wrong. Only then can he say, "I have sinned against the Lord," repent, and live in a new way.

At forty, Samuel was aware of himself as a man of prudence and piety. Looking back on his life, he was conscious of having made many decisions that advanced himself and his family in the world. This may be true of many people, as we do our best on the playing field, at school or at work, and at home. But for Samuel, prudent striving had led him unjustly to condemn and execute twenty other human beings. It was now time to abandon prudence.

In looking back on his work on the witchcraft court, Samuel felt he had violated the laws of humanity and the laws of God. There was no question that in accepting spectral evidence the Court of Oyer and Terminer had violated the laws of England. Samuel may have lacked legal training, but he inherited from his Puritan forebears a deep respect for English common law. In Puritan-run England during the

1640s and 1650s Parliament forged close ties with the Inns of Court, England's law schools. In general, Puritans promoted common law as against royal policy, which they considered "Papist" or Anglican.

Far worse, though, was Samuel's violation of the law of God. In convicting and condemning suspects without solid evidence, he had broken God's commandment, "Thou shalt not bear false witness." With his colleagues on the Court of Oyer and Terminer, Samuel had violated the covenant between New England and God.

Even after he recognized his sin, he did not know how to respond. His personal writings do not clarify the timing of his awareness, although the Reverend Samuel Willard, who had opposed the witch hunt in sermons and in writing as it occurred, was surely his Nathan. It appears to have taken Sewall months if not years of prayer and Scripture study to determine to repent. He felt increasing remorse. He became aware of his lack of discernment. He felt that his will was not in concert with God's. Fitfully he moved toward a spiritual stance that had been brilliantly articulated a century and a half earlier by the Catholic Counter-Reformation leader Saint Ignatius of Loyola: "We should not prefer health to sickness, riches to poverty, honor to dishonor, a long life to a short life." No longer would Samuel seek health, riches, and honor. He might enjoy all these things, but to seek them any longer would prevent him from honoring God.

Still, his family life continued as before. By the beginning of 1693 Hannah was again pregnant. (The average time between her pregnancies, which began when she was nineteen and ended just before she turned forty-four, was nineteen months.) On Monday, August 7, "about 4 *mane* I go for the midwife; about 4 p.m. my wife was brought to bed of a daughter. Thanks be to God." Samuel Willard baptized the baby on August 13. Samuel named her Jane, after his mother and his sister and her daughter, his niece who lived with the family.

A month later, on September 9, Samuel returned from a two-week court trip to Rhode Island to "find little Jane not well." The Reverend Willard and others came to pray with the month-old baby, but Samuel feared the worst. "Methinks she looks like [baby] Henry in his sickness." He prayed, "Good Lord, prepare her and us for the issue, and help us to choose the things that please You." He recorded that "Nurse Judd watches" the baby. Before one on the morning of September 14,

"Little Jane expires, much as Henry did, in [next-door] neighbor [Matthias] Smith's lap, Nurse Hill and I being by." The next afternoon at four, Samuel delivered another child to the grave. The Reverend Willard's teenage son John "carried the corpse" into the tomb. Samuel prayed, "Lord, teach me to profit" from this blow. Jane was the sixth child he had buried.

Meanwhile, he warmed to his new judicial responsibilities on the Superior Court of Judicature. This circuit court covered widely spaced New England towns including Plymouth, Massachusetts; Bristol, Rhode Island; York in Maine; and Springfield and Westfield in western Massachusetts. He enjoyed the regular journeys to these towns, which he made at first on horseback and in later years in horse-drawn chariots or coaches. He relished the meals and hospitality he encountered at the taverns and inns, whose proprietors came to be his friends over the years.

The circuit court would enlarge his mental world, exposing him to new people and ideas. Some years later, on a September visit to Narragansett, Rhode Island, for the sitting of the court, Samuel happened upon a folio of Ben Jonson's plays while his innkeeper prepared his dinner. He was struck by the language of *The Poetaster*, a "comical satire" that Johnson composed in 1601 soon after converting to Catholicism. Samuel was taken by the scene in the fourth act when characters dress up as Roman deities to praise wine, music, and "feasts of sense" such as "Delicious nectar for the taste; For the touch a lady's waist." He scribbled several passages in the traveling diary he carried in his waistcoat pocket:

> Wake, our mirth begins to die,
> Quicken it with tunes and wine.
> Raise your notes; you're out, *fie, fie,*
> This drowsiness is an ill sign.

In the post-1692 years, though, such lighthearted abandon lay still in his future. Hannah nearly died at her next childbirth, in November 1694. "Mother [Hull] said that my wife was in great and more than ordinary extremity," Samuel noted. He asked the Reverends Willard and Torrey to pray with Hannah in the bedchamber. Samuel struggled uncharacteristically over this baby's name. Should she be Sarah or Mehitabel?

At the baptism, which Samuel Willard performed on November 25, Samuel chose Sarah, which means "lady" in Hebrew. The Reverend Torrey had advised him, "Call her Sarah and make a Madame of her."

Four months later, on March 17, 1695, amid a "great snowfall," Samuel woke from a nightmare that "all my children were dead except Sarah." Rising from bed in distress, he went to prayer. He reflected on "my omission of duty towards them." Later that day he prayed, "The Lord help me thankfully and fruitfully to enjoy [my children], and let that be a means to awaken me" to Christ.

A few months later he was again roused in the night, but this time it was not a dream. At one in the morning on June 21 he heard the sound of his niece Jane Tappan's "unusual gait" as she climbed the stairs to his and Hannah's bedchamber. He saw Jane rush into the room and heard a flood of words. Hannah's mother had taken ill. Judith Hull was unable to speak, probably due to a stroke, although the diagnosis was then unknown.

Samuel sent a servant to Cambridge to summon Dr. Oliver, the rare physician his mother-in-law trusted. Hannah stayed by her mother's bed. After breakfast Judith gestured to Samuel as if she wished to pray. He asked her if she desired the Reverend Samuel Willard. She nodded. Willard came quickly and prayed. After his departure, Samuel and Judith were left alone. Observing her "great weakness," Samuel "took the opportunity" to say to her, "Thank you for all your labors of love to me and mine." Without addressing any particular misbehavior, he added, "I ask your pardon of our undutifulness." Judith granted Samuel pardon without words.

Around noon someone in the room mentioned that Judith would need a constant "watcher." Judith, who had said nothing since the day before, muttered, "I should need no watchers. I shall be above, at rest."

Just before sunset, "to our very surprising grief and sorrow," Judith Quincy Hull died, aged sixty-eight. Three days later her daughter, son-in-law, grandchildren, and relatives and friends stood by as her body found its final rest in the family tomb.

The Hull property now belonged to the Sewalls. Within a month Samuel gave away a five-hundred-acre farm in Pettaquamscutt, in

Narragansett country, now Kingston, Rhode Island. This donation to Harvard College was for "the support and education at the said college of such youths whose parents may not be of sufficient ability to maintain them there, especially" those from Pettaquamscutt, "English or Indians, if any such there be." As recently as the late twentieth century Harvard had a Sewall Scholarship Fund.

Even as Samuel helped to educate Indian boys, Indians remained among his enemies. In a letter to a relative in England in July 1695 Samuel observed, "We are grievously oppressed by our French and pagan [Native American] enemies by land and sea. Our blood and estates are running out apace. As several captives escaped inform us, our heads are set [priced] at a certain rate by the governor of Quebec, as foreskins of the Philistines were of old. God will in his time confound all the worshippers of graven images," by which he meant Anglicans and Catholics.

Death affected Samuel's children more deeply now. On December 23, 1695, Sam Jr. accompanied his father to the sunset burial of their longtime neighbor "Dame" Sarah Walker. She had been the widow of Robert Walker, who became a freeman of the colony in 1634. Samuel had prayed with the old woman on her deathbed, "insisting on God's being a present help in time of need, and ... that she might enter into His rest." He meant to ask the Reverend Willard "to give her one lift more heavenward," but Dame Walker died first. Samuel remarked, "God fulfilled his good word in her and kept her leaf from withering." At home after the crowded funeral seventeen-year-old Sam Jr. "was exceedingly affected" by her death, "shed many tears, and is even overwhelmed with sorrow." His father prayed for him. "The Lord grant that the removal of one of his best friends may put him upon seeking unto God betimes and making Him his hiding place."

A week later Samuel kept a private fast day "with prayer for the conversion of my son," Sam Jr., "and his settlement in a trade that might be good for soul and body." Sam Jr. was apprenticed to a printer, which seemed a poor fit. He later worked for a Boston bookseller. While he ultimately chose farming as his career, bookselling was a practical choice for a wealthy young man not headed to Harvard. By 1719 Boston had five printing presses and many bookshops clustered around the Town House, according to a visiting minister, Daniel Neal, author of *History of the Puritans.* This was the highest concentration of media in English America. "In the city of New York there is but one bookshop, and in the Plantations of Virginia, Maryland, Carolina, Barbados, and the Islands none at all."

Sam Jr. was not the only Sewall child in distress. His thirteen-year-old sister, Betty, was undergoing a religious crisis. This was not unusual for a serious Puritan adolescent. Many of New England's male founders experienced God's grace for the first time at fourteen or fifteen. Betty had long shown spiritual sensitivity. At only eight she had burst into tears while reading aloud with her family the twenty-fourth chapter of Isaiah:

> Behold, the Lord maketh the earth empty, and maketh it waste, and turneth it upside down, and scattereth abroad the inhabitants.... The land shall be utterly emptied, and utterly spoiled.... Therefore the inhabitants of the earth are burned, and few men left.... Fear, and the pit, and the snare, [are] upon thee, O inhabitant of the earth.

"Sympathy with her draws tears from me as well," her father had noted then. Many years later Joseph Sewall would write that Betty "was much [our father's] delight." She was "indeed very amiable, the flower and ornament of the family."

In the fall of 1695, when Betty was thirteen, Samuel and Hannah sent her to Salem to spend several months visiting her uncle Stephen Sewall's family. "Sending out" adolescent children to relatives or close friends was customary. In Betty's case it may have contributed to her decision, several years later, to accept a proposal of marriage from the son of a wealthy Salem family.

Samuel never commented on the other Betty, the daughter of the Salem Village minister, who had preceded his daughter, during the summer of 1692, in staying at Stephen's house. It is not even clear that Betty Sewall was aware of her predecessor or, if so, what she felt about her father's central role in the witch hunt. We have no comment from Betty or her sisters on the witchcraft frenzy for the simple reason that we have no written record of any of their thoughts except those few utterances their father jotted in his diary.

Betty did needlework during her stay in Salem and was home again in Boston for her fourteenth birthday, on December 29, 1695. A few weeks later her anxiety about her spiritual estate spilled out before her whole family. At the family's morning prayer session Samuel read aloud from a sermon by the Reverend John Norton on a passage in the Gospel of John—"Ye shall seek me, and shall die in your sins; whither I go, ye cannot come"—that the sermon rendered as, "Ye shall seek me and shall not find me. Ye shall seek me and die in your sins."

This terrified Betty. She would die in her sins. At first she said nothing. Her father went out to the Town House, and the rest of the family dispersed. Her terror stayed. To calm herself she took another religious text from a pile of her father's papers. The sermon she happened upon was Cotton Mather's "Why hath Satan filled thy heart?" This increased her fear.

Betty sat through dinner with her siblings and mother, who noticed she was "sad and dejected." Finally unable to contain herself, Betty burst into an "amazing cry," which "caused all the family"—from seventeen-year-old Sam Jr. to one-year-old Sarah—"to cry, too."

Her mother asked Betty the reason for her distress. Betty would give none. Finally she admitted, "I am afraid I should go to Hell. My sins are not pardoned."

Hannah asked her daughter whether she prayed.

"Yes, but I fear my prayers are not heard, because my sins are not pardoned."

That evening after seven, when Samuel returned home, Hannah met him in the entryway and reported all that had happened. A month later he encountered Betty's spiritual anguish directly. She came into his bedchamber one morning "almost as soon as I was up and tells me the disquiet she had when [she] waked." She said, "I am afraid I should go to Hell.... I fear I am not elected" by God.

"What should I pray for?" Samuel asked his fourteen-year-old daughter.

"That God would pardon my sin and give me a new heart," she replied. Samuel "answered her fears as well as I could, and [we] prayed with many tears on either part. [I] hope God heard us. I gave her solemnly to God." Samuel of course shared Betty's fear of damnation. More now than ever, he was aware of his own vileness.

He was exquisitely aware of the public nature of his shame. That summer, while chatting on the street with an old acquaintance named Jacob Melyen, he realized that Melyen was mocking him "very sharply about the Salem witchcraft." Referring to the court's presumption of the Reverend George Burroughs's guilt on account of his physical strength, Melyen said to Samuel, "If a man should take Beacon Hill on his back and carry it away, I should not make any thing of it."

A few months earlier, in May 1696, Samuel had been the only member of the General Court excluded from an elegant wedding. The merchant Samuel Shrimpton's son was to marry his first cousin, Elizabeth Richardson, a daughter of Mistress Elizabeth Shrimpton's sister. The Shrimptons invited "all of the Council in the town" and "many others," Samuel lamented. "Only I was not spoken to."

Feeling slighted, he defended himself in private. "I was glad not to be there," he noted in his diary, "because [of] the [un]lawfulness of the intermarrying cousins...."

At the same time "it grieves me to be taken up in the lips of talkers and to be in such a condition that Colonel Shrimpton shall be under temptation *in defense of himself* to wound me, if any should happen to say [to him], Why was not such a one here?" To console himself Samuel prayed, "The Lord help me not to do or neglect anything that should prevent the dwelling of brethren together in unity. Oh, most bountiful and gracious God, who givest liberally and upbraidest not," he begged, "admit me humbly to bespeak an invitation to the marriage of the Lamb." This marriage—of Jesus Christ to the church of which Samuel was a part, thus in some sense a marriage between Samuel and Christ—was surely more worthy than the Shrimptons' questionable nuptials.

"Let Thy Grace with me and in me be sufficient for me in making myself ready" for death. "Though I am beyond conception vile," he went on, outdoing his human enemies in castigating himself, "out of Thy infinite and unaccountable compassions place me among those who shall not be left, but shall be accepted by Thee here and taken into glory hereafter." Samuel did not record whether in the aftermath of the witch hunt he was brooding on the twenty innocent people he had sent to their deaths.

"And O Lord, forgive all my unsuitable deportment at Thy table the last Sabbath day, that wedding day," a reference to his still wavering faith. "And if ever I be again invited … —Invite me once again!… help me entirely to give myself to Thy Son as to my most endeared Lord and Husband. And let my dear wife and all my children partake in this privilege and that not as *umbras*," or as shadows of him, "but on their own account."

Two weeks later Hannah delivered a stillborn son. Samuel did not name his "abortive son," whom he buried on May 22, 1696. Making his private devotions he blamed his personal "sin, wandering, and neglect" for his son's death.

It occurred to him later that on the very afternoon he had buried his dead baby he was excluded from a prayer meeting at the Reverend Willard's house. Neither Samuel nor Hannah was "admitted of God to be there" at the Willards' May 22 prayer meeting, he noted with regret. "And now the owners of the family admit us not. It may be I must never more hear a sermon there."

Their daughter Betty's troubles persisted. In May she told him she could not read the Bible without weeping. She "does not taste that sweetness in reading the Word that she once did," he noted after praying alone with his daughter. That fall she spent three months with her Salem cousins at Stephen and Margaret Sewall's house, working on needlepoint. Samuel visited her in November and "set" her to read Ezekiel 37, which begins,

The hand of the Lord was upon me, and carried me out in the spirit of the Lord, and set me down in the midst of the valley which was full of bones,… and, lo, they were very dry. And he said unto me, Son of man, can these bones live? And I answered, O Lord God, thou knowest. Again he said unto me, prophesy upon these bones, and say unto them, O ye dry bones, hear the word of the Lord.

Betty burst into tears. She could not continue. She told her father she was "a reprobate," who "loved not God's people as she should." A few weeks later she returned home. The day she arrived in Boston two

Harvard students drowned while skating on Fresh Pond in Cambridge. One of them, John Eyre Jr., was the child of a longtime member of Samuel's private prayer group, who "cried out bitterly" on learning of his son's fate.

Was this another omen? Everywhere Samuel looked he saw signs of God's anger at New England. Bad weather cut short the latest harvest. Never "was there ... so great a scarcity of food" as in 1696, Thomas Hutchinson noted a century later, "nor was grain ever at a higher price." Ship after ship was lost at sea. Indians and French continued to raid frontier towns. And always there was the memory of the "late tragedy raised among us by Satan," as the General Court officially referred to the Salem witch hunt.

As always when faced with trouble, the General Court and the governor ordered a day of fasting and prayer. This fast day, to be held on January 14, 1697, was aimed specifically at the Salem tragedy. On December 11, 1696, Samuel wrote the statement announcing the fast.

By the Honorable Lieutenant Governor, Council & Assembly of his Majesty's Province of the Massachusetts Bay; in General Court Assembled.

Whereas the anger of God is not yet turned away; but His hand is still stretched out against His people, in manifold judgments; particularly in drawing out to such a length, the troubles of Europe, by a perplexing war. And more especially, respecting our selves in this Province, in that God is pleased still to go on in diminishing our substance, cutting short our harvest; blasting our most promising undertakings; ... And although, considering the many sins prevailing in the midst of us, we cannot but wonder at the patience and mercy moderating these rebukes; yet we cannot but also fear, that there is something still wanting to accompany our supplications. And doubtless there are some particular sins, which God is angry with our Israel for, that have not been duly seen and resented by us, about which God expects to be sought....

Wherefore it's commanded and appointed that Thursday the fourteenth of January next be observed as a day of prayer and fasting throughout the Province ... so all God's people may offer up fervent supplications unto him for the preservation and prosperity of his Majesty's royal person and government and success to attend his affairs both at home and abroad; that all iniquity may be put away, which hath stirred God's holy jealousy against this land; that He would show us what we know not, and help us, wherein we have done amiss, to do so no more. And, especially, that whatever mistakes, on either hand, have been fallen into, either by the body of this people, or any orders of men, referring to the late tragedy raised amongst us by Satan and his instruments, through the awful judgment of God, He would humble us therefore, and pardon all the errors of His servants and people that desire to love his name; and be atoned to His land. That He would remove the rod of the wicked from off the lot of the righteous; that He would bring the American heathen, and cause them to hear and obey His voice.

William Stoughton, as chief justice of the superior court, agreed to the January fast day. He urged, however, that there be no public apologies for the actions of the Court of Oyer and Terminer.

The general chaos and despair hit Samuel directly in mid-December 1696 when his two-year-old, Sarah, took to her bed. Like several of her older brothers, Sarah had suffered from convulsions since infancy. In the late summer Samuel and Hannah had sent her to Newbury in hopes of curing her fits. She had returned home in the fall, and her seizures had continued. Now she appeared to be dying. He called for a doctor, Thomas Oakes, but there was little he could do to help the child.

Samuel woke on December 21 to "a very great snow" on the ground. This would prove to be New England's coldest winter since 1630, when the English record keepers arrived. The ice on the harbor was so deep and wide that sleighs could drive several miles out to the tip of Nantasket, a peninsula to the south of the town. Ships could not enter the harbor to dock and unload, so trade stopped.

Samuel was most worried about his daughter. He dressed warmly and walked out to his pastor's house, where he asked Willard "to choose your own time to come and pray with little Sarah." That evening Willard came and prayed "very fully and well," Samuel noted. Increase Mather and Ezekiel Cheever both called at the house to pray with the child.

The next morning Samuel sent a note to Willard requesting public prayer. He brought Sarah to bed with him and Hannah that evening. Nurse Hannah Cowell ministered to the toddler through the night in the parents' bedchamber. At dawn the next morning, while Samuel and Hannah slept, Sarah "gave up the ghost" in the nurse's arms.

"Dear little Sarah dies," Samuel reported. Thinking of his own inattention, he added, "I thought of Christ's words" in the Garden of Gethsemane to Peter and his other disciples, "Could you not watch with me one hour?"

Later that morning as the family prayed together, his other children were anxious and upset. The reading was Deuteronomy 22, which begins, "Thou shalt not see thy brother's ox or his sheep go astray, and hide thyself from them: thou shalt in any case bring them again unto thy brother." This made Samuel "sadly reflect that I had not been so thoroughly tender of my daughter, nor so effectually careful of her defense and preservation as I should have been." He prayed that "the good Lord pity and pardon and help for the future as to those God has still left me."

The next day it was Sam Jr.'s turn to recite from the Bible. The youth elected to read the Gospel of Matthew in Latin. Listening to the seventh verse—in English, "If ye had known what this meaneth, I will have mercy and not sacrifice, ye would not have condemned the guiltless"—Samuel was overcome with remorse. He had "condemned the guiltless." He observed that this verse "did awfully bring to mind the Salem tragedy," which he had been going over and over in his mind.

On December 25, before burying Sarah, the family gathered for prayers. Eight-year-old Joseph read aloud Ecclesiastes 3: "To every thing there is a season, and a time to every purpose under the heaven...." Betty, now nearly fifteen, recited the twenty-second chapter of the book of Revelation, which begins, "And he showed me a pure river of water of life, clear as crystal, proceeding out of the throne of God and of the Lamb." Samuel asked Hannah Jr. and Sam Jr. each to read a psalm. He spoke to each child in turn, "to our mutual comfort I hope." He asked four boys who were sons of his friends to "bear my little daughter to the tomb."

After the funeral the Sewalls and many other mourners returned to the mansion for the usual meal. Samuel went back alone to the tomb to see "in what order things were set." The tomb, which extended several steps below ground, was lined with bricks and covered with slabs of brown stone. No one was present but a gravedigger, who adjusted some coffins at Samuel's request.

Samuel stood in the tomb, meditating on death. He was "entertained with a view of, and convers[ation] with, the coffins of my dead Father Hull, Mother Hull, Cousin [Daniel] Quincy, and my six children"—Johnny, Hullie, Henry, Stephen, Judith, and the unnamed stillborn. The coffins were stacked so "the little posthumous" Sarah lay two tiers above her grandfather Hull. "My mother [Judith Hull] lies on a lower bench at the end, with [her] head to her husband's head. And I ordered little Sarah to be set on her grandmother's feet."

Samuel found this experience of communion with his dead relatives "an awful yet pleasing treat." The tomb contained so many people he loved that it seemed to him a second home. "The Lord knows who shall be brought hither next," he thought, aware that he might be next. He was already comfortable here and sometimes felt so heavy on account of his sin that he might already be dead.

A few hours later, at his mansion, Samuel arranged to send mourning rings as gifts to the Reverend Increase Mather, who did not attend the funeral because of his gout, Sarah's doctor, Governor Phips, and the Reverend Willard. His minister, Samuel noted, had "prayed with us the night before" but chose not to attend the funeral. In his private meditations, the grieving father noted, "God helped me to pray more than ordinarily, that He would make up our loss in the burial of our little daughter and other children, and that would give us a child to serve Him, pleading with Him as the institutor of marriage and the author of every good work."

A week after the funeral, on January 1, 1697, Samuel and Hannah were again not included in the Reverend Willard's prayer meeting at his home. "We had no invitation to be there as is usual," Samuel observed ruefully. This was the second time the minister had excluded him, both times immediately following the death of a child.

Willard did not record his reasons for excluding the Sewalls and avoiding their baby's funeral, but his sermons offer clues. Two years earlier at the Third Church, Willard had preached that "there is a great noise and cry that some make, the Devil, the Devil, he hath

tempted me, he was too sly and hard for me, and a great deal of anger
seems to be vented upon him."

At the Town House on September 16, 1696, at a special prayer service for government officials, "Mr. Willard preached" and then "spoke
smartly at last about the Salem witchcrafts," Samuel noted in his diary.
The minister regretted "that no order had suffered to come forth by
[public] authority to ask God's pardon" for the witch hunt.

Looking back on the events of the summer of 1692, the Reverend
Willard believed that the Devil's true role was to delude the accusers,
"as a fruit of the[ir] native corruptions," rather than to influence those
condemned and killed. In 1694 Willard had warned his congregation,
which included Samuel Sewall, "The Devil shall bear his own blame,
and God will punish him for all the malicious practices which he useth
against his people. But *you* must bear your *own* blame, which is due *you*
for yielding to the temptation." The Devil can only "keep us from a
due sense of and sorrow for our own folly which we have acted in it,
and thereby hinder our true and soaking repentance."

15

THE BLAME AND SHAME OF IT

On the morning of Thursday, January 14, 1697, as the town crier beat the drum announcing the gathering of saints, thousands of Bostonians made their way through ice and snow to the town's three churches for the obligatory day of fasting and prayer. At the Third Church the Sewalls walked to their benches at the front. Samuel, now forty-four, and his sons, ages eighteen and eight, sat to the left of the aisle, across from his wife, now thirty-eight, in her mourning clothes, and three daughters, ages sixteen, fifteen, and five.

The congregation sang a psalm as the Reverend Samuel Willard strode up the center aisle toward the side of the church where the pulpit was. As the fifty-six-year-old minister passed Samuel Sewall, the judge reached out his hand to him. Willard paused just long enough to receive the note in Sewall's hand, continued the few steps to his pulpit, and opened the service with a prayer to acknowledge the fast day. Slightly later he took up the paper Sewall had given him and looked at Samuel, who rose to his feet. Everyone else remained seated. In the silence, before hundreds of other saints, Samuel Sewall bowed his head.

"Samuel Sewall," the minister began, addressing the unusually large congregation, "sensible that as to the guilt contracted upon the opening of the late Commission of Oyer and Terminer at Salem, to which the order for this day relates ..."

All eyes were on Samuel. The minister continued, "He is, upon many accounts, more concerned than any that he knows of," a reference to the other Salem witch judges and perhaps some ministers and other leading men. "And he desires to take the blame and shame of it, asking pardon of men, and especially desiring prayers that God, who has an unlimited authority, would pardon that sin and all other of his sins, personal and relative."

Finally, Willard prayed that "God, according to his infinite benignity and sovereignty, not visit the sin of [Samuel Sewall] upon himself or any of his, nor upon the land, but that He would powerfully defend him against all temptations to sin, for the future, and vouchsafe him the efficacious, saving conduct of his word and spirit."

It was done. Samuel bowed deeply before sitting down on his bench. His repentance had begun. He hoped now that the Lord might help him to see, as Paul wrote in opening his letter to the Ephesians, "with the eyes of the heart."

Following the service he walked home in the snow with his family. That afternoon the Sewalls read Scripture and prayed together, as always. He excused himself to write in his diary. He had recorded his thoughts about the witchcraft court sparingly until now because the subject seemed so confusing and shadowy. Now, though, he felt utter clarity as to his behavior on that court. He inscribed clearly, once again, the text that he had handed to Willard.

Samuel Sewall, sensible of the reiterated strokes of God upon himself and family; and being sensible, that as to the guilt contracted upon the opening of the late commission of Oyer and Terminer at Salem (to which the order for this day relates) he is, upon many accounts, more concerned than any that he knows of, desires to take the blame and shame of it, asking pardon of men, and especially desiring prayers that God, who has an unlimited authority, would pardon that sin and all other his sins, personal and relative, and according to his infinite benignity and sovereignty, not visit the sin of him, or of any other, upon himself or any of his, nor upon the Land. But that He would powerfully defend him against all temptations to sin, for the future; and vouchsafe him the efficacious, saving conduct of his word and spirit.

He experienced spiritual relief within a week. On the night of January 26, while the new court met at Charlestown, he lodged in the Charlestown house of Anne Tyng Shepard. Mistress Shepard mentioned to Samuel that John Harvard had built and lived in her house. John Harvard, a new immigrant to Boston in 1636, had died a year later in his thirties, leaving his library and half his estate to the proposed colonial college. The board of overseers of the new college named it after him in acknowledgment of his bequest.

That night in bed in John Harvard's house, Samuel lay awake for hours. He was struck by "how long ago God made provision for my comfortable lodging this night, seeing this is Mr. Harvard's house." This led him to meditate on heaven, "the house not made with hands, which God for many thousands of years has stored with the richest furniture: saints that are from time to time placed there." It occurred to Samuel that he might now "have some hopes of being entertained in this magnificent, convenient palace, every way fitted and furnished." He felt the consolation of a new intimacy with Christ.

Around this time, according to Samuel's great-great-great-great-granddaughter, my late great-aunt Charlotte May Wilson, Samuel began wearing a hair shirt. Christian ascetics have long used the hair shirt for bodily mortification and to resist temptations of the flesh. Saint Jerome in the fourth century described rich laymen wearing hair shirts beneath their ornate robes to offset their luxuries and to remind them of Christ. Early Benedictine monks and later members of other religious orders routinely used the hair shirt, although now only the Carthusian and Carmelite orders wear it by rule.

The nineteenth-century historian James Savage used a slightly different term to describe Samuel's garment. In *A Genealogical Dictionary of the First Settlers of New England, Before 1692*, Savage wrote that the "amiable Sewall ... most bitterly repented in public sackcloth." Sackcloth is a biblical symbol of penance. Puritans sometimes wore sackcloth externally during church services to symbolize penitence. But Samuel's use of sackcloth as an undergarment—as described by my Aunt Charlotte, whose information was passed down within the family—makes it sound like the hair shirt worn next to the skin as an instrument of self-mortification, usually associated with Catholicism.

In fact, the two terms *sackcloth* and *hair shirt* derive from a single Latin word, *cilicium*. Moreover, according to the *Catholic Dictionary*, the two are "probably the same thing." Both hark back to the garment of camel hair that John the Baptist wore. The word *cilicium*, from the Roman province of Cilicia in Asia Minor, refers to a rough shirt or girdle of goat hair worn for penance and mortification. The Latin *cilicium* appears in the Vulgate version of Psalm 34:13, "*Ego autem, cum mihi molesti essent, induebar cilicio.*" This word was translated as "haircloth" in the Catholic Douay Bible and as "sackcloth" in the authorized Anglican Bible and Book of Common Prayer. That difference explains the misconception of a denominational divide.

In donning a hair shirt, Samuel abandoned the prudence that had served him well for more than forty years. He determined to abandon himself to Christ. "Lord," he had prayed just before the recent fast day, "take away my filthy garments, and give me change of raiment." This image arises from a passage in the book of Zechariah (3:1–5) in which the high priest Joshua, "clothed in filthy garments," stands before the angel of the Lord, alongside Satan. The Lord rebukes Satan and calls Joshua "a brand plucked out of the fire." The angel says, "Take away the filthy garments from him." God says to Joshua, "Behold, I have caused thine iniquity to pass from thee, and I will clothe thee with change of raiment." And "so they set a fair mitre upon his head, and clothed him with garments. And the angel of the Lord stood by."

The same Scripture would come to mind years later when Samuel was called to speak at the May 5, 1713, inauguration of the new Town House. The old Town House was destroyed in the Great Fire of 1711. Its replacement, in which Samuel spoke, still stands today, as Boston's Old State House. Before all the other leaders of the province, Samuel prayed "that God would take away our filthy garments, and clothe us with change of raiment."

The rising of the new Town House from the ruins of the old reminded him of his own sin and repentance. "The former decayed building is consumed, and a better [one] built," he said. He prayed "that our former sins may be buried in the ruins and rubbish of the

former house, and not be suffered to follow us into this." Pointing to a
framed mirror on the wall, he said, "Let this large, transparent, costly
glass serve to oblige the attorneys always to set things in a true
light.... Let them remember they are to advise the court as well as
plead for their clients. The oaths that prescribe our duty run all upon
truth; God is truth. Let Him communicate to us of His light and truth;
let the jurors and witnesses swear in truth, in judgment, and in righteousness. If we thus improve this house,... the days of this people
shall be as the days of a tree, and they shall long enjoy the work of
their hands." As the fire showed, "our God is a consuming fire, but it
[the people] hath repented Him of the evil. And since He had declared
that He takes delight in them that hope in his mercy, we firmly believe
that He will be a dwelling place to us throughout all generations."

The theme of changing raiment would reappear even later, when he
thought he might be dying. In April 1724, at seventy-two, suffering
from fever and a sore leg, he prayed privately, "God, may I be clothed
up before unclothed."

For a devout Puritan to adopt a traditionally Catholic tool of self-
mortification seems surprising given the Puritans' suspicion of Rome
and the history of mistrust between American Protestants and Catholics. Yet scholars have found remarkable links between seventeenth-
century Puritan (Reformation) and Catholic (Counter-Reformation)
devotional practices. The religious historian Terence Cave called it "le-
gitimate ... to speak of a Protestant devotional tradition running parallel to the Catholic one and encouraging private prayer and meditation
[with] a great deal of common ground between the two traditions." In
*The Practice of Piety: Puritan Devotional Disciplines in Seventeenth-Century
New England*, the scholar Charles Hambrick-Stowe concluded that "Puritans knew and used classic Catholic devotional works.... To a large
extent the Puritan devotional writing that blossomed in the early seventeenth century was modeled on earlier Roman Catholic devotional literature.... Puritans did engage in devotional exercises quite similar to
those of their Catholic forebears, contemporaries, and adversaries."

In the seventeenth century, strikingly, both Puritans and Catholics
looked back to the fourth-century writings of Augustine of Hippo.
Hambrick-Stowe explained, "A far broader stream than the Puritan
or even the Reformed movement issued from the meditations and

mystical tradition of [Augustine's] *Confessions*.... Augustine had Catholic and non-Puritan Church of England heirs as well," including the meditative poets John Donne and George Herbert. "The tradition was passed to all parties in the seventeenth century through the writings of medieval Catholic mystics, which ... were increasingly available in England. Saint Teresa of Avila ... acknowledged her debt to Augustine in a passage that a Puritan could easily have penned: 'Scarcely had I begun to read the *Confessions* of Saint Augustine than I seemed to have discovered myself [and my] frivolous and dissipated life....'"

Just as Saint Teresa can seem Puritan, Cotton Mather can seem Catholic. He periodically fasted and denied himself sleep, like medieval mystics. He reported speaking with angels while praying. At least once the Reverend Mather imaginatively experienced the crucifixion of Christ. "There was a kind of voluptuousness in Cotton Mather's immersion in denial, sacrifice, and finally as an old man, in martyrdom," his biographer Robert Middlekauff wrote. He "increasingly found fulfillment in ... the imitation of Christ." Mather admonished his congregation to meditate on their own deaths, as a spiritual exercise and to avoid pride. The minister often prostrated himself to meditate, a prayer position also recommended by Saint Ignatius of Loyola, a leader of the Catholic Counter-Reformation.

Saint Ignatius, who was born in Catholic Spain in 1491, founded the Society of Jesus, which sent Jesuit missionaries around the globe. Ignatian spirituality presumes an ongoing global combat between the forces of good led by Christ, and the forces of evil led by Satan—not unlike the Puritan worldview. Saint Ignatius's most influential work, *Spiritual Exercises*, presents a system of daily prayer and meditation aimed at achieving utter devotion to God and a profound indifference to this world. Jesuits, like Puritans, spread their message through small prayer groups. Their shared goal was global spiritual reformation. At the same time that Samuel was funding the Indian Bible and "gospelizing" the native people of Cape Cod, Martha's Vineyard, and Maine, Jesuits were sending prayer groups from Europe to such distant spots as Mexico in the New World and Macau on China's southern coast.

Like the Society of Jesus, Puritanism "was from the start a devotional movement, and traditional practices such as meditation and prayer were integral to its formation and persistence," Charles Hambrick-Stowe wrote. "Most important was the use of the imagination and the senses in the exercise known as composition of place"—imagining oneself physically present at moments in Christ's life—which is "the usual point of departure in Catholic meditation." Hambrick-Stowe noted the strong influence on seventeenth-century Puritanism of Catholic methods of prayer and meditation, including Jesuit practices, Saint Teresa's *Interior Castle*, and Saint Francis de Sales's *Introduction to the Devout Life*. "All of them, and the lesser works they generated, were part of the 'Augustinian strain of piety' within Puritanism.... Puritan devotion, like that practiced by Roman Catholics and by other non-Puritans in England, depended upon the use of the imagination for putting oneself into the biblical drama of redemption."

Samuel Sewall's repentance was thus a turning back to the Middle Ages, to the Scholastics, and to the early Christian church. In fact, even before this penitential period of his life Samuel had not looked forward. He was not a man of the Enlightenment, nor would he ever be. There is no evidence that he ever read the works of René Descartes, who died in 1650, before Samuel was born, or even the English thinkers John Locke (1632–1704), Joseph Addison (1672–1719), or Sir Isaac Newton (1642–1727). Sewall's apparent lack of curiosity about Newton is noteworthy because Leonard Hoar, the Harvard president who was close to Samuel's family, was friendly with both Newton and Sir Robert Boyle, another English Enlightenment figure. As for Samuel, he displayed irritation at the burgeoning sciences. In December 1714, after Cotton Mather remarked in a sermon that "the sun is in the center of our system," Samuel noted privately, "I think it inconvenient to assert such problems." The historian M. Halsey Thomas wrote that the Copernican system "was well established at Harvard a decade before Sewall entered" the college. Yet Samuel looked the other way, back to the Ptolemaic, geocentric past. He chose to write and sometimes speak in Latin. So it was natural for him, after acknowledging his guilt in the witch trials, to return to the roots of his faith. As much as possible he wished to live as Christ and his early followers had lived.

True repentance consists of more than a single act, as Samuel was aware. Unlike election, which is momentary, repentance is a long process, entailing many steps. These include contrition, confession, compensation to those wronged, and finally a change of heart.

To accomplish this complex process of repentance, Samuel threw himself with new intensity into the book of Revelation. He roamed through other texts too, including the Old Testament, books of world history, and the poems of George Herbert. He struggled to answer the questions: When will Christ reappear on the earth? Where does America fit in the drama of history? What region will Christ choose for his next coming?

The physical location of Christ's Second Coming held special meaning for Samuel. As an English Puritan he was raised on the notion that Jesus would return to Europe, which to a European was the center of the world. Rome was thought to be a possible setting for Christ's return. But to a Puritan Rome would show an untenable preference for the Roman Catholic Church. Some Puritan ministers proposed Jerusalem. Others mentioned France. Fifteen years earlier Cotton Mather dared to wonder if America might be "part" of the New Jerusalem. He and Samuel had discussed this, after which Samuel wrote to ask him, "Please, when you can spare the time, give me your reasons why the heart of America may not be the seat of the New Jerusalem?"

This was a subject worth pondering. On February 24, 1686, at Samuel's neighborhood prayer group, the Reverend Willard had led a discussion of the first chapter of the Acts of the Apostles, which describes the days immediately after the resurrection of Jesus. The apostles ask Jesus, "Wilt thou at this time restore again the kingdom to Israel?"

Jesus replies, "It is not for you to know the times or the seasons, which the Father hath put in his own power. But ye shall receive power, after … the Holy Ghost is come upon you; and ye shall be witnesses unto me both in Jerusalem … and unto the uttermost part of the earth."

Like Jesus's apostles, Samuel and his peers still wondered, When will the Second Coming occur? As part of his repentance, Samuel spent hours probing this question in his private chamber on the second floor of his mansion. During the summer after his public acceptance of blame he began to write a long essay, which the historian

Perry Miller later called a "prose poem." This was Sewall's "attempt, amid a staggering array of pedantry, to calculate the place of America in the future drama of history," Miller added. "Dedicated to deciphering the often baffling history of the Covenant of Grace, Sewall occupied his leisure with an examination of Biblical prophesies."

While writing this work, which in published form ran to more than sixty pages of English prose punctuated by occasional Latin paragraphs, Samuel tried to place himself outside time and place, in the realm of the divine. "Not to begin to be, and so not to be limited by the concernments of time and place, is the prerogative of God alone," he wrote. He tried to connect the past with the future. At the beginning of "New England, and Boston of the Massachusetts,... the families and churches which first ventured to follow Christ through the Atlantic ocean, into a strange land,... were so religious, their end so holy, their self-denial in pursuing of it so extraordinary, that I can't but hope that the plantation ... will not be of one or two or three centuries only, but very long lasting."

His mind roved back to his youth in Newbury, when his "ever honored master, the late Reverend, learned, and holy Mr. Thomas Parker," taught him that the end of the world was at hand. In the book of Revelation the pouring out of seven vials signals the apocalypse. Parker had said, "I am so far from thinking that no vial is yet poured forth, that I am apt to conclude that no less than five angels have already poured out their vials," meaning that only two vials remained to be poured.

Fifty years later, in Boston in 1697, Parker's former student observed that Christianity invigorated the world's "four quarters": Asia, Africa, Europe, and America. He considered the possibility that the New Jerusalem might be in Asia or Spanish North America. "Why may not [America] be the place of New Jerusalem?" he wondered again.

Mexico struck him as a likely locale. Some years later, after hearing Increase Mather refer in a sermon to the bright morning star as "a sign in the heaven," Samuel was amazed to observe a comet pass over his house. It was "a large cometical blaze, something fine and dim, pointing from the westward, a little below Orion," the dominant constellation in New England's night sky. Samuel used a ship's globe to show a sea captain, Timothy Clark, how the comet's trajectory pointed to Mexico. "I have long prayed for Mexico," he said, "that God would open the Mexican fountain." Mexico City was far more populous than any other town in North America. In 1700 Mexico City had more than 100,000 residents, roughly the number of people in all of New England.

There were practical reasons to make America the New Jerusalem, Samuel observed. From the perspective of someone in England, "the situation of Jerusalem [in the Middle East] is not so central.... A voyage may be made from London to Mexico in as little time as from London to Jerusalem. In that respect, if the New World should be made the seat of the New Jerusalem, if the city of the Great King should be set on the Northern side of it, Englishmen would meet with no inconvenience thereby, and they would find this convenience, that they might visit the citizens of New Jerusalem and their countrymen all under one."

As he was trained at Harvard, he took the opposite view from the one he wished to propound. "What concernment hath America in these things?" he asked rhetorically. "America is not any part of the Apocalyptical stage. The promise of preaching the Gospel to the whole world is to be understood of the Roman Empire only," which "contained about a third part of the old World, and this triental [third] only was to be concerned with the Apocalypse." The standard view was, "The prophesies of the Revelation extend ... not to the West Indians, not Tartarians, nor Chinese, nor East Indians."

He turned a corner with a biblical metaphor: "But what shall we say if the stone which these builders have refused should be made the head of the corner?" The Acts of the Apostles 4:11 describes Jesus Christ as "the stone which was set at nought of you builders, which is become the head of the corner." In other words, America, which like Jesus Christ was at first rejected, might become the cornerstone of the new kingdom of God on earth. Samuel justified his foray by saying, "The word of God is not bound."

By the end of that summer following his public confession, Sewall sensed that his pastor no longer ostracized him. Relieved, he invited Willard's family to attend a picnic he hosted on Hog Island on October 1. He arranged for boats to transport his own five children, who now ranged in age from nineteen to six, and his twenty-three-year-old niece, Jane Tappan, Jeremy Belcher's three sons, who were ages eighteen to twenty-eight, and four children and one nephew (eleven-year-old Edward Tyng) of the Willards. Hannah Sewall stayed home "through indisposition," but Samuel "prevailed with Mr. Willard to go" too.

The party had "a very comfortable passage thither." On the island they snacked on "butter, honey, curds," and cream. Their dinner consisted of "very good roast lamb, turkey, fowls, [and] apple pie." Hannah had sent bottles of "spirits" to drink. Carelessly, someone left a glass of spirits on a joint-stool. Simon Willard, who was twenty-one, inadvertently knocked the glass to the ground, breaking it "all to shivers."

"'Tis a lively emblem of our fragility and mortality," Samuel remarked to his pastor. Willard understood exactly. For these Puritans, the historian David Hall noted, "the unexpected crash of a glass to the floor was like the crash of God's anger breaking in upon the flow of time." Time was not regular for them because time belonged to God. "Though prophecy unfolded, though the clock ticked away the hours by an unvarying beat, though the seven days of Genesis were stamped immutably upon the calendar, the will of God stood over and above any structures.... All existence was contingent, all forms of time suspended, on his will." As Samuel himself would say two years later, when a downpour of rain destroyed orchards and cedars throughout his neighborhood, "How suddenly and with surprise can God destroy!"

Before departing Hog Island Samuel led the group in singing Psalm 121, which he considered appropriate to the setting.

Psalm 121

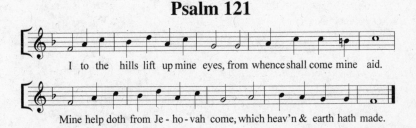

I to the hills lift up mine eyes, from whence shall come mine aid.

Mine help doth from Je-ho-vah come, which heav'n & earth hath made.

York Tune

I to the hills lift up mine eyes,
  from whence shall come mine aid.
2 Mine help doth from Jehovah come,
  which heav'n & earth hath made.

3 Hee will not let thy foot be mov'd,
  nor slumber: that thee keeps.
4 Loe hee that keepeth Israell,
  hee slumbreth not, nor sleeps.

5 The Lord thy keeper is, the Lord
  on thy right hand the shade.
6 The Sun by day, nor Moone by night,
  shall thee by stroke *invade.*

7 The Lord will keep thee from all ill:
  thy soule hee keeps alway,
8 Thy going out, & thy income,
  The Lord keeps now & aye.

That autumn Samuel continued to work on his prose poem. Again and again he returned to the same questions: What place will Jesus Christ choose for his New Heaven? Will the inhabitants be Protestant or Catholic? Where on earth will the apocalypse begin?

16

WISDOM AND REVELATION

A salt marsh alongside the mouth of the Merrimac River in north-eastern Massachusetts overlooks the landscape of Samuel's musings on the book of Revelation, as outlined in his 1697 essay, *Phaenomena quaedam Apocalyptica ad Aspectum Novi Orbis Configurata*, or, as he translated his own Latin, "Some few lines towards a description of the New Heaven, as it makes to those who stand upon the New Earth." In this coastal region to which he had arrived as a boy of nine, the repentant judge envisioned the future Second Coming of Jesus Christ.

How many times had Samuel set out from here by boat? He could no longer say. This was the usual point of departure to Plum Island, a slender barrier island dotted with scrub pines and junipers running parallel to the coast for nearly nine miles. He knew Plum Island almost as well as Newbury. A few people inhabited it, countless cattle grazed there, and farmers stacked salt-marsh hay on the island. Plum Island offered protection to Newbury by keeping the rough, cold Atlantic Ocean at bay, literally, and making the inland waters warm, shallow, and calm.

As a boy Samuel often rowed his dory south from here along Plum Island River, the narrow estuary between Newbury and Plum Island. Looking all around he could see only water, sky, and lime green marsh grass. Now and then a snowy egret dug for food in the mud. Hardly two miles to the south, near the mouth of the Parker River, Plum Island Sound opened up and spread out. The sound, an oval body of water between Plum Island and the mainland with a depth of only six to eight feet, teemed with striped bass, cod, haddock, herring, flounder, mackerel, and sturgeon. Plum Island Sound was roughly the center of the Great Marsh, a vast wetland area extending about seventeen miles along the northern Massachusetts coast from the towns of Salisbury to Gloucester. It was here, Samuel prophesied, that Christ would return to earth.

"As long as Plum Island shall faithfully keep the commanded post," he wrote in the magnificent part of *Phaenomena quaedam Apocalyptica*

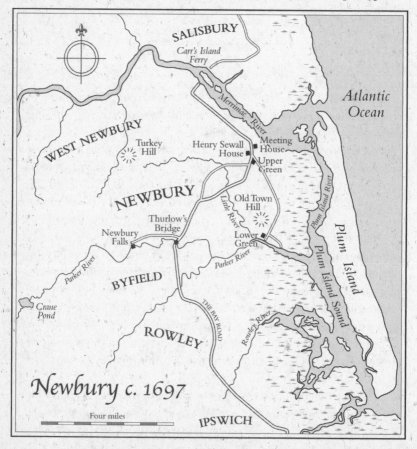

that is often excerpted in collections of colonial American literature and that foreshadows much later pastoral odes such as "To Autumn," by John Keats.

As long as Plum Island shall faithfully keep the commanded post; Notwithstanding all the hectoring words, and hard blows of the proud and boisterous ocean; as long as any salmon, or sturgeon shall swim in the streams of Merrimac, or any perch, or pickerel, in Crane Pond; as long as the sea-fowl shall know the time of their coming, and not neglect seasonably to visit the places of their acquaintance; as long as any cattle shall be fed with the grass growing in the meadows, which do humbly bow themselves down before Turkey Hill; as long as any sheep shall walk upon Old Town Hill, and shall from thence pleasantly look down upon the River Parker, and the fruitful marshes lying beneath; as long as any free and harmless doves shall find a white oak, or other tree within the township, to perch, or feed, or build a careless nest upon, and shall voluntarily present themselves to perform the office of gleaners after barley harvest; as long as nature shall not grow old and dote, but shall constantly remember to give the rows of Indian corn their education, by pairs: So long shall Christians be born there; and being first made meet [fitting], shall from thence be translated, to be made partakers of the inheritance of the saints in light.

Samuel perceived the beauty of this landscape as evidence of its spiritual truth. In his view God granted this gorgeous New Israel to his people, the "saints in light," so they might worship him. "Now," he went on, "seeing the inhabitants of Newbury, and of New England, upon the due observance of their tenure, may expect that their rich and gracious Lord will continue and confirm them in the possession of these invaluable privileges: *Let us have grace, whereby we may serve God acceptably with reverence and godly fear, for our God is a consuming fire.* Heb. 12:28–29." After much consideration, Samuel now believed that Christ would choose America, and more specifically Plum Island on Boston's North Shore, as the location of his kingdom of God on earth.

Literary scholars point to the Plum Island passage, as it is known, in *Phaenomena quaedam Apocalyptica* as the beginning of American literature as such—conscious of itself as American rather than European and with a positive stance toward the land. (The text of *Phaenomena quaedam Apocalyptica* begins on page 289.) Prior to *Phaenomena quaedam Apocalyptica*, the historian Perry Miller wrote, English-American writers portrayed America as a frightening, obscure, threatening "wilderness" full of beasts and French and Indian terrorists. In Samuel's new vision the wilderness is beautiful and godly, a place where Jesus Christ might and would reside.

"It is not too much to say that this cry of the heart signalizes a point at which the English Puritan had, hardly with conscious knowledge, become an American, rooted in the American soil," Miller added. "Suddenly reminded of Plum Island,... where he himself had played as a boy," Sewall was "carried away into this prose poem on the earthly, the sensuous, delicacies of the land [that] he, good Puritan as he resolutely was, had learned to love with a fervor as passionate as that which he held in reserve for the heavenly kingdom." In this essay Sewall "yielded—as no Puritan could have contrived to do without subsuming his love under a millennial destination—to that delight in the American prospect which for over half a century had been perversely nourished under the canopy of his jeremiads."

Sewall's newfound feeling—of love for the land itself—reappears throughout American literature. "The land was ours before we were the land's," the poet Robert Frost wrote in "The Gift Outright." Frost's poem was itself an echo of the Reverend John Cotton's 1630 argument that "the land belonged to them [English Puritans] before they belonged to the land," according to the scholar Sacvan Bercovitch. Claiming the land by charter or deed did not make it thereby one's true home. Bercovitch observed that *Phaenomena quaedam Apocalyptica* puts Sewall in a select group of New England writers who "successfully pierced natural images to reveal supernatural truths," a group that includes Jonathan Edwards, Ralph Waldo Emerson, and Henry David Thoreau. David Lovejoy, another scholar, said Sewall's essay marked the moment when English settlers "took [America] into themselves." This distinguishes Sewall from the early New England poet Anne Bradstreet, who, according to Perry Miller, "wrote only of English streams and English birds." With *Phaenomena quaedam Apocalyptica*, Miller added, "Sewall seems to have put his spiritual crisis behind him, for he 'found salvation in surrender' to the land and its people."

Sewall's concept of America was new in another way. Rather than linking the land's spiritual significance to the arrival of Christian Europeans, he considered America's divinity inborn, thus present before those settlers arrived. For Sewall, America's people included not only Puritans and other new arrivals but also its native tribes. Indians became central to his argument about America's role in the apocalypse. Decades before, the Reverend John Eliot had conjectured that American Indians were not savages, as so many English thought, but a holy people—members of one of the ten lost tribes of Israel. Many Indians are "true believers," Sewall added in his essay on Revelation. "Mr. Eliot was wont to say the New English churches are a preface to the New Heavens.... If Mr. Eliot's opinion prove true—that the aboriginal natives of America are of Jacob's posterity, part of the long since captivated ten tribes, and that their brethren the Jews shall come unto them—the dispute will quickly be at an end."

The dispute was whether Native Americans might, as a lost tribe of Israel, be another sign of Revelation. Samuel argued, "It is no heresy to say [that] Christ means the ten tribes [in] John 10:16." This passage comes immediately after Christ says, "I lay down my life for the sheep." He goes on, "And other sheep I have, which are not of this fold: them also I must bring, and they shall hear my voice; and there shall be one fold, [and] one shepherd." Proceeding logically, Samuel wrote, "If it be no heresy to say, the Ten Tribes are the sheep, why should it be accounted heresy to say, America is the distinct fold there implied? For Christ doth not affirm that there shall be one fold, but there shall be ONE FLOCK, ONE SHEPHERD!"

This argument suggested kinship between Native Americans and New England Puritans, who saw themselves as God's covenanted people. To buttress the argument that the natives and the settlers were equal in God's eyes, Samuel quoted a poem by the early Massachusetts divine Roger Williams. In 1636 the General Court had banished Williams from Massachusetts for his "dangerous" refusal to support the forced conversion and killing of Indians in the name of Christ. The Reverend Williams wrote:

Boast not, proud English, of thy birth and blood.
Thy brother Indian is by birth as good.
Make sure thy Second Birth, else thou shalt see
Heaven ope' to Indians wild, but shut to thee.

Samuel admonished his fellow Englishmen to treat Indians better. "Instead of being branded for slaves with hot irons in the face, and arms, and driven by scores in mortal chains," Indians should "wear the name of God in their foreheads, and ... [be] delivered unto the glorious liberty of the children of God."

Describing the Indians as a lost tribe of Israel led Samuel back to the Jews, whose conversion to Christianity he and his peers considered another hopeful sign. "Now it is manifest to all that very considerable numbers of Jews are seated in the New World"—in Barbados, Jamaica, Port Royal, Suriname, and Curaçao. He anticipated that "these Jews will be converted before any great numbers of the Indians." Some Catholics too were turning Protestant, he noted. After castigating Spanish colonists for their cruelty to Native Americans, he concluded, "What [evangelism] is done or prepared by Papists among Indians is not to be despised, but improved by Protestants. There may be some sincere laborers and converts among them...." Roaming over European history, he referred to Montezuma, Columbus, Pope Alexander VI ("that horrible monster" the second Borgia pope), Emperor Charles V, Calvin, and the English Puritan theologians Joseph Mede and William Twisse. His aim was to prove that America could be the New Jerusalem and its native people could be holy.

"Captain John Smith, in his History published *anno* 1624, affirms that he found New England well inhabited with a goodly, strong and well-proportioned people," the native tribes. The newcomers from England "need not fear subsisting where ash, chestnut, hazel, oak and walnut do naturally and plentifully grow." Samuel cited his own teacher, the Reverend Parker, stating that "the passengers [from England] came over upon good grounds, and that God would multiply them as He did the children of Israel. And as Mr. Nicholas Noyes, who was an auditor [to this] and is yet living, lately informed me, Mr. Parker was at this time (1634) principally concerned in beginning Newbury...."

This complex vision—of Captain John Smith, "Mr. Parker," the Reverend Noyes, godly Indians, converted Jews, and even missionary Catholics—finally crystallized for Samuel in the body of an old Englishwoman whom he had known since he was a child. Mary Brown Godfrey, who was the first English baby born in Newbury after its settlement in 1635, was "yet alive, and is become the mother and grandmother of many children. And so many have been born after her in the town that they make two assemblies [meetinghouses], wherein God is solemnly worshiped every Sabbath day." Decades later, in a second printing of this essay, Samuel would add a note on Godfrey: "She died April 14, 1716, in the 82 year of her age, having obtained a good repose as maid, and wife, and widow; and leaving a numerous posterity." To him the physical presence of old Goodwife Godfrey and her large family was another sign, in addition to the magnificent landscape, of God's affection for New England.

In its praise of the natural world, Samuel's *Phaenomena quaedam Apocalyptica* is now considered a harbinger of the environmental movement. "Sewall's aesthetic response ... to the beauty of regular natural cycles and processes," the literary scholar Timothy Sweet observed, "draws forth a hope of their continuance and of the covenanted community's 'privilege[d]' relation to them. The interplay of social ecology and apocalypse thus links Sewall to later apocalyptic writers such as George Perkins Marsh and Rachel Carson."

In the same vein many years later Samuel would compose a broadside poem, "On the Drying up of that Ancient River, the River Merrimac," in which he would again connect "an image of environmental degradation with an apocalyptic text," Timothy Sweet noted. This "bagatelle," which Samuel published in January 1720, was prompted by a boundary dispute between New Hampshire and Massachusetts over the upper portion of the river. New Hampshire had won the dispute and proceeded to dam the river at its northern end, altering and reducing its flow to the south. As a boy Samuel had spent many happy hours on the Merrimac River, which ran less than a mile from his parents' house. In his poem the river is an idealized embodiment of the Christian heaven, as Plum Island was in *Phaenomena quaedam Apocalyptica*.

Long did Euphrates make us glad,
Such pleasant, steady course he had:
Fight white, fight chestnut, all was one,
In peace profound our river run
From his remote and lofty head,
Until he with the ocean wed....
Dutiful salmon, once a year,
Still visited their parent dear:
And royal sturgeon saw it good
To sport in the renowned flood.
All sorts of geese, and ducks, and teal,
In their allotments fared well.
Many a moose, and thirsty deer
Drank to full satisfaction here.
The fox, the wolf, the angry bear,
Of drink were not denied their share....
At length, an ambushment was laid
Near Powwow Hill, when none afraid;
And unawares, at one hug sup,
Hydropic Hampshire drunk it up!
Look to thyself! Wachusett Hill;
And bold Monadnock, fear some ill!
Envied earth knows no certain bound;
In Heaven alone, content is found.

Powwow Hill, near where New Hampshire "ambushed" the river, was (and is) at 332 feet the highest elevation in Essex County. Its summit, on the northern side of the Merrimac River in the town of Amesbury, Massachusetts, just north of Newbury, affords views of coastal Cape Ann, New Hampshire's White Mountains, and Mount Agamenticus in Maine. The hill and adjacent Powwow River, which was created by the damming of the Merrimac, were named for the Indian powwows once held there.

One of Samuel's goals in writing *Phaenomena quaedam Apocalyptica*, beyond locating the Second Coming, was to place Native Americans in God's scheme. Preaching the gospel to the Indians was essential for two reasons. First, they were descendants of Israel. Second, their conversion, like the conversion of the Jews and other Christians, would usher in the end of the world. Samuel had worried over this for years. He had funded a meetinghouse on Cape Cod and given money and time to the Society for the Preservation of the Gospel in New England. At the age of seventy-five he would send ten shillings per Sabbath to an Englishman named John Cleverly to preach to Indians at Arrowsic Island on the Kennebec River in Maine. In middle age, when he and Hannah had a house full of children, they hosted several gifted Indian boys, who lived with the Sewalls while preparing for Harvard. Samuel delivered the youths to college and paid for their educations.

In July 1714 he mourned the death of one of these teenagers, who was "an acute grammarian" and "an extraordinary Latin poet," according to the Reverend Benjamin Wadsworth, who later became Harvard's president. The youth, Benjamin Larnell of Taunton, had lived with the Sewalls for several years, during which he graduated from Boston Latin and began studies at the college. At the Sewall mansion during his summer vacation in 1714, Larnell developed a high fever. Samuel called for doctors and ministers to tend to his young Indian boarder. Then he put up a note at the Third Church requesting the community's prayers. His son Joseph came to the house on July 20 to pray with Samuel, Hannah, and Hannah Jr. for the youth, who died the next day. The Sewalls held a funeral—"I and the president [of Harvard, John Leverett] went next [to] the corpse"—and buried Larnell in the New Burying Place. Samuel gave memorial scarves and gloves to the pallbearers. "God," he asked, "graciously grant a suitable improvement of the death of Benjamin Larnell, student of Harvard College."

Another Native American, John Neesnummin, knocked on the door of the Sewall mansion on the afternoon of January 30, 1708. Samuel had not previously met Neesnummin, a preacher to the Indians, who bore a letter of recommendation from the Reverend John Cotton III of Plymouth. Neesnummin was on his way to Natick and needed a place to stay overnight. Samuel suggested a nearby tavern run by Matthias Smith. The preacher departed for Smith's tavern. An hour or so later a boy brought Samuel a note saying that Smith would not host an Indian, even one who preached the gospel.

"I was fain to lodge [Neesnummin] in my study" that night, Samuel noted. The next day "I send him on his way towards Natick, with a letter to John Trowbridge to take him in…."

Twenty years later Samuel wrote plaintively to the Reverend Benjamin Wadsworth, who was then the president of Harvard College, "Why isn't New England a preface" to the New Jerusalem? "God will as readily tabernacle in our Indian wigwams as enter into them. What does signify the most sumptuous and magnificent buildings of Europe? I hold that He set his right foot in the New World and His left, in the Old."

In a similar vein he wrote in April 1706 to the Reverend John Higginson of Salem to ask "Whether it be not for the honor of God and of New England to reserve entire and untouched the Indian plantation of Natick [Massachusetts] and other lands under the same circumstance?" His hope was "that the lying of those lands unoccupied by the English may be a valid and lasting evidence that we desire the conversion and welfare of the natives, and would by no means extirpate them as the Spaniards did."

In 1721, after the court resolved to send an expedition to Maine to repell Indian uprisings, Samuel published a "Memorial to the Kennebeck Indians," a journal of his two-week journey in the summer of 1717 to several Maine islands, then inhabited mostly by Indians, that the Corporation for the Propagation of the Gospel claimed for evangelical work. Setting sail from Boston on August 1, 1717, Samuel's ship arrived in Casco Bay (now Portland, Maine) three days later. He stepped ashore on an unnamed island in Casco Bay and "desired the [other] gentlemen" with him, including the Massachusetts governor, Samuel Shute, "to take notice and bear witness that as attorney to the honorable Company for Propagating the Gospel in New England … I did enter upon and take possession of that island in the name and on the behalf of the company." Samuel proceeded to cut a branch of a "thorntree" and "eat very good gooseberries and raspberries gathered there." He gathered apples and "cut fresh and salt grass for the sheep aboard" their ship.

The ship continued north to the Kennebec River, turned inland, and "came to an anchor in the slack water of Arrowsic Head" around noon on August 7. "Many canoes of Indians came aboard," among them the Penobscot sachem, or leader, and "Caesar and August, the two sons of Moxis," another sachem. On board the ship the English and Indian men shared an ox killed by the Indians and delivered by canoe. On the Sabbath, August 11, an English minister preached to the group beneath a tent on Arrowsic Island. The next day the Indians signed the Englishmen's treaty. In response the English "gave them all to drink. The young men gave volleys, made a dance, and all was managed with great joy."

During their negotiations, Samuel noted, the "Natives desired a line might be run" between the two cultures, "and [they] seemed to be against a [lot] more houses being built." In considering the ongoing conflicts between English and Indians, Samuel felt the English bore more fault. Unlike many of his peers, he believed the Indians should manage their own lands and English settlers should respect the Indians' rights. He had heard the Indians on Arrowsic express "a great reluctancy against erecting forts higher up the [Kennebeck] river." In addition, they opposed "the arrival of a multitude of new inhabitants, lest they should prove unable heartily to embrace them.... But no proposals for fixing boundaries were offered to them" by the English. Samuel believed, "Boundaries are necessary for the preservation of honesty and peace among those that border one upon another." It seemed "necessary to state and settle plain and lasting bounds between the English and the Indians, that so the natives may have a certain and established enjoyment of their own country, and that the English may have *Deus Nobiscum*"—"God is with us"—"legibly embroidered in their banners."

Bit by bit over the summer and fall of 1697 Samuel delivered pages of his lengthy manuscript to the printers Bartholomew Green and John Allen, who set them in type and printed them. In dedicating this work, Samuel set aside his and William Stoughton's differences over the witch hunt. The new court's chief justice was now also the acting governor of the province, as he had been since Sir William Phips's death in 1695 in London. Samuel dedicated *Phaenomena quaedam Apocalyptica* jointly "to William Stoughton, as Lieutenant Governor and Commander in Chief of His Majesties' Province of Massachusetts Bay in New England, and to William Ashurst," a leader in England of the "gospelizing" movement, "and the Company for the Propagation of

the Gospel in New England." Samuel arranged with a Boston bookseller to sell the forthcoming book in his shop, where Sam Jr. was now
working as an apprentice. *Phaenomena quaedam Apocalyptica* first appeared for sale in Boston on November 9, 1697.

Samuel exulted, "The epistle [dedication] to the Lieutenant Governor, which is the last half-sheet, is wrought off" the press, "and the book
is set to sale in Mr. Wilkins's shop. One is sold." A little later, "Mr. Flint
of Norwich came into the printing-room. I gave him a book stitched up,
which is the first perfect book I have given away." The next day, at the
Council Chamber in the Town House, Samuel "took the opportunity to
present the Lieutenant Governor [Stoughton] with seven *Phaenomena!*" Over the next few days he handed out copies to a Mistress Hillers,
"my brother in Salem," the father of Sheriff Bradford, and the eighty-
one-year-old Salem minister, John Higginson.

Samuel's sense of pride in this work grew over the years. Near the
end of his life, in 1727, he paid for the publication of a second edition
of *Phaenomena quaedam Apocalyptica*, with no changes. Fourteen years
before that he had published an "appendix" to it, "Proposals Touching
the Accomplishment of Prophecies Humbly Offered," in which he promoted even more evangelizing of Indians in order to hasten the
coming of Christ.

Although America "stands fair for being made the seat of the divine
metropolis," he wrote in this appendix, Americans should not be com-
placent with God. "Do you so love ... to say, ... *Come Lord Jesus! Come
quickly!*

"Are you in earnest?" Samuel demanded. "Desire then, pray that the
Gospel may be preached in all the world; in this Indian end of it. For
till then, Christ himself tells you, He will not, He cannot come. The
door is, as it were, shut against Him.... For love, or shame, get up!
And open the door!"

17

❦

EVIL MUST NOT
BE DONE

In the waning months of the seventeenth century, with the labor of *Phaenomena quaedam Apocalyptica* behind him, Samuel turned his attention to another social problem, the New England slave trade. By this time wealthy men of Boston and other New England towns routinely bought and sold Native Americans and Africans as slaves. Samuel regretted "the numerousness of slaves at this day in the Province, and the uneasiness of them under their slavery." Doubting that "the foundation of [slavery] be firmly and well laid," Samuel decided to attack slavery at its foundation. He would do so systematically, as in *Phaenomena quaedam Apocalyptica*. He would present a thesis, list all possible objections to it, and then, using the Bible and other ancient documents, attempt to counter each objection.

His thesis, composed in July 1700, was, "Forasmuch as liberty is in real value next unto life, none ought to part with it themselves, or deprive others of it, but upon most mature consideration. It is most certain that all men, as they are the sons of Adam,... have equal right unto liberty, and all other outward comforts of life." And "through the indulgence of God to our first parents after the Fall, the outward estate of all and every of the children, remains the same, as to one another. So that originally, and naturally, there is no such thing as slavery."

Samuel had been prompted to compose this thesis upon returning home from the June 19, 1700, funeral of John Eyre, a forty-four-year-old member of his private prayer group who owned slaves. (It was Eyre who had cried out "bitterly" after learning of his son's drowning while skating in Cambridge.) Following the burial Samuel spoke warmly to the widow, Katharine Brattle Eyre, whom he would later woo after Hannah Sewall's death. "I pray God to be favorably present with you," he said to Madame Eyre, "and to comfort you in the absence of so near and dear a relation."

Walking home from John Eyre's funeral, Samuel fixed on a thought. "Having been long and much dissatisfied with the trade of fetching Negroes from Guinea, at last I had a strong inclination to write something about it." Over several days, while reading a Puritan theologian's 1618 *Commentary upon the First Chapter of the Epistle of Saint Paul, written to the Ephesians,* "I began to be uneasy that I had so long neglected doing anything" about slavery. "When I was thus thinking, in came Brother [Joseph] Belknap to show me a petition he intended to present to the General Court for the freeing of a Negro and his wife, who were unjustly held in bondage. And there is a motion by a Boston committee to get a law that all importers of Negroes shall pay forty shillings per head, to discourage the bringing of them." And so he began.

The year before, Samuel had attempted to adjudicate a conflict between two slave owners over slaves who wished to marry. Sebastian, a "Negro servant of John Wait," became engaged to "Jane, Negro servant of Debora Thayer," but their owners could not agree to terms. In September 1699, Sewall noted, "Mrs. Thayer insisted that Sebastian might have one day in six allowed him for the support of Jane, his intended wife and her children.... Mr. Wait now wholly declined that, but freely offered to allow 'Bastian five pounds in money per annum toward the support of his children by said Jane...." After many rounds of negotiation between the owners, Samuel "persuaded Jane and Mrs. Thayer to agree to it and so it was concluded; and Mrs. Thayer [gave] the note of publication [of banns] to Mr. Wait for him to carry it to" the town clerk. Still, the couple had to wait eighteen months before their owners finally permitted them to marry, on February 13, 1701. Judge Samuel Sewall officiated at the ceremony.

Samuel owned no slaves. His numerous household employees, who served for a term with a salary, included his relatives and many other people of various backgrounds. But roughly one in five families in late seventeenth-century New England did own slaves. For instance, in September 1714 Samuel's nephew and namesake, his brother Stephen's son Samuel, then a twenty-four-year-old Boston merchant, advertised in the Boston *News-letter* "several Irish maid servants' time, most of them for five years [indenture], one Irish man servant's time ... [and] also four or five likely Negro boys." Historians estimate that by 1750, just twenty years after the death of Judge Sewall, New England had more than 10,000 slaves. Of that number, Connecticut had an estimated 6,400 slaves. Rhode Island had 3,700, and New Hampshire had 650. Massachusetts and Maine together had about 500 slaves, most of them in Boston.

New England's slave trade had begun soon after the first English settlement. In 1638 Emmanuel Downing, Governor John Winthrop's brother-in-law, suggested that colonists trade Indian captives of war for West Indian "Moors." Downing, who was in the West Indies, introduced slavery to Massachusetts, where many traders and entrepreneurs soon relied on slave labor. Even liberal-minded Rhode Island was not immune to slavery. The port of Bristol, Rhode Island, was a major arrival point for slave ships, which boosted the local economy. England ended the Royal African Company's monopoly of the slave trade in 1697, allowing competitors to join the profitable business. From that year forward the number of slaves in New England grew rapidly. Most slaves worked as shipwrights, rope makers, cooks, gardeners, potters, and seamstresses.

"How horrible," Samuel Sewall wrote in 1700, "is the uncleanness, mortality, if not murder, that the ships are guilty of that bring great crowds of these miserable men and women [whom we are] forcing ... to become slaves amongst our selves." Many of his landowning English peers considered slavery necessary. Contemporaneous death records for Boston-area "Negroes" include "William Cottle's Negro" (1667), "Robin, belonging to Lt. Stephen Greenleaf" (1689), and "Jack, belonging to Capt. Edward Sargeant" (1708).

In considering slavery, Samuel started with the Bible, in which, he believed, "Man stealing is ranked amongst the most atrocious of capital crimes. God hath said, 'He that stealeth a man and selleth him, or if he be found in his hand, he shall surely be put to death.' Exodus 21:16. What louder cry can there be made of the celebrated warning, *caveat emptor!* The Old Testament figure Joseph, son of Jacob, whose brothers sold him to Ishmaelite traders for twenty pieces of silver, "was rightfully no more a slave to his brethren than they were to him, and they had no more authority to sell him than they had to slay him. Neither could Potiphar," the Egyptian who purchased Joseph from the Ishmaelites, "have any better interest in him than the Ishmaelites had.... There is no proportion between twenty pieces of silver and liberty." It was a "pity there should be more caution used in buying a horse, or a little lifeless dust, than there is in purchasing men and women, [who] are the offspring of God, and their liberty is *auro pretiosior omni*," or "more precious than all gold."

Before raising objections to his thesis, Samuel mused that it would be better for New England to have "white servants for a term of years than to have slaves for life. Few [masters] can endure to hear of a Negro's being made free." Moreover, slaves' "continual aspiring after" freedom "renders them unwilling servants." He added that it was "most lamentable to think, how in taking Negroes out of Africa and selling of them here, that which God has joined together men do boldly rend asunder—men from their country, husbands from their wives, parents from their children. Methinks, when we are bemoaning the barbarous usage of our friends and kinsfolk in Africa, it might not be unseasonable to enquire whether we are not culpable in forcing the Africans to become slaves amongst ourselves." Throughout the previous century, to the horror of many Englishmen, North African pirates known as Barbary corsairs had seized hundreds of British and European ships and sold thousands of their sailors into slavery in Africa. Samuel, who had sent money to redeem friends from "Algerian captivity," appreciated the hypocrisy of condemning the enslavement of English and Europeans but not that of Africans.

Logically, he presented the standard arguments in support of slavery. "Objection 1" to his thesis was that Africans "are of the posterity of Cham, and therefore are under the curse of slavery. Genesis 9:25–27."

He replied that no one should wish "to be an executioner of the vindictive wrath of God." In addition, the standard reading of "this text may have been mistaken." Correctly read, "Black men ... are not descended of Canaan, but of Cush," an ancient name of Ethiopia. He cited Psalm 68, Jerimiah 13:23, and Ovid to prove that Africa "shall soon stretch out her hands unto God."

Objection 2: "Negroes are brought out of a pagan country into places where the Gospel is preached."

He dismissed this argument with the line, "Evil must not be done, that good may come of it." He added an example. "The extraordinary and comprehensive benefit accruing to the Church of God, and to Joseph personally, did not rectify his brethren's sale of him."

Objection 3: "The Africans have wars with one another. Our ships bring lawful captives taken in those wars."

Samuel's response was, "An unlawful war cannot make lawful captives." He offered another example, aimed at his well-to-do Boston peers. "I am sure, if some Gentlemen should go down to Brewster [on Cape Cod] to take the air and fish, and a stronger party from Hull should surprise them and sell them for slaves to a ship outward bound, they would think themselves unjustly dealt with, both by sellers and buyers."

Samuel concluded with Matthew 7:12, *"Quaecunque volueritis ut faciant vobis homines, ita & vos facite eis,"* the Golden Rule, generally translated as, "Do unto others as you would have them do unto you." He added an excerpt from an English law text, Ames's *Cases of Conscience:*

Perfecta servitus poenae, non potest jure locum habere, nisi ex delicto gravi quod ultimum supplicium aliquo modo meretur; quia Libertas ex naturali aestimatione proxime accedit ad vitam ipsam, & eidem a multis praeferri solet.

A servitude carried out as a penalty cannot have a place in law, unless from a serious crime because the greatest penalty is in some way deserved, because liberty from a natural valuation comes close to life itself and is normally preferred by many to the same degree.

The judge who had sent twenty innocent people to their deaths was well aware, by their example, that "liberty ... comes close to life itself and is normally preferred by many to the same degree."

He anticipated the standard objection to his thesis, from the Old Testament, that was often used to justify slavery: "Abraham had servants bought with his money, and born in his house." Samuel replied, "Until the circumstances of Abraham's purchase be recorded, no argument can be drawn from it." He cited Leviticus 25, Jeremiah 34, and Deuteronomy 15 in pointing out that "the Israelites were strictly forbidden the buying or selling of one another for slaves."

"God expects that Christians should be of a more ingenuous and benign frame of spirit," the judge added. "For men obstinately to persist in holding their neighbors and brethren under the rigor of perpetual bondage seems to be no proper way of gaining assurance that God has given them spiritual freedom." Using a musical metaphor, Samuel said, "Our Blessed Savior has altered the measures of the ancient love-song and set it to a most excellent new tune, which all ought to be ambitious of learning. Matthew 5:43–44, John 13:34. These Ethiopians, as black as they are, seeing they are the sons and daughters of the first Adam, the brethren and sisters of the last Adam [Jesus Christ], and the offspring of God, they ought to be treated with a respect agreeable."

There is caution, perhaps even defensiveness, in Samuel's tone. He was aware that his "defense of liberty" was out of time and place. Nevertheless, he presented it in public. He titled the pamphlet *The Selling of Joseph, a Memorial*, and paid Bartholomew Green and John Allen to print it. (The complete text of *The Selling of Joseph* begins on page 300.) Bartholomew Green, a son of Samuel Green, patriarch of the famous seventeenth-century printing family, was a deacon of the Third Church who later took as his second wife Samuel's niece, Jane Tappan, who had spent many years in the Sewall home. The Greens lived a few blocks up the main road, above his printing house.

Samuel received many "frowns and hard words" in response to *The Selling of Joseph*, many copies of which he handed out in Boston during the fall of 1700. John Saffin, a magistrate, merchant, and slave trader in his late sixties, attacked Sewall's pamphlet in writing. Saffin had personal as well as political reasons for opposing Judge Sewall, who was then trying to help one of Saffin's slaves, a man named Adam, to gain his freedom through the courts. In his own pamphlet, *A Brief and Candid Answer to A Late Printed Sheet, Entitled, The Selling of Joseph*

(1701), Saffin rejected Sewall's comparison of the biblical Joseph with African slaves. In Saffin's view, Africans were suited to enslavement because they were "deceitful," "cowardly and cruel," and "prone to revenge," with "mischief and murder in their very eyes...." Africans benefited from living "among Christians," he added. Colonial and provincial laws against stealing men did not apply to "strangers."

Saffin repeated the standard proslavery arguments that Sewall had dismissed. Abraham owned slaves, so "our imitation of him in his moral action is as warrantable as that of adopting his faith." God intentionally set "different orders and degrees of men in the world." Equality would "invert the order that God had set." God ordained "some to be high and honorable, some to be low and despicable; some to be monarchs, kings, princes, and governors, masters and commanders, others to be subjects, and to be commanded; servants of sundry sorts and degrees, bound to obey; yea, some to be born slaves, and so to remain during their lives."

Saffin's reasoning disgusted Samuel. At first, though, Samuel made no public statement in response to Saffin's attack. "I forbore troubling the province with any reply," he explained. He continued in his judicial work to oppose chattel slavery and other racial inequities. And four years later, in 1705, when a bill to prohibit interracial marriage—an "Act for the Better Preventing of Spurious and Mixt Issue"—came before the court, Samuel revised *The Selling of Joseph* for publication in a London magazine, the *Athenian Oracle*. He also composed an opinion piece for a local newspaper, the *Boston News-letter*, in which he restated his earlier point that New England would fare better with servants than with slaves.

Samuel's antislavery statements appeared seven decades before the Bill of Rights and a century and a half before the Civil War. *The Selling of Joseph* was in fact the first antislavery tract ever published in America. The historian David Brion Davis noted that Samuel's "break with the traditional Christian acceptance of slavery as a necessary part of a sinful world would help to inspire ... later radical opponents of slavery.... Despite the rarity and novelty of moral repudiations of slavery before the mid-eighteenth century," Samuel's essay was one of only "two early antislavery documents [that] serve as examples of the misgivings felt by a few Northern colonists before racial slavery became both widely accepted and deeply entrenched." The other document, written in 1688 in Germantown, Pennsylvania, was a petition against slavery that several Dutch-speaking Quakers sent to their local Quaker gathering. They stated that buying and selling humans contradicted their faith. The local meeting sent the petition to Quaker authorities, who "quietly buried it," according to Davis. Both Puritans and Quakers engaged in the slave trade on both sides of the Atlantic.

In a society that rejected racial equality—and had not yet conceived of civil rights—Samuel continued to work for these causes. In the summer of 1716 the Provincial Council passed a bill taxing Indians and Negroes at the same rate as cattle. Samuel voted against it. On June 16 of that year he wrote in his diary, "I essayed to prevent Indians and Negroes being rated with horses and hogs, but could not prevail." A few years later, in a letter to another judge, he remarked, "The poorest boys and girls within this province, such as of the lowest condition, whether they be English or Indians or Ethiopians, they have the same right to religion and life, that the richest heirs have. And they who go about to deprive them of this right, they attempt the bombarding of Heaven; and the shells they throw shall fall down upon their own heads."

The year 1700, in which Samuel composed *The Selling of Joseph*, also marked the end of a century. Despite Samuel's loyalty to the Julian calendar, in this case he acknowledged January 1 as the start of a year. As the new century approached he sought to celebrate what seemed a harbinger of the Christian millennium that he hoped would soon arrive.

Well before dawn on the first day of the eighteenth century, Wednesday, January 1, 1701, four trumpet players hired by Samuel met on Boston Common, where cows still grazed. The brass band gave a blast before the sun showed over the ocean. The trumpeters walked the few blocks to the Town House, where they sounded their instruments until sunrise.

During the fanfare the bellman, who kept time for the town, declaimed a poem that Samuel had composed for the occasion. He may also have sung it, to the Old Hundredth tune, to which Samuel set it. In rhymed couplets, "My Verses upon [the] New Century" was addressed to God:

Once more! Our God, vouchsafe to shine:
Correct the coldness of our clime.
Make haste with Thy impartial light,
And terminate this long dark night.

Let the transplanted English vine
Spread further still: still call it thine.
Prune it with skill: for yield it can
More fruit to Thee the husbandman.

Give the poor Indians eyes to see
The light of life: and set them free;
That they religion may profess,
Denying all ungodliness....

So false religions shall decay,
And darkness fly before bright day:
So men shall God in Christ adore;
And worship idols vain, no more.

So Asia, and Africa,
Europa, with America;
All four, in consort joined, shall sing
New songs of praise to Christ our king.

One of the trumpeters, whom Samuel paid extra, rode to Cambridge to play a fanfare at the college. He delivered to its library a donation from Samuel, two volumes of Dr. John Owen's *Exercitations on the Epistle to the Hebrews*, published in London in 1670. These volumes were destroyed in a fire in 1764, along with many other books donated to Harvard by Samuel.

After all the fanfares and the public reading of his verses on the new century, Samuel observed, "My mind was at quiet, and all seemed to run smooth."

Samuel Sewall at age seventy-seven, painted by John Smibert in Boston in 1729.

18

CHIEF JUSTICE, PATERFAMILIAS

As Samuel approached the age of fifty, his first family began passing away. His brother John died in his midforties in August 1699, and his older sister, Hannah Tappan, followed three months later. Samuel felt these losses deeply. "We [siblings] have lived, eight of us together, thirty years and were wont to speak of it (it may be too vainly). But now God begins to part us apace. Two are taken away in about a quarter of a year's time. And methinks, now my dear brother and sister are laid in the grave I am as it were laid there in proxy. The Lord help me to carry it more suitably, more fruitfully, toward the five remaining; and put me in a preparedness for my own dissolution. And help me to live upon Him alone."

Samuel learned of his father's demise while on the legal circuit in Portsmouth, New Hampshire, on May 16, 1700. This death, unlike those of his siblings, was expected. Two weeks earlier his father had told him, "I cannot go to meeting" at church "but I hope to go shortly to a greater assembly."

Samuel rode south for the burial on May 19. He was pleased to hear the Reverend Christopher Tappan of Newbury call his father "a true Nathaniel"—a man without guile. "Lord," Samuel prayed in private, "pardon all my sins of omission and commission toward my father and help me to prepare to die. Accept of any little labor of love towards my dear parents." To assuage his guilt over his perceived failures of attention to his father, he noted, "I had just sent [him] four pounds of raisins, which with the canary [wine] were very refreshing to him." Samuel paid an engraver to record his father's history on a gravestone carved with flowers and a winged skull.

Hardly six months later Samuel's "dear mother" was dead. Due to extremely cold weather Samuel did not hear this news until the following day, January 14, when his nephew John Sewall arrived in Boston. That night, in a thick fog, Samuel and his oldest son set out for Newbury. They hired horses across the river, in Charlestown. They ate and lodged at a tavern in Ipswich.

In Newbury the family awaited its oldest son. As such Samuel "followed the bier" by himself. The January 16 funeral began around four at the meetinghouse across from the family house. The ministers prayed. The mourners wept. The grave digger began to cover the coffin with dirt.

"Forbear a little," Samuel said to the grave digger. Turning to face the crowd, he went on, "Suffer me to say that, amidst our bereaving sorrows, we have the comfort of beholding this saint put into the rightful possession of the happiness of living desired and dying lamented."

Everyone stopped, seeing that Jane Dummer Sewall's oldest son, the forty-eight-year-old judge, had a speech. "She lived commendably four and fifty years with her dear husband, my dear father," Samuel told the assembled people. "She was a true and constant lover of God's work, worship, and saints; and she always with a patient cheerfulness submitted to the divine decree of providing bread for herself and others in the sweat of her brows. Now her infinitely gracious and bountiful master has promoted her to the honor of higher employments, fully and absolutely discharged from all manner of toil and sweat.

"My honored and beloved friends and neighbors!" he said, tears streaking his face. "My dear mother never thought much of doing the most frequent and homely offices of love for me, and she lavished away many thousands of words upon me before I could return one word in answer." It occurred to him that his mother's simple gifts were superior to his sophisticated skills. "Therefore, I ask and hope that none will be offended that I have now ventured to speak one word in her behalf; when she herself is become speechless."

He could not continue. As he noted later, "I could hardly speak for passion and tears." He motioned with his hand for the grave digger to resume his work.

That evening at his parents' home, "Mr. Tappan prayed with us," Samuel noted. "The two brothers and four sisters being together, we took leave [of each other] by singing of the 90th Psalm, from the 8th to the 15th verses inclusively."

Psalm 90

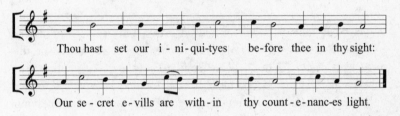

Thou hast set our i-ni-qui-tyes be-fore thee in thy sight:

Our se-cret e-vills are with-in thy count-e-nanc-es light.

Low Dutch Tune

8 Thou hast set our iniquityes
   before thee in thy sight:
   Our secret evills are within
   thy countenances light.

9 Because in thine exceeding wrath
   our dayes all passe away:
   our years wee have consumed quite,
   ev'n as a tale *are they.*

10 Threescore & ten yeares are the dayes
   of our yeares which remaine,
   & if through strength they fourscore be,
   their strength is grief & paine:

   For it's cut off soone, & wee flye
11   away: Who is't doth know
   thine angers strength? according as
   thy feare thy wrath is so.

12   Teach us to count our dayes: our hearts
         so wee'l on wisdome set.
13   Turne Lord, how long? of thy servants
         let it repent thee yet?

14   O give us satisfacti-on
         betimes with thy mercee:
     That so rejoyce, & be right glad,
         through all our dayes may wee.

15   According to the dayes *wherin*
         affliction wee have had,
     and yeares *wherin* we have seen ill,
         now also make us glad.

The next morning Samuel headed back to Boston on the rutted road he knew so well. Now that his mother was dead, "almost all my memory is dead with her." As the familiar landscape receded, he felt he was leaving Newbury—and his early life—behind forever.

Several months later Samuel attended at the deathbed of the chief of the witchcraft court. Aware that seventy-one-year-old William Stoughton, who was both the province's acting governor and chief justice of its highest court, was ill, Samuel had ridden to Stoughton's house in Dorchester on court business on July 4, 1701. The old man lay on a couch in his parlor. "The court," Samuel began, "is affected with the sense of your Honor's affliction."

Stoughton struggled to raise himself to a seated position but could not. He reached a hand to Samuel, who took it. "Pray for me!" Stoughton said. Samuel kissed his hand. Three days later Stoughton was dead.

A neighbor rushed into Samuel's garden one day in September 1707 to announce that the Reverend Willard had taken ill. The sixty-seven-year-old minister was now the president of Harvard College, the symbolic leader of New England's Congregationalist clergy.

Samuel raced to Willard's bedside. The Reverend Ebenezer Pemberton was already there with a crowd, praying. At one point most people drifted away. Samuel stayed and so was with "my dear pastor" when he died. A "doleful cry rose throughout the house." After

Willard's grand funeral, his body lay in the Sewall tomb until his tomb could be built.

So many of the older generation were passing away. Ninety-two-year-old Simon Bradstreet had died on March 27, 1697, in Salem, where he first set foot on American soil in 1630. More than eight ministers officiated at the funeral of a man who, in the words of Shelby Foote, "seemed to concentrate in himself the dignity and wisdom of the first century of Massachusetts life." As a pallbearer Samuel proudly "bore the feet of the corpse into [the] tomb" at the Salem cemetery now known as the Charter Street Burying Ground.

But it was the stern Stoughton, not the humane Willard and Bradstreet, who reappeared in Samuel Sewall's dreams. During the February after Stoughton's death Samuel dreamed, "I was in company with Mr. Stoughton and Mr. N. Higginson." Nathaniel Higginson, a son of the Salem minister John Higginson, was a member of the Harvard class of 1670, thus a classmate of the late Reverend George Burroughs. A merchant who had emigrated to England and then Madras, India, Higginson had been governor of the East India Trading Company since 1692. Now that Stoughton was dead, Samuel hoped that the younger Higginson, forty-nine, might return to New England as its royal governor. Samuel was eager to find someone other than the man who would actually be chosen, Joseph Dudley, who was soon to become Sam Jr.'s father-in-law.

Sam Jr., twenty-three, was courting twenty-year-old Rebecca Dudley. The couple wed at her parents' elegant Roxbury home on September 15, 1702, with the Roxbury pastor, Nehemiah Walter, presiding. Samuel had even "played Cupid" for his son the previous year, sending the young lady a piece of silver embossed with the Latin motto *plus ultra*, which means, "beyond which there is none." Samuel included this note:

> The enclosed piece of silver ... bespeaks your favor for a certain young man in town.... By your generous acceptance, you may make both it and the giver great.
> Madam, I am
> Your affectionate friend, SS

Nevertheless, Samuel disliked Rebecca's father. Joseph Dudley, a son of Thomas Dudley, the colony's overbearing second governor, had been born in 1647 in Roxbury, one of seventeenth-century Boston's tonier addresses. If Dudley's legendary arrogance did not offend Samuel, then his Anglicanism and his fashionably aristocratic white powder wigs did. Increase and Cotton Mather despised Dudley, with whom they had a long public feud. Samuel could find both sides disagreeable, but he usually sympathized with the Reverends Mather.

A member of Harvard's class of 1663, Dudley had married Rebecca Tyng, with whom he had a large family. Elected to the General Court in 1673, he showed loyalty to the royal governor Edmund Andros, who made him president of the council in 1684. Five years later, when Samuel's friends ousted Governor Andros, they put Dudley under house arrest and then shipped both men back to England. The English court appointed Dudley to high positions in colonial New York and on the Isle of Wight. Now, though, he was back in Massachusetts, eager once again to assume power.

In a few years, following the 1702 ascension to the throne of Queen Anne, Dudley would be named Massachusetts's royal governor. Five years after that Boston merchants would petition for his removal, saying he consorted with smugglers and other illicit traders. Their published attack on him, *The Deplorable State of New England by Reason of a Covetous and Treacherous Governor*, appeared in London in 1708. In a letter to Sir Henry Ashurst in England, Samuel Sewall noted hopefully that "Dudley's government is near its end. If he should indeed be removed, I apprehend you would do this province excellent service if you could procure that Mr. Nathaniel Higginson might be made our governor...." These efforts compromised Dudley's power, but he did not actually leave office until 1715. The historian Thomas Hutchinson concluded that Dudley "had as many virtues as can consist with so great a thirst for honor and power."

The marriage of the progeny of Dudley and Sewall was not happy. Most of Sam Jr. and Rebecca's children died early. There were other strains, some detectable to Samuel and Hannah, who often worried about the young couple. Sam Jr. was a "practical, fallible, ordinary man ... beset by earthly troubles," the historian Judith Graham wrote. He left school early, did not attend college, struggled to find a career, and now farmed the family land in Brookline. He was also a justice of the peace and the first town manager of Brookline, which was incorporated as a separate town, with fewer than two hundred residents, in 1705. Now his marriage was in trouble.

One day in February 1712, when Samuel was alone with his daughter-in-law, he took the opportunity to ask her, in private, "What is the cause of my son's indisposition?"

Rebecca Dudley Sewall did not reply.

Samuel asked, more pointedly, "Are you so kindly affectioned towards [one] another as you should be?"

"I do my duty," she said.

Samuel dropped the subject. The next week he learned that his son had discussed their marital troubles with the Reverend Nehemiah Walter. Not long after, Samuel returned home to find his daughter-in-law and his wife engaged in "very sharp discourse." Rebecca had accused Sam Jr. of seducing their maids. She "wholly justified herself," Samuel noted, "and said, if it were not for her, no maid could be able to dwell at their house.... At last Daughter Sewall burst out with tears, and called for the calash," her coach, in which to depart. "My wife relented also, and said she did not design to grieve her."

Not long afterward, Samuel rode to Brookline to visit his son's family. He found Sam Jr. dining alone, which worried him. Eventually Rebecca arrived. "I propounded to her that Mr. Walter might be desired to come to them and pray with them. She seemed not to like the notion, and said she knew not wherefore she should be called before a minister."

Samuel explained that the minister seemed "the fittest moderator" of their difficulties. "The Governor [her father] or I might be thought partial" to one side.

In reply Rebecca pleaded, "I perform my duty.... How much I have borne...." During the next year Rebecca took a lover, William Ilsly, who moved into her and Sam Jr.'s house in January 1714.

Sam Jr., who was now thirty-five years old, moved back into his parents' house. His parents, particularly his mother, urged him never to return to his wife, who on December 19, 1716, gave birth to an illegitimate baby boy.

"Nobody knows whose it is," Governor Dudley admitted to Samuel, who had said the infant "should not be chargeable to [Sam Jr.'s] estate."

Samuel had often prayed "for good matches for my children as they grow up, that they may be yoked equally." With the exception of Sam Jr. and Hannah Jr. (who remained single), his prayers appear to have been answered. His younger son, Joseph, was everything Sam Jr. was not. Joseph succeeded at school, attended Harvard (class of 1707), and earned a master's degree in divinity, following the early path of his prudent father. Outdoing his father in pursuit of a religious career, Joseph was ordained a minister, serving for more than half a century at the church his grandfather Hull helped to found. Humble, pious, and "of a deliberate and cautious disposition," according the historian Hamilton Andrews Hill, Joseph Sewall was eventually offered the presidency of Harvard College, the highest honor given a New England divine.

Joseph's choice of a wife was equally perspicacious. His betrothed, Mistress Elizabeth Walley, a member since 1711 of the Third Church, was a daughter of Samuel's good friend Major John Walley, a fellow magistrate and Third Church member. Samuel liked this daughter-in-law so much that he gave her his wife's wedding ring two months after Hannah died. "I hope you will wear it with the same nobility as she did who was the first owner of it."

Samuel's oldest daughter, Hannah Jr., who was infirm by her thirties as a result of injuries to her legs that never healed, apparently had no suitors. His second daughter, Betty, whose spiritual crisis passed without comment by her father, was first courted by Captain Zechariah Tuthill in 1699. Samuel, who learned that Tuthill was without "blot" and worth six hundred pounds, encouraged the courtship. One afternoon before Tuthill was to call on her, Samuel took seventeen-year-old Betty alone into his chamber. He read aloud to her the biblical story of Adam and Eve "as a soothing and alluring preparation for the thought of matrimony," he explained. To his regret, Betty was nowhere to be found by the time Tuthill arrived. Only after the disappointed captain departed did Samuel discover that she had been hiding outside in one of the stables. "At last she came in," he reported, "and looked very wild."

Betty, it turned out, was already acquainted with the young man she would marry, Grove Hirst, of Salem, from her sojourns there. The couple had a complex courtship, which in its later stages her father actively guided. He sometimes advised her in writing, although she lived in his house. "Elizabeth," began one such missive, dated October 26, 1699, which is forceful yet respectful of his seventeen-year-old daughter:

Mr. Hirst waits on you once more to see if you can bid him welcome. It ought to be seriously considered, that your drawing back from him after all that has passed between you, will be to your prejudice; and will tend to discourage persons of worth from making their court to you. And you had need well to consider whether you be able to bear his final leaving of you, howsoever it may seem grateful to you at present.

When persons come toward us, we are apt to look upon their undesirable circumstances mostly; and thereupon to shun them. But when persons retire from us for good and ill, we are in danger of looking only on that which is desirable in them, to our woeful disquiet. Whereas 'tis the property of a good balance to turn where the most weight is, though there be some also in the other scale. I do not see but the match is well liked by judicious persons, and such as are your cordial friends, and mine also.

Yet notwithstanding, if you find in yourself an immovable, incurable aversion from him, and cannot love and honor and obey him, I shall say no more, nor give you any further trouble in this matter. It had better be off than on. So praying God to pardon us, and pity our undeserving, and to direct and strengthen and settle you in making a right judgment, I take leave, who am, dear child,
    Your loving father

The Reverend Cotton Mather performed the wedding of Grove Hirst and Elizabeth Sewall on October 17, 1700. Samuel gave the couple a "house of wood" with a large garden on Cotton Hill (later Pemberton Hill) in Boston that he had purchased more than a decade earlier as a rental property. The Hirsts had five children at the time of Betty's death, probably of consumption, on July 10, 1716.

"When my flesh and my heart faileth me," Samuel said at this daughter's deathbed, "God is the strength of my heart and my portion forever. Thus I have parted with a very desirable child. She lived desired and died lamented. The Lord fit me to follow, and help me to prepare my wife and children for a dying hour."

His next-youngest daughter Mary's beau was Samuel Gerrish, a young man from the North Shore. Gerrish's father, the Reverend Joseph Gerrish of Wenham, had been a classmate of Samuel Sewall's in Newbury. Mary informed her parents of her intentions in January 1709. One evening Samuel and Hannah prayed with Mary, who displayed "considerable agony and importunity with many tears." Samuel said, "The Lord hear and help."

Two days later, feeling "uneasy" after learning from Grove Hirst that Gerrish courted another young lady, Samuel inquired about Gerrish of his cousin. The cousin "answered not directly, but said [Gerrish] would come [visit Mary] if he might have admittance. I told him I heard [gossip that Gerrish] went to [court] Mr. Coney's daughter. He said he knew nothing of that. I desired him to enquire and tell me. I understood he undertook it; but he came no more."

Samuel's efforts continued. Returning from a funeral on February 4, he asked the Reverend Ebenezer Pemberton, of the Third Church, whether Samuel Gerrish "courted Mr. Coney's daughter."

"Not now," the minister said. "Mr. Coney thought his daughter young." Samuel, placated, asked Samuel Gerrish to take a letter regarding the courtship to his father. A week or so later Samuel received the senior Gerrish's reply and assent.

Twenty-three-year-old Samuel Gerrish, a member of the Third Church, was a bookseller, the town clerk for Boston, and the register of deeds of Suffolk County. He and Mary Sewall were married by the Reverend Ebenezer Pemberton that August at her father's house. Mary was not quite eighteen. A little more than a year later, on November 9, 1710, she gave birth to a girl, Hannah. Eight days later nineteen-year-old Mary Sewall Gerrish died as a result of complications of childbirth. The baby died a few months after that, and Mary's widower later married Mr. Coney's daughter.

Samuel's youngest daughter, Judith, rejected two suitors—the Reverend Thomas Prince, of the Third Church, who was a classmate of her brother Joseph, and Colonel William Dudley, a son of Joseph and brother of Rebecca—before accepting one. The man she married was the Reverend William Cooper of the Church in Brattle Square, which had gathered in 1698 as Boston's fourth church. At the Sewall mansion on May 12, 1720, a few hours after Joseph Sewall's lecture at the Third Church, Samuel prepared to "join the Reverend Mr. William Cooper and Mistress Judith Sewall in marriage."

First the bride's father addressed the groom's widowed mother. "The great honor you have conferred on the bridegroom and bride, by being present at this solemnity, does very conveniently supersede any further enquiry after your consent. And the part I am desired to take in this wedding renders the way of my giving my consent very compendious. There's no manner of room left for that previous question, Who giveth this woman to be married to this man?"

To his daughter Judith, who was twenty, he said, "Dear child, you give me your hand for one moment, and the bridegroom forever." And to his new son, twenty-four-year-old William Cooper: "Spouse, you accept and receive this woman now given you." After the ceremony Samuel set Psalm 115 to St. David's tune while his servants passed around glasses of sack-posset and plates of bride-cake.

Judith's wedding was the only one that Hannah Sewall missed. She had "taken very sick" in the summer of 1717, perhaps due to malaria, according to historians. She suffered "extraordinary" pain and fainting spells. Her condition improved somewhat in August and September, but she "relapsed" on October 15. Samuel had servants move her to the dining room, on the ground floor, where she could more easily be attended. Dr. Thomas Oakes came to the house that evening and stayed with her and Samuel all night.

The next day her weakness and "distemper" increased. That night, though, she told Samuel to go to bed rather than stay by her side. He needed sleep.

October 17 was Thursday, lecture day. "Shall I go to lecture to pray?" he asked her tenderly. He wished discreetly to know if she expected still to be alive when he returned.

"I can't tell," she replied.

Samuel stayed home. He sent out a note requesting prayers to be posted at the Third Church. Everyone at church noticed his absence, he learned later. After the gathering his old friend Justice Wait Still Winthrop and his wife, who was known as Madame Winthrop, called at the house to see Hannah. Taking leave of them at the door, Samuel said, "Thank you for visiting my poor wife."

The next day Hannah was "worse and exceeding restless." Samuel prayed to God "to look upon her." He and John Cutler, a doctor, stayed at her bedside through the night.

Samuel sent a note to Cotton Mather, who came to pray with Hannah the next morning. The Reverend Benjamin Wadsworth arrived. He prayed with Samuel in his chamber "when 'twas supposed my wife took little notice." Then, at "about a quarter of an hour past four," on Saturday, October 19, 1717, "my dear wife expired." Hannah was fifty-nine years old.

"The chamber filled with a flood of tears," Samuel noted. Immediately reaching out to the divine, he added, "God is teaching me a new lesson—to live a widower's life. Lord, help me to learn, and be a sun and shield to me, now [that] so much of my comfort and defense are taken away." In a letter announcing the awful news to his cousin Jeremiah Dummer, Samuel wrote a couplet:

What signify these locks, and bolts, and bars?
My treasure's gone, and with it all my fears.

The next day was the Sabbath, so Samuel went out to public worship. He had earlier sent yet another note requesting prayers. Before the congregation of the Third Church, where their son Joseph now preached, "my son has much ado to read the note ... being overwhelmed with tears."

Hannah was disemboweled due to the hot weather. Her body, wrapped in cerecloth, was placed in a coffin. Her funeral was to be Wednesday, October 23. Cotton Mather gave the sermon, which he later published under the title *The Valley of Baca. The Divine Sovereignty, Displayed and Adored; More Particularly in Bereaving Dispensations, of the Divine Providence. A Sermon Preached on the Death of Mrs. Hannah Sewall, the Religious and Honorable Consort of Samuel Sewall Esq.*

At her funeral the other absence that Samuel felt most acutely was that of his son-in-law Grove Hirst, Betty's forty-two-year-old widower. Grove Hirst too was now seriously ill. A day or two later Samuel visited Hirst and found him "very sick." He told his son-in-law, "You are in a great degree the stay and comfort of my life."

The following day, from his bed Hirst said to Samuel, "Please take my son Samuel," who was twelve, "home to your house." Samuel did so. Two days later Hirst requested that Samuel take eleven-year-old Elizabeth Hirst to the home of a paternal uncle "until the controversy should be ended." Samuel wrote in his diary, "I did it late at night." Then he added, "Mr. Hirst expired between 3 and 4 past midnight."

At his son-in-law's funeral two days later, Samuel led the five orphans—his grandchildren Samuel; Elizabeth; Mary, who was thirteen; nine-year-old Hannah; and Jane, who was eight. The task of raising several of them would fall to Samuel, a sixty-five-year-old widower.

A few months later, against the wishes of his late mother, Sam Jr. returned to Brookline to live with his wife.

Meanwhile, Samuel Sewall began to consider courting again. He spent hours in prayer on whether to live single or marry. On the morning of February 6, 1718, not quite four months after Hannah's death, he had "a sweet and very affection meditation concerning the Lord Jesus," the spouse of the church of which Samuel was a member. "Nothing was to be objected against [Jesus's] person, parentage, relations, estate, house, home! Why did [I] not resolutely, presently close with Him! And I cried mightily to God that He would help me so to do!" Now and then he prayed with his son Joseph for divine guidance in the matter.

Late that winter he wrote to Governor Shute requesting the top post on the Superior Court of Judicature, which Wait Still Winthrop had recently vacated. "It comes to pass by the disposal of divine sovereignty that I am the last of the councilors left standing in the [1692] Charter, and the last of the justices left standing in the Superior Court, of those that were of it from the beginning [of the province] which was in the year 1692. And by reason of the inability of the late Honorable Chief Justice Winthrop to ride the remoter circuits, I have frequently presided" over the court. "As to my real estate in New England it is considerable." Governor Shute made Samuel the court's chief justice that April.

A year later in the summer Samuel, who was now sixty-seven, began to "visit Mrs. Tilley, and speak with her in her chamber," and "ask her to come and dwell at my house." Abigail Melyen Woodmansey Tilley, a widow just past fifty whom he had known for years, was of Dutch and English descent and born in Elizabeth, New Jersey. Samuel had known her father and officiated at her 1686 wedding to her first husband, James Woodmansey, who died in 1694. The Reverend Willard performed her second wedding, in 1703, to William Tilley, who died the same year as Samuel's wife. Both couples attended the Third Church. Samuel and Abigail speedily arranged a marriage settlement. His son Joseph married them before a large crowd "in the best room below stairs" at her house on October 29, 1719.

A strange scene ensued that evening. Samuel reported that his new wife's sister "introduced me into my bride's chamber after [Abigail] was abed." He thanked his sister-in-law, who left. Samuel undressed, presumably to his hair shirt, and joined his bride in her bed. "Quickly after our being abed my bride grew so very bad" and "under great consternation" that "she was fain to sit up in her bed."

Samuel was alarmed. He rose "to get her petticoats about her. I was exceedingly amazed, fearing lest she should have died. Through the favor of God she recovered in some considerable time of this fit of the tissick," or coughing.

Madame Abigail Sewall never returned to health. Seven months later, in May 1720, she was dead, "to our great astonishment, especially mine." This sharp loss reminded him again that "I had cause to be ashamed of my sin, and to loath[e] myself for it." He prayed, "May the sovereign Lord pardon my sin, and sanctify to me this very extraordinary, awful dispensation."

A few months later, feeling even "more lonesome" than before, Samuel began the courtship for which he is best known. Not a few readers of Samuel Sewall's diary, including my late Aunt Charlotte, have considered his new love object, Madame Winthrop, to be that book's second most important character. In late-nineteenth-century Boston several interested parties, including Winthrop descendants, the minister of the Old South (formerly Third) Church, and the vice president of the Massachusetts Historical Society, engaged in public debate over which party in this courtship was more at fault.

Katharine Winthrop, the widow of Samuel's friend and colleague Wait Still, was a daughter of Thomas Brattle Sr. and Elizabeth Tyng and a younger sibling of the mathematician Thomas Brattle. Born in Boston in 1664, she married John Eyre in 1680 and was widowed a decade later. Her second husband, Winthrop, by then the chief justice of the Superior Court of Judicature, died in November 1717, just weeks after Hannah Sewall. Samuel, a pallbearer for Wait Still, noted that the "streets were crowded with people" for the funeral. The "regiment attended in arms" as Winthrop's coffin was carried from the Town House to the old burying place" beside King's Chapel and "laid in Governor Winthrop's tomb."

Not long after his second wife's death, Samuel eyed the widows' seats at the Third Church. He "fixed on" Madame Winthrop, who was fifty-six. Their courtship began at the end of September and was over by early November, a period of six weeks that has received undue attention because of its emotional intensity, at least on Samuel's part, the detail and volume of his writings on it, and the couple's harsh negotiations for a marriage settlement.

That September Samuel was riding the court circuit, an impressive feat for a man nearing seventy. On September 13 he presided over a civil action in Bristol, Rhode Island, where he remained until the 17th, when he rode to Rehoboth. Dining and lodging along the way, as was his custom while serving on the Superior Court of Judicature, he reached Boston on the 21st. On September 30, at the Third Church after the Thursday lecture service, his "Daughter Sewall," Joseph's wife, "acquaints Madam Winthrop that if she pleased to be within at 3 p.m. I would wait on her. She answered she would be at home."

On his first visit he told her, "My loving wife died so soon and suddenly, 'twas hardly convenient for me to think of marrying again. However, I came to this resolution, that I not make my court to any person without first consulting with you."

Madame Winthrop "propounded one and another" of the other widows of the Third Church "for me, but none would do."

Two days later he came again to her house, on the Boston Common side of what is now Beacon Hill. "I pray that you, Katharine, might be the person assigned for me." She "instantly took it up in way of denial." Aware that he would wish to remain in his mansion, she said, "I believe I should not, cannot leave my children."

Samuel tried to convince her to change her mind. Every few days he visited, bearing gifts of fruit, published sermons, and Canary wine. He chatted with her children and their spouses and children, some of whom lived with her, and gave coins to her many servants. He wrote her love letters, and sometimes she seemed to encourage him. On the evening of October 10 "she treated me with a great deal of courtesy, serving wine and marmalade," and they likely kissed. Two days later, though, she let him into her parlor looking "dark and lowering" and worked on needlepoint the entire time they conversed. He asked permission to remove her glove. She enquired why. He said, "'Tis great odds between handling a dead goat and a living lady."

Eventually he removed the glove and took her hand. "I have one petition to ask of you, that you would take off the negative you laid on me the 3rd of October."

"I cannot leave my house, children, neighbors, business," she said.

He told her, as he had before, that "she might do her children" who lived in her house "as much or more good by bestowing what she laid out in housekeeping on them."

A few days later, frustrated with the courtship, he turned on himself. Praying alone at home on the Sabbath, October 16, he "upbraided myself that [I] could be so solicitous about earthly things; and so cold and indifferent as to the love of Christ, who is altogether lovely."

At his next visit Madame Winthrop began to bargain with him. She "was courteous to me, but took occasion to speak pretty earnestly about my keeping a coach" rather than renting one when needed, which was his practice. "I said 'twould cost a hundred pounds per annum. She said 'twould cost but forty pounds."

A few days later she told him, "You need a wig." Unlike many of his peers, who covered their bald spots with fashionable English periwigs, Samuel gratefully accepted whatever hair God gave. As he'd explained in a letter remonstrating the Roxbury minister, Nehemiah Walter, for his "head dress," "A Great Person has furnished me with perukes, gratis, these two and fifty years...."

To Madame Winthrop he said, "My best and greatest Friend—I could not possibly have a greater—began to find me with hair before I was born, and continued to do so ever since, and I can not find in my heart to go to another."

The court was sitting in Salem, so Samuel had to depart Boston again. On November 2 he returned to Madame Winthrop with an offering of half a pound of expensive sugared almonds. "She seemed pleased with them," he observed, and "asked what they cost."

In negotiations over glasses of Canary wine, he offered her "a hundred pounds per annum" if he died first. Teasingly, he inquired, "What sum would you give me, if you should die first?" She did not reply. He offered, "I will give you time to consider of it." She told him that someone said he had already given his entire estate to his children "by deeds and gift."

"That is a mistake," he said, noting that he still held land, including Point Judith in Rhode Island.

On the evening of November 7, after praying at home with his son Joseph in regard to this emotionally exhausting courtship and then reading two psalms, Samuel walked once more to Madame Winthrop's house. A servant let him into the parlor. Madame Winthrop was rocking her little granddaughter Katie in a cradle.

"Excuse me for coming so late," he said. It was already eight. She showed him to a cushioned armchair positioned so the cradle separated them. He could not reach to touch her. He gave her more sweet almonds. She did not eat them as she had before, to his regret, but put them away.

"I came to inquire whether you have altered your mind since Friday, or remain of the same mind still," he said. "I love you, and am so fond to think that you love me."

"I have a great respect for you."

"I made you an offer without asking any advice. You have so many to advise with that it is a hindrance." He reminded her that she had "already entered the fourth year of your widowhood." The flames in the fireplace were dying down, he noticed. The room grew chilly. Madame Winthrop did not call a servant to add more firewood. He stared at the hearth. Silently, he observed that "at last the one short brand ... fell to pieces, and no recruit was made." Yet she gave him a glass of wine.

"I will go home and bewail my rashness in making more haste than good speed," he said. "I will endeavor to contain myself, and not go on to solicit you to do that which you cannot consent to."

Then he left. "As [I] came down the steps she bid me have a care." She "treated me courteously.... I did not bid her to draw off her glove as sometime I had done. Her dress was not so clean as sometime it had been. *Jehovah jireh!*" That is the Hebrew for "The Lord will provide."

Indeed, seventeen months later, Samuel married Mary Shrimpton Gibbs, a widow of fifty-four. Samuel's son-in-law William Cooper, Judith's husband, performed the ceremony at the Sewall mansion on March 29, 1722. Madame Mary Sewall, as she was now known, was a daughter of Jonathan Shrimpton and Mary Oliver. Her first husband, Robert Gibbs, was a Boston selectman and Third Church member who had died suddenly of smallpox in December 1702, "much lamented," Samuel noted. It was "a great stroke to our church and congregation." As for Madame Winthrop, Samuel remained friendly with her. When she died at the age of sixty, in August 1725, he and his son Joseph were present, and Samuel was one of her pallbearers.

19

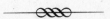

MAIDEN, ARISE

As Samuel set out to create a new life with his third wife, his house was filled with people from his past lives. Several of his Hirst grand-children lived with him. His daughter Hannah, who was an invalid by her thirties, never moved away. She broke her right knee in the summer of 1714, when she was thirty-four, and the next summer she tumbled down stairs and broke the other knee. "Lord, sanctify this smarting rod to me and mine," her father prayed. Not long afterward, on January 6, 1717, she became a member of the Third Church, where her younger brother now preached. Her sixty-five-year-old father petitioned God "that it may be in order to her being taken into Heaven!" Her health worsened after 1720. She could no longer walk, her injuries having never fully healed. She took a bedchamber on the first floor, where she received visitors and engaged in family life. For more than two years she did not leave the house. One of her legs became infected. In the summer of 1724, apparently, it became gangrenous.

Samuel did the only thing he could to help her. He frequently invited ministers, including her brother and brother-in-law, to come pray with her. At night, when Hannah Jr. was in too much pain to sleep, he and his wife, Mary, and her sister sat with her. To pass the time Samuel prayed with his daughter and read or sang psalms.

In the midst of this crisis, Harvard College invited Joseph Sewall, thirty-five, to be its president. This infuriated Cotton Mather, who wanted the job, which his father had once held. Cotton Mather hissed that the college had chosen "a modest young man, of whose piety (and little else) everyone gives a laudable character." Satan "has quarters at the College," Mather added. Joseph, though not privy to Cotton Mather's private thoughts as recorded in his diary, declined the offer because he preferred not to leave Boston and its Third Church.

Cotton Mather also kept private his feelings about Joseph's father's public acceptance of blame for the witch hunt. According to his diary entry on the day after Samuel's public apology, the minister could not sleep. "Discouraging thoughts ... afflicted me," he confessed, "as if unavoidable marks of divine displeasure must overtake my family for [my] not appearing with vigor enough to stop the proceedings of the judges [of the witchcraft court], when the inextricable storm from the invisible world assaulted the country." Unlike Samuel Sewall and Samuel Willard, Cotton Mather suspected that "wicked sorceries" and "Devils" were to blame for the crisis. But he lacked confidence in his view and feared God's wrath. He continued to ponder and study witchcraft in a manner that had the flavor of incipient psychiatry. His sincere interest in medicine and science led Cotton Mather in the summer of 1721 to pioneer the use of inoculation against smallpox, for which he received much public ridicule. For most educated men of Boston, including Samuel Sewall, such medical advancements were almost as frightening as witchcraft.

In the Sewall mansion on Sunday, August 16, 1724, at two in the morning, Samuel heard his daughter Hannah "expostulate." He rose from bed and went downstairs to her. She could not sleep and was afraid. He called his wife, who joined them at Hannah's bedside. Samuel comforted Hannah by reading the Twenty-third Psalm. By dawn Joseph Sewall and William Cooper were in the room praying with Hannah. Samuel recited Psalms 34 and 27. He sent notes to be posted on the doors of the First and Third Churches: "Prayers desired for Hannah Sewall as drawing near her end."

Samuel left the house to attend the morning service at his church. Upon his return a little more than an hour later, he found his oldest daughter already laid out. She had expired at half past ten, while he was at meeting. Sitting beside her body, now at rest, he found "her pleasant countenance ... very refreshing. I hope God has delivered her from all her fears!"

She had asked not to be disemboweled, as her mother had been. As a result of that, the warm weather, and her gangrene, she had to be buried quickly. Samuel noted that his servants "put her into her coffin in a good cere cloth, and bestow a convenient quantity of lime, whereby the noxious humor from her leg may be suppressed and absorbed." One servant, a man named Boston, "will not have her put into the cellar," which was relatively cool, "so she is only removed into the best room. And because the casements were opened for coolness, Boston [said he] would watch [her corpse] all night."

Hannah Jr. was interred in the tomb with her mother, grandparents, and late siblings on August 18. Samuel handed the customary black gloves and rings to notable guests: "Twelve ministers of the town had rings, and two out of town." At the house after the burial, the Reverend Joseph Sewall led family and friends in prayer for his sister. "*Laus Deo,*" his father said.

Two days later the family gathered yet again. The fourteen-month-old son that had been born to Sam Jr. and his wife after their reconciliation was dead. The baby's body was brought to Samuel's house in a coach and buried from the Third Church on August 20, with his uncle Joseph presiding. Less than a month later, fourteen-month-old Mehetabel Cooper, the "dear babe" of William and Judith Cooper, was interred in the family tomb.

During his daughter Hannah's last few years, Samuel had spent long hours at her bedside. While "waiting on my dear child in her last sickness," as he put it, he had worked through a stack of books. One book first struck his interest because it seemed a suitable antidote to long hours in or near a deathbed. Titled *The British Apollo* and published in London in 1711, it contained "about two thousand answers to curious questions in most arts & sciences, serious, comical & humorous," approved of "by many of the most learned & ingenious of both universities & of the Royal Society."

Samuel read several of these questions and answers to Hannah, by way of entertainment. On page 200 he came to a question that both captivated him and also seemed unsuitable for reading aloud on this occasion: "Is there now, or will there be at the resurrection, any females in Heaven?" This was a relevant question, according to the text, "since there seems to be no need of them there."

The *British Apollo*'s reply was, "Since sexes are corporal distinctions, it follows that there can be now no distinction of sex in Heaven, since the souls only of the saints (which are immaterial substances) are as yet in that happy place. And that our rising bodies will not be distinguished into sexes we may fairly gather from those expressions of our Lord's—In the resurrection they neither give nor are given in marriage, but are as the angels of God"—that is, male.

This "malapert question" troubled Samuel. The embedded assumption—*since there seems to be no need of them there*—especially irritated him. In his view, "It is most certain there will be no needless impertinent persons or things in Heaven," because "Heaven is a roomy" and "magnificent palace, furnished with the most rich and splendid entertainments, and the noblest guests are invited to partake of them."

"But why," he wondered, "should there seem to be no need of women in Heaven!" So many of the women whom Samuel loved were dead—his wife Hannah, his brief wife Abigail, his daughter Mary, and his daughter Betty—and now his daughter Hannah. Thinking on them, he felt sure that "God is their father" and "therefore Heaven is their country."

Samuel saw no convincing evidence that women's bodies were less likely to be resurrected than men's although this was the teaching of his church. Puritan theology envisioned heaven as masculine. Men's physical bodies were resurrected as such, but women, once their reproductive function on earth was fulfilled, had no physical role in the afterlife. After death, according to Cotton Mather, the souls of male saints escape their worldly bodies but can still see and hear. They float with angels in a heavenly realm while awaiting the Second Coming. After Christ has destroyed the world and the Devil, he will rule the new world as king. In this Puritan vision the bodies and souls of resurrected saints live and join with Christ in a manner that defies earthly understanding. Cotton Mather conceived of Luther and Zwingli hugging each other and the prophets Moses and Abraham conversing. In the City of God, Mather wrote, the "self will be entirely dethroned," and God's love "will govern every motion." Every body will be male.

Samuel, in his early seventies, desired to record his thoughts on this matter. He took up an old diary and commonplace book that he had bought nearly a half century before. It contained matters of decades past, such as his accounting of his wife Hannah's dowry, paid to him in installments in 1676 by John Hull. It contained his list of accounts received for his father-in-law in the same year for bushels of wheat, barrels of salt, kegs of Madeira wine, and a chestnut mare. It also contained an early draft of *Phaenomena quaedam Apocalyptica* from March 1696.

In the summer of 1724, probably at the bedside of his dying daughter, Samuel began to address the issue of "whether the bodies of women deceased shall be again raised up, and remain in their own sex." He titled his work, *Talitha Cumi*, or An Invitation to Women to Look After Their Inheritance in the Heavenly Mansions." *Talitha cumi*, an Aramaic expression found in the fifth chapter of the Gospel of Mark, means, "Maiden, arise," or "Damsel, arise." He added the author's name, "Samuel Sewall, M.A., sometime fellow of Harvard College in Cambridge in New England," as if he might someday publish these pages. (The complete text of *Talitha Cumi* begins on page 304.) He jotted down two biblical quotes: 2 Corinthians 6:18, "Ye shall be my sons and daughters, saith the Lord Almighty," and Galatians 3:28, "There is neither male nor female: for ye are all one in Christ Jesus." Samuel gathered additional texts he might need, including works of prominent Puritan divines, several "formularies" of the Churches of England and of Scotland, and Tertullian, Jerome, Augustine, and Ambrose. Finally, he stated his thesis: "He that instituted both sexes will restore both" in heaven.

"Is there no need for a daughter to go and see her father when he sends for her?" he wrote. Is there no need for her "to see God, who, though He be a great king, yet is a most loving and tender hearted father?"

Need is not relevant, Samuel concluded. "God has no *need* of any creature," he determined. "By the same argument there will be no angels nor men in Heaven, because there is no *need* of them there. God created all things for his pleasure that he might communicate of his goodness ... and glory. And that this end may be attained, there is need of angels in Heaven and of men and women." Erasmus and

Augustine provided "plain and undeniable proof" that "women have an equal share in the resurrection until eternal life and heavenly glory." In heaven "there is no other change for women than for men. Both men and women shall be freed from sin...."

Samuel was convinced that three biblical women—Eve, Sarah, and Mary—"shall rise again." If "these three rise again," he reasoned, "without doubt all will." Regarding "the blessed Mary, the Mother of our Lord," he added, "for my part I had rather with the Roman Catholics believe that she is in Heaven already, than imagine that she shall never be there." For a Puritan this was a surprising preference.

Elaborating on the mother of Jesus Christ, he wrote, "Never was there so great and honorable a wooing as Mary had.... That blessed womb of hers was the bride chamber wherein the Holy Ghost did knit that indissoluble knot betwixt our human nature and His deity. Our glorious Bridegroom will not demolish the chamber, which He made and dearly bought and paid for, from whence He proceeded, but will repair it with permanent and wonderful magnificence" for eternity. "In the heavenly choir she will indeed appear to be blessed among women." Samuel cited several biblical stories of women cured or raised from the dead. "If the Lord had been minded to deny women a share in the general resurrection from the dead, He would not have provided and recorded for us these preambulatory resurrections."

In the style learned at Harvard, Samuel stated the known objections to his theme. Some commentators had questioned whether "there will be any distinction of sexes" in heaven. Samuel responded by noting "the beautiful variety with which [God] has been pleased to adorn" his works. This prompted Samuel to conclude that "He will have sons and daughters as like Himself as can be."

Another objection someone had raised was that "the ancients are divided" on this question. "That is a shrewd thing indeed!" he noted before dismissing it. "If we should wait till all the ancients are agreed in their opinions, neither men nor women would ever get to Heaven." Finally, in expressing disgust at the *British Apollo*, he scribbled, "One might have thought that the translation of Augustine's excellent book, *De Civitate Dei* [*The City of God*], into English one hundred years ago would have proved a sovereign sufficient antidote against this poison, and would have prevented this wildfire of the *British Apollo* from being thrown about the streets of our great city.

"According to these authorities 'tis past dispute that in the resurrected world Mary shall enjoy her own body, and John shall enjoy his."

Samuel remarked on the "right of women," a most unusual phrase in the early eighteenth century. "If any controversy shall be moved injurious to the right of women before ancient or modern men, in my opinion their safest and surest way is to plead that they are *Coram non judice*," a legal phrase that means "not before a judge or the proper tribunal," and thus to be dismissed. "'Tis not what ... men say concerning the freehold of the moiety of mankind, but what God says who is their creator and redeemer and sanctifier. To this their own Master they stand or fall.... And many [women] are such good lawyers, and are of such quick understanding in the fear of the Lord, and have entertained such an able, faithful, and successful an advocate, they have no reason to be afraid ... seeing [that] all is to be tried and decided by the word of God...."

At one point he addressed his "Courteous Reader," suggesting again his hope that these words would find their way into print. "I have written these few lines from a detestation of that Sadducean argument, There shall be no weddings in Heaven [because] there shall be no women there. And out of a due regard to my dear parents, my mother Eve, and my immediate mother, whose very valuable company I hope shortly to enjoy, and through the (to me) unaccountable grace of God, recover an opportunity of rendering them the honor due to them according to the invaluable and eternal obligation of the Fifth Commandment," which is of course, "Honor thy father and thy mother."

This is far from Governor John Winthrop's use of that commandment to argue for the banishment and excommunication of his powerful neighbor Anne Hutchinson. In 1637 in the Cambridge meetinghouse that served as the Massachusetts court, Winthrop had interpreted the fifth commandment to mean, "Honor the fathers of the commonwealth," in order to silence Hutchinson. As he put it to her, "We do not mean to discourse with those of your sex." And even after Samuel

Sewall composed *Talitha Cumi*, nearly two hundred years would pass before women in America were granted the right to vote.

Most historians have assumed that Sewall's essay on gender equality was never published in its entirety. However, in January 1625 Samuel recorded in his ledger that he paid two pounds to Bartholomew Green, his niece's husband, "for printing and folding 3/2 sheets *Talitha Cumi*." No copies of this twenty-four-page octavo remain.

By this time in his long life, of course, most of Samuel's thoughts were private. His last significant public appearance was on January 2, 1723, when he was called on to address yet another new governor. The previous day the royal governor, Samuel Shute, had returned to England to report to the Privy Council. Now, in the Governor's Council chamber at the Town House, Deputy Governor William Dummer, a son of Samuel's mother's cousin Jeremiah Dummer, the late silversmith, took the oath of office to lead the province in Shute's absence.

Samuel stood up to speak. He was now the senior member of the council. At seventy he was the only magistrate alive who had served under the old charter. He was not only alive and relatively healthy, but he still enjoyed wide public support. In contrast, Cotton Mather had alienated many, Increase Mather was deathly ill, and Samuel Willard had died. As for Samuel Sewall, he was "the crusty conservative of such recognizable probity that all sides trusted him," according to the historian Stephen Foster, which made him "irreproachably independent and in a partisan sense nonpolitical."

Addressing his cousin who was now the acting governor, Samuel followed John Winthrop in referring to New England as a land specially favored by God. "You have this for your encouragement, that the people [here] are a part of the Israel of God, and you may expect to have ... the prudence and patience of Moses.... It is evident that our almighty Savior counseled the first planters to remove hither and settle here," and that "He will never leave nor forsake them nor theirs." He closed with an epigraph from the *Adagia* of Erasmus, "*Difficilia quae pulchra*," which translates to, "Difficult things are beautiful."

Samuel took his seat. All the men in the council chamber rose up to applaud him, which he found delightful and embarrassing in roughly equal parts. In his diary he wrote that the Council "expressed a handsome acceptance of what I had said. *Laus Deo.*"

20

∞∞∞

FIT ME FOR
MY CHANGE

By 1728, the year he turned seventy-five, Samuel Sewall had outlived eleven of his fourteen children. He had outlived two wives. He had outlived every other member of his college class and many of his friends. Both the Reverends Mather were dead, Increase in 1724 and Cotton on February 28, 1728. As for the nine Salem witch judges, Samuel was the only one left.

In old age Samuel was deeply grateful for his remaining fruits, his children and grandchildren. "There is all my stock," he had remarked of his sons and daughters to a Dorchester minister in 1698; "I desire your blessing of them." Writing in 1720 to Sam Jr., who had asked him to put down his early memories, Samuel said, "It pleased God to favor us" in 1677 "with the birth of your brother John Sewall," their firstborn. "In June 1678 you were born. Your brother lived till the September following, and then died. So that by the undeserved goodness of God your mother and I never were without a child after the second of April 1677.

"And now what shall I render to the Lord for all His benefits?" Samuel asked his son. "The good Lord help me to walk humbly and thankfully with Him all my days, and profit by mercies and by afflictions, that through faith and patience I may also in due time fully inherit the promises. Let us incessantly pray for each other, that it may be so!"

Samuel's long public life was coming to a close. In 1728 he resigned as chief justice of the most powerful court in New England, a position he had occupied since 1718. He resigned from the Suffolk County Probate Court, on which he had served since 1715. Including the nine years prior to 1692 that he was a magistrate of the General Court of the colony as well as his thirty-five years on the Superior Court of Judicature, he had served New England as a judge for close to half a century.

His legacy was a concern. He had tried to be fair and wise. Yet he was, and would always be, a Salem witch judge. On April 23, 1720, as he scanned the contemporary historian Daniel Neal's new two-volume *History of New England to 1700*, he was shocked to find New England's "nakedness" there "laid open in the businesses of the Quakers, Anabaptists, witchcraft." In regard to the latter he flushed to see his own name in the text. "The judges' names are mentioned [on] page 502" of the second volume, and "my confession" is on page 536. He prayed, "Good and gracious God, be pleased to save New England and me, and my family!"

As for the dependency of old age, Samuel accepted it gracefully. Over the decades he had prayed for his children. Now they prayed for him. On April 3, 1726, after hearing his son preach on Genesis 1:26, Samuel prayed, "I desire with humble thankfulness to bless God who has favored me with such an excellent discourse to begin my 75th year, withal delivered by my own son, making him as a parent to his father."

Repentance was a continuing process. In November 1707, during one of the public battles over the tenure and behavior of Governor Joseph Dudley, Samuel prayed, "Lord, do not depart from me, but pardon my sin; and fly to me in a way of favorable protection!" Seven years later, in Plymouth on court business, he was called to view the body of a "poor Indian" who slipped off a boat to his death. Samuel knew that the man, twenty-six-year-old Samuel Toon, was "not disordered by drink." He mused, "I, in many respects a greater sinner [than he], am suffered to go well away, when my poor namesake, by an unlucky accident, has a full stop put to his proceedings, and not half as old as I." He was still repenting in April 1718, when he wrote on the

occasion of the death of his old friend Elisha Hutchinson, "The Lord
help me, that as He is anointing me with fresh oil, as to my office, so
He would graciously pardon my sin, and furnish me with renewed and
augmented ability for the rightful discharge of the trust reposed in
me!" Five years later, a December 1723 sermon on Revelation 2:21
prompted seventy-one-year-old Samuel to pray, "Lord, help me to hear
and obey the pungent exhortations to repentance, and that the godliness may be and appear in me! I humbly bless You ... and earnestly
pray that You would pardon my unworthiness ... and that You would
condescend to know me and be known of me!"

Samuel had many models in preparing for death. Christ was first.
The old schoolmaster Ezekiel Cheever was another. Samuel visited
Cheever often in August 1707 as the ninety-four-year-old weakened
and died. In Cheever's bedchamber the two men discussed the "afflictions"—human losses and suffering—which, they agreed, were God's
way of testing and improving humanity. Referring to New Englanders' afflictions, Cheever said to Samuel, "God did by them as a goldsmith" does. "Knock, knock, knock. Knock, knock, knock, to finish the
plate. It was to perfect them, not to punish them."

Even after the dying Cheever no longer recognized his own son
Thomas, whose scandalous behavior cost him his pulpit in 1686, he
still knew Samuel. The latter reported, "August 13. I go to see
[Cheever], went in with his son Thomas.... His son spake to him, and
he knew him not. I spake to him, and he bid me speak again. Then he
said, 'Now I know you,' and speaking cheerily mentioned my name."
Samuel requested Cheever's blessing for himself and his family.

"You are blessed, and it cannot be reversed," the dying man prophesied.

At another visit Cheever took Samuel's hand and begged him to
pray with him.

"The last enemy is death," Samuel reassured him, "and God hath
made that a friend, too." Cheever lifted his bony hand from beneath
the bedcovers and "held it up, to signify his assent." Samuel, who had
observed Cheever enjoy a slice of orange, returned later with a dish of
marmalade and "a few of the best figs I could get."

The next morning Cheever was dead. Samuel wrote in his diary
this final note on his friend: "Came over to New England 1637, to

Boston. ... Labored in that calling [of teaching] skillfully, diligently, constantly, religiously, seventy years. A rare instance of piety, health, strength, serviceableness. The welfare of the Province was much upon his spirit. He abominated periwigs." For Boston's old guard, the wig remained a powerful symbol of evil. A few years before, in January 1703, Samuel had copied six pages "transcribed out of the original manuscript of the Reverend Mr. Nicholas Noyes (of Salem), ... 'Reasons against wearing of Periwigs made of women's hair, as the custom now is, deduced from Scripture and reason.'"

Another inspiration in preparing for death was the Reverend John Eliot. At the grave of Eliot's wife in 1687 the widower had wept at his inability to join her. Years later, on his own deathbed, Eliot's last words were "Welcome joy!" Eliot had preached, in a sermon recorded by Cotton Mather, that "our employment lies in heaven. In the morning, if we ask, 'Where am I to be today?' our souls must answer, 'In heaven.' In the evening, if we ask, 'Where have I been today?' our souls may answer, 'In heaven.' If thou art a believer, thou art no stranger to heaven while thou livest; and when thou diest, heaven will be no strange place to thee; no, thou hast been there a thousand times before."

Samuel's health declined. By 1725 he was "a lame fainting soldier." His "locomotive facility" was "enfeebled." He had weak hands, back trouble, and "feeble knees." His upper and lower teeth fell out. He took this as a "warning that I must shortly resign my head."

"Lord," he prayed, "help me to do it cheerfully."

The greatest loss was his ability to sing, which had been a problem for some time. In 1705, when he was only in his early fifties, Samuel had tried to set the Windsor tune for the twentieth verse of Psalm 66 but somehow "fell into" High Dutch. Trying to revert to Windsor, he found himself in "a key much too high." He felt foolish and asked another man to set the tune, "which he did well," choosing the Litchfield tune. At church a few years later, in the summer of 1713, he tried to set Low Dutch "and failed. Tried again and fell into the tune of the 119th Psalm." He wondered if he was too old to "line out" the psalm tune so people could hear him and follow. Five years later, also at meeting, Samuel set the York tune, which at the second verse the congregation in the gallery "carried ... irresistibly to Saint David's."

Bay Psalm Book, 9th Edition, 1698

York Tune

St. David's Tune

This melodic shift "discouraged me very much," Samuel noted. He resigned his post as deacon of the Third Church.

One night in July 1728, after an "extraordinary sickness of flux and vomiting," he felt it was "high time for me to be favored with some leisure, that I may prepare for the entertainments of another world."

A month later, though, the seventy-six-year-old retired chief justice went out for a walk after the meeting one Sabbath afternoon. Following a brilliant thundershower, the sun was out. As Samuel strolled through his neighborhood on the Shawmut Peninsula, a "noble" rainbow emerged from a cloud.

Amazed, he stopped, leaned on his cane, and watched the rainbow. It seemed to penetrate the cloud. The "eastern end" of the rainbow "stood upon Dorchester Neck, and the other foot stood upon the town" of Boston.

A rainbow was a biblical symbol of God's covenant with Israel. As such it was a "cause for celebration," according to David Hall. In the ninth chapter of the book of Genesis, after saving Noah from the flood, God tells Noah that he places a rainbow and clouds in the sky to show that he will send no more floods. "This is the token of the covenant which I make between me and you ... for perpetual generations: I do set my [rain]bow in the cloud, and it shall be for a token of a covenant between me and the earth ... and the waters shall no more become a flood to destroy all flesh. And the bow shall be in the cloud; and I will look upon it, that I may remember the everlasting covenant...."

Samuel watched the rainbow for a long time so he could describe it in detail and try to discern its meaning. It was so bright that "the reflection of it caused another faint rainbow to the westward of it. But the entire completeness of it, throughout the whole arch, and for its duration, the like has been rarely seen. It lasted about a quarter of an hour. The middle parts were discontinued for a while; but the former integrity and splendor were quickly recovered. I hope this is a sure token that Christ remembers His covenant for His beloved Jews under their captivity and dispersion; and that He will make haste to prepare for them a city that has foundations, whose builder and maker is God."

In referring to God's "beloved Jews," Samuel meant not only the Jewish people, whose conversion to Christianity he awaited, but also the saints of Boston, the members of his church.

Meanwhile, the physical structure of that church was crumbling. The male members of the Third Church had decided by a vote of forty-one to twenty to build a new church on the same spot as the old. Samuel opposed this decision. He preferred to renovate the cedar meeting-house in which so much of his spiritual life, including his statement of repentance for the witch hunt, had occurred. In February 1729 he wrote a letter to the church's pastors, his son and Joseph Prince:

That our meeting house needs repairing is apparent, and I apprehend that it ought to be done as soon as the season of the year will admit. But ... the building of a new meeting house ... is now unseemly. God in his holy providence preserving this, seems plainly to advise us to the contrary. This is a very good meeting house, and we have not convenient room to build a new one in, while this is standing. And considering the terrible earthquakes we have had, shaking all our foundations, it behooves us to walk humbly with our God and to observe the divine counsel given to Barach by the Prophet Jeremiah in the forty-fifth chapter, and to take care that we do not say in the pride and greatness of heart, "We will cut down the sycamores, and change them into cedars," Isaiah 9:10.

This did not move the pastors. They proceeded with construction of a new church, during which the congregations of the Third and First Churches both worshipped at the First Church.

Samuel must have come round to this plan, for in the fall of 1729 he marked his initials on the granite cornerstone of the new Third Church. A stonemason carved the distinctive *S*'s into the stone, where they can still be found on the cornerstone of the Old South Meeting House, as the church is now known. Samuel was also asked to name that street, then Cornhill Road, which passed his church and his house on its way to Roxbury. Samuel chose to call it Newbury Street, after his hometown. In the nineteenth century, after that main road became Washington Street, "Newbury Street" moved about a mile northwest, into the Back Bay. Today Boston is a metropolitan area of several million people, but its population then was less than 15,000, according to John Bonner's 1722 map, which indicates three hundred houses in Boston, Dorchester, Charlestown, and Roxbury. New England had only 30,000 inhabitants.

Many of Samuel's best qualities—warmth, eagerness to solve problems, delight in making a good match—remained intact even as his body "mouldered down apace." On October 13, 1729, eleven weeks before he died, he wrote what was to be the final entry in his diary. The subject was the engagement of his granddaughter, Betty Hirst's daughter Jane, who lived in his mansion. He enjoyed his power in such matters and tried to wield it wisely. That autumn morning, "Judge [Addington] Davenport," one of his former colleagues on the Superior Court, "comes to me ... and speaks to me on behalf of Mr. Addington Davenport, his eldest son, that he might have liberty to wait upon Jane Hirst, now at my house, in way of courtship."

The elder Davenport, a member of Harvard's class of 1689, told Samuel he would build a house for the couple if they married and give his son his pew at church. The son, a twenty-eight-year-old lawyer, had graduated from Harvard in 1719.

Judge Davenport's generous offer pleased Samuel. He had spoken at length with his twenty-two-year-old granddaughter, as he had previously done with her mother and his other daughters. He knew she loved the young man.

At the conclusion of these pleasant negotiations Samuel would have liked to walk Judge Davenport to the gate, an obligatory gesture of courtesy to departing guests. Thirty years earlier he had paid a stonemason to carve and set up "cherubim's heads" atop the two gateposts at the street before his house. In Exodus 25:18–22, God asks Moses to make "two cherubims of gold," with outstretched wings, "and their faces shall look one to another." God promises Israel, "I will commune with thee from … between the two cherubims…." Over the decades—until January 1725, when a windstorm toppled the statuary—Samuel had enjoyed taking leave of guests between the stone cherubim with outstretched wings.

But now he was too feeble to walk outside. So "I gave [Davenport] my hand at his going away and acknowledged his respect to me and granted his desire."

Soon afterward, Samuel's maternal cousin, fifty-two-year-old William Dummer—"His Honor the Lieutenant Governor"—arrived at the mansion for a visit. Samuel "informed his Honor of what Mr. Davenport had been about; his Honor approved it much, commended the young man, and reckoned it a very good match."

With this match Samuel Sewall's diary concludes as a comedy. The Reverend Joseph Sewall joined Addington Davenport and Jane Hirst in marriage at the Sewall mansion on December 23, 1729, in the Great Hall in which the bride's parents, grandparents, and great-grandparents had exchanged vows.

Samuel Sewall went to bed for the last time a day or two after their wedding, which he was apparently too weak to attend. He spent his final short days and long nights in his bedchamber in the house that he and John Hull had each renovated, which Hannah's grandfather had built almost a century before. He lay in the bed in which Hannah and all their children were born. He had prayed here at the deathbeds of his babies and his wives. Now it was his turn to die.

His son Joseph visited him on the day after Christmas. "My father seems to grow weaker," he noted in his own diary, recording his father's final days. Sensing the end was near, Joseph spent as much time as possible with his father.

Samuel could no longer sing a psalm, but he occasionally roused himself to pray. He repeated the Creed and the Lord's Prayer. His recitation of the Our Father was not flawless, like that of the Reverend George Burroughs on the gallows, but it too was heartfelt.

As Samuel pondered his final end and his just deserts, he said to Joseph, "If any man sin, we have an advocate with the Father." Joseph knew the reference, 1 John 2:1: "My little children, these things write I unto you, that ye sin not. And if any man sin, we have an advocate with the Father, Jesus Christ the righteous."

"For what do you wish to pray?" Joseph asked him.

"That I might follow the captain of my salvation." Father and son prayed together that Samuel would be saved and know God after death.

Every day he spoke less. Yet his mind remained keen. He listened attentively on December 29 as Joseph read to him John 11:23–27, in which Jesus tells Martha, a sister of the deceased Lazarus, "Thy brother shall rise again."

Martha replies with faith. "I know that he shall rise again in the resurrection at the last day."

Jesus says, "I am the resurrection, and the life: he that believeth in me, though he were dead, yet shall he live: And whosoever liveth and believeth in me shall never die. Believest thou this?"

"Yea, Lord," Martha says. "I believe that thou art the Christ, the Son of God, which should come into the world."

Samuel considered this story, which he knew by heart, once more. He raised his head slightly to say something to his son. His long, white hair cascaded over his pillow. "We are beholden to Martha," he said. Martha was one of the women around Jesus Christ whose examples had suggested that women's bodies are as worthy of resurrection as men's.

As so often happened to Samuel, his mind wandered back to sin. He could not forget the sinfulness that underlay his repentance as well as his continued effort to turn back to God. He murmured something about "the brazen serpent."

Joseph knew that the serpent on a cruciform stake, resembling the cross of Christ, was a biblical image of saving faith. In Numbers 21 God sends a plague of serpents to punish his people for their lack of faith. Moses intercedes for Israel and offers that the people of Israel will repent. God tells Moses, "Make thee a fiery serpent, and set it upon a pole: and it shall come to pass, that every one that is bitten, when he looketh upon it, shall live." The New Testament takes up this story in John 3:14: "And as Moses lifted up the serpent in the wilderness, even so must the Son of man be lifted up: That whosoever believeth in him should not perish, but have eternal life."

For a long time no one said anything. Samuel was praying. "Looking to Jesus," he muttered. "He [is] the only remedy."

Joseph stayed overnight at his father's house on Wednesday, December 31, 1729. While the son slept for a few hours the servants kept a fire burning in Samuel's room. Well before dawn on the first day of 1730, Massachusetts Bay Colony's centennial, a servant summoned Joseph to his father's bed.

Samuel's breathing was labored. Still, he could pray with his son. Servants sent word through the dark town that the judge was near his earthly end. The Reverend William Cooper, husband of Samuel's only surviving daughter, and the Reverend Charles Chauncy, the young First Church pastor who was married to Samuel's granddaughter Elizabeth Hirst, arrived to join the circle of prayer. "Cousin Chauncy," a namesake and great-grandson of Harvard's second president, was doubly related to Samuel: his mother was a sister of Joseph's wife. Chauncy, a member of the Harvard class of 1721, would preach at the First Church for more than half a century, become a patriot in the Revolutionary period, and die in 1787.

Three ministers attended Samuel at his deathbed—his twenty-five-year-old grandson-in-law; a son-in-law, thirty-three; and his forty-one-year-old son. Amid their many prayers Joseph observed that his father "seemed to enjoy the use of his reason." This had almost always been true of Samuel.

"My honored father expired" at 5:35 in the morning on January 1, Joseph reported. The hour was "near the time in which 29 years ago he was so affected upon the beginning of the century, when he made those verses to usher in the New Year, once more our God vouchsafe to shine." As the family and servants tended to Samuel's body, the sun rose over the town that he once referred to, in a letter, as "our Boston peninsula, which I am a little fond of."

At long last Samuel had completed his earthly career as a follower of Christ. Rather than "groaning under the heavy consequences of his cruelties," as Nathaniel Hawthorne imaged his ancestor the Salem witch judge doing, Samuel had sought forgiveness and expiation of sin. As a result, Samuel freed his descendants from the guilt that Hawthorne apparently felt. In the preface to *The Scarlet Letter*, Hawthorne wrote of his ancestors, "I, the present writer, as their representative, hereby take shame upon myself for their sakes, and pray that any curse incurred by them ... may be now and henceforth removed." Scholars interpret the *A* carved by the Reverend Arthur Dimmesdale onto his own flesh as the author's symbolic self-mortification for the sins of Judge John Hathorne.

Samuel Sewall's servants wrapped his body in a linen pall for burial. They did not remove his hair shirt, my late great-aunt Charlotte May Wilson told me, because he had asked to be buried in it. Burial in a hair shirt was unusual for a Puritan, but it had precedents among devout Christians. Charlemagne, the ninth-century Holy Roman Emperor, and the twelfth-century martyr Saint Thomas Becket, Archbishop of Canterbury, were buried in their hair shirts. Decades earlier, during his memorable visit to the Winchester College library, Samuel had viewed Becket's earliest-known portrait, in the early-thirteenth-century manuscript of the *Life of St. Thomas Becket*.

On Wednesday, January 7, a "fair cold day," Samuel was interred in the family tomb. His body still lies there, in Boston's Old Granary Burying Ground, alongside the remains of his wife Hannah, fourteen children, and more than twenty other relatives. Hundreds of people gathered for his funeral at the Third Church, of which he had been a member for fifty-three years.

At that church the next day the Reverend Thomas Prince, Joseph's Harvard classmate, took as the text for his Thursday lecture 1 Samuel 7:15–17: "And Samuel judged Israel all the days of his life; and he went from year to year in circuit to Bethel and Gilgal and Mispeh, and judged Israel in all those places: and his return was to Ramah, for there was his house, and there he judged Israel, and there he built an altar to the Lord." This was an apt Scripture to honor a judge who rode from year to year in circuit to Bristol and Plymouth and York and always returned to Boston.

Scores of friends and family, including his widow, Madame Mary Sewall, who lived another sixteen years, his three surviving children, and their spouses and children, listened to Prince's lecture. Prince, a fellow lover of the psalms, would later publish the *Revisal of the New England Version of the Psalms*.

In Prince's words, Samuel Sewall was "esteemed and beloved among us for his eminent piety," "cheerful conversation," "regard to justice," "compassionate heart," "neglect of the world," "catholic and public" spirit, "critical acquaintance with the Holy Scriptures in their inspired originals," "zeal for the purity of instituted worship," "tender concern for the aboriginal natives," and, "as the crown of all, his moderation, peaceableness and humility."

Joseph gave the second sermon, which he titled *The Orphan's Best Legacy.* His text was the tenth verse of Psalm 27: "When my father and my mother forsake me, then the Lord will take me up." Had Samuel been able, he would surely have lined out the psalm for the congregation to sing.

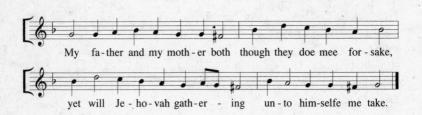

My fa-ther and my moth-er both though they doe mee for-sake,
yet will Je-ho-vah gath-er - ing un-to him-selfe me take.

EPILOGUE

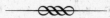

Samuel Sewall had carefully overseen scores of wills in his role as a probate judge, but he died intestate, trusting his two sons agreeably to settle his estate. His mansion went to forty-one-year-old Joseph. Because Joseph chose to remain in the parsonage of the Third Church, he turned over the mansion to his older brother, fifty-one-year-old Sam Jr., who lived in it with his family.

Samuel's youngest daughter, Judith, the only one of his seven daughters who survived him, was twenty-nine when he died. She died a decade later, at thirty-nine, on December 23, 1740, of unknown causes. Her oldest son, William Cooper Jr., a Boston town clerk, was a prominent Patriot in the Revolution, one of whose great-grandsons was Oliver Wendell Holmes Jr., a justice of the Supreme Court of the United States. Judith's second son, the Reverend Samuel Cooper, preached at the Brattle Square Church like his father and was a founder of the American Academy of Arts and Sciences.

Sam Jr. and Joseph were the only Sewall offspring who enjoyed old age. In December 1738 Sam Jr. asked the Massachusetts House of Representatives to appoint a committee to determine "the circumstances of the persons and families who suffered in the calamity of the times in and about the year 1692." Samuel's son "entered into the matter with great zeal," the historian Charles Upham noted, and the court unanimously supported his order. As head of the committee then formed, Sam Jr. wrote letters asking his cousin Mitchell Sewall, of Salem, Stephen's son, and John Higginson, whose father had partici-pated in the hunt until the accusation of his wife, to help the cause. As a result of these and other efforts, Governor Jonathan Belcher in No-vember 1740 determined to "inquire into the sufferings of the people called Quakers ... and also into the descendants of such families as were in a manner ruined in the mistaken management of the terrible affair called witchcraft. I really think there is something incumbent on this government to be done for relieving the estates and reputations of the posterities of the unhappy families that so suffered...."

Sam Jr. died at the Sewall mansion in Boston in 1751 at seventy-two, survived only by his son, Henry. Henry inherited the Sewall farm in Brookline, which extended from what is now the western campus of Boston University to Fenway Park and the Muddy River in the Long-wood Medical Area. Tens of thousands of people, including me, now live on this land.

Joseph was the most enduring Sewall child, living until he was eighty, even longer than his father had. Joseph served a "long and mostly serene" ministry at the Third Church. At the end of his life he supported colonial America's independence from England and allowed the Third Church to become "a shrine of the American cause." He preached into his eightieth year and died on June 27, 1769, survived by only one of his and Elizabeth's two sons, Samuel (1715–1771). That Samuel Sewall married his distant cousin Elizabeth Quincy, the sister of John Hancock's wife, Dorothy. They too had a son, Samuel Sewall, who, like his great-grandfather, attended Harvard (class of 1776) and grew up to be chief justice of the Superior Court of Judicature. That Judge Samuel Sewall's son the Reverend Samuel Sewall, of Burling-ton, Massachusetts, in the nineteenth century donated the diaries and letters of his great-great-grandfather to the Massachusetts Historical Society, where they remain.

Another great-grandchild of Joseph Sewall was my great-great-great-grandfather the Reverend Samuel Joseph May (1797–1871), a Unitarian minister and abolitionist. The Reverend May (Harvard class of 1817) noted defensively in his memoir that our ancestor partici-pated in the Salem witch trials only "as a junior judge." He "was among the first to suspect, and afterward to expose, the delusion" of the witch hunt, and he "strove in so many ways to atone for that early wrong." The "early" suggests Sewall's youth, but the Reverend May must have known that in 1692 Sewall was forty years old.

Samuel Joseph May's sister, Abigail May Alcott (1800–1877), was the mother of Louisa May Alcott, another lineal descendant of Samuel Sewall. The May and Sewall families had merged in 1784 with the wedding of Colonel Joseph May (1760–1841), a founder of Massachusetts General Hospital, and Dorothy Sewall, a great-granddaughter of Samuel Sewall through his son Joseph.

Repentance was the subject of a sermon that the Reverend Joseph Sewall addressed to the governor and council of New England at Boston's Town House on December 3, 1740. Addressing the passage in the Old Testament Book of Jonah in which Jonah warns the city of Nineveh of its need to repent, Joseph Sewall envisioned Jonah walking around the present world warning people to repent. "No greatness or worldly glory will be any security against God's destroying judgments," Samuel's son preached, "if such places go on obstinately in their sins. O let not London! Let not Boston, presume to deal unjustly in the land of uprightness, lest the holy God say of them, as of his ancient people,... 'I will punish you for all your iniquities.'" The king of Nineveh "humbled himself before the most high" and "arose from his throne, and laid his robe from him, and covered him[self] with sackcloth, and sat in ashes."

Joseph Sewall continued, "We must believe our Lord Jesus when he says to us, *Except ye repent, yet shall all likewise perish*. ... We must abhor ourselves, lie down before God in deep abasement, and humble ourselves under his mighty hand." Finally, he assured his listeners, quoting Ezekiel, "A new heart also will I give you, and a new spirit will I put within you, and I will take away [your] stony heart ... and I will give you a heart of flesh...." It is hard to imagine that this sermon, "Nineveh's repentance and deliverance," was not inspired by Joseph's father.

More than a century later the historian Charles Upham closed his seminal study of the witch hunt, *Salem Witchcraft* (1867), with the story of Samuel Sewall. Having traversed "scenes of the most distressing and revolting character," Upham wished to "leave before your imagination one [scene] bright with all the beauty of Christian virtue." That was "Judge Sewall standing forth in the house of his God and in the presence of his fellow-worshippers, making a public declaration of his sorrow and regret of the mistaken judgment he had co-operated with others in pronouncing. Here you have a representation of a truly great and magnanimous spirit," which had achieved a "victory over itself; a spirit so noble and pure, that it felt no shame in acknowledging an error, and publicly imploring, for a great wrong done to his fellow-creatures, the forgiveness of God and man."

Upham warned, "Elements of the witchcraft delusion of 1692 are slumbering still," and "always will be.... The human mind feels instinctively its connection with a higher sphere. Some will ever be impatient of the restraints of our present mode of being, and ... eager to pry into the secrets of the invisible world, willing to venture beyond the bounds of ascertainable knowledge, and ... to aspire where the laws of evidence cannot follow them." Or, as the twentieth-century historian Keith Thomas observed, "If magic is to be defined as the employment of ineffective techniques to allay anxiety when effective ones are not available, then ... no society will ever be free from it."

Rectifying the wrong of the witch hunt took centuries and remains incomplete. Not until 2001 were the last five victims of the Salem witch hunt exonerated. The legislative act to pardon Susanna Martin, Bridget Bishop, Alice Parker, Margaret Scott, and Wilmot Reed was signed that year on Halloween by Massachusetts governor Jane Swift, John Winthrop's first female successor. "The fear of malefic witchcraft is still a problem in many parts of the world," the historian Marilynne Roach noted in 2002. Witchcraft executions occurred in Switzerland as late as 1782, in Germany until 1793, and in Mexico in the twentieth century. Even today "neighbors and witch-finders in Africa, India, Slovakia, the Ukraine, and elsewhere blame suspects—often women—for causing local misfortunes," Roach noted. During the last decade of the twentieth century, for instance, authorities in Bihar, India, killed more than four hundred suspected witches.

Samuel Sewall's world is less distant than it seems. We too may never transcend superstition and misjudgment. Yet he can be our guide in acknowledging and rectifying our wrongs. Like him, we are capable of a change of heart.

EXPLORING
SAMUEL SEWALL'S
AMERICA AND ENGLAND

Although he was peripatetic for his day, thrice crossing the Atlantic Ocean, Samuel Sewall never traveled far beyond southern England, where he was born, and Massachusetts, where he spent most of his life. In sixty-eight years in New England he rode or sailed only as far north as Maine's Kennebec River, as far west as Albany, New York, and as far south as Manhattan. As a result of this—and his frequent, detailed diary entries—it is not hard for us to follow his steps.

Samuel's favorite place on earth, where he envisioned the Second Coming of Jesus Christ, was the Great Marsh on Massachusetts's North Shore. Much of New England's coastal wetlands have been destroyed to make way for cities and suburbs. But the Great Marsh is still there, protected by the federal government and local groups as a wildlife preserve. As a result, the Great Marsh provides a rare glimpse of Samuel's seventeenth-century world.

An edge of the Great Marsh can be seen from a car on Interstate 95 just north of the Scotland Road, Newbury, exit. For a closer look, visit Perley's Marina, a boatyard along the Rowley River just south of Newbury. Perley's sells fishing tackle, worms, and cold drinks. Nautical maps of the Rowley River, Ipswich Bay, and Plum Island Sound plaster the walls. On the hot July morning that I explored these waters with a local fisherman, the greenhead flies were biting, especially at the low speed required near shore. (They bothered Samuel, who also reported "much affliction ... by the mosquitoes" on the Maine coast in August 1717.) A few hundred yards east of Perley's Marina the Rowley River passes under the bridge that conveys the Boston-Newburyport commuter rail. Just beyond the bridge the Great Marsh opens up and spreads out. Water, sky, and marsh grass predominate. A few duck-hunting cabins and houses on stilts, accessible only by boat, dot the marsh. That morning an osprey flew overhead. In the mud beside the estuary a snowy egret dug for food.

A mile or so east of the marina the river meets Plum Island Sound, the warm, calm, shallow bay that is protected by the slender, sandy strip of Plum Island. The sound teems with blue fish, sea bass, cod, haddock, flounder, and mackerel. A few herring remain, but the sturgeon, which were plentiful in Samuel's day, are gone. From a boat in the middle of Plum Island Sound, you can roll back the centuries. With the exceptions of thickly settled Ipswich Neck and occasional structures in the Rowley marsh, this landscape bears almost no sign of European settlement. The view is remarkably like what Samuel Sewall saw from here as a boy and remembered as a man. It is not unlike Governor John Winthrop's first view of Boston, from Charlestown in the summer of 1630. Most of the city we know as Boston was then underwater at high tide, including the land beneath Faneuil Hall, Quincy Market, the Prudential and John Hancock buildings, the Public Garden, Massachusetts General Hospital, the Back Bay, and the South End. The Great Marsh now conveys an image of coastal New England when it was inhabited only by Native American tribes.

Two-thirds of Plum Island—accessible by boat or a bridge at its northern end—is a nature preserve. The unprotected, northern third of the island is thickly settled, crowded with summer homes and convenience stores. A single road leads south to the preserve, which is populated by scrub pines and junipers, great blue herons, and occasionally a glossy ibis. In the 1950s the federal government banned all development on this part of Plum Island and restricted owners of existing houses from altering them, selling them, or bequeathing them to anyone but a direct heir. As the final heir of each house died, the government razed it. By the early twenty-first century only one house remained in the preserve, a wind-worn Victorian with a wraparound porch overlooking a grassy lawn and private dock. The house belonged to a childless man in his nineties who still swept the sidewalk in front of a Rowley gas station, which he owned.

Duck hunters were the intended beneficiaries of the federal government's action on Plum Island, according to Kathryn Glenn, an official of the Massachusetts Office of Coastal Zone Management. "Migratory birds use Plum Island as a flyway, which the federal government saved, to protect ducks for hunting." Local environmental groups soon became involved and the philosophy changed. Now the birds—and landscape—are saved for themselves. In the wake of the preservation of most of Plum Island, the Essex County Greenbelt Association, Massachusetts Audubon Society, and Trustees of Reservations collaborated with local officials to protect a much larger swath of the North Shore. Locals now refer to a Great Marsh spanning seventeen miles of the northern Massachusetts coast, from Salisbury on the New Hampshire border south to West Gloucester.

The Great Marsh includes every place that Samuel Sewall mentioned in *Phaenomena quaedam Apocalyptica*, his 1697 essay prophesying the location of Christ's return. The Merrimac and Parker rivers still flow in from the sea near the northern tip of Plum Island. Hiking trails meander through woods and marsh at the Parker River Wildlife Refuge, a haven for birders in Newbury and Rowley. Crane Pond, a widening of the Parker River several miles inland, is on protected land along the border between West Newbury and Groveland. Turkey Hill, at an elevation of 135 feet, stands on the southeast shore of Artichoke Reservoir, just west of Interstate 95 at the border of Newbury and West Newbury. From the summit of Newbury's Old Town Hill, which the Trustees of Reservations maintains, the public can view an expanse of coastal Massachusetts, New Hampshire, and Maine. These and many more sites that Samuel knew and loved are marked on *Protected Open Space of Essex County*, a 2004 map published by the Essex County Greenbelt Association (www.ecga.org).

In the center of modern Newbury, the seventeenth-century house of Sewall's parents still stands and is occupied. It sits beside a gas

station on the western side of bustling Route 1A just north of the intersection of Parker Street, near the Town Green. Newbury's First
Church Congregational, erected in the early 1900s, is on the same side
of Route 1A, slightly to the north. The site of the meetinghouse that
Samuel and his family attended, where he once filled in for his teacher
the Reverend Parker, was across the road, at the southerly portion of
Newbury's Old Burying Ground. At the northern edge of this cemetery, among the oldest gravestones, are slates purchased by Samuel to
honor his parents, Henry and Jane, and his son Hull (1684–1686).

The original village of Newbury, which Samuel's grandfather and
father and other English settlers founded in 1635, was about two
miles south on Route 1A, at the Lower Green, between the Parker
River and Old Town Hill. The landing place of the first settlers is
marked by a stone alongside the river. Across the river, below the
Route 1A bridge, Fernald's Marina rents kayaks for exploring the
river and sound. Inland along the Parker River, a mile east of Interstate 95 on Central Street in Byfield, one can still see the waterfall
beside which Samuel enjoyed strawberries and cream with his sister
Anne Longfellow in June 1686 while visiting his twenty-two-month-
old son Hull. "The Falls," as he called it, is just one of many places on
the North Shore where members of Samuel's family owned acreage.
Not long ago I discovered that land along the Ipswich River owned by
my aunt Judith, who was named for Samuel's youngest daughter, was
in the mid-seventeenth century the property of Samuel's father.

About twenty-five miles south of Newbury is Salem, which now ad-
vertises itself as the "Witch City." Salem's Peabody Essex Museum has
a large collection of documents and artifacts from the witch hunt. Adjacent to the museum, beside the seventeenth-century cemetery in which
Judge John Hathorne and Governor Simon Bradstreet are buried, is a
stone memorial to those who died during the 1692 witch hunt. The
cemetery, now named after Charter Street, was then the Burying Point.
The house of Samuel's brother Stephen is long gone, as are most houses
linked to the witch hunt. However, Judge Jonathan Corwin's house, at
310½ Essex Street, is open as a museum, the Witch House of Salem.

In 1992, the tercentenary of the witch hunt, the nearby town of
Danvers, which was then Salem Village, erected a roadside memorial
at 176 Hobart Street to honor those hanged as witches. The handsome

house and hillside farm of Rebecca Nurse, at 149 Pine Street in Danvers, are open to the public and well worth a visit. Nurse was the basis for the heroic central character in the film *Two Sovereigns for Sarah.* Her body was buried on Gallows Hill, but her family erected a memorial stone beneath a tree down the hill from her house.

Twenty miles to the south one can still find Samuel's grave, a large gray slab marked SEWALL, near the back of the Old Granary Burying Ground on Tremont Street in downtown Boston. This cemetery, a short walk from the Park Street subway station, opened in 1660 and closed for health reasons in 1879. Many prominent early Bostonians, including forty members of the Sewall, Hull, and Quincy families, are buried here. A few short blocks away, at the Old South Meeting House, at 308 Washington Street, Samuel's initials—*S.S.*—are still visible in the granite cornerstone. Old South was built in stone in 1629–30 to replace the cedar Third, or South, Church in which Samuel worshipped for half a century. In 1773 Old South was the site of tax protests that led to the Boston Tea Party. One of Boston's oldest public buildings, it was scheduled for demolition in 1876 but saved by preservationists. While Samuel's church and his family crypt remain today, the city surrounding them has dramatically changed. Not only have Boston's wetlands and bays been filled in and built over, but also its population has increased roughly a hundredfold—from fifteen thousand people then to nearly two million today.

To see Sewall's farm, Brooklin, which gave the suburb of Brookline its name, take the Green Line subway train outbound to Brookline Village or Coolidge Corner. While the exact extent of Samuel's vast acreage here is no longer known, it included much of Brookline Village and Coolidge Corner, Beacon Street between Coolidge Corner and Kenmore Square, the Minot Rose Garden, most of Cottage Farm, the Graffam-McKay Historic District between Coolidge Corner and Commonwealth Avenue at the western edge of the campus of Boston University, and a portion of the Massachusetts Turnpike in Brighton. The Smelt Brook, a tributary of the Charles River that exists today only in the form of damp basements north of Coolidge Corner, was the farm's northern border, which suggested to Samuel its name, Brook-lying, which he shortened to Brooklin. Several Brookline streets still carry his family names, such as Dummer Street and Sewall

Avenue, near Coolidge Corner. A good way to view Sewall's now densely settled farm is to walk the portion of Frederick Law Olmsted's Emerald Necklace from Jamaica Pond, at the Boston-Brookline border, north past Hall Pond to the Muddy River, alongside the Longwood Medical Area, to the Fens and, finally, Kenmore Square, where the Red Sox play at Fenway Park. Kenmore Square, which was known as Sewall's Point in the eighteenth and nineteenth centuries, was the easternmost—and marshiest—part of his farm.

Cambridge, just north of Brookline across the Charles River, is much changed from Samuel's day. No building he knew at Harvard College remains. The nearby town of Malden too bears little resemblance to the village Samuel visited in 1686 for the trial of the Reverend Thomas Cheever. Still, the names of towns around Boston area recall men of Samuel's era. The towns of Hull (after his father-in-law), Quincy (for his mother-in-law's family), and Stoughton (after the chief justice) are south of the city. (William Stoughton's elaborately carved gravestone can be found at the Dorchester North Burying Ground, at the intersection of Columbia Road and Stoughton Street in Dorchester's Uphams Corner.) The town of Winthrop—named for the first governor, who officiated at the 1647 marriage of Samuel's parents-in-law—lies just north of Boston, beyond Logan International Airport. Beneath the pavement of the airport are several former islands, including Hog Island, which Samuel purchased for family outings in 1687.

Located directly across Boston Harbor from the airport to the south, behind the John F. Kennedy Library, in Dorchester, the Big Dig Museum at the Commonwealth of Massachusetts Archives contains a remarkable collection of the discarded belongings of a Sewall contemporary. Katherine Wheelwright Nanny Naylor (1630–1714), a daughter of the Reverend John Wheelwright and a sister-in-law of Nathaniel Williams, a member of Samuel's private prayer group, lived in the North End in the late seventeenth century. She married in succession two Boston merchants, Robert Nanny and Edward Naylor, and occupied a house on Cross Street beside Mill Pond near the landing place for the Charlestown ferry. Three hundred years later, during the massive downtown roadway reconstruction project dubbed the "Big Dig," archeologists unearthed her backyard privy, a stone-lined chamber dug into the ground for use as an outhouse and trash disposal.

The Big Dig Museum offers a permanent display of many of Nanny Naylor's discards, giving us an intimate look inside the home of a high-status seventeenth-century Bostonian. The exhibit includes imported ceramic tableware, English pottery, iron keys and belt buckles, decorative fireplace tiles, pewter spoons and knife blades, leather shoes, and a tiny brass pincushion. The privy contained more than a quarter of a million pits and seeds (mostly from cherries, but including thirty-two varieties of plums), animal bones, the wings of granary weevils, herbs, corn and wheat pollen, and parasite eggs.

Continuing south to Quincy, one can visit the canary yellow house in "Braintree" (now a separate town south of Quincy) where Samuel often stopped on his way to and from the South Shore, in which his wife's cousin Daniel Quincy died in August 1691. The Quincy Homestead, as the house is known, is open to the public one Saturday afternoon a month in summer, courtesy of the National Society of the Colonial Dames of America, who call it "one of the few houses in Massachusetts in which the elements of a seventeenth-century building are still clearly visible." Located at the corner of Hancock Street and Butler Road, a quarter mile north of the Quincy National Historic Site, the house occupies part of the farmland that the General Court granted to Judith Quincy Hull's father in 1635. It was built in 1685 by Edmund Quincy Jr. (Samuel's "Uncle Edmund") and renovated in 1706 by his son, Daniel's younger half brother, "Cousin" Edmund Quincy (1681–1738). Five generations of Quincys, including Judith Quincy Hull and Dorothy Quincy Hancock, "Cousin Edmund's" granddaughter, occupied the house. John Hancock's decrepit chariot remains in its garage. John Adams, Josiah Quincy (another grandchild of "Cousin Edmund"), John Hancock, and other patriots gathered here before the American Revolution.

Farther south there are still several Indian meetinghouses on Cape Cod. However, the Indian meetinghouse in Sandwich that Samuel funded in 1688 no longer stands. It was located between Buzzard's Bay and the Herring River on a plateau that forms a watershed in modern-day Bournedale.

In Samuel's thirties, when he was a successful merchant and member of the General Court, he spent almost a year in his native land on a mission to protect colonists' rights. He departed Boston on

November 22, 1688, and landed at Dover, England, seven weeks later. Traveling to England is far easier today, as is following his steps to the usual tourist stops at Canterbury, Salisbury, Stonehenge, Oxford, Cambridge, Hampton Court Castle (where he went "to wait on the king"), Greenwich, and London. At the Tower of London the lions, leopards, and polar bear he enjoyed are not present, but the fourteenth-century mint, royal armory, and crown scepter are.

Samuel's base in England was a flat above his wife's cousin's hat shop, the Hat-in-Hand, in Aldgate, just northeast of the City of London. During a March 1689 perambulation of the East End of London, Samuel toured "the Jews' Burying Place at Mile End," where he told the friendly grave keeper, "I wish we might meet in Heaven." There are now five Jewish cemeteries in the East End, all in disrepair. The one he visited is the Betahayamin Velho cemetery, which is owned by a Sephardic synagogue and closed to the public. Britain's oldest Jewish cemetery, founded in 1657, Betahayamin Velho is near the Stepney Green tube station, up the Mile End Road past the Half Moon Pub. This bedraggled cemetery, not visible from the road, lies behind the Albert Stern House. An effort is afoot in London to restore and open to the public these historic Jewish cemeteries.

A high point of Samuel's tour of England was his visit to Winchester College, where he would likely have been schooled had he not emigrated as a boy of nine. Winchester College is in Hampshire's handsome county seat of Winchester, now an easy hour's car or train ride south of London. Today the college employs a hundred dons to teach seven hundred male students, roughly half of whom go to Oxford or Cambridge and then to positions in government. Visitors to the college enter through iron gates manned by uniformed guards. My guide to the campus was Dr. W. Geoffrey Day, a don and keeper of the library, who led me across the campus to the architectural oddity that Samuel described as "the chapel on the green." At Winchester College, and nowhere else in the world, a fourteenth-century chantry (in which monks chanted for the dead) is set on a grassy lawn inside a cloister.

Dr. Day ushered me inside the chantry and up a spiral marble staircase to the "library around the stairs" that so impressed Samuel on February 25, 1689. A light-filled room with timber beams, white plaster walls, and delicately mullioned Gothic windows, this was then the

Winchester College library. While the collection has since moved to a different building, the books that Samuel encountered remain at the college, including the twelfth-century *Historia Scholastica*, the vellum songbook inscribed by a suitor to Queen Elizabeth I, the early-thirteenth-century *Life of St. Thomas Becket*, and the 1587 Heidelberg Bible.

Samuel's Indian Bible, which he handed to the college librarian that day, is now the most valuable book in the collection. The Bible is kept in a locked vault in a strong room behind an inch of oak and a half inch of steel. There are only four Indian Bibles in all of England, according to Dr. Day, and but twenty in the entire world. Samuel's Indian Bible is brought out for display at Winchester College once every five years. "The boys are here for five years," the don explained, "so they all see it." In his view the Indian Bible "has everything, starting with impeccable provenance. It has had only two owners, and we know exactly where it's been. It has his signature and the date he received it, and his diary tells us the date he gave it to us. It also has wonderful foreshadowing: this Bible was owned by the man who would recant his judgment at the witchcraft trials."

The market town of Romsey, where Samuel's formal education began, lies about ten miles southwest of Winchester. As an adult he returned to Romsey and to the neighboring village of Lee, where his father still owned property. Lee—Saxon for "a gap in the woods"—has changed little in the intervening centuries, according to Don Bryan, a local historian and Blue Badge guide. Lee's one remaining thatched farmhouse is likely to be on the erstwhile Sewall land. Romsey too retains much of its seventeenth-century character. A great Norman abbey, begun in the ninth century and completed in the twelfth, dominates the town. One of four abbeys in Hampshire before the Reformation, this was the only abbey that survived King Henry VIII's dissolution of the monasteries. A Benedictine abbot saved it in 1544 by cleverly transforming it into a parish church. Across the street is King John's House, which dates to the thirteenth century. A Tudor tea room, open for business, occupies its early-seventeenth-century addition. The River Test, one of Europe's finest trout and salmon rivers, runs just west of Romsey, crossed by a seventeenth-century bridge.

Samuel also returned as an adult to Baddesley, the village where he had lived between the ages of two and nine. Baddesley's town center has moved since then and been renamed North Baddesley, but the small medieval church he knew, where his father occasionally preached, remains amid farmland, rolling fields, and woods. In the burying place beside the Parish Church of Saint John the Baptist (or, simply, the South Baddesley Church), one can still find the gravestone of Samuel's "Aunt Rider," Anne Dummer Rider, which he viewed in February 1689, not quite a year after she died. The neighboring property is now the Rider Farm.

Samuel's parents came to Baddesley in 1654 from the (then) slightly larger village of Bishopstoke, where Samuel was born in 1652. Bishopstoke lies between Winchester and Southampton in the Itchen Valley. In Samuel's time this region was open heath and fields not divided by the blackthorn hedges and hawthorn boundaries that are ubiquitous now. Local roads have changed dramatically too as a result of nineteenth-century Enclosure Acts, which split huge medieval estates into small parcels. The few surviving seventeenth-century roads, according to Don Bryan, are the ones that now appear "narrow and sunken" below the fields. "A road in a hollow, like Bishopstoke Lane, is an old road, which his family would have known."

The house in which Samuel Sewall was born is gone, although the Itchen Valley offers several examples of the sort of timber-framed, thatched cottage the Sewalls occupied. As for the church in which five-week-old Samuel was baptized on May 4, 1652, it burned down years ago. Only its altar stone remains, embedded in a meadow on the eastern bank of the River Itchen Canal, which flows where a tributary of the River Itchen ran then. These words are etched into the stone:

Here lyeth buried the body of
Henry Cox gentleman
Late pastor of the church of Christ at Stoke
Died June 30 1697

Parish records indicate that the Reverend Cox baptized Samuel's younger siblings John in October 1654, Stephen in August 1657, and Jane in October 1659. Beside the altar stone a sign announces, "The place where you stand is holy ground."

CHRONOLOGY

1652	Born in Bishopstoke, Hampshire, England, to Henry and Jane Dummer Sewall, March 28
1658	Future wife Hannah Hull born in Boston to John and Judith Quincy Hull, February 14
1661	Samuel, his siblings, and his mother followed his father to Massachusetts and settled in Newbury, north of Boston, which his grandfather and father had helped to found in 1635
1667	Began studies at Harvard College, age fifteen
1671	Earned BA at Harvard
1674	Earned MA at Harvard, met Hannah Hull
1676	Married Hannah Hull in Boston, February 28
1677	Accepted as a member of the Third Church of Christ in Boston
1677	First child, John, born (died at seventeen months)
1678	Made a freeman (voter) of the colony
1678	Second child, Samuel, born
1680	Third child, Hannah, born
1681	Fourth child, Elizabeth, born
1683	Elected to the General Court as a deputy (antecedent of representative)
1684	Fifth child, Hull, born (died at twenty-three months)

1684　Elected to the General Court as an assistant (antecedent of senator)

1685　Sixth child, Henry, born (died at two weeks)

1687　Seventh child, Stephen, born (died at six months)

1688　Eighth child, Joseph, born

1690　Ninth child, Judith, born (died at six weeks)

1691　Chosen to serve on the Provincial Council, successor of the General Court

1691　Tenth child, Mary, born

1692　Appointed judge of the witchcraft court in Salem, May to October

1692　Appointed judge of the Superior Court of Judicature, America's first independent judiciary, December

1693　Eleventh child, Jane, born (died at five weeks)

1694　Twelfth child, Sarah, born (died at two years)

1696　Thirteenth child stillborn

1697　Publicly repented for his role in the witchcraft trials and executions, January 14

1697　Published his essay on Revelation, *Phaenomena quaedam Apocalyptica ad Aspectum Novi Orbis configurata*, stating the godliness of America and Native Americans

1699　Became commissioner of the Corporation for the Propagation of the Gospel Among the Indians in New England

1700　Wrote and published America's first antislavery tract, *The Selling of Joseph, A Memorial*, June

1702　Fourteenth child, Judith, born

1710　Death of daughter Mary (age nineteen, in childbirth)

1713　Published "Proposals Touching the Accomplishment of Prophecies Humbly Offered," appendix to *Phaenomena quaedam Apocalyptica*

1715　Appointed judge of probate for Suffolk County

1716　Death of daughter Elizabeth (age thirty-four)

1717　Death of wife Hannah (age fifty-nine)

1718　Became chief justice of the Superior Court of Judicature

1719　Married Abigail Woodmansey Tilley, who died seven months later

1722   Married Mary Shrimpton Gibbs, who survived him

1724   Death of daughter Hannah (age forty-four)

1724   Wrote essay *Talitha Cumi*, arguing that women's bodies as well as men's are resurrected in heaven

1725   Resigned from the Provincial Council

1727   Published second edition of *Phaenomena quaedam Apocalyptica*, November

1728   Resigned from Superior Court of Judicature and Probate Court due to advanced age and ill health

1730   Died at home on January 1, age seventy-seven, survived by three children, Sam Jr., Joseph, and Judith

WRITINGS OF SAMUEL SEWALL

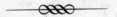

Phaenomena quaedam *APOCALYPTICA* *Ad Aspectum NOVI ORBIS configurata*

Or, some few Lines towards a
description of the NEW HEAVEN
As It makes to those who stand
upon the NEW EARTH

(1697)

Psalm 45:10. Forget also thy own people, and thy fathers house.
Isai. 11:14. But they shall fly upon the shoulders of the Philistins toward the west.
Act. 1:6–8. Lord, wilt thou at this time restore again the kingdom to Israel?...
Luke 15:24. For this My Son was dead, and is alive again; he was lost, and is found....

MASSACHUSET; Boston, Printed by Bartholomew Green, and John Allen, and are to be sold by Richard Wilkins, 1697

[Dedicated] To the honorable, William Stoughton Esq., Lieut. Governour and Commander in Chief, in and over His Majesties Province of the Massachusets Bay in New-England ... [and] To the honorable, Sir William Ashurst, Knight, Governour, and the Company for the Propagation of the GOSPEL to the Indians in New-England, and places adjacent, in AMERICA ... For I can't but think that either England, or New-England, or both (Together is best) is the only Bride Maid mentioned by Name in David's prophetical Epithalamium, to assist at the Great Wedding now shortly to be made. And for ought I know, this Noble Gift, Administered by your hands, may be partly intended. Angels Incognito have sometimes made themselves guests to Men, designing thereby to surprise them with a Requital of their Love to Strangers. In like manner the English Nation, in shewing Kindness to the Aboriginal Natives of America, may possibly, shew Kindness to Israelites unawares.... Instead of being branded for Slaves with hot Irons in the Face and arms; and driven by scores in mortal Chains: they shall wear the Name of God in their foreheads, and they shall be delivered into the glorious Liberty of the Children of God.... Now that their Miseries be very inveterate, yet GOD can speedily, and easily give them a New Name, and in a moment, change the Scene. Asia, Africa, and Europe have, each of them, had a glorious Gospel Day: None therefore will be grieved at any ones pleading that America may be made a Coparcener with her Sisters in the Free, and Soveraign Grace of God. God many times sets one thing against another: and we may hope that Unparallel'd Severity will be succeeded by Superabundant BENIGNITY. And when the Messiah shall have gathered his Sheep belonging to this his American Fold: His Churches Musick being then compleat in the Harmony of Four Parts: The whole Universe shall ring again with Seraphick Acclamations, ONE FLOCK! ONE SHEPHERD!

Your Honours most humble Servant,

S. SEWALL

Not to begin to be; and so not to be limited by the concernments of Time, and Place; is the Prerogative of GOD alone. But as it is the Priviledge of creatures, that GOD has given them a beginning: so to deny their actions, or them, the respect they bear to Place, and successive duration, is, under a pretence of Promotion, to take away their very Being. Yet notwithstanding, some Things have had this to glory of; that they have been time out of mind; and their Continuance refuses to be measured by the memory of Man.

Whereas New-England, and Boston of the Massachusets have this to make mention of; that they can tell their Ages; and account it their Honour to have their Birth, and Parentage kept in everlasting Remembrance. And in very deed, the Families and Churches which first ventured to follow Christ thorow the Atlantick Ocean, into a strange Land, full of wild men, were so Religious; their End so Holy; their Selfdenyal in pursuing of it, so Extraordinary; that I can't but hope that the Plantation has thereby gaind a very strong Craft; and that it will not be of one or two, or three Centuries only; but very long lasting. Some who peremptorily conclude that Asia must afford situation for New-Jerusalem, are of the mind, when that divine City comes to be built, the Commodities of It will be so inviting as will drain disconsolate America of all Its Christian Inhabitants, as not able to brook so remote a distance from the beloved City. But if Asia shoald be again thus highly favored, and the eldest daughter be still made the darling; yet 'tis known there will be a River, the Streams whereof shall make glad the City of God.

The Correspondence, and Commerce of the little cities, and villages in the three Kingdoms, and Plantations, do make LONDON glad. And so it will be with New Jerusalem: the Nations of them which are saved, shall walk in the light of it: and the Kings of the Earth do bring their glory and honour into it. New Jerusalem will not straiten, and enfeeble; but wonderfully dilate, and invigorate Christianity in the several Quarters of the World; in Asia, in Africa, in Europe, and in America. And one that has been born, or but liv'd in America, between thirty, and fourty years; it may be pardonable for him to ask. Why may not that be the place of New Jerusalem?

Problematical Questions do circulate; and this was set up by Dr. Twisse above threescore years ago, the newness of it in its return after so considerable a space of time, will, I hope, render it gratefull; or at least, will procure leave for one, with a little alteration, to enquire, Why may not New-Spain be the place of New Jerusalem? Its being part of the New World, one would think, carries with it no contradiction thereunto.

Places are usually called new from the newness of their situation, and not from their being built anew; as New-Spain, New-England, New-London.

For certain, If Mr. Eliot's Opinion prove true; viz. that the aboriginal Natives of America are of Jacob's Posterity, part of the long since captivated Ten Tribes; and that their Brethren the Jews shall come unto them, the dispute will quickly be at an end. Manasseh-Ben-Israel is said to have published a book entitled, The hope of Israel, endeavouring to prove this Position. For my own part, what Mr. Downam, and Mr. Thorowgood have written on this head, seems to be of far more weight with me than what Hornius, or any other that I have seen, have guess'd to the contrary. Mr. Eliot was wont to say The New-English Churches are a preface to the New Heavens: and if so, I hope the preface and Book will be bound up together, and this Mexican Continent shall comprehend them both.

Who can tell, but that David may thus fetch a compass behind his Antichristian enemies and come upon them over against the Mulberry trees, and utterly destroy them by the brightness of his coming? Who can tell but that Christ may in this manner expose the lewd fondness of the Unholy War, and happily umpire the Difference about the holiness of Places by causing New Jerusalem to come down from God out of Heaven, upon that Earth wherein Satan, for many Ages, has peaceably possessed an entire, and far more large empire than any where else in the whole world besides? No body doubts but that our Saviour can enter into this strong man's house, bind him, and spoil his goods: Let us wait till He revive us by saying, I am willing. If I mistake not we have a warrant sufficient enough to encourage us unto a perseverance in hoping, and waiting upon God for this Salvation. ...

Some judicious and learned Divines have conjectured that America is prophesied of in the thirty seventh of Ezekiel, under the denomination of a Valley. Certainly, no part of the habitable World, can shew more Bones; or bones more dry, than these vast Regions do. Mr. Downam thinks that Mr. Eliot's taking his Text from thence when he first preached to the Indians, has its weight. His Appendix to the Letters from New England, is well worth the reading. The Prophet is said to be carried out in the spirit: and for ought I know, he might be carried beyond the limits of the then known World.

Dan. 11:45. *And he shall plant the tabernacles of his palace between the seas in the glorious holy Mountain; yet he shall come to his end, and none shall help him.*

The complexion of this portion of Scripture is such, as constrains me to imagin, that the place designed by the Holy Spirit, is no other than America. Every word almost, has an emphasis carrying in it, to me, the perswasion of this sence. They who remove from one Land to another, there to dwell; that settlement of theirs is call'd a Plantation. Especially, when a Land, before rude and unfurnish'd, is by the New-comers replenished with usefull Arts, Vegetables, Animals. Thus when in the year 1492 Christopher Columbus had opened the way, the Spaniards planted themselves in the spatious Regions of America; and, too much, planted Antichristianisme in the room of Heathenisme....

Upon all, or some of these Considerations, it seems to me probable that Five of the Vials are already poured out. Not but that they hold on their course still; and will do so, until the Confluence of them all do with irresistible Force ingulf Antichristianisme in utter Ruine. The truth is, all the Vials may in some sence be said to have been poured out together at the beginning of this Period of Rome's gradual Decay.... And the Sixth Angel seems now to stand ready with his Vial, waiting only for the Word to be given for the pouring of it out. The pouring out of this vial will dry up the Antichristian Interests in the New World: and thereby prepare the way for the Kings of the East....

What Concernment hath America in these Things? America is not any part of the Apocalyptical Stage. The Promise of preaching the Gospel to the whole World, is to be understood of the Roman Empire only, according to the extent of it in John's time: As it is said Augustus made a decree that all the world should be taxed. The Roman Empire contained about a third part of the Old World: and this Triental only was to be concern'd with the Apocalypse. The Prophesies of the Revelation extend but to such Kingdoms or Monarchies of the World, where the Church in all Ages still was: therefore not to the West-Indians, nor Tartarians, nor Chinese, nor East-Indians.

But what shall we say, if the Stone which these Builders have refused, should be made the Head of the Corner? Lo, we heard of Ephratah: we found it in the fields of the wood. Or if it be not made a

Corner-stone: that it should be quite thrown by, and not be at all laid in the Building: is more than can be proved from the Scriptures. I suppose there is *nec vola, nec vestigium* of any such thing to be found there....

1492. Christopher Columbus found out the New World for Castile and Leon. And altho the New World was not yet made ready for the Entertainment of the ejected Jews; or else the Jews were not yet fit to dwell in a place of their Own: Yet considering the Synchronicisme of this Banishment, and Discovery; with the marvelous Perplexity the distressed Outcasts were in, not knowing whither to go: As also the great Gain that this Navigation afforded; the hopes some might conceive of managing themselves more safely with their feigned Religion, which they had not proved, in a remote Place, than at home: Considering also the mixture those Nations by Inter Marriages; and that the great and best part of America is peopled by Spaniards, and Portugals: It is not improbable, but many Jews may reside there, tho covered with a Spanish Vail. Manasseh-Ben-Israel, Downam, Thorowgood, Eliot, and others were of Opinion that America was first peopled by the Ten Tribes. God's removing Israel out of his sight, is no less than three times mentioned (2 Kings 17), which may insinuate the Remoteness of that Land, into which God by his Providence intended to call them. And none was so remote, and so much out of sight, as America. Mr. Greenbil thinks it is no Heresie to say, Christ meant the Ten Tribes, John, 10:16, alluding to Ezek. 37:22, 24. If it be no Heresie to say, the Ten Tribes are the Sheep: Why should it be accounted Heresie to say, America is the distinct Fold, there implied? For Christ doth not affirm that there shall be one Fold; but that there shall be ONE FLOCK, ONE SHEPHERD!

But however it might be when Mr. Mede writ, Now it is manifest to all, that very considerable Numbers of Jews are seated in the New World; where they merchandize, have their Synagogues, and places of Burial. At Spikes in Barbados there is a Street called Jews Street; tho most live at the Bridge; and there is the Burying Place for both Towns. At Jamaica there are a great many; and Port-Royal also hath its Jews Street; by the same Token, that the Formidable Earthquake left that standing; tho their Synagogue, which stood in another Street, was thrown down by it. This Earthquake happened upon the Third day of the Week, about a Quarter of an hour before Noon; being the Seventh of June, 1692.... There are several Families of them at New York; and New England is seldom without them....

Probably, these Jews will be converted, before any great Numbers of the Indians, shall I say, or Israelites be brought in. That that ancient Prophesie may be fulfilled, Zech. 12: 7. The LORD also shall save the tents of Judah First, that the glory of the house of David, and the glory of the Inhabitants of Jerusalem do not magnifie themselves against Judah. To be for some time defrauded and deprived of her Husband, was Rachel's disgrace and grief; which was renewed and multiplied by Barrrenness after her enjoyment of him. Gen. 30: 1. And when Rachel saw that she bare Jacob no children, Rachel envied her sister. But when the Times of Refreshing by the New Jerusalem, shall come, Joseph shall take away his Mothers Reproach, and her Children shall be more & mightier than her Sisters. Insomuch that there will be need of the forementioned Expedient, to keep the balance. Isa. 11:13. The envie also of Ephraim shall depart, and the Adversaries of Judah shall be cut off: Ephraim shall not envie Judah, and Judah shall not vex Ephraim. Isa. 54:1. Sing, O barren, thou that didst not bear: Break forth into singing, and cry aloud, thou that didst not travail with child: for more are the children of the desolate, than the children of the married wife, saith the LORD. That America hath been desolate and unmarried for innumerable Ages, is a most sad and awfull Truth: That she may now receive Jesus Christ as her Husband; will be the desire and Prayer of all that favour the dust of Zion....

What a Pity it is, that because the American Mulbery trees are not so early in putting forth as some other: therefore they must all presently be condemned to the Fire! Seeing the First Resurrection is near at hand; it were better to wait a little, and see what God will do for them therein. For we are certain that if they have a part given them in the first Resurrection; they will not be obnoxious to the mentioned Judgment. *In orbis nostri meditullio sitae.* The situation of Jerusalem is not so Central; but that a Voyage may be made from London, to Mexico, in as little time, as from London, to Jerusalem. In that respect, If the New World should be made the seat of New Jerusalem; if the City of the Great KING should be set on the Northern side of it: Englishmen would meet with no Inconvenience thereby; and they would

find this Convenience; that they might visit the Citizens of New Jerusalem and their Countrymen, all under one. As they go thether, Barbados stands advanced three hundred Leagues Eastward, ready to
meet them with a Welcome to the New World. And Jamaica is posted
just in the way, to invite them thether, or to salute them in their passing by, and to pilot them to St Juan de Ulva, if there be occasion.
When homeward bound, Providence will firstly take care of them; and
after that, they will have their Countrymen to friend all along shoar.
Solitary Bermuda will be overjoyd, if they happen to touch there. And
if in that Latitude, any Captain shall command, Helm a-Starboard, on
purpose to visit our New English Tirzab; they will be met with an-
swerable Respect; & mutual kindness shall render the Congress happy.
Yea, if the Spending of a Mast, or springing of a Leak, do oblige them
to such a Diversion, the Pleasantness of the Effect, in bringing good
Company together, shall help to qualifie the bitterness of the Cause.
*Ad cujus minimum fines, Regnum Christi portentum ire, testantur Propheta-
rum oracula.* This word Minimum contains in it the most Light for
America, of any one in the whole Chapter. The worthy Author seems
here to begin to relent. By this means being fairly got without the Invisible walls of the Imperial Prison, and expatiating as far as Japan,
and the Cape of Good Hope; I know nothing should hinder, but that
we may from thence take Shipping for the New World. As for Psalm
72:8 and Isa. 49:6 they are summoned to speak on our side. And there
are no less than Six times Three very Credible Witnesses, who have
given their Affidavit, that the Conversion of American Indians is an
Accomplishment of those glorious Prophesies. Their Testimony is to
be seen at large in their Epistle set before a Book Published at London
in the Year 1652 entitled, *Strength Out of Weakness.* Or a Glorious
MANIFESTATION of the further Progress of the GOSPEL AMONGST THE IN-
DIANS IN NEW ENGLAND. &c...

As for the Dearness of the Gospel in New England; being Fore-
warnd we ought to be Forearmed, that we may not be outbid. Truth is
a Kind of Gold that cannot be bought too dear.... My honoured
Pastor, the Reverend Mr Samuel Willard, a person eminent for Soundness of Judgment, and clearness of Expression; lately preached and
printed some Excellent Sermons, the Text & Title whereof is *Buy the
Truth, and Sell it not....* If we consult the memorable Epistle of Mr.

Shepard of Cambridge, and Mr. Allin of Dedham, before their Answer to the *Nine Positions;* Or, if we inquire of the Learned and Judicious Mr. Jonathan Mitchel, and Mr. Urian Oakes; we shall finde, they reckoned that the Planters had a good Bargain. And this Amiable Quaternion were all born in England, but chose to have their Graves here at our Cambridge and Dedham.

... Upon the Resettlement of Virginia by the Lord la Ware, June, 9. 1610. there is this remark; *This was the Arm of the Lord of Hosts, who would have his People pass the Red Sea & Wilderness; and then to possesse the Land of Canaan.* Altho there were not Ten to One, yet there were Ten to Two of those who went to search the Land of Canaan; who reported A Land that eateth up the Inhabitants thereof! Num. 13.32. And some pious honest man, being surrounded with Difficulties at his first coming hither; might Unadvisedly write a discouraging Letter: Unto which, his never Returning to England, and the flourishing circumstances of his Grandson at this day in New England, are a very desirable and pleasant Contradiction. Capt. John Smith in his History published *Anno* 1624 affirms that he found New England well inhabited by a goodly, strong, and well proportioned People. And the Proverb is, *Show me the Man, and not the Meat.* And if men can be contented with the Food and Raiment intended in 1 Tim. 6:8 they need not fear subsisting where Ash, Chesnut, Hazel, Oak & Walnut do naturally and plentifully grow. But for this, let Mr. Morden be consoled, to whom N.E. is beholden for the fair character given them in his Geographie. It is remarkable, that Mr. Parker, who was a successful schoolmaster at Newbury in Barkshire, in the happy days of Dr. Twisse; was much about this time preaching and Proving at Ipswich in Essex, That the Passengers came over upon good Grounds, and that GOD would multiply them as He did the Children of Israel. His Text was Exod. 1:7. As Mr. Nicholas Noyes, who was an Auditor, and is yet living, lately informed me. Mr. Parker was at this time; 1634 principally concerned in beginning Newbury, where the Learned & Ingenious Mr. Benjamin Woodbridge, Dr. Twisse's Successor, had part of his Education under his Unckle Parker. Mary Brown (now Godfry) the first-born of Newbury, is yet alive; and is become the Mother and Grandmother of many children. And so many have been born after her in the Town, that they make three or four large Assemblies, wherein GOD is solemnly worshipped every Sabbath Day. And

As long as Plum Island shall faithfully keep the commanded Post; Notwithstanding all the hectoring Words, and hard Blows of the proud and boisterous Ocean; As long as any Salmon, or Sturgeon shall swim in the streams of Merrimack; or any Perch, or Pickeril, in Crane-Pond; As long as the Sea-Fowl shall know the Time of their coming, and not neglect seasonably to visit the Places of their Acquaintance; As long as any Cattel shall be fed with the Grass growing in the Medows, which do humbly bow down themselves before Turkie-Hill; As long as any Sheep shall walk upon Old Town Hills, and shall from thence pleasantly look down upon the River Parker, and the fruitful Marishes lying beneath; As long as any free & harmless Doves shall find a White Oak, or other Tree within the Township, to perch, or feed, or build a careless Nest upon; and shall voluntarily present themselves to perform the office of Gleaners after Barley-Harvest; As long as Nature shall not grow Old and dote; but shall constantly remember to give the rows of Indian Corn their education, by Pairs: So long shall Christians be born there; and being first made meet, shall from thence be Translated, to be made partakers of the Inheritance of the Saints in Light. Now, seeing the Inhabitants of Newbury, and of New England, upon the due Observance of their Tenure, may expect that their Rich and Gracious LORD will continue & confirm them in the Possession of these invaluable Privileges: *Let us have Grace, whereby we may serve GOD acceptably with Reverence and godly Fear, For our GOD is a consuming Fire.* Heb. 12:28–29.

The mention of Mary Brown brings to mind an idle Whimsey, as if Persons born in New-England would be short liv'd, Whereas the Natives live long. And a Judgment concerning English men cannot well be made till Twenty or Thirty years hence. Capt. Peregrine White born Novemb. 1620 is yet alive, and like to live. Major William Bradford (whose honorable Father Governour Bradford married here) is more than 73 years old; and hath worn a Bullet in his Flesh above 20 of them. Elizabeth Alden (now Paybody), Capt. John Alden her brother, Alexander Standish, and John Howland have lived more than Seventy years.

This Summer Ensign James Noyes hath happily discovered a Boddy of Marble at Newbury, within half a mile of the Navigable part of the Little River; by which means much better Lime may be made, than of Oyster shells or West-Indian Lime-stones; and afforded at a much cheaper rate. This Summer a Contribution hath been made at Rode Island and Narraganset; but firstly and principally at Connecticut, by a Brief from the honorable the Governour & Council there: By the continuance of which brotherly Love, many Hundreds in this Province, almost quite slain with Hunger, have been rescued and revived. It is observable that by far the greatest part of our Divines have received their Birth and Education here: Who by Solidity of Learning, Soundness of Doctrine, and Integrity of Life, do give much honour to their Lord and Master. And as Dr. Twisse's VINDICIAE came out, *Anno* 1632, quickly after the Settlement of New England, which was in the Years 1620, 1628, 1630. So that Faith which the Doctor did Earnestly and Victoriously contend for; is no where more Unanimously, Skillfully, and Resolutely defended than here. As a Memorial for the Plantations of JESUS CHRIST in New England, a worthy Divine [Shepard], whose honorable Parents were born here, is erecting a Testimonial Pillar more ornamental and durable than polished Marble. And this very Year, notwithstanding the Blast, the Worm, the Frost, the Drought, the War: The Inhabitants of Fairfield, Newton, Rowley, and Exeter, have been at the Charge to build themselves very fair and large Meeting Houses for the publick worship of GOD. I would fain hope, that the End of the Lord with New England, will be such as was with Job: Because the Language of this Thing seemeth to be, *Tho He Slay us, yet will we Trust in HIM*. October, 7. 1697.

The Selling of Joseph

A Memorial

(1700)

Forasmuch as Liberty is in real value next unto Life: None ought to part with it themselves, or deprive others of it, but upon most mature Consideration.

The Numerousness of Slaves at this day in the Province, and the Uneasiness of them under their Slavery, hath put many upon thinking whether the Foundation of it be firmly and well laid; so as to sustain the Vast Weight that is built upon it. It is most certain that all Men, as they are the Sons of Adam, are Coheirs; and have equal Right unto Liberty, and all other outward Comforts of Life. GOD hath given the Earth (with all its Commodities) unto the Sons of Adam. Psalm 115:16. And hath made of One Blood, all Nations of Men, for to dwell on all the face of the Earth, and hath determined the Times before appointed, and the bounds of their habitation: That they should seek the Lord. Forasmuch then as we are the Offspring of God etc. Acts 17:26–29. Now although the Title given by the last ADAM, doth infinitely better Mens Estates, respecting GOD and themselves; and grants them a most beneficial and inviolable Lease under the Broad Seal of Heaven, who were before only Tenants at Will: Yet through the Indulgence of GOD to our First Parents after the Fall, the outward Estate of all and every of their Children, remains the same, as to one another. So that Originally, and Naturally, there is no such thing as Slavery. Joseph was rightfully no more a Slave to his Brethren, than they were to him: and they had no more Authority to *Sell* him, than they had to *Slay* him. And if they had nothing to do to Sell him; the Ishmaelites bargaining with them, and paying down Twenty pieces of Silver, could not make a Title. Neither could Potiphar have any better Interest in him than the

Ishmaelites had. Gen. 37:20, 27–28. For he that shall in this case plead Alteration of Property, seems to have forfeited a great part of his own claim to Humanity. There is no proportion between Twenty Pieces of Silver, and LIBERTY. The Commodity it self is the Claimer. If Arabian Gold be imported in any quantities, most are afraid to meddle with it, though they might have it at easy rates; lest if it should have been wrongfully taken from the Owners, it should kindle a fire to the Consumption of their whole Estate. 'Tis pity there should be more Caution used in buying a Horse, or a little lifeless dust; than there is in purchasing Men and Women: Whenas they are the Offspring of GOD, and their Liberty is,

… *Auro pretiosior Omni.*

And seeing GOD hath said, He that Stealeth a Man and Selleth him, or if he be found in his hand, he shall surely be put to Death. Exod. 21:16. This Law being of Everlasting Equity, wherein Man Stealing is ranked amongst the most atrocious of Capital Crimes: What louder Cry can there be made of that Celebrated Warning,

CAVEAT EMPTOR!

And all things considered, it would conduce more to the Welfare of the Province, to have White Servants for a Term of Years, than to have Slaves for Life. Few can endure to hear of a Negro's being made free; and indeed they can seldom use their freedom well; yet their continual aspiring after their forbidden Liberty, renders them Unwilling Servants. And there is such a disparity in their Conditions, Colour & Hair, that they can never embody with us, and grow up into orderly Families, to the Peopling of the Land: but still remain in our Body Politick as a kind of extravasat Blood. As many Negro men as there are among us, so many empty places there are in our Train Bands, and the places taken up of Men that might make Husbands for our Daughters. And the Sons and Daughters of New England would become more like Jacob, and Rachel, if this Slavery were thrust quite out of doors. Moreover it is too well known what Temptations Masters are under, to connive at the Fornication of their Slaves; lest they should be obliged to find them Wives, or pay their Fines. It seems to be practically pleaded that they might be Lawless; 'tis thought much of, that the Law should have Satisfaction for their Thefts, and other Immoralities; by which means, Holiness to the Lord, is more rarely engraven upon this sort of

Servitude. It is likewise most lamentable to think, how in taking Negroes out of Africa, and Selling of them here, That which GOD has joyned together men do boldly rend asunder; Men from their Country, Husbands from their Wives, Parents from their Children. How horrible is the Uncleanness, Mortality, if not Murder, that the Ships are guilty of that bring great Crouds of these miserable Men, and Women. Methinks, when we are bemoaning the barbarous Usage of our Friends and Kinsfolk in Africa: it might not be unseasonable to enquire whether we are not culpable in forcing the Africans to become Slaves amongst our selves. And it may be a question whether all the Benefit received by Negro Slaves, will balance the Accompt of Cash laid out upon them; and for the Redemption of our own enslaved Friends out of Africa. Besides all the Persons and Estates that have perished there.

Obj[ection].1. *These Blackamores are of the Posterity of Cham, and therefore are under the Curse of Slavery.* Gen. 9:25–27.

Answ[er]. Of all Offices, one would not begg this; *viz.* Uncall'd for, to be an Executioner of the Vindictive Wrath of God; the extent and duration of which is to us uncertain. If this ever was a Commission; How do we know but that it is long since out of Date? Many have found it to their Cost, that a Prophetical Denunciation of Judgment against a Person or People, would not warrant them to inflict that evil. If it would, Hazael might justify himself in all he did against his Master, and the Israelites, from 2 Kings 8:10–12.

But it is possible that by cursory reading, this Text may have been mistaken. For Canaan is the Person Cursed three times over, without the mentioning of Cham. Good Expositors suppose the Curse entail'd on him, and that this Prophesie was accomplished in the Extirpation of the Canaanites, and in the Servitude of the Gibeonites. *Vide Pareum.* Whereas the Blackmores are not descended of Canaan, but of Cush. Psal. 68:31. Princes shall come out of Egypt [Mizraim], Ethiopia [Cush] shall soon stretch out her hands unto God. Under which Names, all Africa may be comprehended; and their Promised Conversion ought to be prayed for. Jer. 13:23. Can the Ethiopian change his skin? This shows that Black Men are the Posterity of Cush: Who time out of mind have been distinguished by their Colour. And for want of the true, Ovid assigns a fabulous cause of it.

Sanguine tum credunt in corpora summa vocato
Aethiopum populus nigrum traxisse colorem.

Metamorph. Lib. 2.

Obj. 2. *The Nigers are brought out of a Pagan Country, into places where the Gospel is Preached.*

Answ. Evil must not be done, that good may come of it. The extraordinary and comprehensive Benefit accruing to the Church of God, and to Joseph personally, did not rectify his brethrens Sale of him.

Obj. 3. *The Africans have Wars one with another: Our Ships bring lawful Captives taken in those Wars.*

Answ. For ought is known, their Wars are much such as were between Jacob's Sons and their Brother Joseph. If they be between Town and Town; Provincial, or National: Every War is upon one side Unjust. An Unlawful War can't make lawful Captives. And by Receiving, we are in danger to promote, and partake in their Barbarous Cruelties. I am sure, if some Gentlemen should go down to the Brewsters to take the Air, and Fish: And a stronger party from Hull should Surprise them, and Sell them for Slaves to a Ship outward bound: they would think themselves unjustly dealt with; both by Sellers and Buyers. And yet 'tis to be feared, we have no other kind of Title to our Nigers. Therefore all things whatsoever ye would that men should do to you, do ye even so to them: for this is the Law and the Prophets. Matt. 7:12.

Obj. 4. *Abraham had Servants bought with his Money, and born in his House.*

Answ. Until the Circumstances of Abraham's purchase be recorded, no Argument can be drawn from it. In the mean time, Charity obliges us to conclude, that He knew it was lawful and good.

It is Observable that the Israelites were strictly forbidden the buying, or selling one another for Slaves. Levit. 25:39–46. Jer. 34:8–22. And GOD gaged His Blessing in lieu of any loss they might conceipt they suffered thereby. Deut. 15: 18. And since the partition Wall is broken down, inordinate Self love should likewise be demolished. GOD expects that Christians should be of a more Ingenuous and benign frame of spirit. Christians should carry it to all the World, as the Israelites were to carry it one towards another. And for men obstinately to persist in holding their Neighbours and Brethren under the Rigor of perpetual Bondage, seems to be no proper way of gaining Assurance that God ha's given them Spiritual Freedom. Our Blessed Saviour has altered the Measures of the ancient Love-Song, and set it to a most Excellent New Tune, which all ought to be ambitious of Learning. Matt. 5:43–44. John 13:34. These Ethiopians, as black as they are; seeing they are the Sons and Daughters of the First Adam, the Brethren and Sisters of the Last ADAM, and the Offspring of GOD; They ought to be treated with a Respect agreeable.

> *Servitus perfecta voluntaria, inter Christianum & Christianum, ex parte servi patientis saepe est licita, quia est necessaria: sed ex parte domini agentis, & procurando & exercendo, vix potest esse licita: quia non convenit regulae illi generali: Quaecunque volueritis ut faciant vobis homines, ita & vos facite eis.* Matt. 7:12.

> *Perfecta servitus poenae, non potest jure locum habere, nisi ex delicto gravi quod ultimum supplicium aliquo modo meretur; quia Libertas ex naturali aestimatione proxime accedit ad vitam ipsam, & eidem a multis praeferri solet.*

Ames, Cases of Conscience, Lib. 5 Cap. 23 Thes. 2, 3.

BOSTON **of the Massachusets; Printed by Bartholomew Green, and John Allen, June 24ᵗʰ, 1700.**

TALITHA CUMI

Or An Invitation to WOMEN to look after their Inheritance in the HEAVENLY MANSIONS

(1724)

By Samuel Sewall M.A. and sometime Fellow
of Harvard College at Cambridge in New-England.

2 Cor. 6:18. Ye shall be my Sons & Daughters, saith the LORD Almighty.

Gal. 3:28. There is neither Male nor Female: for ye are all One in CHRIST JESUS.

Qui utrumque Sexum instituit, utrumque restituit. Augustine *de Civit. Dei.*

Honi soit qui mal y pense.

Resurget igitur Caro, et quidem omnis, et quidem ipsa, et quidem integra. Tertullian p. 347. l. 41.

— *absit vafrities in qua multi nimis sibi placent, dum ad suos methodos inflectunt Dei Verbum, & philosophiam nescio quam &c. Evangelium ut suis figmentis mixtum, nobis fabricant.*—Calvin. Act. 20.26, p. 185. col. 2.

When I was waiting upon a dear child in her last sickness, I met with a Book the Title page whereof was this; 'The British Apollo: Containing about Two Thousand Answers to Curious Questions in most Arts & Sciences, Serious, Comical & Humorous. Approved of by many of the most Learned & Ingenious of both Universities & of the Royal Society. Performed by a Society of Gentlemen. Vol. I. The Second Edition. London, Printed 1711.'

In page 200, I met with this surprising Question: *Is there now, or will there be at the Resurrection, any Females in Heaven, Since there seems to be no need of them there?*

A[nswer]. Since Sexes are Corporeal Distinctions, it follows, that there can be now no distinction of Sex in Heaven, since the Souls only of the Saints, (which are Immaterial Substances) are as yet in that Happy Place. And that our rising Bodies will not be distinguished into Sexes, we may fairly gather from those Expressions of our Lord's—*In the Resurrection they neither give, nor are given in Marriage, but are as the Angels of God.*

This Malapert Question had not patience to stay for an Answer, as appears by the Conclusion of it, *Since there seems to be no need of them there.* 'Tis most certain there will be no needless impertinent persons or things in Heaven. Heaven is a roomy, a most magnificent Palace, furnished with the most Rich & Splendid Entertainments; and the Noblest Guests are invited to partake of them. But why should there seem to be no need of Women in Heaven! Since GOD is their Father, and therefore Heaven is their Country: *Ubi Pater ibi*

Patria. Is there no need for a Daughter to go and see her Father when he sends for her; to see God, who, though He be a Great King, yet is a most Loving & tender hearted Father? To speak the Truth, GOD has no need of any Creature. His Name is exalted far above all Blessing & Praise. But by the same Argument there will be no Angels nor Men in Heaven, because there is no need of them there. God created all Things for his pleasure that he might communicat of his Goodness, & for his declarative Glory; And that this End may be attained, there is need of Angels in Heaven, and of Men and Women. As for the Argument taken from Mat. 22:30, *For in the Resurrection they neither marry, nor are given in marriage, but as the Angels of God in heaven.* The most learned and best Expositors conclude that the words are a plain and undeniable Proof that Women have an Equal Share in the Resurrection until Eternal Life and heavenly Glory. [Quotation from Erasmus in Greek and English.] To which the Dutch Annotations agree. For in the Resurrection they (viz. men) take not in marriage; neither are they (viz. women) given out in marriage. And Augustine, who has been deservedly styled *Ecclesiae Catholicae Fulgor*, is of the same opinion; as may be seen in the seventeenth chapter of his two and twentieth book *De Civitate Dei.* [Quotations from *De Civitate Dei*, chaps. 17, 18; Gen. 2; Eph. 4; Matt. 22; 1 Cor.; Col..; and Ps. 109, in Latin.]

Those that shall be left alive at the Last Judgment. 1 Thess. 4:14, 15. For if we believe that Jesus died, and rose again, even so them also which sleep in Jesus, will God bring with him —

The opposition is between the Godly deceased; and the Godly remaining alive, compared with 1. Cor. 15:51, 52. Behold, I shew you a mystery; we shall not all sleep, but we shall all be changed, In a moment —

Here [there] is no other change for Women than for Men. Both Men and Women shall be freed from sin, and the Corruption introduced thereby.

There are three Women that shall rise again; EVE, the Mother of all living; SARAH, the Mother of the Faithfull; and MARY, the Mother of our LORD. And if these three rise again without doubt all will. As for EVE she was created in the Image of God as well as ADAM. Gen. 1:27.

So God created man in his own Image, in the Image of God created him him; male & female created he them. Gen. 9:6. Whoso sheddeth man's blood, by man shall his blood be shed: for in the image of God made he man. So that Eve was perfected and walked with God in Righteousness and true Holiness as the Saints shall do in Heaven, free from Sin and Sorrow. And when our first parents fell by their sinning against God, God provided a Coat for Eve as well as for Adam, and left her not to the miserable shift of her own Fig Leaves. For tho' Eve had just cause to be ashamed of her Transgression, yet God had no cause to be ashamed of his Workmanship. And as Christ was sent to destroy the work of the Devil; so he will give a demonstration of His Power, Wisdom, and Goodness in raising up Eve and causing her to stand forever, Eve the mother of all Living, Lightfoot, Gen. 3. p. 690. [Latin quote from Lightfoot.]

Sarah, whom God chose to be the Mother of the Jewish Church, Sarah to whom God gave a new Name; Sarah so renowned in the Old Testament, and her Faith & Piety celebrated in the New. It cannot be that so many millions of her natural & spiritual children should obtain a Resurrection unto Life and Glory, and that she should be Left Behind. Her Son Jesus will not suffer it to be so. Mr. Perkins has these words upon Heb. 11:11. Saving Faith, and Consequently Salvation itself, is not proper to one Sex, but to both; Man, and Woman. The Woman indeed was the first that brought in sinne—And for that cause, grievous calamities, and much bitterness was laid upon that Sex, in bearing and bringing up children, and in subjection. In which regards they might think themselves forsaken of God for this fault. For the preventing whereof, the Apostle here, or rather the Holy Ghost by him, teacheth us that true Faith, and Salvation by this [illegible], belongeth to SARAH, as well as ABRAHAM; to Women as well as to men. p. 84. col. 2. [Quotation from Perkins on Heb.]

It is the concurrent opinion of Divines that Funerals have Respect to the Resurrection. They that follow Christians to their Grave, profess their Faith of their Resurrection from the dead. Now the first Funeral Recorded in the holy Scriptures is that of Sarah, which is very Considerable. Abraham was the principal mourner. Sarah handsels the Grave for Abraham himself, and the following Patriarchs. She died in Faith.

And by her Burial Abraham took Possession of the Whole Land of Canaan, the Type of Heaven. Of the most Renowned case of Machpellah 'tis said, Gen. 49:31. There they buried Abraham, and Sarah his wife; then they buried Isaac, and Rebekah his wife, and then they buried Leah. Gen. 25:10. There was Abraham Buried and Sarah his wife. Gen. 35. gives an account of the sole solemn burial of Deborah & Rachel, and Isaac.

These all died in Faith, not having received the Promises, but having seen them afar off, and were persuaded of them, and embraced them, and confess that they were strangers and pilgrims on the Earth. For they that seeing such things, declare plainly that they seek a country. And truly if they had been mindfull of that country, from whence they came out, they might have had opportunity to have returned: But now they define a better country, that is, an heavenly: Wherefore God is not ashamed to be called their God: for he hath prepared for them a city.

In the book of Genesis containing the History of Two Thousand three hundred and Sixty Eight years, one whole Chapter is taken up in describing the Circumstances of Sarah's Interment. We find but eight Funerals recorded in the Book, & five of these are godly Women, viz. Sarah, Rebekah, Leah, Debora & Rachel.

As for the blessed Mary the Mother of our LORD, for my part I had rather with the Roman Catholics, believe that she is in Heaven already; than imagine that she shall never be there. Never was there so Great & Honorable a wooing as Mary had; Whether we consider the Immensity & Greatness of the Person, The Holy Spirit, or the Superiority of the Ambassador the Angel Gabriel. Well might the Blessed Virgin upon mature Consideration, after the Example of Rebekah, speedily give her full Consent and say, Behold the Handmaid of the Lord, Be it unto me according to they Word.

Bp. Usher in his Emanuel speaks thus, That blessed Womb of hers was the Bride-Chamber, wherein the Holy Ghost did knit that indissoluble knot betwixt our human nature & his Deity. P. 5.

Our glorious Bridegroom will not demolish the Chamber, which He built & made & dearly bought & paid for, from whence He proceeded, but will Repair it with permanent & Wonderful Magnificence *In Perpetuam Rei Memoriam*. In the heavenly Choir she will indeed appear to be Blessed among Women, When Christ shall set her at his

Right Hand, as Solomon did Bathsheba his Mother.

Now God in his alwise Providence Raised Women from the dead as well as men; thereby signifying that they shall equally partake in the last Resurrection. The Fame of the Raising Jairus his Daughter from the dead is gon abroad not only into the Land of Judea; but into the whole world, into Asia, Africa, Europe, & America. Tis remarkable that this illustrious Story is Recorded in three of the Evangelists, Matthew, Mark, & Luke. And the Cure wrought on the Woman in the way, who had laboured under a Chronical Disease was a very suitable Prologue to this glorious Miracle. The Raising of Dorcas from the dead by the ministry of Peter, is at large recorded in the Ninth of the Acts, and the happy effect it had, v. 42. And it was known throughout all Joppa, and many believed in the Lord. As God revealed to Mano-ah's wife, Jud. 13, that she should bear a Nazarite; so He strengthened her Faith and honoured her in making her instrumental to encourage her husband [who was] overcome with fear, v. 23.

So it may be argued in this case, If the Lord had been minded to deny Women a share in the General Resurrection from the dead, He would not have provided and Recorded for us these preambulatory Resurrections.

Objection. Whether in glorified Bodies there will be any distinction of Sexes, some too curiously dispute.

Answer. Is it so? But can there be too much Curiosity employed in maintaining the Words and Works of GOD; and in preserving the beautifull Variety with which He has been pleased to adorn them? Mat. 10:30. But the very hairs of your head are all numbered.... 2 Cor. 16:17, 18. Ye are the temple of the living God; as God hath said, I will dwell in them, and walk in them; and I will be their GOD, and they shall be my People, Wherefore come out from among them, and be ye separate, saith the Lord, and touch not the unclean thing; and I will receive you, and will be a Father unto you, and ye shall be my Sons and Daughters, saith the Lord Almighty. 'Tis plain that 'tis the Everlasting Covenant that is here spoken of. As God is Al-mighty; so He is Eternal & Unchangeable. And He will have Sons & Daughters as like Himself as can be.

Obj[ection]. The Ancients are divided in their Opinions about it; but whether there will be a distinction, or no —

Ans[wer]. That is a shrewd thing indeed! But if we should wait till all the Ancients are agreed in their Opinions; neither Men nor Women would ever get to Heaven. I should have been glad if the learned Gentleman had mentioned the Ancients he refers to; that it might have been seen who & who are of a side: and then I am persuaded the voice of the standers by would have been *Impar Congressus!* It will not be easy to match the Sanctity, the Zeal, the Learning, the Natural Power & Industry of Tertullian, Jerome, Ambrose, Augustine. And one might have hoped that the Translation of Augustine's excellent Book, *De Civitate Dei*, into English One Hundred Years agoe would have proved a sovereign sufficient Antidote against this Poyson; and would have prevented this Wild-Fire of the British Apollo from being thrown about the Streets of our great City. [Quotations from Bp. Babbington on Gen. 23; *De Vita Contemplativa;* Ovid; and Deut. 4:16.]

Modern testimonies may be added to the Ancients. Office for the Burial of the Dead: *This our dear Sister,* as the constant practice is to read when a woman is buried. The Church of England is very full for this purpose, as appears by the order for the Burial of the Dead—the soul of our dead brother here departed; we therefore commit his body to the ground—in sure and certain hope of the Resurrection to eternal Life, throughout Lord Jesus Christ. For I am informed that when a Woman comes to be buried the form of words then is, Our dear Sister, here, we commit her body. I observe in later editions, the word *Brother* is printed in Italics, intimating I presume, that it is to give place to *Sister* when the Funeral of a Woman is solemnified. I could wish a *mutatis mutandis* had been prescribed the better to prevent the stumblings of Weak Brethren.

In like manner speaks the incomparable Apologist [Jewell], This our self-same Flesh, wherein we live, altho' it die and come to dirt, yet at the last shall return again to Life, by the means of Christ's Spirit.... [Quotations: Jewell, *Apol.,* chap. 21; Usher, *Sum of Christian Religion,* p. 447; 1597 Confession of Faith of the Church of Scotland; Erasmus; and Decisions of the Synod of Dort, in Latin.] According to these Authorities 'tis past dispute, that in the Resurrection World, Mary shall enjoy her own Body; and John shall enjoy his.

And yet after all, if any Controversy shall be moved injurious to the Right of Women before ancient or modern Men, in my opinion their safest and surest way is to plead, that they are *Coram non judice.* 'Tis not what ancient & modern Divines, or Learned and Philosophical men say concerning the Freehold of the Moiety of Mankind; but what GOD says who is their Creator, and Redeemer and Sanctifier: To this their own Master, they stand, or fall. 'Yea, they shall be holden up.' (Rom. 14:4.) For GOD is able to make them stand. They are impowered to say, For the LORD is our Judge, the LORD is our Law-giver, the LORD is our KING, He will Save us. (Isa. 33:22.) And many of them [women] are such good Lawyers, & are of such quick understanding in the Fear of the LORD, and have entertained such an able, Faithfull, and Success-ful an Advocat; they have no reason to be afraid. The Heavenly Inheri-tance is inconceivably great & good wherein there are innumerable Conveniences, and no inconvenience. And it is no small Injury to have the Title to this Inheritance defamed or questioned. But seeing all is to be Tried & decided by the WORD of GOD, they need not be afraid with any amazement.

The first Statute brought against their Interest is mentioned by Augustine in the 17th Chapter of his 22nd book *de Civitate Dei.* Ephes. 4:13. Till we all come in the Unity of the Faith, and of the knowledge of the Son of God, unto a perfect man, unto the measure of the stature of the fullness of Christ.

Peroratio. Courteous Reader. I have written these few Lines from a Detestation of that Sadducean argument, There shall be no Weddings in Heaven, [because] there shall be no Women there—and out of a due Regard to my dear Parents, my Mother EVE, and my immediat Mother, whose very valuable Company I hope shortly to enjoy, and through the (to me) unaccountable Grace of God, Recover an Oppor-tunity of rendering them the Honour due to them according to the invaluable & Eternal obligation of the Fifth Commandment.

GENEALOGY

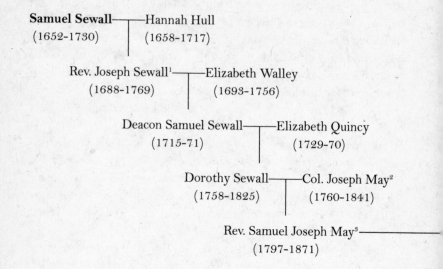

Samuel Sewall——Hannah Hull
(1652-1730)   (1658-1717)

Rev. Joseph Sewall[1]——Elizabeth Walley
(1688-1769)   (1693-1756)

Deacon Samuel Sewall——Elizabeth Quincy
(1715-71)   (1729-70)

Dorothy Sewall——Col. Joseph May[2]
(1758-1825)   (1760-1841)

Rev. Samuel Joseph May[3]——
(1797-1871)

1 Minister of Third (Old South) Church, Boston
2 Founder of Massachusetts General Hospital, Boston
3 Prominent abolitionist Unitarian minister, brother of Abigail May Alcott

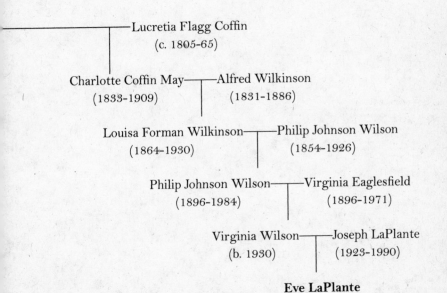

Lucretia Flagg Coffin
(c. 1805-65)

Charlotte Coffin May——————Alfred Wilkinson
(1833-1909)   (1831-1886)

Louisa Forman Wilkinson——————Philip Johnson Wilson
(1864-1930)   (1854-1926)

Philip Johnson Wilson——————Virginia Eaglesfield
(1896-1984)   (1896-1971)

Virginia Wilson——————Joseph LaPlante
(b. 1930)   (1923-1990)

Eve LaPlante

ACKNOWLEDGMENTS

Leo Collins, Samuel Sewall's successor as deacon of a Boston church, opened up for me the depth of Sewall's musical life. Several years ago Leo introduced himself to me as "a resident of John Cotton's farm," part of which was later Sewall's. Leo taught me the melodies to which Sewall and his peers sang the psalms, and provided the musical examples that accompany the text. The other graphic accompaniments to the text, maps of the sites of Sewall's life, were created by Kelly Sandefer and Jonathan Wyss, of Topaz Maps, in Watertown, Massachusetts.

Once again I am grateful to the historian and curator Edward Furgol, D.Phil., who answered hundreds of questions and read and commented on the manuscript. My former history teacher, Bradford Wright, again offered books, articles, and advice. Other historians who helped are David D. Hall, the John Bartlett Professor of New England Church History at Harvard Divinity School, and Adrian Chastain Weimer, a Ph.D. candidate in the Study of Religion at Harvard, who guided my reading in seventeenth-century Puritan piety. Mary Ann McLaughlin and the Rev. John Sassani, S.J., introduced me to the Spiritual Exercises of Saint Ignatius of Loyola, which are similar to Puritan devotional practices. I am grateful to them and to all participants in the Nineteenth Annotation Retreat of 2004–2005. Timothy Sweet, Ph.D., of West Virginia University, graciously shared with me a prepublication draft of his essay on Sewall's *Phaenomena quaedam Apocalyptica*, "What Concernment hath America in these Things!"

On Boston's North Shore I wish to thank Richard Cunningham, the historian of Newbury, Massachusetts. A retired dairy farmer who was born there in 1920, Cunningham showed me the sights of Old Newbury, including its old burying grounds. Nancy Thurlow and Marge Motes provided assistance at the Historical Society of Old Newbury, in Newburyport. At the Peabody Essex Museum and the Phillips Library, in Salem, I am grateful to Peter McKay and to curators Kathy Flynn, Kristen Weiss, and Dean Lahikainen. Charlotte Moody, of the Historical Society of Wells & Ogunquit, Maine, assisted with research.

In Boston I wish to thank D. Brenton Simons, executive director of the New England Historical and Genealogical Society; Marilynne Roach, author of studies of the Salem witchcraft crisis; Marta Pardy-King, research librarian at the Boston Public Library; Jay Brinkerhoff, a court officer, and Joan Kenney, public information officer, at the Supreme Judicial Court of Massachusetts; Anne C. Peters and Brian Harkins of the Social Law Library; and Edgar Bellefontaine, retired librarian of the Social Law Library. Eben Graves, author of a Sewall genealogy, and Judith Graham, Ph.D., author of a study of Sewall's family life, graciously answered queries. Mary Collins assisted in preparing the musical examples. At the Massachusetts State House, Susan Greendyke LaChevre, Art Collections Manager of the Massachusetts Art Commission, provided images of and historical information about Albert Herter's 1942 mural of Samuel Sewall repenting. The Museum of Fine Arts granted permission to use the 1729 portrait of Sewall by John Smibert that appears on the cover and inside the book. At the Massachusetts Historical Society, which holds the Samuel Sewall Papers, I am grateful to librarians Peter Drummey, Rakashi Chand, Elaine Grublin, Carolle Morini, Kimberly Nusco, and Carrie Supple. The Massachusetts Historical Society generously permitted me to quote from the Samuel Sewall papers and to include the texts of Sewall's major essays.

In England I am grateful to all who made my research there pleasant and informative. The Blue Badge guide Don Bryan, a lecturer in archaeology and history at Hampshire County's Eastleigh College, drove me around Bishopstoke, Baddesley, and Romsey, describing Hampshire's seventeenth-century landscape and, occasionally, knocking on doors of houses that the Sewalls might have occupied. In Winchester the staff at the Hampshire Records Office, the Lending Library, and the Local Studies Library helped me find and copy documents and historic maps of the region; archivists Nicky Pink and Adrienne Allen were particularly helpful. Local historians Phoebe Merrick, Barbara Burbridge, Nancy Kelly, Pat Gench, Helen Robinson, and Una Lonergan added details of seventeenth-century Hampshire. At Winchester College I wish to thank Prue Martin, Lachlan MacKinnon, the librarian F. Hugh Eveleigh, and W. G. Day, Ph.D., keeper of the Indian Bible that Sewall deposited there in 1689. Dr. Day showed me the Indian Bible, led me on a tour of "the chapel on the green and the library around the stairs" that Sewall described, answered numerous questions, and provided the image of Sewall's signature that appears here by permission of the Warden and Scholars of Winchester College. Thanks to Kate Miller and Doreen Rennert of the Wykeham Arms Inn, in Winchester, and to Zinnia Watson, a guide at Salisbury Cathedral. I am grateful to two guards, one at Westminster Abbey, who allowed me in to see Henry VII's room after hours, and another at the Queen's House in Greenwich, who let me peek at the Painted Room of William III during a wedding. Thanks to Lutz Clausen, Kirsi Norlamo, Anthony Lee, and Angela Hartnett, of the Connaught Hotel, in London, to Jacqueline Gazzard and Vikki Wood, of Historic Royal Palaces, and to Clive Bettington, who determined exactly which Jewish cemetery Sewall visited at Mile End in East London in 1689.

Among the many people who have sustained my family and me, I wish in particular to thank the Rev. Jack Ahern, Teodora Arias, Bob and Ida Bolster, Amy Bowles, the Rev. Brian Clary, Mark Conry, Glenn and Rebecca Gibbs, Susan Harvey, Liza Hirsch, Julianne Johnston, Jane Larsen, Kim Manasevit, Andrea and Danielle Mazandi, Alison McGandy, Richard Moriarty (who lent me a historic map of Brookline that shows the expanse of Sewall's farm), Gayle Robertson, Mary Sheldon, Pipier Smith-Mumford, Rebecca Sneider, and David

Weinstein. Glenn Gibbs arranged for me to spend a day touring the Great Marsh and Plum Island Sound with his friend Dave Voci, who generously shared his knowledge of Sewall's favorite place on earth.

Many family members helped me. Virginia LaPlante, Carl Dreyfus, and Deanie and Gerry Blank provided support and counsel. Tony Dreyfus made translations from the Latin and corrected others. Phoebe Hoss recalled family stories she heard as a child. Judith and Don Fouser gave me a tour of their land along the Ipswich River that Henry Sewall once owned. Gregory and Anne Bridgman provided a mariner's view of the Kennebec region, which Samuel Sewall visited in 1717. The book is dedicated to my great-aunt Charlotte May Wilson, who introduced me to Sewall, and to my father, Joseph LaPlante, who grew up speaking French in Salem, Massachusetts, was the first member of his large family to attend college, and became a professor of law.

I could not have written this book without the emotional and editorial support of my husband, David. To our four "fruits," thank you for motivating me to write because you were at school, and for interrupting me when you're home. A special thanks to Rose, Clara, and Charlotte for bringing Philip home safe from school every day.

Finally, I wish to thank Katharine Cluverius, of International Creative Management; Renée Sedliar, who acquired this book and its prequel, *American Jezebel*; and everyone at HarperOne who brought it to life. Eric Brandt skillfully edited the manuscript and guided its author. I am also grateful to assistant editor Kris Ashley, production editor Carolyn Allison-Holland, copy editor Priscilla Stuckey, book designer Joseph Rutt, cover designer Le Van Fisher, managing editor Terri Leonard, as well as Krista Holmstrom, Laina Adler, Jennifer Johns, Julie Michaels, Claudia Boutote, Helena Brantley, and Greg Mowery.

BIBLIOGRAPHY

ARCHIVAL COLLECTIONS

Commonwealth of Massachusetts Archives, Boston

Correspondence of Samuel Sewall.
Court records of Massachusetts Bay Colony. Vols. 5–12.

Hampshire (England) Record Office

Berrow, Phoebe. *A Tour of Old Romsey.* Hampshire: Lower Test Valley Archaeological Society, 1979.

Berrow, Phoebe, Barbara Burbridge, and Pat Genge. *The Story of Romsey.* Newbury, Berkshire: Local Heritage Books, 1984.

Laxton, Paul. *Two Hundred and Fifty Years of Map-making in the County of Hampshire: A Collection of Reproductions of Printed Maps Published Between the Years 1575 and 1826.* Kent, England: Harry Margery, 1976.

Lonergan, Una, and Beryl Green. *The Changing Face of North Baddesley.* Pamphlet. Hampshire, 1996.

Merrick, Phoebe. *The History of Romsey.* Romsey, Hampshire: Lower Test Valley Archaeological Society Group Publications, 2000.

Merrick, Phoebe. Dr. John Latham manuscripts. Vols. 3, 4. From seven volumes of notes held by the British Library Add Mss 26774–267780.

Ritchie, K. J. *Short History of North Baddesley Church and Village.* Winchester: Warren and Son, 1949.

Suckling, F. H. *Bye-Gone Romsey.* Collection of reprinted articles from the *Romsey Advertiser* of 1915–16.

Suckling. F. H. "North Baddesley." *Hampshire Chronicle*, August 1919. Reprinted in Winchester, 1919.

Walker, Rev. F., ed. *A Short History of Romsey.* Hampshire, 1896.

When the Nuns Ruled Romsey. Pamphlet. Hampshire: Lower Test Valley Archaeological Society, 1978.

Historical Society of Old Newburyport, Massachusetts

Know Your Town. Pamphlet from League of Women Voters of Greater Newburyport, MA, n.d.

Mary Adams Rolfe papers.

Historical Society of Wells & Ogunquit, Maine

Grave marker inscriptions for Rev. George Burroughs from First Church of Wells Museum; Boston's Old North Church; Harvard University; and First Church of Danvers.

Shelley, Hope M., and 350th Celebration History Committee. *My Name Is Wells: I Am the Town. A History of the Town of Wells, Maine, on the Occasion of Its 350th Anniversary.* Rockland, ME: Penobscot Press, 2003.

Massachusetts Historical Society, Boston

Samuel Sewall Papers, 1672–1729:
 Diary, 1674–1729. 3 vols.
  Account book, 1688–1692.
  Almanacs, 1689–1729, annotated.

Bill of lading book, 1686–1698.

Common-place book, 1677–1698.

Diary, 1672–1677.

Diary and common-place book, 1675–1721, containing drafts of
   Phaenomena quaedam Apocalyptica and *Talitha Cumi.*

Diary, 1685–1703.

Diary, 1703–1712.

Diary, 1712–1729.

Diary, 1714–1729.

Diary, 1717–1726.

Journal of his visit to England, 1688–1690.

Letterbook, 1686–1737.

Memoranda from the Diary, 1685–1728.

Notes on sermons, 1672–1674.

Probate Court Records, 1715–1728.

Phaenomena quaedam Apocalyptica. Boston: Bartholomew Green,
   1697, 1727.

The Selling of Joseph: A Memorial. Boston: Bartholomew Green, 1700.

Sewall, Samuel Jr. "Arithmetick and Commonplace Book." 1698.

Sewall, Rev. Samuel. "A Brief Memoir of Samuel Sewall, Harvard College
   1671." Compiled by the Rev. Samuel Sewall of Burlington, 1838.

PUBLISHED PRIMARY SOURCES

Cotton, John, and other New England ministers. *The Bay Psalm Book,*
   or *The Whole Book of Psalms, Faithfully Translated into English Meter.*
   Facsimile reprint of the first edition of 1640. Chicago, IL: Univ. of
   Chicago Press, 1956. Facsimile including the 1640 preface by the
   Rev. John Cotton is at http://www.thedcl.org/bible/bpb/baypslbk.
   pdf.

Green, Joseph. *Biographical Sketch and Diary of Rev. Joseph Green, of
   Salem Village.* 1866. Reprinted in *A Library of American Puritan
   Writings: The Seventeenth Century.* Vol. 7. Puritan Personal Writings:
   Diaries. New York: AMS Press, 1983.

Hull, John. *Diaries of John Hull, Mint-master and Treasurer of the
   Colony of Massachusetts Bay,* with a Memoir of the Author. 1857.
   Reprinted in *A Library of American Puritan Writings: The Seventeenth*

Century. Vol. 7. Puritan Personal Writings: Diaries. New York: AMS Press, 1983.

Mather, Cotton. *Diary of Cotton Mather, 1681–1724.* 2 vols. Collections of the Massachusetts Historical Society, 7th ser., vols. 7 and 8. Boston: Massachusetts Historical Society, 1911–1912.

―――. *On Witchcraft: Being the Wonders of the Invisible World.* 1692. Reprint. New York: Bell Publishing, 1974.

Old South Church. *An Historical Catalogue of the Old South Church (Third Church) Boston, 1669–1882.* Boston: David Clapp and Son, 1883.

Ravenscroft, Thomas. *The Whole booke of psalmes with the hymnes euangelicall.* London: Sternhold, Thomas, 1621. Available on microfilm from UMI (Early English books, 1475–1640; 1809:12) and online at http://www.cgmusic.com/workshop.

Salem Witchcraft Papers. Verbatim transcriptions of the court records in three volumes. Revised, corrected, and augmented by Benjamin C. Ray and Tara S. Wood. Cambridge, MA: DaCapo, 1977. The Salem Witchcraft Web site at the University of Virginia is http://etext.lib.virginia.edu/salem/witchcraft.

Sandoz, Ellis, ed. *Political Sermons of the American Founding Era, 1730–1805.* Indianapolis: Liberty Press, 1991.

Sewall, Joseph. Diary. Excerpts on his father's decline, death, and funeral appear in Hill, H. A., *History of the Old South Church (Third Church), Boston, 1669–1884,* vol. 1: 442-444.

Sewall, Samuel. *Diary of Samuel Sewall, 1674–1729.* Edited by M. Halsey Thomas. New York: Farrar, Straus and Giroux, 1973. Includes *The Selling of Joseph* (1700) and *Sewall's Journey to Arrowsick* (1717).

―――. *Letter-Book of Samuel Sewall, 1685–1729.* 2 vols. New York: AMS Press, n.d. Collections of the Massachusetts Historical Society, 6th Series, 1886–1888.

―――. *Phaenomena quaedam Apocalyptica.* Boston: Bartholomew Green, 1697. Early American Imprints, Series I: Evans Readex Digital Collections, 813.

―――. *The Selling of Joseph.* Boston: Bartholomew Green, 1700. Early American Imprints, Series I: Evans Readex Digital Collections, 951.

————. *Talitha cumi*, or "An Invitation to Women to Look After Their Inheritance in the Heavenly Mansions." Reprinted in part in an essay by the Rev. George E. Ellis in Massachusetts Historical Society Proceedings 12 (1871–73): 358–85.

Shurtleff, Nathaniel B., MD, ed. *Records of the Governor and Company of the Massachusetts Bay in New England.* Boston: William White Press, 1853.

Walter, Thomas, MA. *The grounds and rules of Musick Explained: Or, An Introduction to the Art of Singing by Note. Fitted to the Meanest Capacities.* Boston, MA: Benjamin Mecom for Thomas Johnston, 1721. Reprinted by University Microfilms International, Ann Arbor, MI, 1979.

SECONDARY SOURCES

Adams, Charles Francis. *Three Episodes of Massachusetts History.* Vols. 1 and 2. New York: Russell and Russell, 1965.

Adams, James T. *Dictionary of American History.* New York: Scribner, 1940.

Ahlstrom, Sydney E. *A Religious History of the American People.* New Haven, CT: Yale Univ. Press, 1972.

Anderson, Fred. *Crucible of War: The Seven Years' War and the Fate of Empire in British North America, 1754–1766.* New York: Knopf, 2000.

Andrews, Charles M. *The Colonial Period of American History.* Vol. 1, *The Settlements.* New Haven, CT: Yale Univ. Press, 1934.

Attwater, Donald, ed. *Catholic Dictionary.* Rockford, IL: Tan Books and Publishers, 1997.

Bailyn, Bernard. *Faces of Revolution: Personalities and Themes in the Struggle for American Independence.* New York: Vintage Books, 1990.

————. *The New England Merchants in the Seventeenth Century.* Cambridge: Harvard Univ. Press, 1955.

————. *The Ordeal of Thomas Hutchinson.* Cambridge, MA: Harvard Univ. Press, 1974.

————. *The Peopling of British North America: An Introduction.* New York: Knopf, 1986.

Baker, Emerson W., and James Kences. "Maine, Indian Land Speculation, and the Essex County Witchcraft Outbreak of 1692." *Maine
History* 40, no. 3 (Fall 2001): 159–89.

Baker, Emerson W., and John G. Reid. *The New England Knight: Sir
William Phips, 1651–1695.* Toronto: Univ. of Toronto Press, 1998.

Behringer, Wolfgang. *Witches and Witch-Hunts: A Global History.* Cambridge, UK: Polity Press, 2004.

Bercovitch, Sacvan. *A Library of American Puritan Writings: The Seventeenth Century.* Vol. 7. Puritan Personal Writings: Diaries. New
York: AMS Press, 1983.

———. *The Puritan Origins of the American Self.* New Haven, CT: Yale
Univ. Press, 1975.

Berkin, Carol. *First Generations: Women in Colonial America.* New York:
Hill and Wang, 1996.

Blackmon, Joab L., Jr. "Judge Samuel Sewall's Efforts in Behalf of the
First Americans." *Ethnohistory* 16 (Spring 1969): 165–76.

Bobbitt, Philip. *The Shield of Achilles: War, Peace, and the Course of History.* New York: Knopf, 2002.

Bonfanti, Leo. *The Witchcraft Hysteria of 1692.* New England Historical Series, vol. 2, no. 2726A. Burlington, MA: Pride Publications,
1992.

Boyer, Paul, and Stephen Nissenbaum, eds. *Salem Possessed: The Social
Origins of Witchcraft.* Cambridge, MA: Harvard Univ. Press, 1974.

———. *Salem-Village Witchcraft: A Documentary Record of Local Conflict in Colonial New England.* Boston: Northeastern Univ. Press, 1993.

Breen, Louise A. "Religious Radicalism in the Puritan Officer Corps:
Heterodoxy, the Artillery Company, and Cultural Integration in
Seventeenth-Century Boston." *New England Quarterly* 68 (1995):
3–43.

———. *Transgressing the Bounds: Subversive Enterprises Among the Puritan Elite in Massachusetts, 1630–1692.* New York: Oxford Univ.
Press, 2001.

Bridenbaugh, Carl. *Cities in the Wilderness: The First Century of Urban
Life in America, 1625–1742.* New York: Knopf, 1955.

Briggs, Robin. *Witches and Neighbors: The Social and Cultural Context of
European Witchcraft.* New York: Viking, 1996.

Brown, David D. *A Guide to the Salem Witchcraft Hysteria of 1692.* Worcester, MA: Mercantile Printing, 1984.

Brown, John Perkins, and Eleanor Ransom. *The Thomas Creese House: being the Description of a typical townhouse of the early Eighteenth century and containing a History of the site thereof.* Boston: Little, Brown, 1939.

Buell, Lawrence. *The Environmental Imagination: Thoreau, Nature Writing, and the Formation of American Culture.* Cambridge, MA: Harvard Univ. Press, 1995.

Burns, Eric. *Infamous Scribblers: The Founding Fathers and the Rowdy Beginnings of American Journalism.* New York: Public Affairs, 2006.

Burr, G. L., ed. *Narratives of the Witchcraft Cases, 1648–1706.* New York: Charles Scribner's Sons, 1914.

Cahill, Robert Ellis. *The Horrors of Salem's Witch Dungeon (and Other New England Crimes and Punishments).* Peabody, MA: Chandler-Smith, 1986.

Caldwell, Patricia. *The Puritan Conversion Narrative: The Beginnings of American Expression.* Cambridge: Cambridge Univ. Press, 1984.

Carlson, Laurie W. *A Fever in Salem: A New Interpretation of the New England Witch Trials.* Chicago: Ivan R. Dee, 1999.

Carter, Stephen L. *The Culture of Disbelief: How American Law and Politics Trivialize Religious Devotion.* New York: Basic Books, 1993.

Carter, Susan B., et al., eds. *Historical Statistics of the United States.* New York: Cambridge Univ. Press, 2006.

Castillo, Susan, and Ivy Schweitzer, eds. *The Literatures of Colonial America.* Oxford: Blackwell, 2001.

Chamberlain, Nathan H. *Samuel Sewall and the World He Lived In.* 1897. Second edition. New York: Russell and Russell, 1967.

Christ-Janer, Albert, and Charles Hughes. *American Hymns Old and New.* New York: Columbia Univ. Press, 1980.

Clarke, Hermann Frederick. "The Craft of Silversmith in Early New England." *New England Quarterly* 12, No. 1 (Mar. 1939): 68-79.

———. *John Hull, A Builder of the Bay Colony.* Portland, ME: Southworth-Anthoensen Press, 1940.

Coffin, Joshua. *A Sketch of the History of Newbury, Newburyport, and West Newbury.* 1845. Reprint. Hampton, NH: Peter Randall, 1977.

Cohen, Charles L. *God's Caress: The Psychology of Puritan Religious Experience.* New York: Oxford Univ. Press, 1986.

Collins, Joseph B. *Christian Mysticism in the Elizabethan Age.* Baltimore: Johns Hopkins University Press, 1940.

Collins, Leo. *This Is Our Church: The Seven Societies of the First Church in Boston, 1630–2005.* Boston: Society of the First Church in Boston, 2005.

Collinson, Patrick. *The Elizabethan Puritan Movement.* Oxford: Oxford Univ. Press, 1967.

———, ed. *The Sixteenth Century, 1485–1603.* New York: Oxford Univ. Press, 2002.

Collinson, Patrick, and John Craig, eds. *The Reformation in English Towns, 1500–1640.* London: Macmillan, 1998.

Conforti, Joseph. *Imagining New England: Explorations of Regional Identity from the Pilgrims to the Mid-Twentieth Century.* Chapel Hill: Univ. of North Carolina Press, 2001.

Cross, F. L., and E. A. Livingstone, eds. *The Oxford Dictionary of the Christian Church.* New York: Oxford Univ. Press, 1997.

Currier, John J. *History of Newburyport, Mass., 1764–1905.* Newburyport, MA: John J. Currier, 1906.

———. *"Ould Newbury": Historical and Biographical Sketches.* Boston: Damrell and Upham, 1896.

Curtis, John G. *History of the Town of Brookline, Massachusetts.* Boston: Houghton Mifflin, 1933.

Daniels, Bruce. *Puritans at Play: Leisure and Recreation in Colonial New England.* New York: St. Martin's Press, 1995.

Davidson, James W. *The Logic of Millennial Thought: Eighteenth-Century New England.* New Haven, CT: Yale Univ. Press, 1977.

Davis, David Brion. *Challenging the Boundaries of Slavery.* Cambridge, MA: Harvard Univ. Press, 2003.

———. *Inhuman Bondage: The Rise and Fall of Slavery in the New World.* New York: Oxford Univ. Press, 2006.

———. *The Problem of Slavery in Western Culture.* Ithaca, NY: Cornell Univ. Press, 1966.

Davis, David Brion, and Steven Mintz, eds. *The Boisterous Sea of Liberty: A Documentary History of America from Discovery through the Civil War.* New York: Oxford Univ. Press, 1998.

Delbanco, Andrew. *The Puritan Ordeal.* Cambridge, MA: Harvard Univ. Press, 1989.

Demos, John. *Entertaining Satan: Witchcraft and the Culture of Early New England.* New York: Oxford Univ. Press, 1982.

————, ed. *Remarkable Providences, 1600–1760.* New York: Braziller, 1972.

Derby, George. *National Cyclopaedia of American Biography, being the History of the United States Illustrated in Lives.* Vol. 5. New York: James T. White, 1907.

Dietz, James. *In Small Things Forgotten: An Archeology of Early American Life.* New York: Anchor Books, 1977.

Dow, George F. *Every Day Life in the Massachusetts Bay Colony.* 1935. Reprint. New York: Dover, 1988.

Earle, Alice Morse. *Home Life in Colonial Days.* 1898. New York: Berkshire House, 1993.

————. *The Sabbath in Puritan New England.* New York: Scribners, 1909.

Einarsdottir, Jonina. *Tired of Weeping: Mother Love, Child Death, and Poverty in Guinea-Bissau.* Madison: Univ. of Wisconsin Press, 2004.

Elliot, J. H. *Empires of the Atlantic World: Britain and Spain in America, 1492–1830.* New Haven, CT: Yale Univ. Press, 2006.

Erikson, Kai T. *Wayward Puritans: A Study in the Sociology of Deviance.* New York: Wiley, 1966.

Farrow, Anne, Joel Lang, and Jenifer Frank. *Complicity: How the North Promoted, Prolonged, and Profited from Slavery.* New York: Ballantine Books, 2005.

Fiering, Norman S. "Will and Intellect in the New England Mind." *William and Mary Quarterly,* 3rd ser., 29 (1972): 515–58.

Fischer, David Hackett. *Albion's Seed: Four British Folkways in America.* New York: Oxford Univ. Press, 1989.

Flibbert, Joseph. *Salem: Cornerstones of a Historic City.* Beverly, MA: Commonwealth Editions, 1999.

Foster, Stephen. *The Long Argument: English Puritanism and the Shaping of New England Culture, 1570–1700.* Chapel Hill: Univ. of North Carolina Press, 1991.

Frankfurter, David. *Evil Incarnate: Rumors of Demonic Conspiracy and Satanic Abuse in History.* Princeton, NJ: Princeton Univ. Press, 2006.

Fraser, Antonia. *Cromwell: The Lord Protector.* New York: Knopf, 1973.

Frost, Robert. *Selected Poems.* New York: Henry Holt, 1923.

Gaskill, Malcolm. *Witchfinders: A Seventeenth-Century English Tragedy.* Cambridge, MA: Harvard Univ. Press, 2005.

Gaustad, Edwin S. *A Religious History of America.* New York: Harper and Row, 1966.

———, ed. *A Documentary History of Religion in America to the Civil War.* Grand Rapids, MI: Eerdmans, 1982.

Geis, Gilbert, and Ivan Bunn. *A Trial of Witches: A Seventeenth-Century Witchcraft Prosecution.* London: Routledge, 1997.

Gemmill, William N. *The Salem Witch Trials: A Chapter of New England History.* Chicago: McClung, 1924.

Genge, Pat, and Jessica Spinney. *Romsey Schools: 900 until 1940.* Romsey, Hampshire, England: LTVAS Group, 1991.

Godbeer, Richard. *Escaping Salem: The Other Witch Hunt of 1692.* New York: Oxford Univ. Press, 2005.

Goodell, Abner C. "John Saffin and His Slave Adam." *Publications of the Colonial Society of Massachusetts* 1 (1895): 85–112. Includes reprint of John Saffin's *A Brief and Candid Answer to a late Printed Sheet Entitled the Selling of Joseph* (1705) and legal documents concerning Adam's struggle to win his freedom.

Gould, Philip. "New England Witch Hunting and the Politics of Reason in the Early Republic." *New England Quarterly* 68 (1995): 58–82.

Gragg, Larry. *The Salem Witch Crisis.* Westport, CT: Praeger, 1992.

Graham, Judith. *Puritan Family Life: The Diary of Samuel Sewall.* Boston: Northeastern Univ. Press, 2002.

Graves, Eben. "The Death of Henry Sewall in 1628: Puzzles, Evidence, and Solutions." *New England Historical and Genealogical Register* 159 (January 2005): 35–42.

Greven, Philip. *The Protestant Temperament: Patterns of Child-Rearing, Religious Experience, and the Self in Early America.* Chicago: Univ. of Chicago Press, 1977.

Griffin, A. P. C. *Annual Report of the American Historical Society for the Year 1905.* Vol. 2. 1907. Reprint. Detroit: Gale Research Company, 1966.

Hall, David D. *The Faithful Shepherd: A History of the New England Ministry in the Seventeenth Century.* Chapel Hill: Univ. of North Carolina Press, 1972.

————. *Worlds of Wonder, Days of Judgment: Popular Religious Belief in Early New England.* New York: Knopf, 1989.

————, ed. *Lived Religion in America: Toward a History of Practice.* Princeton, NJ: Princeton Univ. Press, 1997.

————, ed. *Puritans in the New World: A Critical Anthology.* Princeton, NJ: Princeton Univ. Press, 2004.

————, ed. *Witch-Hunting in Seventeenth-Century New England: A Documentary History, 1638–1692.* Boston: Northeastern Univ. Press, 1991.

Hambrick-Stowe, Charles. *The Practice of Piety: Puritan Devotional Disciplines in Seventeenth-Century New England.* Chapel Hill: Univ. of North Carolina Press, 1982.

————, ed. *Early New England Meditative Poetry: Anne Bradstreet and Edward Taylor.* New York: Paulist Press, 1988.

Hammond, Jeffrey A. *Sinful Self, Saintly Self: The Puritan Experience of Poetry.* Athens: Univ. of Georgia Press, 1993.

Hansen, Chadwick. *Witchcraft at Salem.* New York: Braziller, 1969.

Harbury, Katharine E. *Colonial Virginia's Cooking Dynasty.* Columbia: Univ. of South Carolina Press, 2004.

Hawke, David F. *The Colonial Experience.* Indianapolis: Bobbs-Merrill, 1966.

————. *Everyday Life in Early America.* New York: Harper and Row, 1988.

Hawthorne, Nathaniel. *The Scarlet Letter.* 1850. Reprint. Boston: Houghton Mifflin, 1960.

————. *Selected Short Stories of Nathaniel Hawthorne.* Edited by Alfred Kazin. New York: Fawcett Premier, 1966.

Heimert, Alan, and Andrew Delbanco, eds. *The Puritans in America: A Narrative Anthology.* Cambridge, MA: Harvard Univ. Press, 1985.

Heyrman, Christine Leigh. *Commerce and Culture: The Maritime Communities of Colonial Massachusetts, 1690–1750.* New York: Norton, 1984.

Higham, John, and Paul K. Conkin, eds. *New Directions in American Intellectual History.* Baltimore: Johns Hopkins Univ. Press, 1979.

Hill, Frances. *A Delusion of Satan: The Full Story of the Salem Witch Trials.* New York: Bantam, 1995.

———. *Hunting for Witches: A Visitor's Guide to the Salem Witch Trials.* New York: Commonwealth Editions, 2002.

———. *The Salem Witch Trials Reader.* Cambridge, MA: Da Capo, 2000.

Hill, Christopher. *God's Englishman: Oliver Cromwell and the English Revolution.* New York: Dial Press, 1970.

———. *The World Turned Upside Down: Radical Ideas During the English Revolution.* London: Penguin, 1972.

Hill, Hamilton Andrews. *History of the Old South Church* (Third Church), Boston, 1669–1884. 2 vols. Boston and New York: Houghton Mifflin, 1890. Contains excerpts from Joseph Sewall's diary.

Hill, Sally D. H. "Marriages Noted by the Rev. Cotton Mather and His Son, the Rev. Samuel Mather, Boston, Massachusetts, 1675–1737." *New England Historical and Genealogical Register* 159 (April 2005): 101–9.

Hillerbrand, Hans J., ed. *The Protestant Reformation.* New York: Harper and Row, 1968.

Hilmer, Mary A. "The Other Diary of Samuel Sewall." *New England Quarterly* 55, no. 3 (September 1982): 354–67.

Hochschild, Adam. *Bury the Chains: Prophets and Rebels in the Fight to Free an Empire's Slaves.* Boston: Houghton Mifflin, 2005.

Hoffer, Peter Charles. *The Devil's Disciples: Makers of the Salem Witchcraft Trials.* Baltimore: Johns Hopkins Univ. Press, 1996.

———. *The Salem Witchcraft Trials: A Legal History.* Lawrence: Univ. Press of Kansas, 1997.

Holifield, E. Brooks. *The Covenant Sealed: The Development of Puritan Sacramental Theology in Old and New England, 1570–1720.* New Haven, CT: Yale Univ. Press, 1974.

———. *Theology in America: Christian Thought from the Age of the Puritans to the Civil War.* New Haven: Yale Univ. Press, 2003.

———. "Peace, Conflict, and Ritual in Puritan Congregations," *Journal of Interdisciplinary History* 23, no. 3 (winter 1993): 551–57.

———. "The Renaissance of Sacremental Piety in Colonial New England." *William and Mary Quarterly* 3rd ser. 29, no. 1 (Jan. 1972): 33–48.

Holliday, Carl. *Woman's Life in Colonial Days.* Williamstown, MA: Corner House Publishers, 1968.

Hollis, Christopher. *Saint Ignatius.* New York: Harper and Brothers, 1931.

Holmes, Thomas J. *Cotton Mather: A Bibliography of His Works.* Cambridge, MA: Harvard Univ. Press, 1940.

Huggett, Jane. *The Book of Children: Children and Childrearing, 1480–1680, Part 1, Birth to Age Seven.* Bristol, England: Stuart Press, 1996.

———. *The Book of Children: Children and Childrearing, 1480–1680, Part 2, Age 7–14.* Bristol, England: Stuart Press, 1998.

Hume, Ivor Noel. *A Guide to Artifacts of Colonial America.* Philadelphia: Univ. of Pennsylvania Press, 1969.

Hutchinson, Thomas. *The History of the Colony and Province of Massachusetts-Bay.* Edited by Lawrence Shaw Mayo. 2 vols. Cambridge, MA: Harvard Univ. Press, 1936.

Innes, Stephen. *Creating the Commonwealth: The Economic Culture of Puritan New England.* New York: Norton, 1995.

Isani, Mukhtar Ali. "The Growth of Sewall's *Phaenomena quaedam Apocalyptica.*" *Early American Literature* 7 (1972): 64–75.

Jantz, Harold S. *The First Century of New England Verse.* New York: Russell and Russell, 1962.

Johnson, Claudia D. *Understanding "The Scarlet Letter": A Student Casebook to Issues, Sources, and Historical Documents.* Westport, CT: Greenwood Press, 1995.

Johnson, Claudia D., and Vernon E. Johnson. *Understanding "The Crucible": A Student Casebook to Issues, Sources, and Historical Documents.* Westport, CT: Greenwood Press, 1998.

Johnson, Edward. *Johnson's Wonder-Working Providence, 1628–1651.* Edited by J. Franklin Jameson. New York: Charles Scribner's Sons, 1910.

Karlsen, Carol H. *The Devil in the Shape of a Woman: Witchcraft in Colonial New England.* New York: Norton, 1987.

Kaufmann, U. Milo. *The Pilgrim's Progress and Traditions in Puritan Meditation.* New Haven: Yale Univ. Press, 1966.

Kellaway, William. *The New England Company, 1649–1776: Missionary Society to the American Indians.* London: Longmans, 1961.

Kibbey, Ann. *The Interpretation of Material Shapes in Puritanism: A Study of Rhetoric, Prejudice, and Violence.* Cambridge: Cambridge Univ. Press, 1986.

Kidd, Thomas S. "Let Hell and Rome Do Their Worst: World News, Anti-Catholicism, and International Protestantism in Early Eighteenth-Century Boston." *New England Quarterly* 76 (2003): 265–90.

Kimball, Everett. *The Public Life of Joseph Dudley: A Study of the Colonial Policy of the Stuarts in New England, 1660-1715.* New York: Longmans, Green, and Co., 1911.

Kittredge, George L. *Witchcraft in Old and New England.* 1929. Reprint. New York: Russell and Russell, 1958.

Knight, Janice. "Learning the Language of God: Jonathan Edwards and the Typology of Nature." *William and Mary Quarterly*, 3rd ser., 48 (1991): 531–51.

————. *Orthodoxies in Massachusetts: Rereading American Puritanism.* Cambridge, MA: Harvard Univ. Press, 1994.

Krieger, Alex, and David Cobb, eds. *Mapping Boston.* Cambridge, MA: MIT Press, 2001.

LaPlante, Eve. *American Jezebel: The Uncommon Life of Anne Hutchinson, the Woman Who Defied the Puritans.* San Francisco: HarperSanFrancisco, 2004.

Lazare, Aaron. *On Apology.* New York: Oxford Univ. Press, 2004.

Le Beau, Bryan F. *The Story of the Salem Witch Trials: "We Walked in Clouds and Could Not See Our Way."* Upper Saddle River, NJ: Prentice Hall, 1998.

Lepore, Jill. *A Is for American: Letters and Other Characters in the Newly United States.* New York: Knopf, 2002.

————. *The Name of War: King Philip's War and the Origins of American Identity.* New York: Knopf, 1998.

————, ed. *Encounters in the New World: A History in Documents.* New York: Oxford Univ. Press, 2000.

Levack, Brian P. *The Witch-Hunt in Early Modern Europe.* New York: Longman, 1987.

Levin, David. *Cotton Mather: The Young Life of the Lord's Remembrancer, 1663–1703.* Cambridge, MA: Harvard Univ. Press, 1978.

Lieven, Anatol. *America Right or Wrong: An Anatomy of American Nationalism.* New York: Oxford Univ. Press, 2004.

Liu, Tai. *Puritan London: A Study of Religion and Society in the City Parishes.* Newark, NJ: Univ. of Delaware Press, 1986.

Lockridge, Kenneth A. *A New England Town: The First Hundred Years, Dedham, Massachusetts, 1636–1736.* New York: Norton, 1970.

Lodge, Henry Cabot. *Studies in History.* Boston: Houghton Mifflin, 1884.

Love, William DeLoss. *Fast and Thanksgiving Days of New England.* Boston: Houghton Mifflin, 1895.

Lovejoy, David S. "Between Hell and Plum Island: Samuel Sewall and the Legacy of the Witches, 1692–97." *New England Quarterly* 70 (1997): 355–67.

Lovelace, Richard F. *The American Pietism of Cotton Mather: Origins of American Evangelism.* Grand Rapids: Christian Univ. Press, 1979.

Lowrie, Ernest B. *The Shape of the Puritan Mind: The Thought of Samuel Willard.* New Haven: Yale Univ. Press, 1974.

MacCulloch, Diarmaid. *The Reformation: A History.* New York: Viking, 2004.

Macfarlane, Alan. *Witchcraft in Tudor and Stuart England: A Regional and Comparative Study.* New York: Harper and Row, 1970.

Mann, Charles C. *1491: New Revelations of the Americas Before Columbus.* New York: Knopf, 2005.

Mappen, Marc. *Witches and Historians: Interpretations of Salem.* New York: Wiley, 1979.

Marrocco, W. Thomas, and Harold Gleason. *Music in America: An Anthology from the Landing of the Pilgrims to the Close of the Civil War, 1620–1865.* New York: Norton, 1964.

Marsden, George M. *Jonathan Edwards: A Life.* New Haven: Yale Univ. Press, 2003.

Marty, Martin. *Martin Luther.* New York: Viking Penguin, 2004.

Mather, Cotton. *Cotton Mather on Witchcraft: The Wonders of the Invisible World.* New York: Dorset Press, 1991.

Matthiesen, F. O. *American Renaissance: Art and Expression in the Age of Emerson and Whitman.* New York: Oxford Univ. Press, 1941.

May, Samuel J. *The Life of Samuel J. May.* Boston: Roberts Brothers, 1874.

Mayo, Lawrence Shaw. *The Winthrop Family in America.* Boston: Massachusetts Historical Society, 1989.

McCusker, John J. *Money and Exchange in Europe and America, 1600–1775: A Handbook.* Institute of Early American History and Culture. Chapel Hill: Univ. of North Carolina Press, 1992.

Meissner, W. W., SJ, MD. *Ignatius of Loyola: The Psychology of a Saint.* New Haven: Yale Univ. Press, 1992.

Meyer, F. B. *Psalms: A Study of the 150 Psalms.* Grand Rapids, MI: Zondervan, 1964.

Michaels, W. B., and Donald E. Pease, eds. *The American Renaissance Reconsidered.* Baltimore: Johns Hopkins Univ. Press, 1985.

Middlekauff, Robert. *The Mathers: Three Generations of Puritan Intellectuals, 1596–1728.* Berkeley and Los Angeles: Univ. of California Press, 1999.

Miller, Arthur. *The Crucible.* New York: Viking, 1954.

Miller, John C., ed. *The Colonial Image: Origins of American Culture.* New York: Braziller, 1962.

Miller, Perry. *Errand into the Wilderness.* Cambridge, MA: Harvard Univ. Press, 1956.

———. *Nature's Nation.* Cambridge, MA: Harvard Univ. Press, 1967.

———. *The New England Mind: From Colony to Province.* Cambridge, MA: Harvard Univ. Press, 1953.

———. *The New England Mind: The Seventeenth Century.* New York: Macmillan, 1939.

———, ed. *The America Puritans: Their Prose and Poetry.* Garden City, NY: Anchor-Doubleday, 1956.

Moore, Margaret B. *The Salem World of Nathaniel Hawthorne.* Columbia: Univ. of Missouri Press, 1998.

Morgan, Edmund S. *The Genuine Article: A Historian Looks at Early America.* New York: Norton, 2004.

———. *The Puritan Family: Religion and Domestic Relations in Seventeenth-Century New England.* New York: Harper, 1966.

———. *Visible Saints: The History of a Puritan Idea.* New York: New York Univ. Press, 1963.

Morison, Samuel Eliot. *Builders of the Bay Colony.* Boston: Houghton Mifflin, 1938.

———. *The Founding of Harvard College.* 1935. Reprint. Cambridge, MA: Harvard Univ. Press, 1995.

Morone, James A. *Hellfire Nation: The Politics of Sin in American History.* New Haven, CT: Yale Univ. Press, 2003.

Morris, Robert. *Clothes of the Common Man and Woman, 1580–1660.* Bristol, England: Stuart Press, 2000.

————. *Headwear, Footwear and Trimmings of the Common Man and Woman, 1580–1660.* Bristol, England: Stuart Press, 2001.

Morrison, Dane Anthony, and Nancy L. Schultz. *Salem: Place, Myth, and Memory.* Boston: Northeastern Univ. Press, 2004.

Mouw, Richard J., and Mark A. Noll, eds. *Wonderful Words of Life: Hymns in American Protestant History and Theology.* Grand Rapids, MI: Eerdmans, 2004.

Mulford, Carla, Angela Vietto, and Amy E. Winans, eds. *Early American Writings.* New York: Oxford Univ. Press, 2002.

Murdock, Kenneth Ballard. *Increase Mather: The Foremost American Puritan.* Cambridge, MA: Harvard Univ. Press, 1925.

Nash, Gary B. *The Urban Crucible: Social Change, Political Consciousness, and the Origins of the American Revolution.* Cambridge, MA: Harvard Univ. Press, 1979.

Nash, Roderick, ed. *Wilderness and the American Mind.* New Haven: Yale Univ. Press, 1973.

Norton, Mary Beth. *Founding Mothers and Fathers: Gendered Power and the Forming of American Society.* New York: Knopf, 1996.

————. "George Burroughs and the Girls from Casco: The Maine Roots of Salem Witchcraft." *Maine History* 40, no. 1 (Winter 2001–2002): 259–77.

————. *In the Devil's Snare: The Salem Witchcraft Crisis of 1692.* New York: Knopf, 2002.

Nuttall, Geoffrey Fillingham. *The Holy Spirit in Puritan Faith and Experience.* New York: Oxford, 1948.

Osgood, Russell K., ed. *The History of the Law in Massachusetts: The Supreme Judicial Court, 1692–1992.* Boston: Supreme Judicial Court Historical Society, 1992.

Parry, R. H., ed. *The English Civil War and After, 1642–1658.* Berkeley and Los Angeles: Univ. of California Press, 1970.

Peterson, Mark A. *The Price of Redemption: The Spiritual Economy of Puritan New England.* Stanford, CA: Stanford Univ. Press, 1997.

————. "The Selling of Joseph: Bostonians, Antislavery, and the Protestant International, 1689–1733." *Massachusetts Historical Review* 4 (2002): 1–22.

Pettit, Norman. *The Heart Prepared: Grace and Conversion in Puritan Spiritual Life.* Middletown, CT: Wesleyan Univ. Press, 1989.

Philbrick, Nathaniel. *Mayflower: A Story of Courage, Community, and War.* New York: Viking, 2006.

Plumstead, A. W., ed. *The Wall and the Garden: Selected Massachusetts Election Sermons, 1670–1775.* Minneapolis: Univ. of Minnesota Press, 1968.

Porterfield, Amanda. *Female Piety in Puritan New England: The Emergence of Religious Humanism.* New York: Oxford Univ. Press, 1992.

Prestowitz, Clyde. *Rogue Nation: American Unilateralism and the Failure of Good Intentions.* New York: Basic Books, 2003.

Pulsipher, Jenny Hale. *Subjects unto the Same King: Indians, English, and the Contest for Authority in Colonial New England.* Philadelphia: Univ. of Pennsylvania Press, 2005.

Ranlet, Philip. *Enemies of the Bay Colony.* New York: P. Lang, 1995.

Reis, Elizabeth. *Damned Women: Sinners and Witches in Puritan New England.* Ithaca, NY: Cornell Univ. Press, 1997.

Richter, Daniel K. *Facing East from Indian Country: A Native History of Early America.* Cambridge, MA: Harvard Univ. Press, 2002.

Roach, Marilynne K. *The Salem Witch Trials: A Day-to-Day Chronicle of a Community Under Siege.* New York: Cooper Square Press, 2002.

Roberts, Gary Boyd. *Ancestors of American Presidents.* Santa Clara, CA: Carl Boyer, 1989.

Robinson, Marilynne. *The Death of Adam: Essays on Modern Thought.* Boston: Houghton Mifflin, 1998.

Rosenthal, Bernard. *Salem Story: Reading the Witch Trials of 1692.* Cambridge: Cambridge Univ. Press, 1993.

Ruchames, Louis, ed. *Racial Thought in America: From the Puritans to Abraham Lincoln.* Amherst: Univ. of Massachusetts Press, 1969.

Rutman, Darrett B. *Winthrop's Boston: A Portrait of a Puritan Town.* Chapel Hill: Univ. of North Carolina Press, 1965.

Sargent, William. *The House on Ipswich Marsh: Exploring the Natural History of New England.* Hanover, NH: Univ. Press of New England, 2005.

Sarti, Raffaella. *Europe at Home: Family and Material Culture, 1500–1800.* New Haven: Yale Univ. Press, 2002.

Savage, James. *A Genealogical Dictionary of the First Settlers of New England, Showing Three Generations of Those Who Came Before May, 1692.* 4 vols. Boston: Little, Brown, 1862.

Scholes, Percy A. *The Puritans and Music in England and New England: A Contribution to the Cultural History of Two Nations.* Oxford: Oxford Univ. Press, 1934.

Seelye, John. *Prophetic Waters: The River in Early American Life and Literature.* New York: Oxford Univ. Press, 1977

Sewall, Samuel. *Diary and Life of Samuel Sewall.* Edited by Mel Yazawa. Boston: Bedford Books, 1998.

Seybolt, Robert F. "The Private Schools of Seventeenth-Century Boston." *New England Quarterly* 8, no. 3 (Sept. 1935): 418–24.

Shurtleff, Nathaniel B. *A Topographical and Historical Description of Boston.* Boston: Noyes, Holmes, 1872.

Silverman, Kenneth. *The Life and Times of Cotton Mather.* New York: Harper & Row, 1984.

Simons, Brenton D. *Witches, Rakes, and Rogues: True Stories of Scam, Scandal, Murder, and Mayhem in Boston, 1630–1775.* Beverly, MA: Commonwealth Editions, 2005.

Simpson, Alan. *Puritanism in Old and New England.* Chicago: Univ. of Chicago Press, 1955.

Smith, Merril D., ed. *Sex and Sexuality in Early America.* New York: New York Univ. Press, 1998.

Smolinski, Reiner. "*Israel Redivivus:* The Eschatological Limits of Puritan Typology in New England." *New England Quarterly* 63 (1990): 357–395.

Stannard, David E. *The Puritan Way of Death: A Study in Religious, Cultural, and Social Change.* New York: Oxford Univ. Press, 1977.

Stark, Rodney. *For the Glory of God: How Monotheism Led to Reformations, Science, Witch-hunts, and the End of Slavery.* Princeton, NJ: Princeton Univ. Press, 2003.

Starkey, Marion L. *The Devil in Massachusetts: A Modern Enquiry into the Salem Witch Trials.* New York: Anchor Books, 1949.

Steele, Ian K., and Nancy L. Rhoden, eds. *The Human Tradition in Colonial America.* Wilmington, DE: Scholarly Resources, 1999.

Stout, Harry S. *The New England Soul: Preaching and Religious Culture in Colonial New England.* New York: Oxford Univ. Press, 1986.

Stout, Harry S., and Daryl Hart, eds. *New Directions in American Religious History.* New York: Oxford Univ. Press, 1997.

Strandness, T. B. *Samuel Sewall: A Puritan Portrait.* Detroit: Michigan State Univ. Press, 1967.

Sweet, Timothy. "'What Concernment Hath America in these Things!' Local and Global in Samuel Sewall's Plum Island Passage." *Early American Literature* 41, no. 2 (2006): 213–40.

Tannenbaum, Rebecca J. "'What Is Best to Be Done for These Fevers': Elizabeth Davenport's Medical Practice in New Haven Colony." *New England Quarterly* 70, no. 2 (June 1997): 265–84.

Taylor, Alan, and Eric Foner, eds. *American Colonies.* Penguin History of the United States, vol. 1. New York: Viking, 2001.

Temin, Peter, ed. *Engines of Enterprise: An Economic History of New England.* Cambridge, MA: Harvard Univ. Press, 2000.

Thomas, Keith. *Religion and the Decline of Magic.* New York: Scribner, 1971.

Thwing, Annie H. *The Crooked and Narrow Streets of Boston.* Boston: Brown, 1949.

Tomalin, Claire. *Samuel Pepys: The Unequalled Self.* New York: Knopf, 2002.

Towner, Lawrence W. "The Sewall-Saffin Dialogue on Slavery." *William and Mary Quarterly* 3rd ser. 21 (1964): 40-52.

Trask, Richard B. *"The Devil Hath Been Raised": A Documentary History of the Salem Village Witchcraft Outbreak of March 1692.* West Kennebunk, ME: Phoenix Publications, 1992.

———. "The Witchcraft Trials of 1692." In *Salem: Cornerstones of a Historic City,* edited by Joseph Flibbert et al., 25–58. Beverly, MA: Commonwealth Editions, 1999.

Tucker, Bruce. "Joseph Sewall's Diary and the Rhythm of Puritan Spirituality." *Early American Literature* 22 (1987): 3-18.

Ulrich, Laurel Thatcher. *The Age of Homespun: Objects and Stories in the Creation of an American Myth.* New York: Knopf, 2001.

Upham, Charles W. *Salem witchcraft; with an account of Salem village and a history of opinions on witchcraft and kindred subjects.* 2 vols. Boston, 1867. Reprint. Williamstown, MA: Corner House Publishers, 1971.

Van Lonkhuyzen, Harold W. "A Reappraisal of the Praying Indians: Acculturation, Conversion, and Identity at Natick, Massachusetts, 1646-1730." *New England Quarterly* 63 (1990): 396-428.

Wakefield, Gordon S. *Puritan Devotion: Its Place in the Development of Christian Piety.* London: Epworth, 1957.

Wakefield, Gordon S., ed. *The Westminster Dictionary of Christian Spirituality.* Philadelphia: Westminster Press, 1983.

Waller, George M., ed. *Puritanism in Early America.* Boston: Heath, 1950.

Waller, Maureen. *1700: Scenes from London Life.* New York: Four Walls Eight Windows, 2000.

————. *Ungrateful Daughters: The Stuart Princesses Who Stole Their Father's Crown.* New York: Saint Martin's Press, 2003.

Watkins, Owen. *The Puritan Experience: Studies in Spiritual Autobiography.* New York: Schocken Books, 1972.

Weare, Nancy V. *Plum Island: The Way It Was.* Newbury, MA: Newburyport Press, 1993.

Weis, Frederick L. *Colonial Clergy of New England.* Lancaster, MA: Descendants of the Colonial Clergy, 1936.

Weisman, Richard. *Witchcraft, Magic, and Religion in Seventeenth-Century Massachusetts.* Amherst: Univ. of Massachusetts Press, 1984.

Whittier, John Greenleaf. "The Prophecy of Samuel Sewall, 1697." *The Complete Poetical Works of John Greenleaf Whittier.* Boston: Houghton Mifflin, 1985.

Williams, Selma R., and P. W. Adelman. *Riding the Nightmare: Women and Witchcraft from the Old World to Colonial Salem.* New York: HarperCollins, 1992.

Williamson, William D. *The History of the State of Maine: From Its First Discovery, A.D. 1602, to the Separation, A.D. 1820, Inclusive.* Hallowell, ME: Glazier, Masters, 1832.

Willis, Deborah. *Malevolent Nurture: Witch-Hunting and Maternal Power in Early Modern England.* Ithaca, NY: Cornell Univ. Press, 1995.

Wilson, Susan. *Boston Sites and Insights.* Boston: Beacon Press, 2003.

Winship, George Parker. *The Cambridge Press, 1638–1692: A Reexamination of the Evidence Concerning the Bay Psalm Book and the Eliot Indian Bible, as Well as Other Contemporary Books and People.* Philadelphia: Univ. of Pennsylvania Press, 1945.

Winship, Michael P. *Seers of God: Puritan Providentialism in the Restoration and Early Enlightenment.* Baltimore: Johns Hopkins Univ. Press, 1996.

Winslow, Ola Elizabeth. *Samuel Sewall of Boston.* New York: Macmillan, 1964.

Wisner, Benjamin B. *The history of the Old South Church in Boston, in four sermons, delivered May 9, & 16, 1830, being the first and second Sabbaths after the completion of a century from the first occupancy of the present meeting house.* Boston: Crocker and Brewer, 1830.

Wolfe, Alan. *One Nation, After All.* New York: Viking, 1998.

Woodson, Carter G., and Charles H. Wesley. *The Negro in Our History.* Washington, DC: Associated Publishers, 1922.

Yazawa, Melvin. *The Diary and Life of Samuel Sewall.* New York: Palgrave Macmillan, 1998.

INDEX

Page numbers of illustrations appear in italics.